W9-BYD-035

Love Me,
Love Me Not

4

IO SAKISAKA

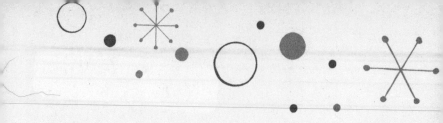

Contents

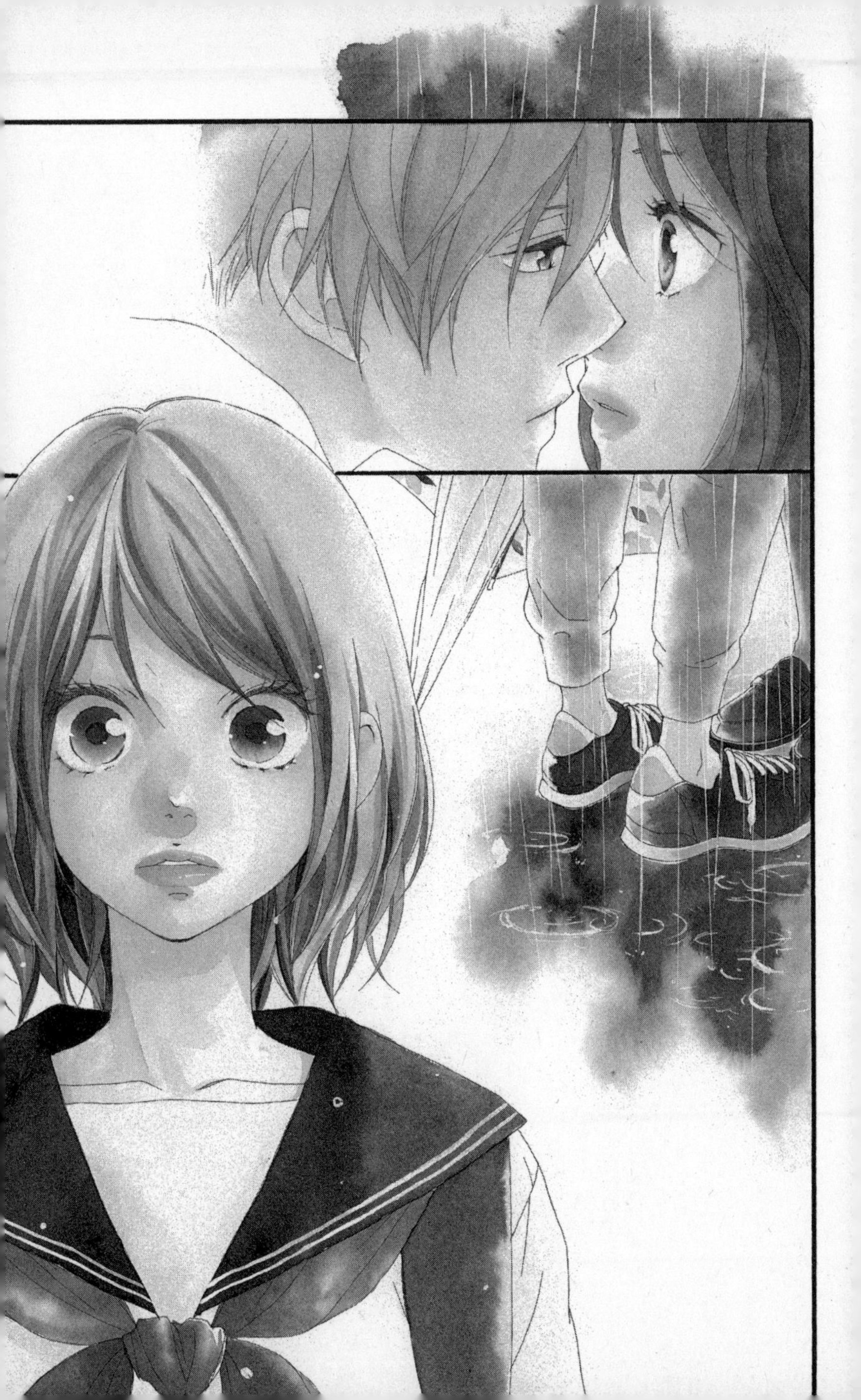

Love Me, Love Me Not

Piece 13

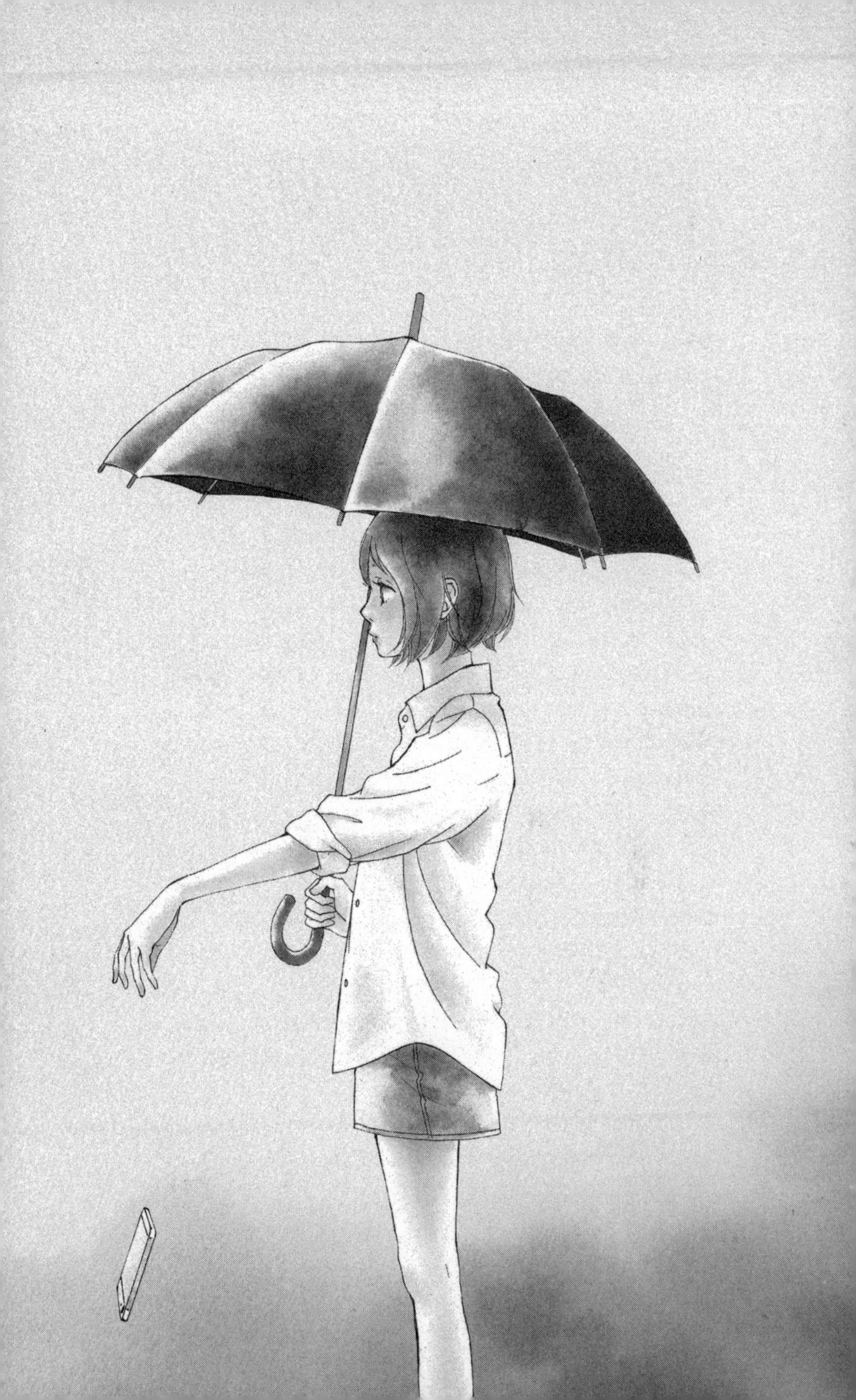

GREETINGS

Hello. I'm Io Sakisaka. Thank you very much for picking up volume 4 of *Love Me, Love Me Not*.

I'm going out! I'm leaving the house! I decided this out of the blue one day. I tend to be a stay-at-home type normally, but I realized the other day that in a certain month, I had left the house only about three days in total. (It was a particularly busy month). But I was happy enough and thought, "Oh, people don't need to go out to survive..." I want to change the feeling that this is normal. I want to chat with lots of people, and I want to hear lots of stories. But if I do it all at once, I think I'll run out of steam quickly. So, little by little, I want to go places I usually wouldn't think of going and do things I wouldn't normally do. I can't picture what an active me will look like, but that's what I'm attracted to at the moment. Just thinking about it makes me excited. I want Yuna and Akari to behave differently than they do usually, and I want them to be excited by that feeling. For that to happen, I need to start first. Then I can confidently get Yuna and Akari to experience various new things. I'm looking forward to it. So please stay with me through the end of *Love Me, Love Me Not* volume 4.

 Io Sakisaka

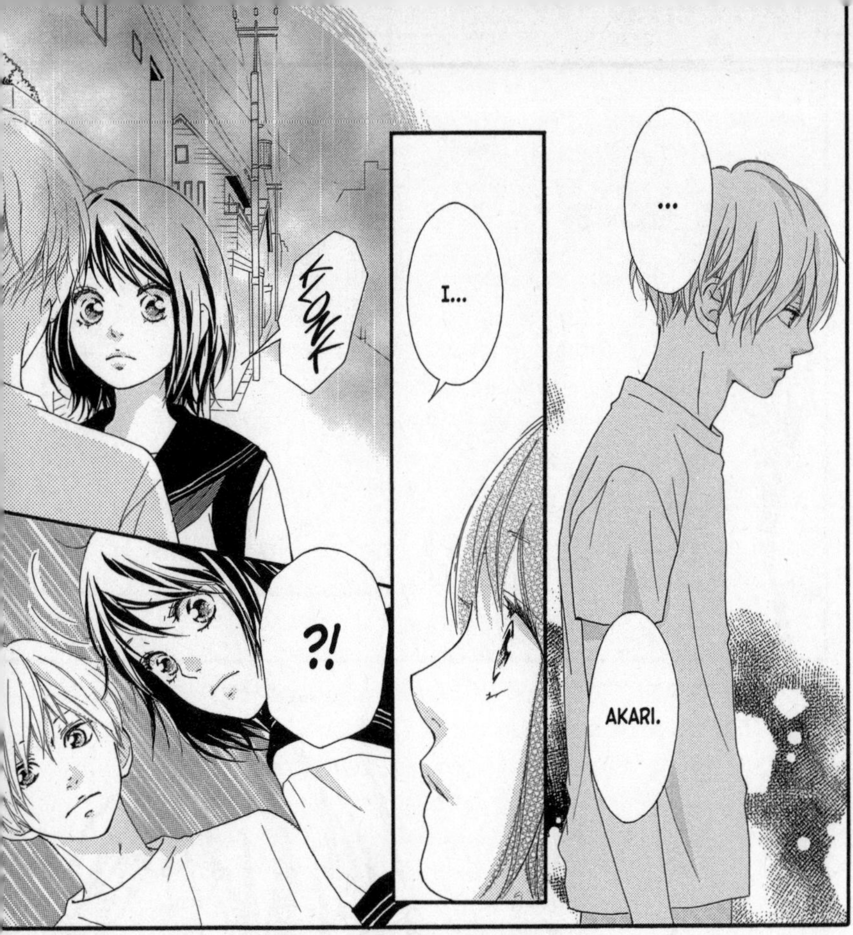
...
AKARI.
I...
KLONK
?!
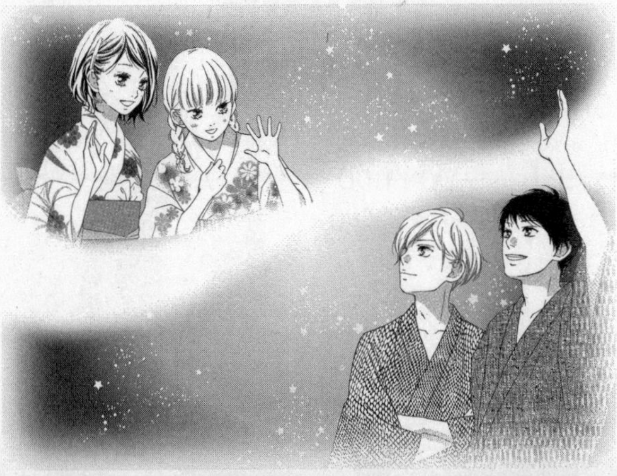

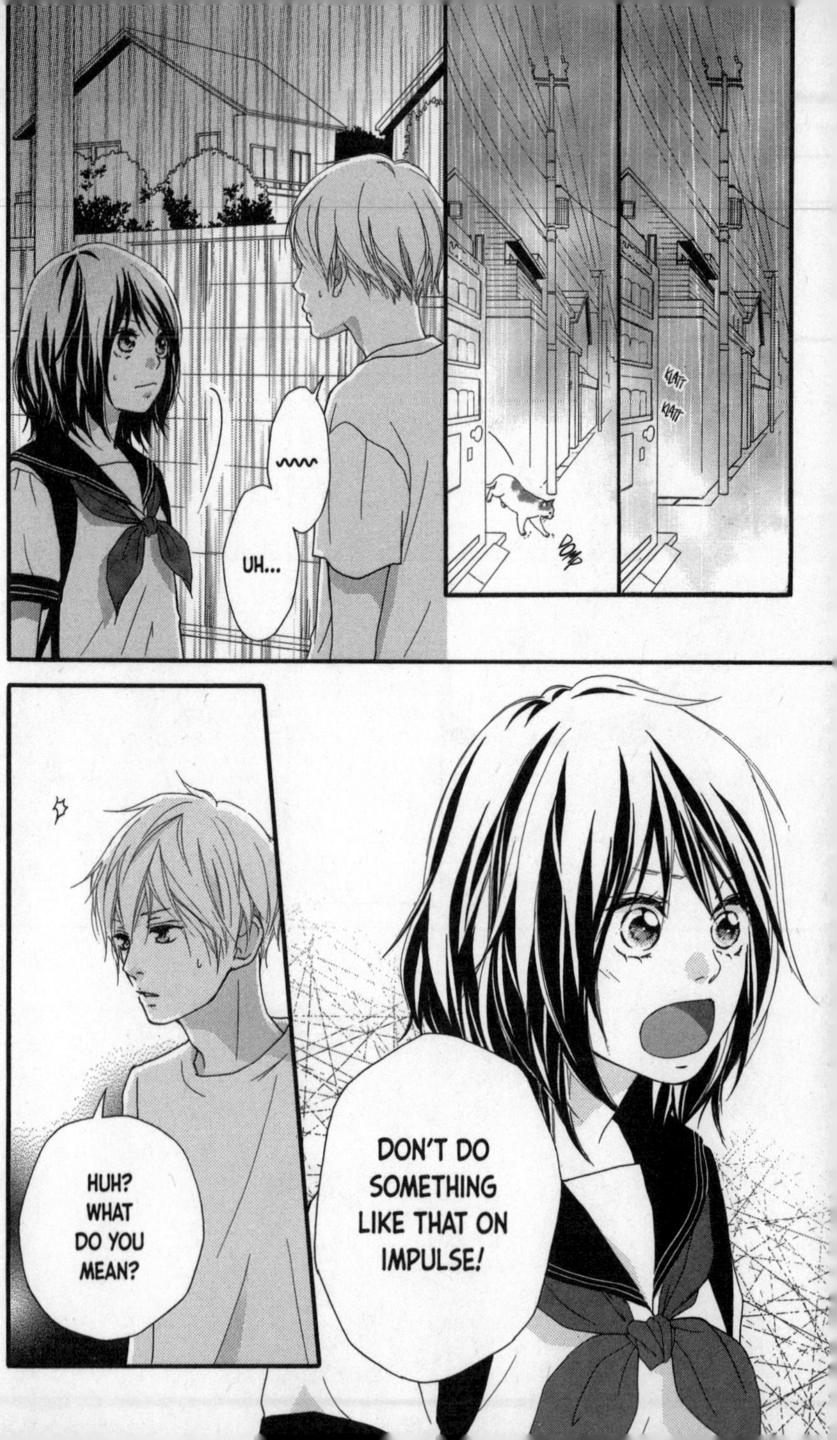
KLATT
KLATT
DOMP
UH...
DON'T DO SOMETHING LIKE THAT ON IMPULSE!
HUH? WHAT DO YOU MEAN?

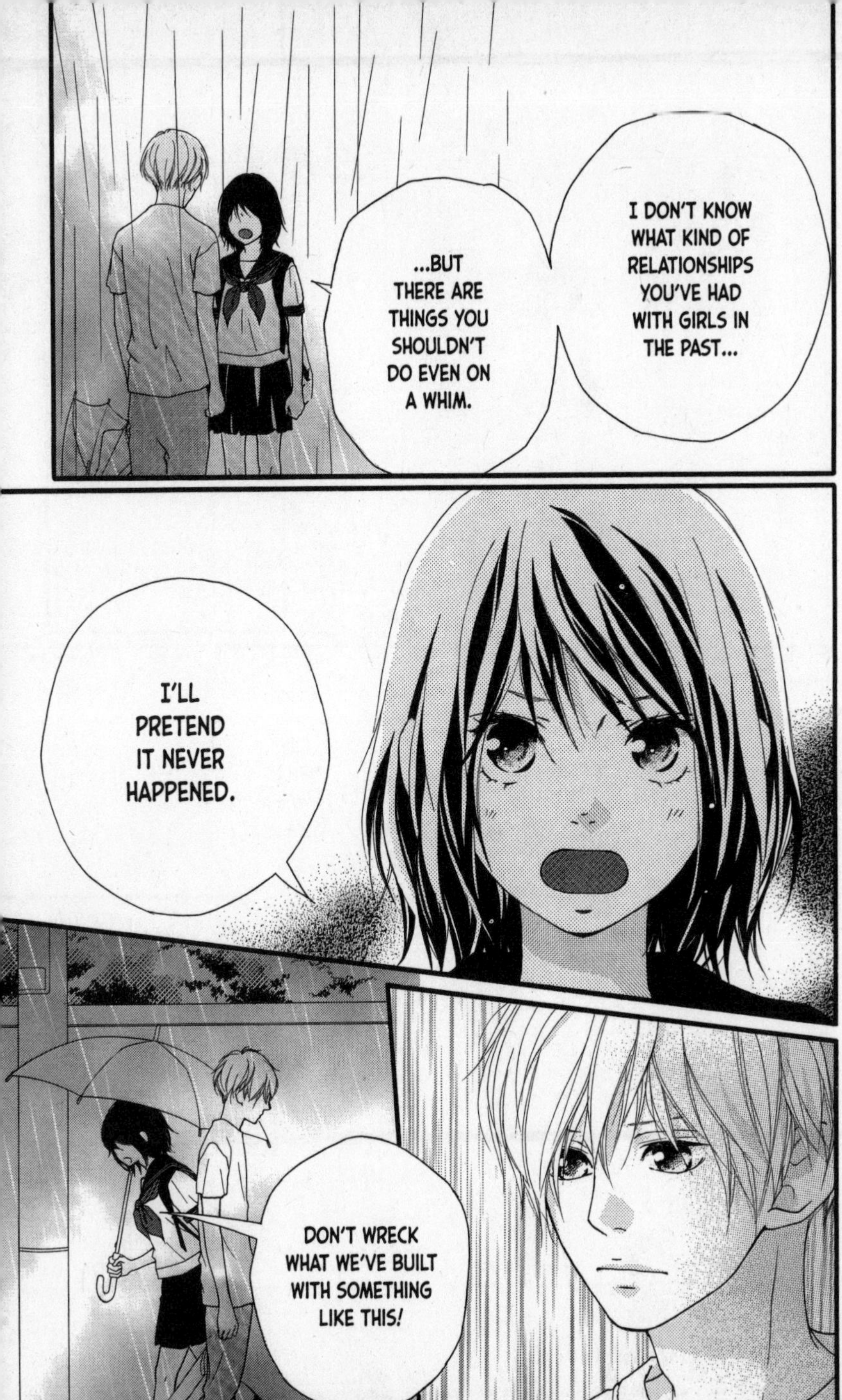
I DON'T KNOW WHAT KIND OF RELATIONSHIPS YOU'VE HAD WITH GIRLS IN THE PAST...
...BUT THERE ARE THINGS YOU SHOULDN'T DO EVEN ON A WHIM.
I'LL PRETEND IT NEVER HAPPENED.
DON'T WRECK WHAT WE'VE BUILT WITH SOMETHING LIKE THIS!

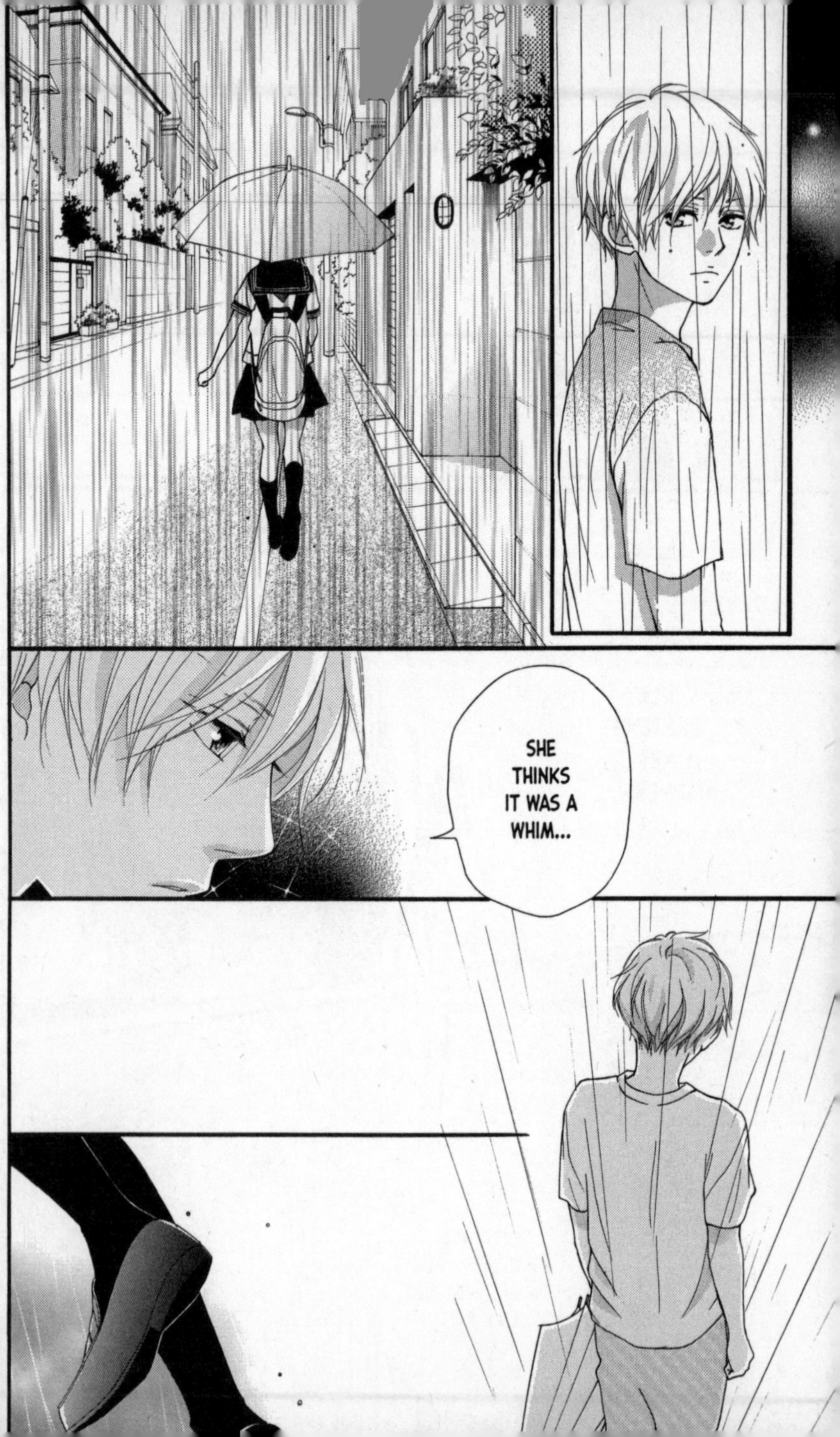
SHE THINKS IT WAS A WHIM...

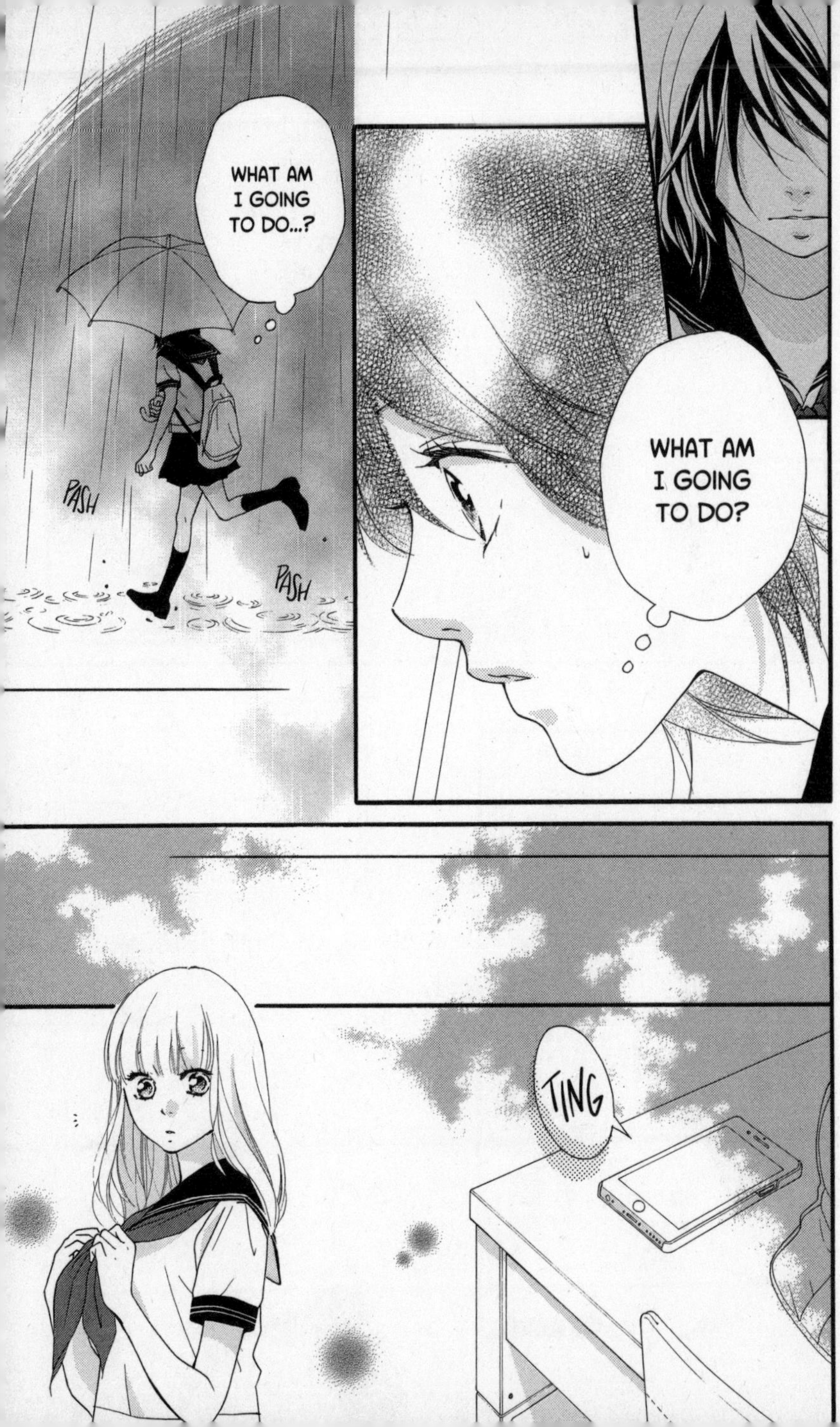
WHAT AM I GOING TO DO?
WHAT AM I GOING TO DO...?
PASH
PASH
TING

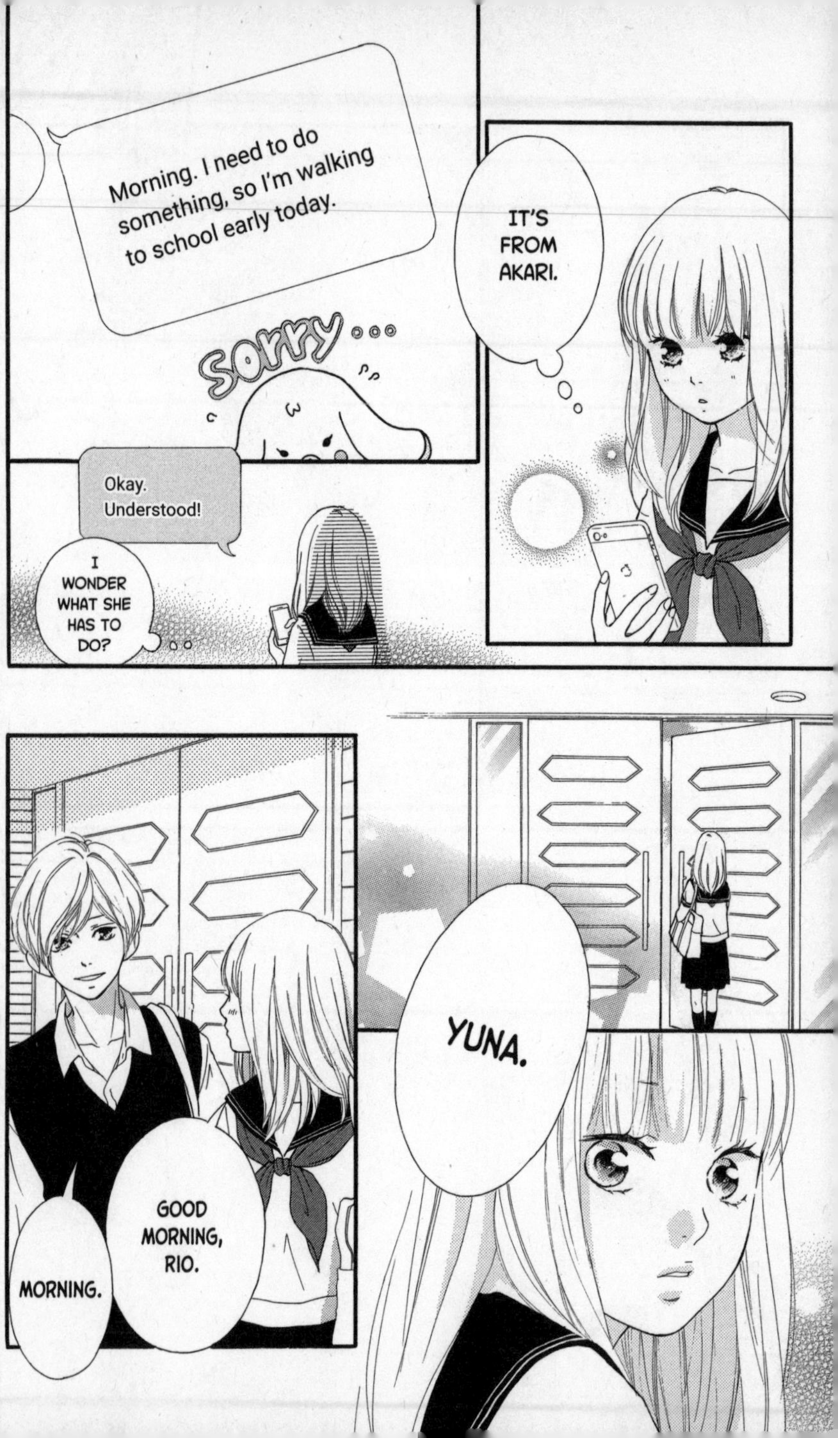
IT'S FROM AKARI.
Morning. I need to do something, so I'm walking to school early today.
Sorry...
Okay. Understood!
I WONDER WHAT SHE HAS TO DO?
YUNA.
GOOD MORNING, RIO.
MORNING.

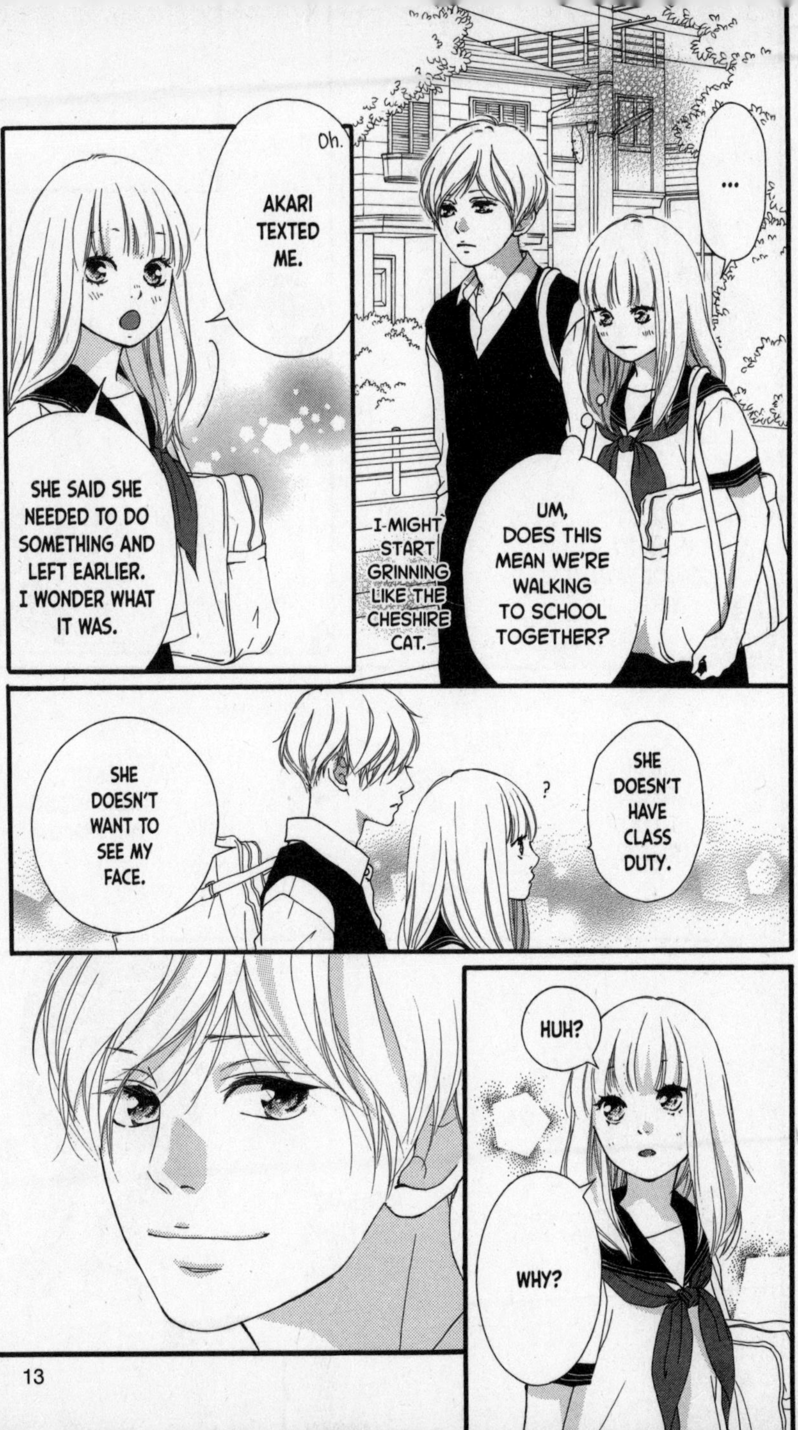
...
UM, DOES THIS MEAN WE'RE WALKING TO SCHOOL TOGETHER?
I-MIGHT START GRINNING LIKE THE CHESHIRE CAT.
Oh.
AKARI TEXTED ME.
SHE SAID SHE NEEDED TO DO SOMETHING AND LEFT EARLIER. I WONDER WHAT IT WAS.
SHE DOESN'T HAVE CLASS DUTY.
?
SHE DOESN'T WANT TO SEE MY FACE.
HUH?
WHY?

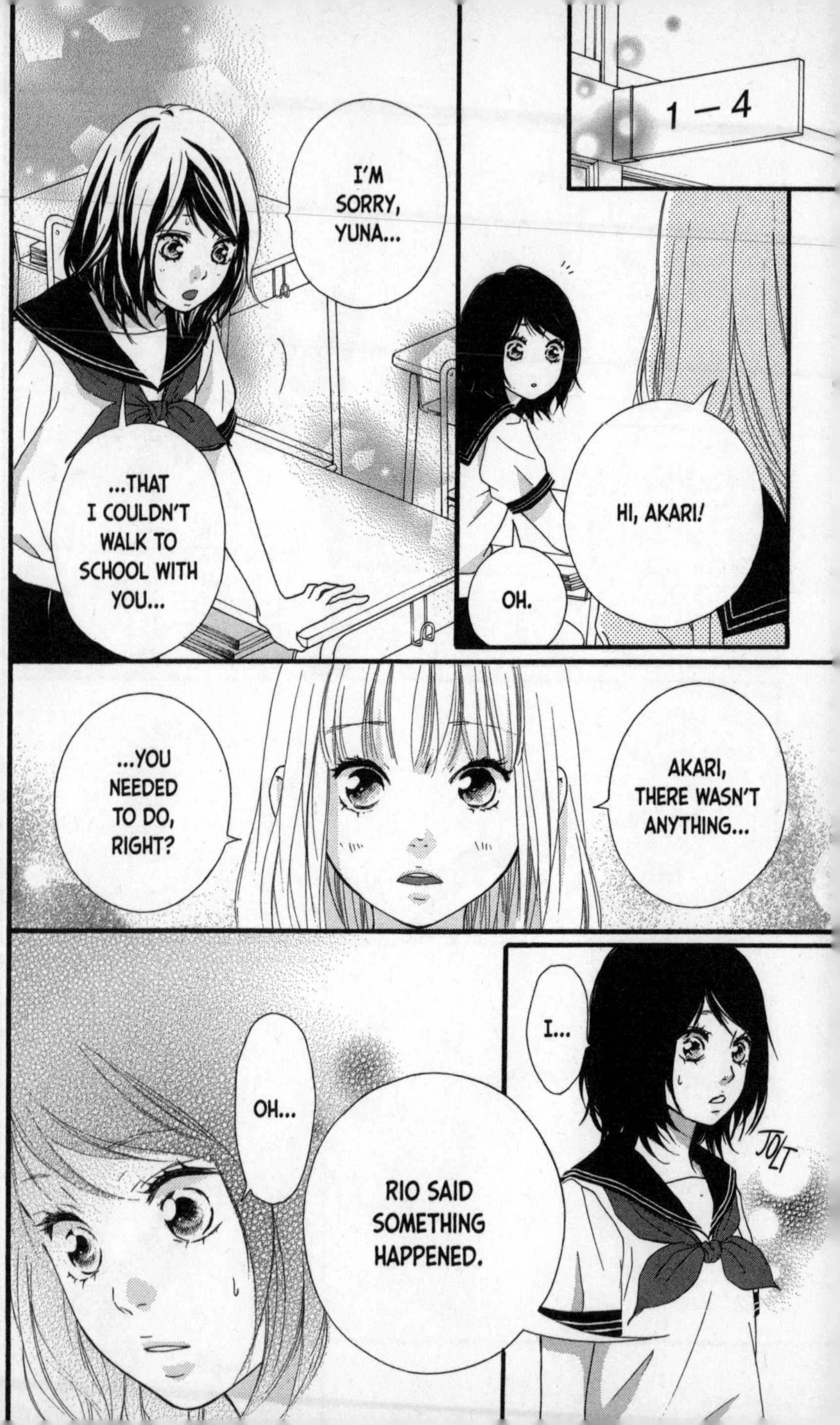
1 — 4
HI, AKARI!
OH.
I'M SORRY, YUNA...
...THAT I COULDN'T WALK TO SCHOOL WITH YOU...
AKARI, THERE WASN'T ANYTHING...
...YOU NEEDED TO DO, RIGHT?
I...
JOLT
RIO SAID SOMETHING HAPPENED.
OH...

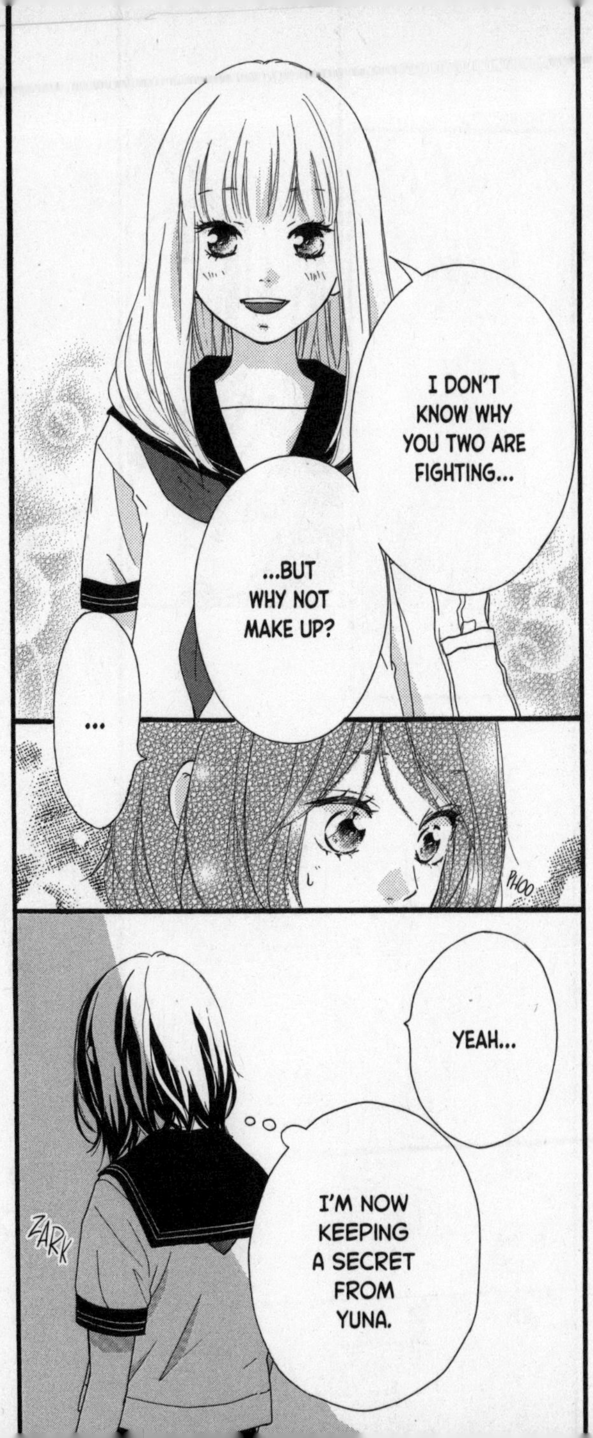
I DON'T KNOW WHY YOU TWO ARE FIGHTING...
...BUT WHY NOT MAKE UP?
...
PHOO
YEAH...
I'M NOW KEEPING A SECRET FROM YUNA.
ZARK

In order to squeeze in some time to read, I tend to read in the bath. My head gets fuzzy if I'm sitting in the hot water for too long trying to read something too complicated, so I'm very careful about my book choice. And just in case I should ever drop the book in the tub, I bring in a paperback rather than an e-reader. (My smartphone is not waterproof.) Well it's not like I submerge my books all that often...or so I thought. But the other day, I did it. It splashed. I had no idea it was so hard to turn the pages of a wet book! (*laugh*) I was at a really good part, so rather than waiting for it to dry, I just kept reading. Not only were the pages hard to turn, the type was hard to read because you could see through to the next page. It was tough going.

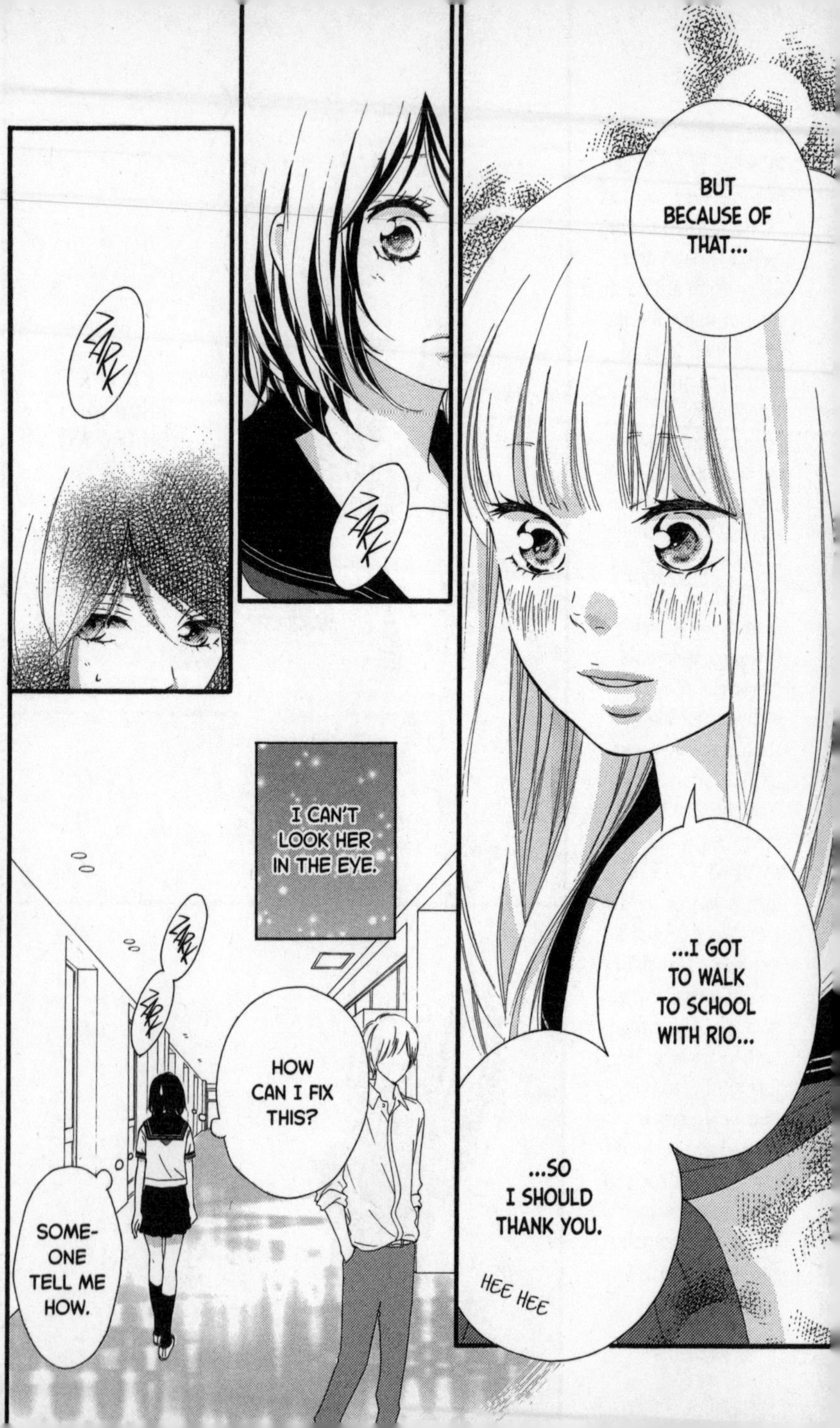
BUT BECAUSE OF THAT...
...I GOT TO WALK TO SCHOOL WITH RIO...
...SO I SHOULD THANK YOU.
HEE HEE
ZARK
ZARK
I CAN'T LOOK HER IN THE EYE.
ZARK
ZARK
HOW CAN I FIX THIS?
SOME-ONE TELL ME HOW.

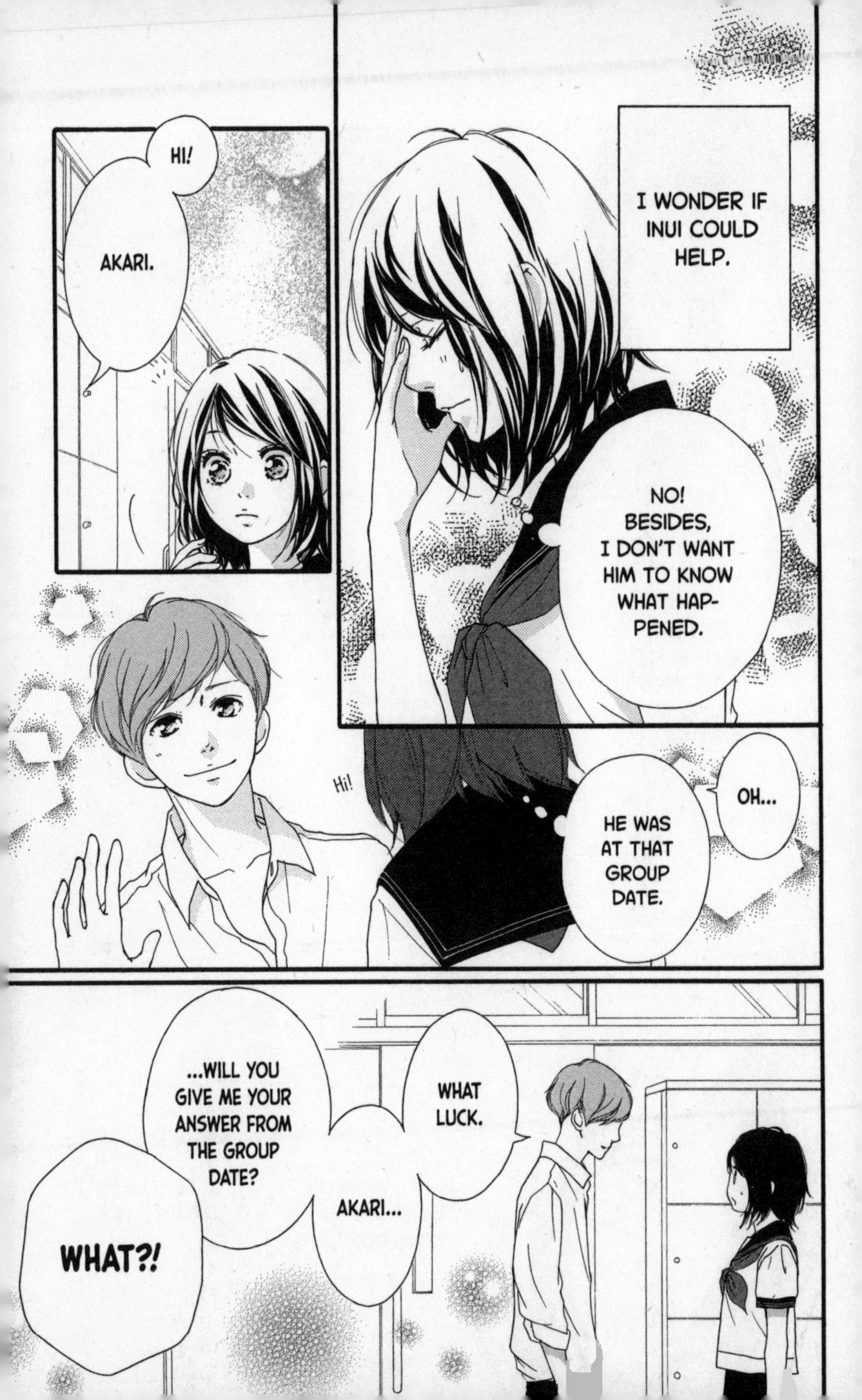
I WONDER IF INUI COULD HELP.
NO! BESIDES, I DON'T WANT HIM TO KNOW WHAT HAP-PENED.
HI!
AKARI.
OH...
HE WAS AT THAT GROUP DATE.
Hi!
WHAT LUCK.
AKARI...
...WILL YOU GIVE ME YOUR ANSWER FROM THE GROUP DATE?
WHAT?!

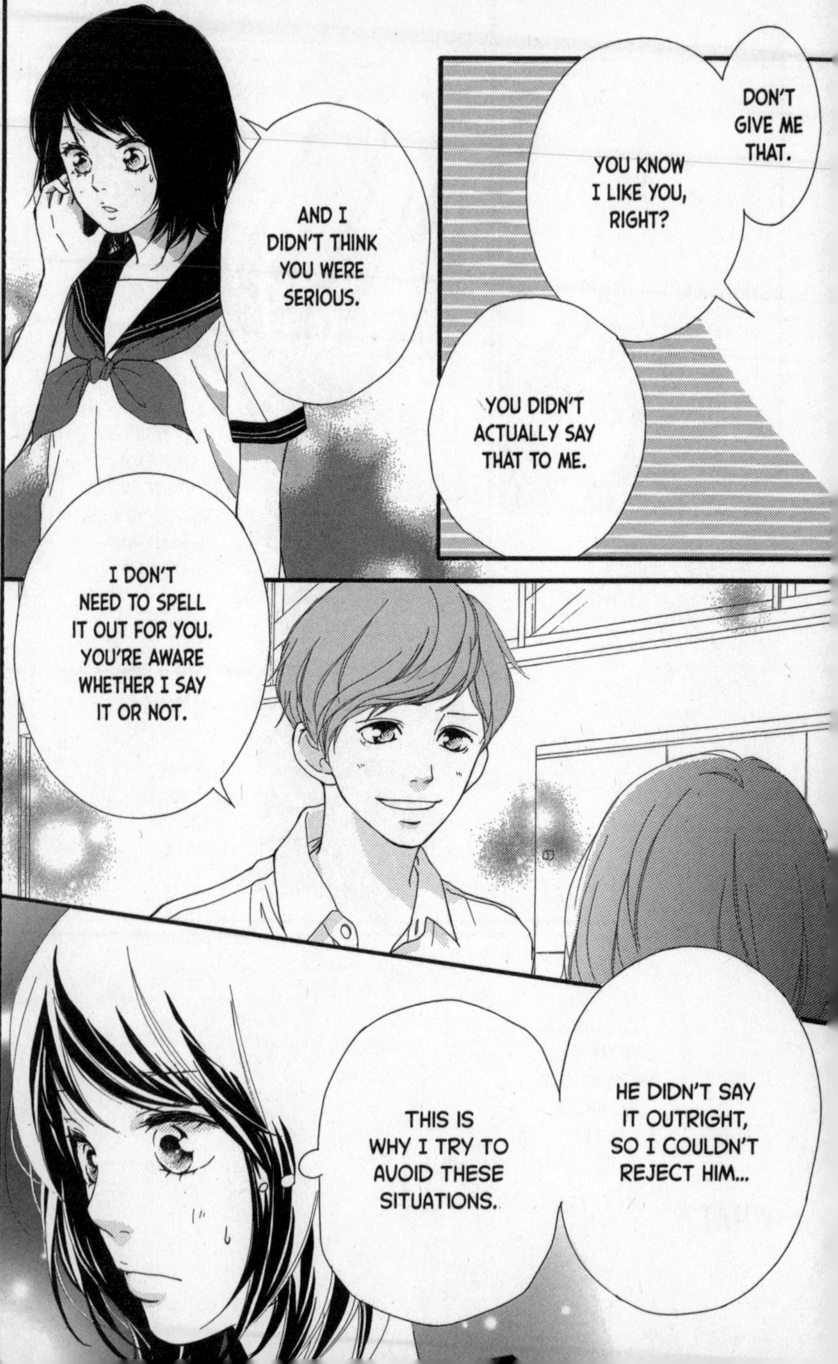
DON'T GIVE ME THAT.
YOU KNOW I LIKE YOU, RIGHT?
YOU DIDN'T ACTUALLY SAY THAT TO ME.
AND I DIDN'T THINK YOU WERE SERIOUS.
I DON'T NEED TO SPELL IT OUT FOR YOU. YOU'RE AWARE WHETHER I SAY IT OR NOT.
HE DIDN'T SAY IT OUTRIGHT, SO I COULDN'T REJECT HIM...
THIS IS WHY I TRY TO AVOID THESE SITUATIONS.

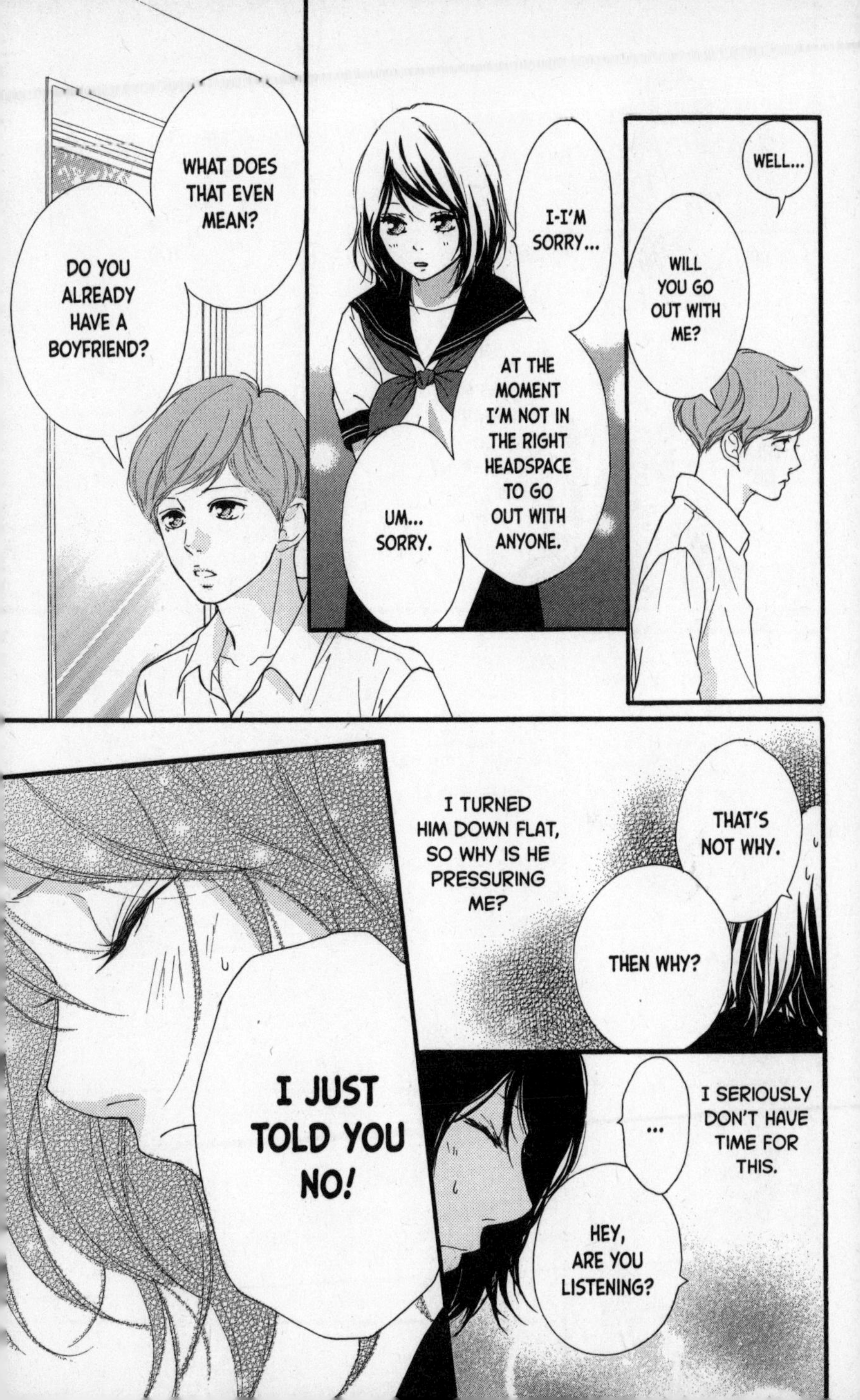
WELL...
WILL YOU GO OUT WITH ME?
I-I'M SORRY...
AT THE MOMENT I'M NOT IN THE RIGHT HEADSPACE TO GO OUT WITH ANYONE.
UM... SORRY.
WHAT DOES THAT EVEN MEAN?
DO YOU ALREADY HAVE A BOYFRIEND?
THAT'S NOT WHY.
THEN WHY?
I TURNED HIM DOWN FLAT, SO WHY IS HE PRESSURING ME?
I SERIOUSLY DON'T HAVE TIME FOR THIS.
...
HEY, ARE YOU LISTENING?
I JUST TOLD YOU NO!

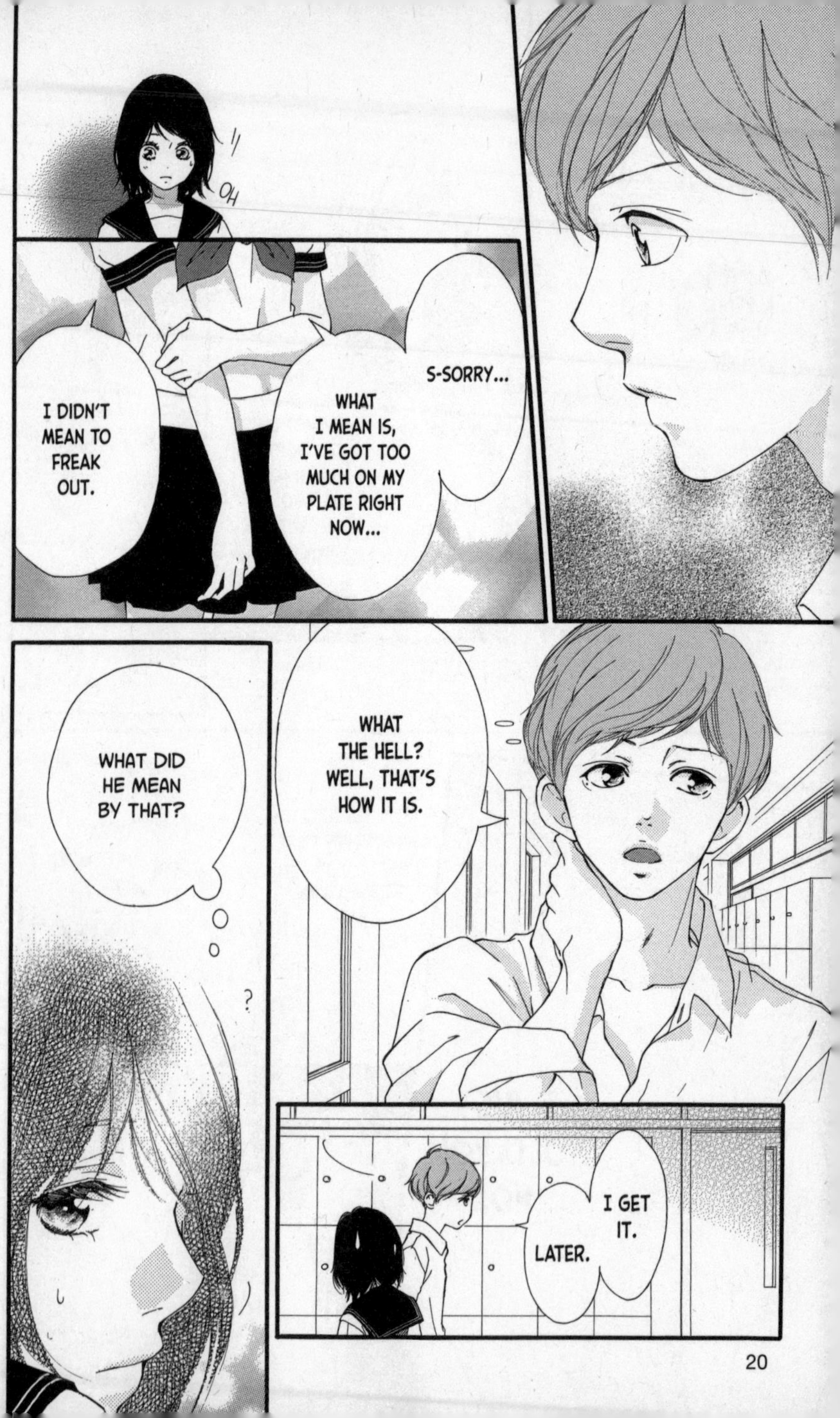
OH
S-SORRY...
WHAT I MEAN IS, I'VE GOT TOO MUCH ON MY PLATE RIGHT NOW...
I DIDN'T MEAN TO FREAK OUT.
WHAT THE HELL? WELL, THAT'S HOW IT IS.
I GET IT.
LATER.
WHAT DID HE MEAN BY THAT?
?

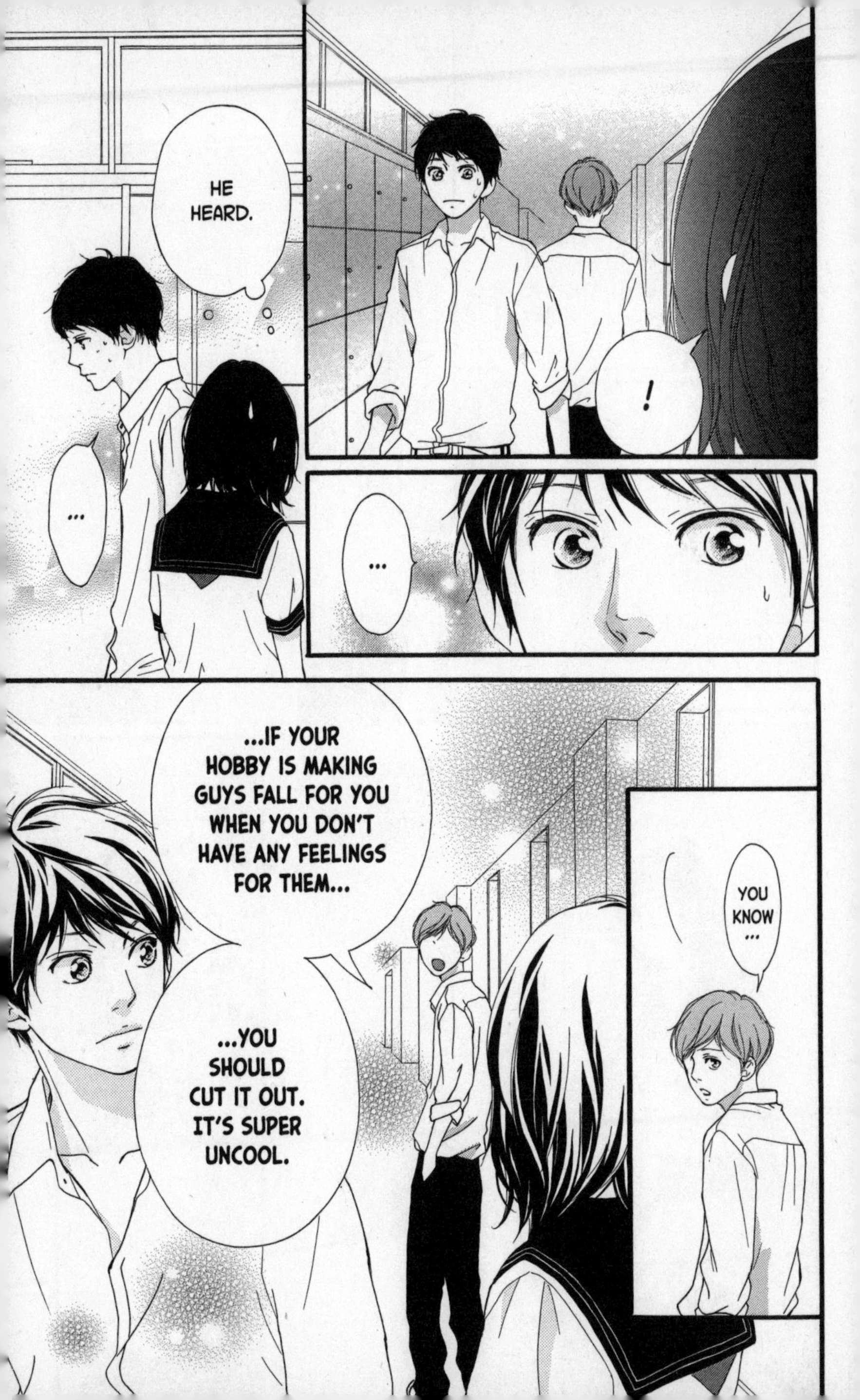
!
...
HE HEARD.
...
YOU KNOW...
...IF YOUR HOBBY IS MAKING GUYS FALL FOR YOU WHEN YOU DON'T HAVE ANY FEELINGS FOR THEM...
...YOU SHOULD CUT IT OUT. IT'S SUPER UNCOOL.

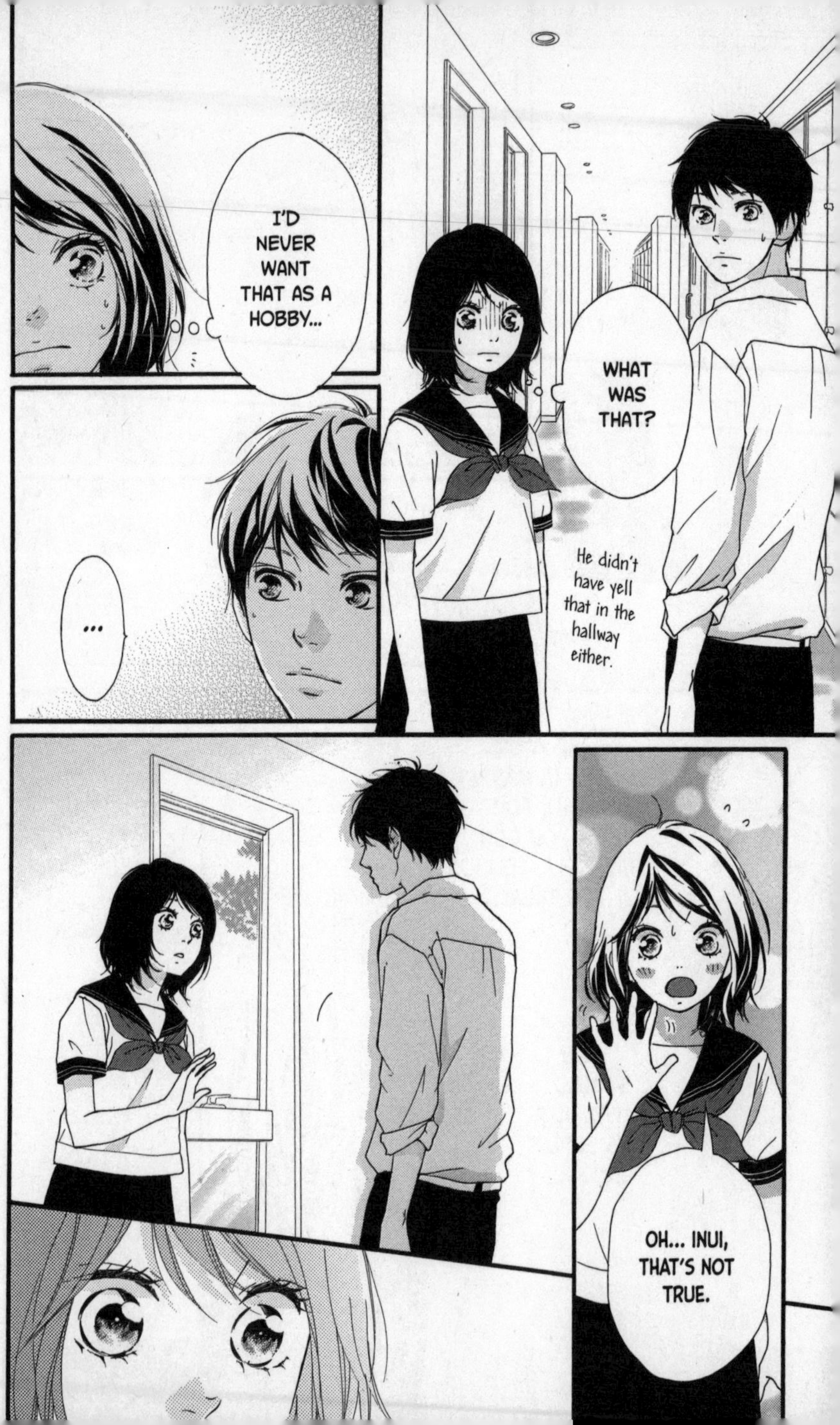
WHAT WAS THAT?
He didn't have yell that in the hallway either.
I'D NEVER WANT THAT AS A HOBBY...
...
OH... INUI, THAT'S NOT TRUE.

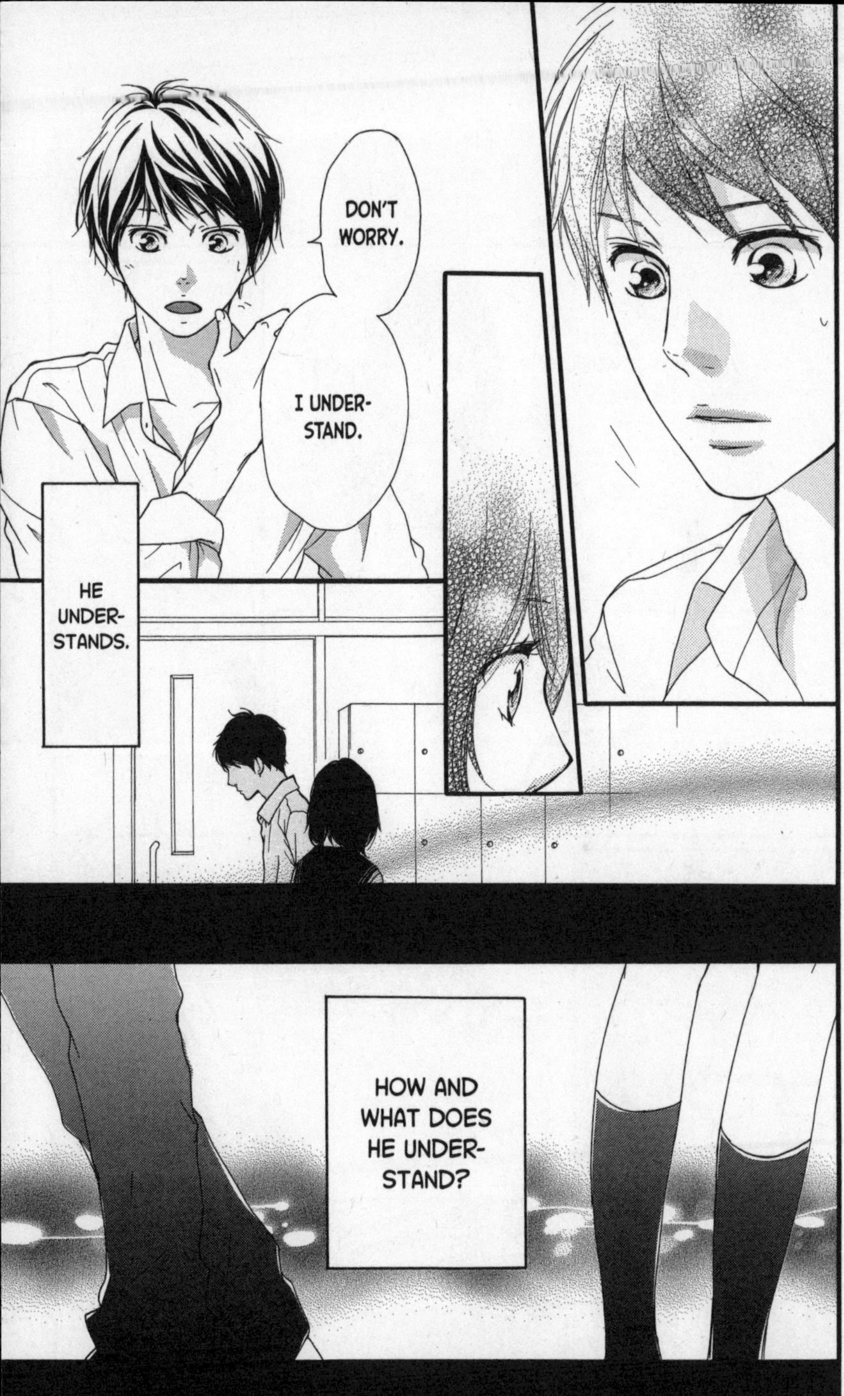
DON'T WORRY.
I UNDER-STAND.
HE UNDER-STANDS.
HOW AND WHAT DOES HE UNDER-STAND?

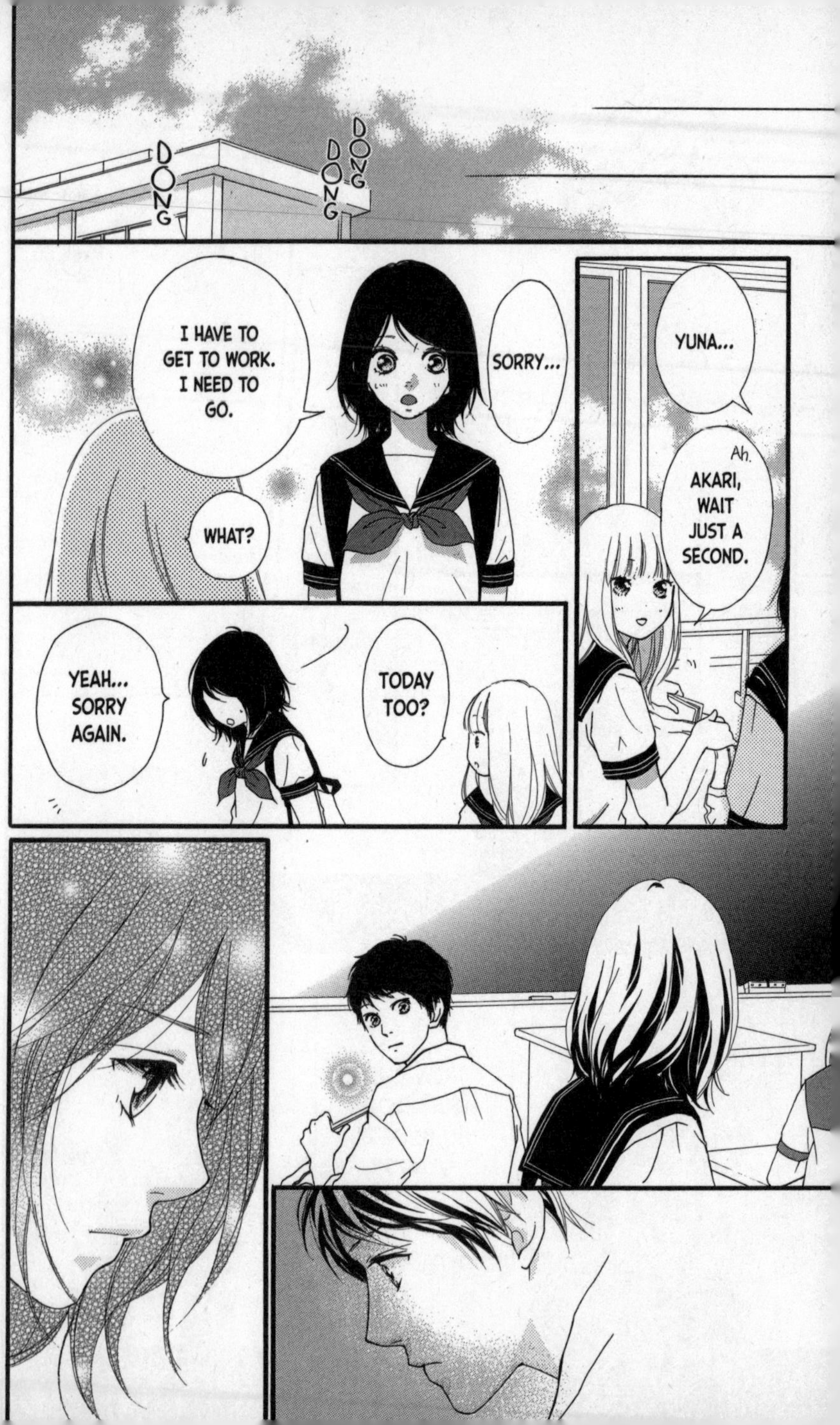
DONG
DONG
DONG
YUNA...
Ah.
AKARI, WAIT JUST A SECOND.
SORRY...
I HAVE TO GET TO WORK. I NEED TO GO.
WHAT?
TODAY TOO?
YEAH... SORRY AGAIN.

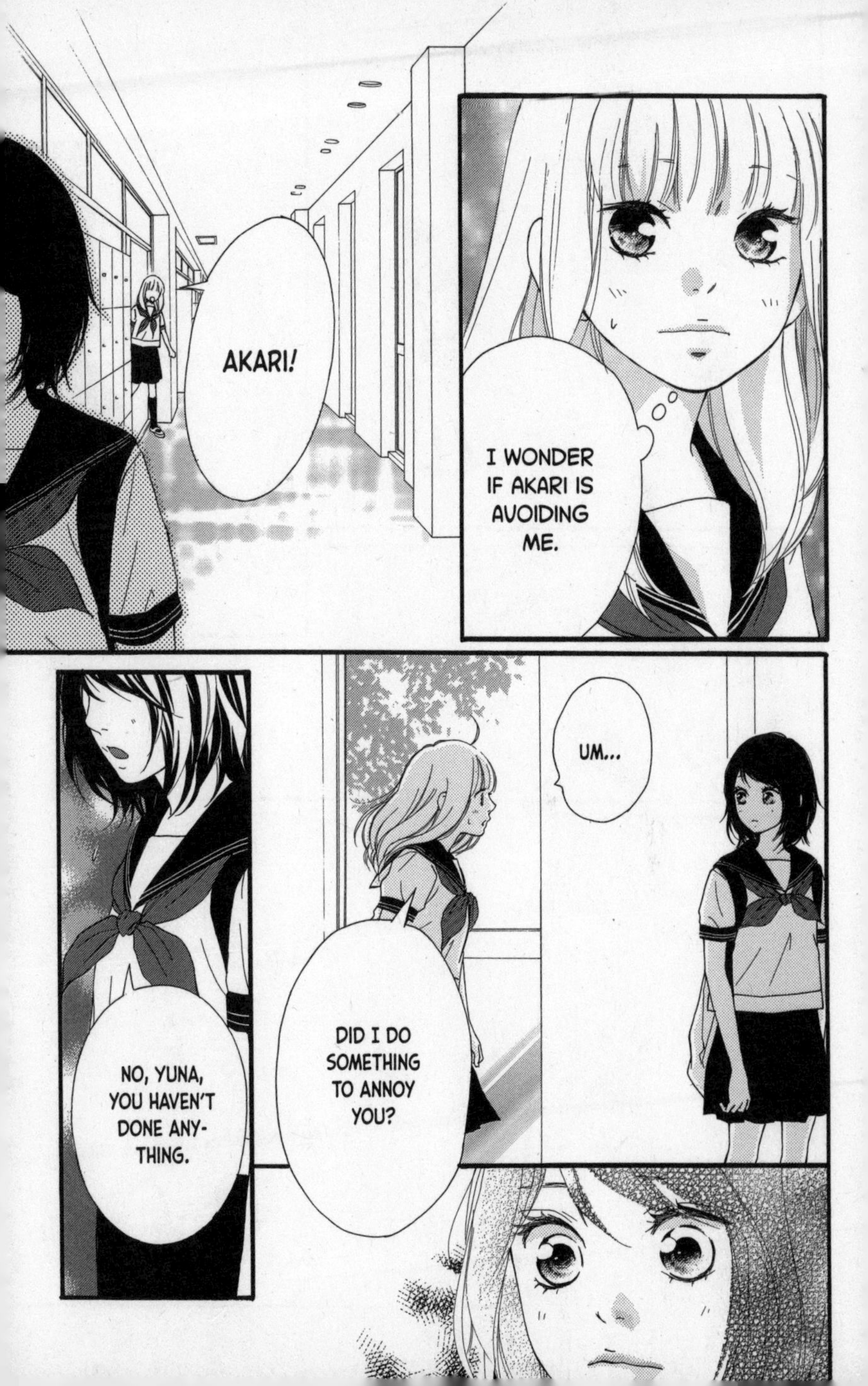
I WONDER IF AKARI IS AVOIDING ME.
AKARI!
UM...
DID I DO SOMETHING TO ANNOY YOU?
NO, YUNA, YOU HAVEN'T DONE ANY-THING.

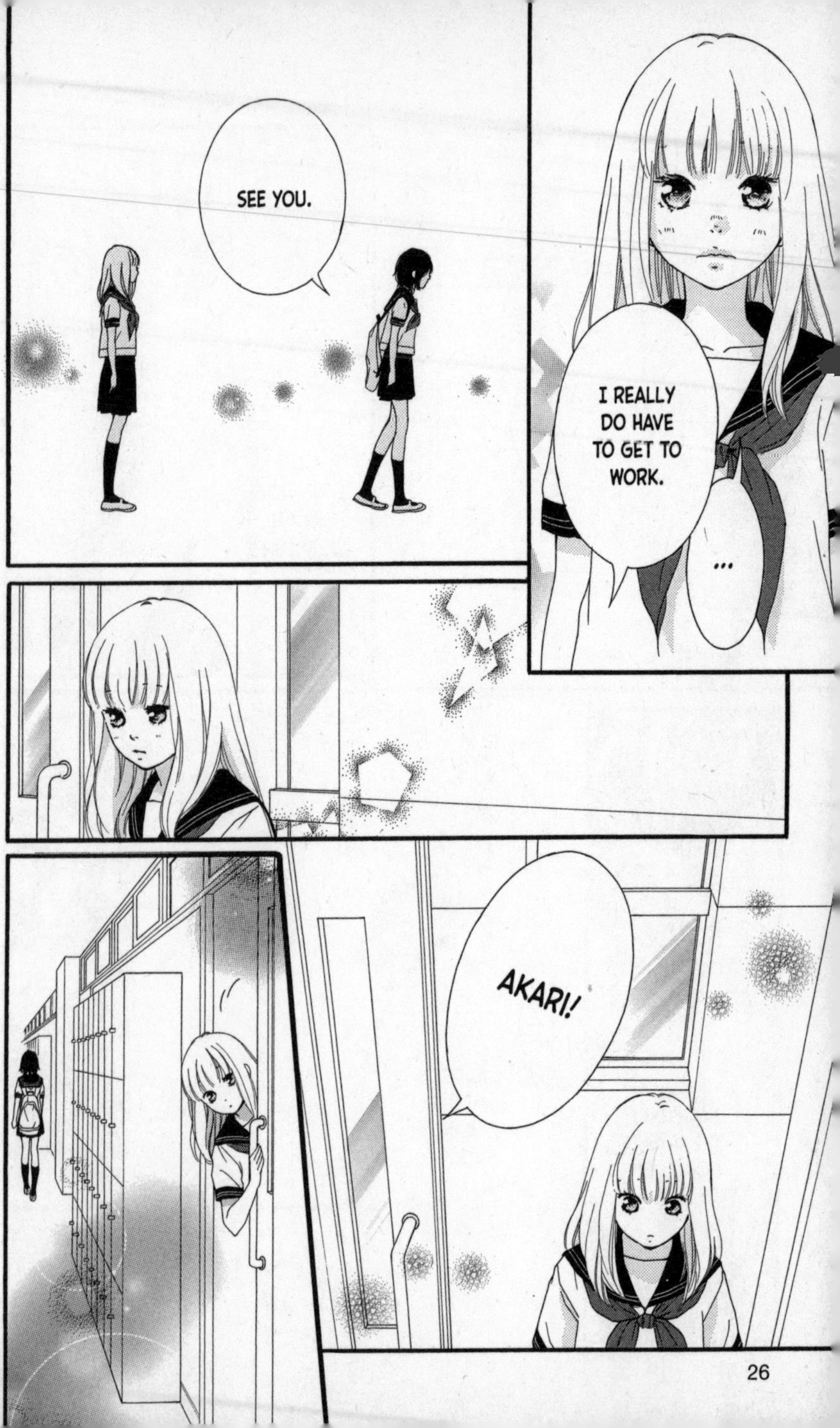
I REALLY DO HAVE TO GET TO WORK.
...
SEE YOU.
AKARI!

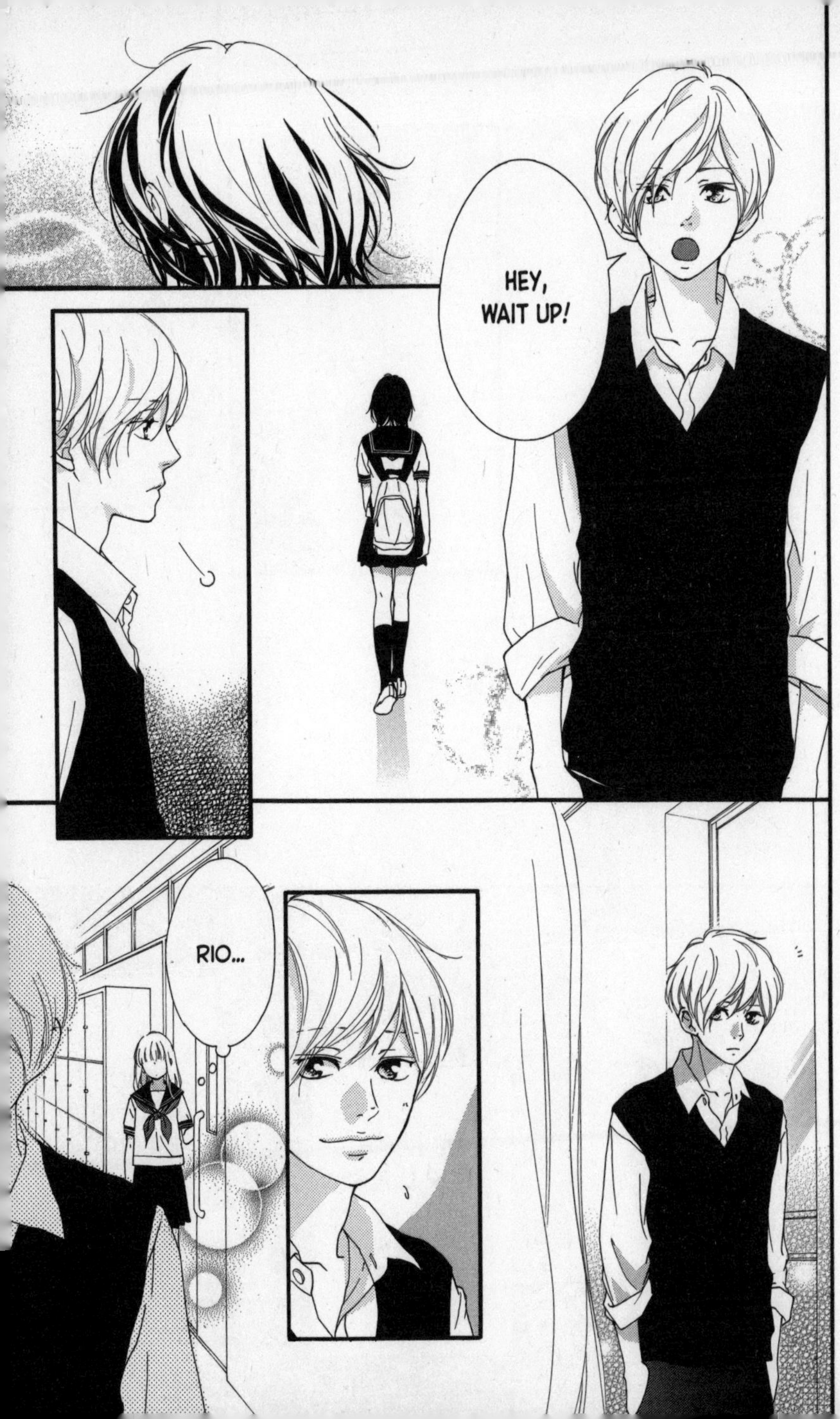
HEY, WAIT UP!
RIO...

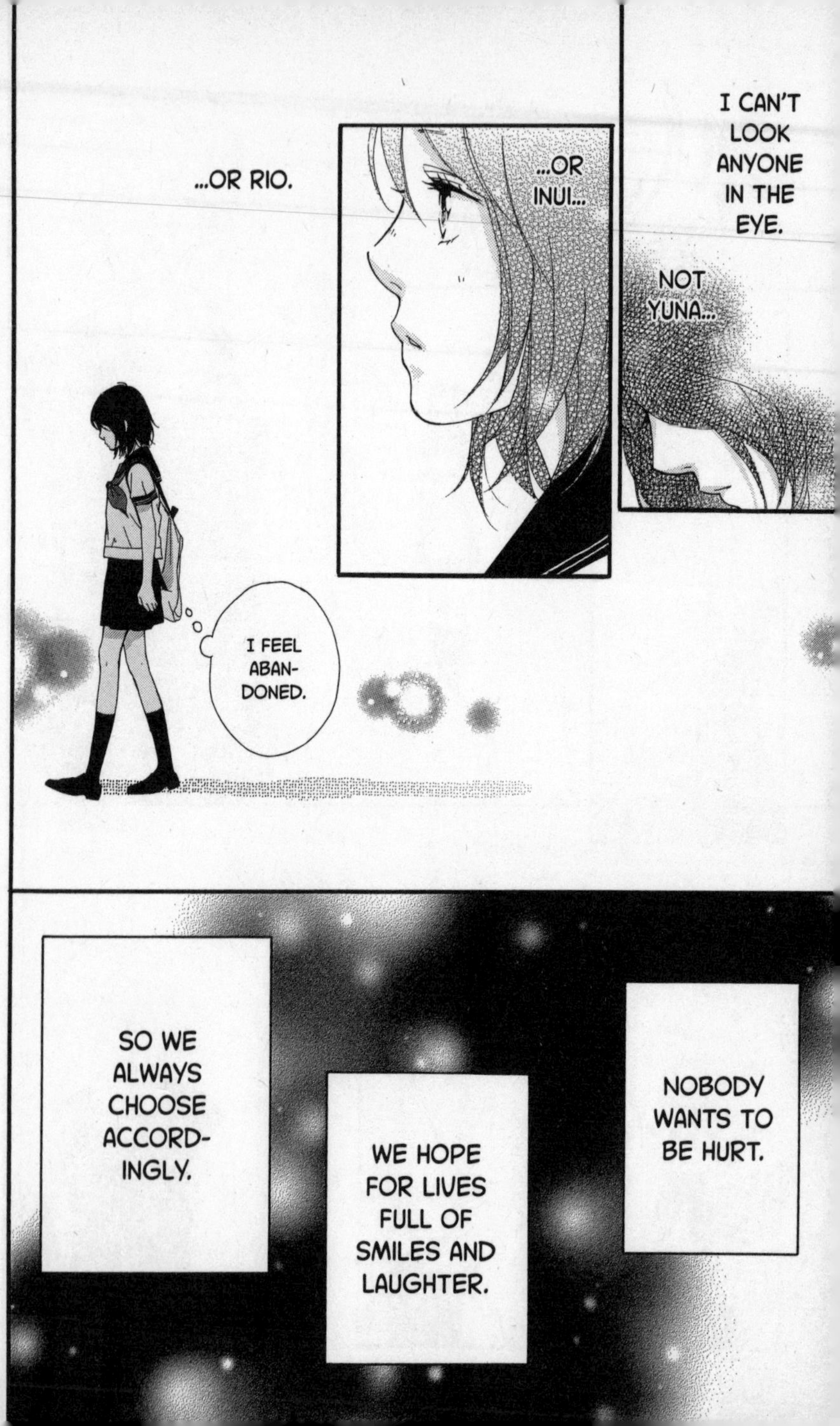
I CAN'T LOOK ANYONE IN THE EYE.
NOT YUNA...
...OR INUI...
...OR RIO.
I FEEL ABAN-DONED.
NOBODY WANTS TO BE HURT.
WE HOPE FOR LIVES FULL OF SMILES AND LAUGHTER.
SO WE ALWAYS CHOOSE ACCORD-INGLY.

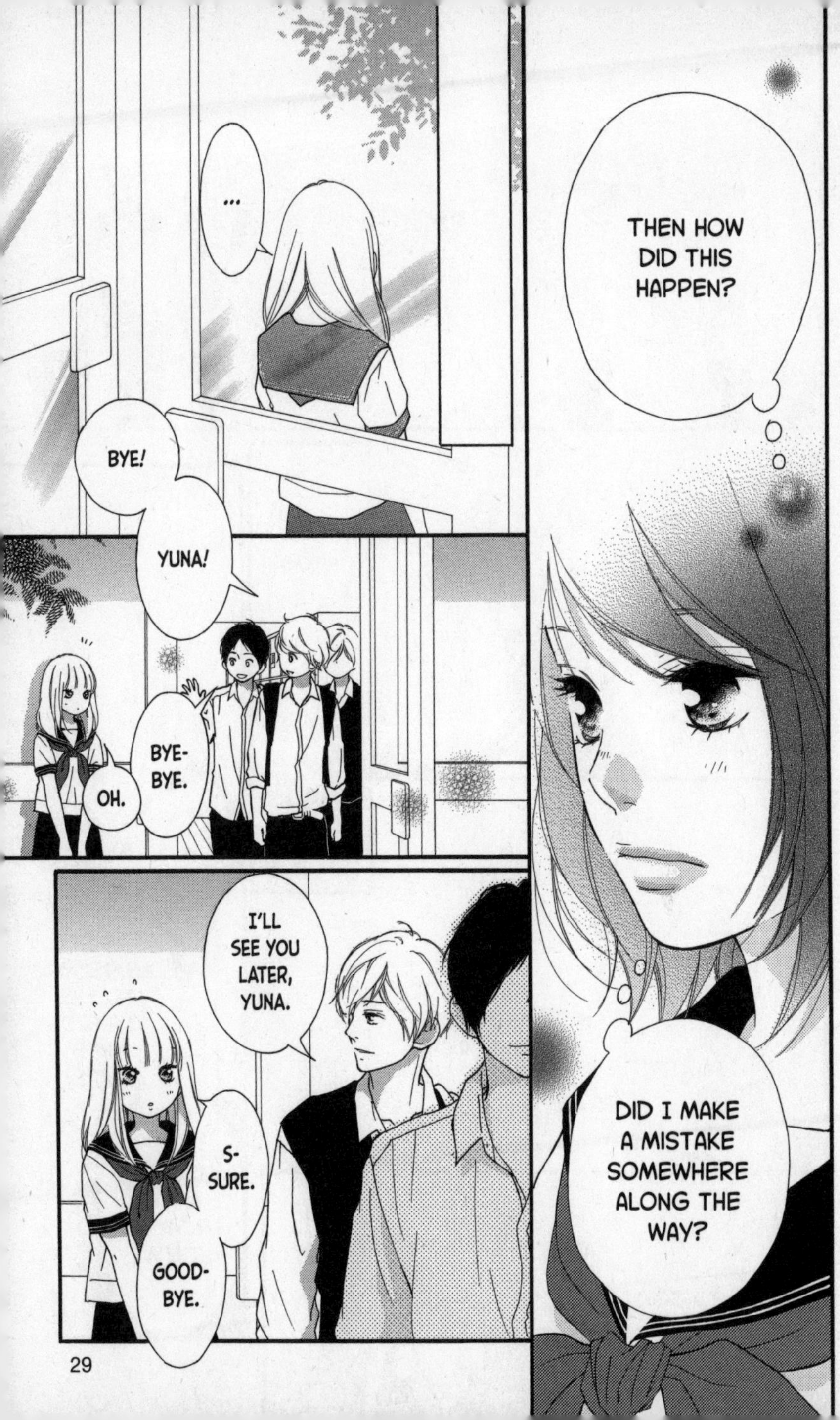
THEN HOW DID THIS HAPPEN?
DID I MAKE A MISTAKE SOMEWHERE ALONG THE WAY?
...
BYE!
YUNA!
BYE-BYE.
OH.
I'LL SEE YOU LATER, YUNA.
S-SURE.
GOOD-BYE.

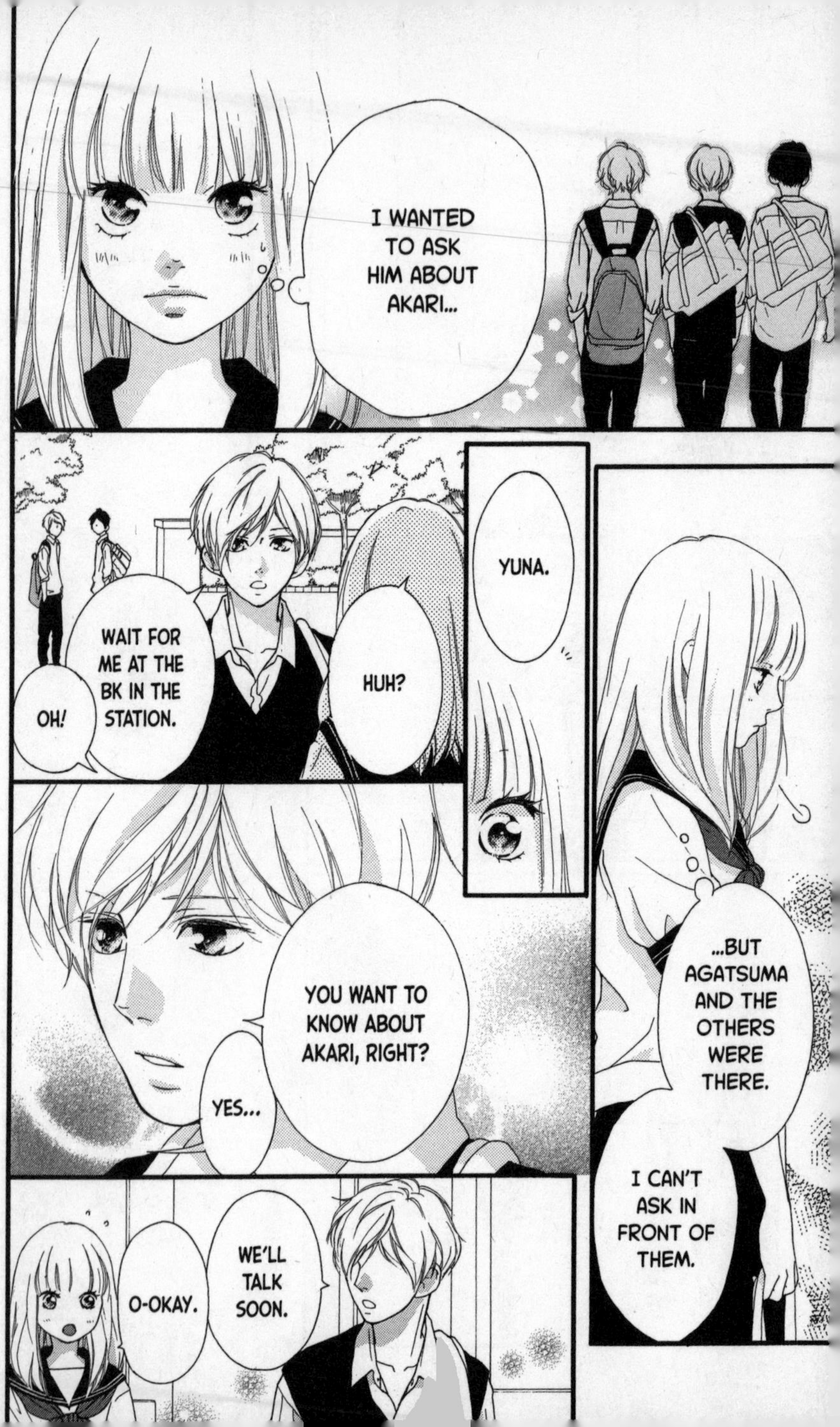
I WANTED TO ASK HIM ABOUT AKARI...
...BUT AGATSUMA AND THE OTHERS WERE THERE.
I CAN'T ASK IN FRONT OF THEM.
YUNA.
HUH?
WAIT FOR ME AT THE BK IN THE STATION.
OH!
YOU WANT TO KNOW ABOUT AKARI, RIGHT?
YES...
WE'LL TALK SOON.
O-OKAY.

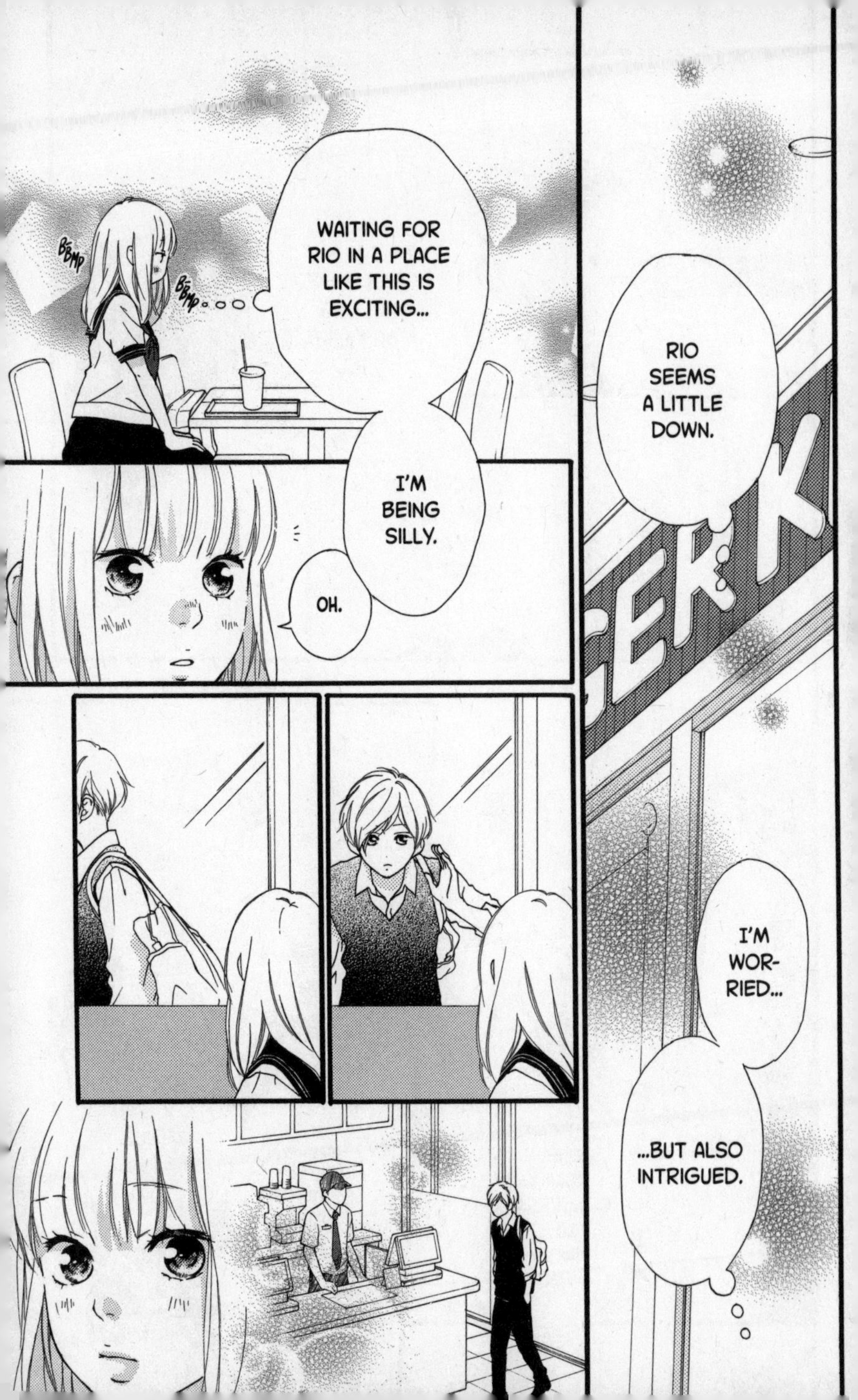

RIO SEEMS A LITTLE DOWN.
I'M WOR-RIED...
...BUT ALSO INTRIGUED.
WAITING FOR RIO IN A PLACE LIKE THIS IS EXCITING...
B-BMP
B-BMP
I'M BEING SILLY.
OH.

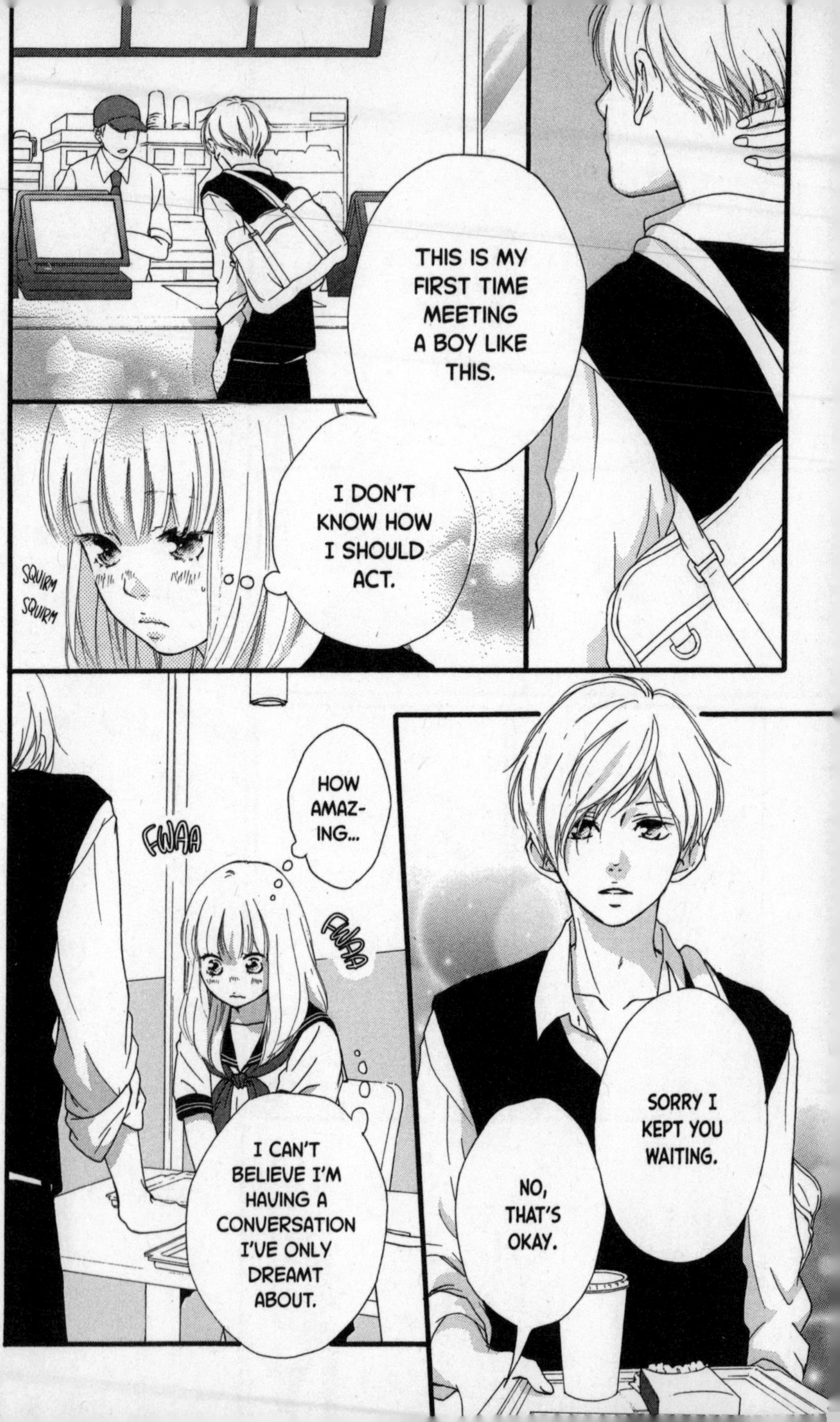
THIS IS MY FIRST TIME MEETING A BOY LIKE THIS.
I DON'T KNOW HOW I SHOULD ACT.
SQUIRM SQUIRM
SORRY I KEPT YOU WAITING.
NO, THAT'S OKAY.
HOW AMAZ-ING...
FWAA
FWAA
I CAN'T BELIEVE I'M HAVING A CONVERSATION I'VE ONLY DREAMT ABOUT.

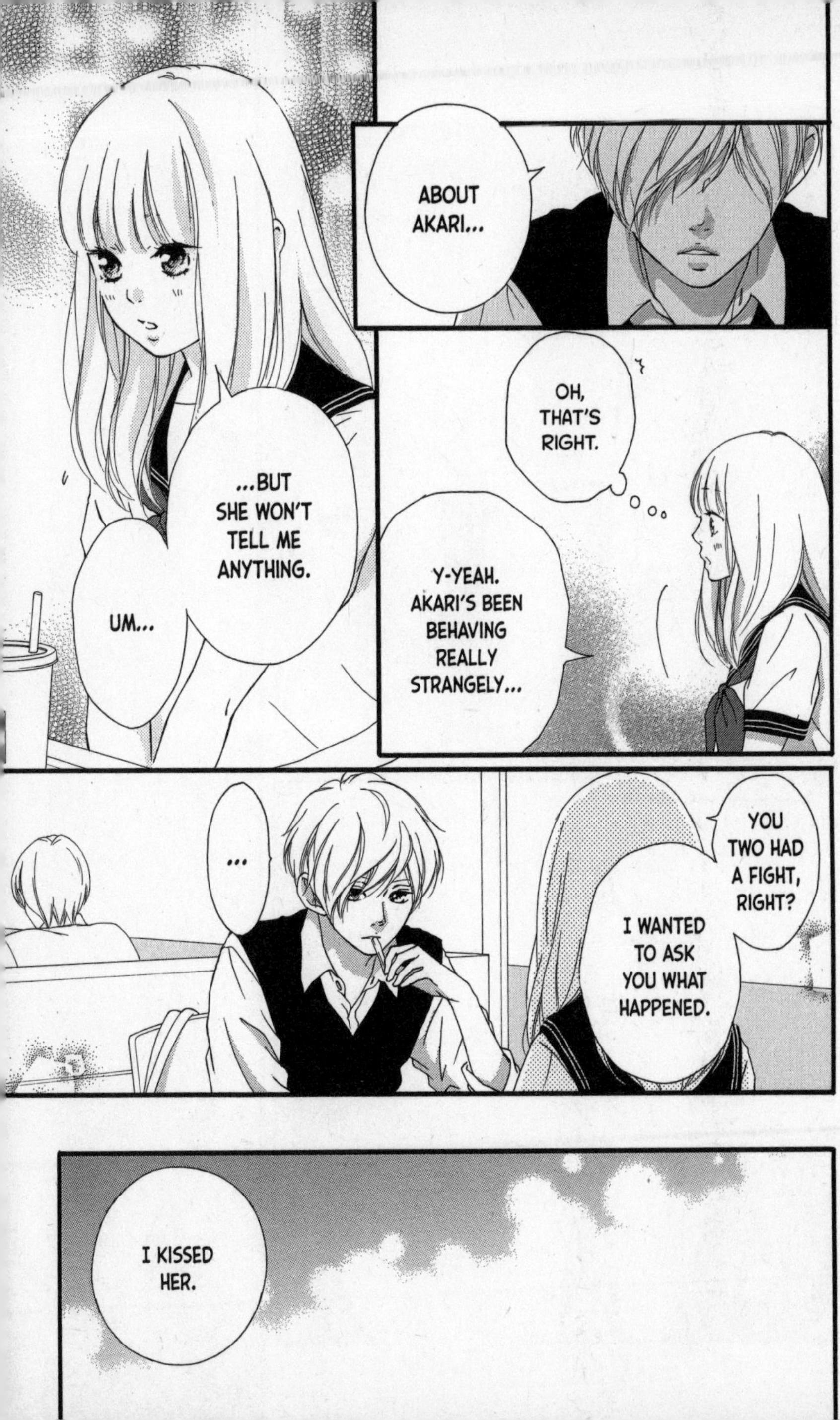
ABOUT AKARI...
OH, THAT'S RIGHT.
Y-YEAH. AKARI'S BEEN BEHAVING REALLY STRANGELY...
...BUT SHE WON'T TELL ME ANYTHING.
UM...
YOU TWO HAD A FIGHT, RIGHT?
I WANTED TO ASK YOU WHAT HAPPENED.
...
I KISSED HER.

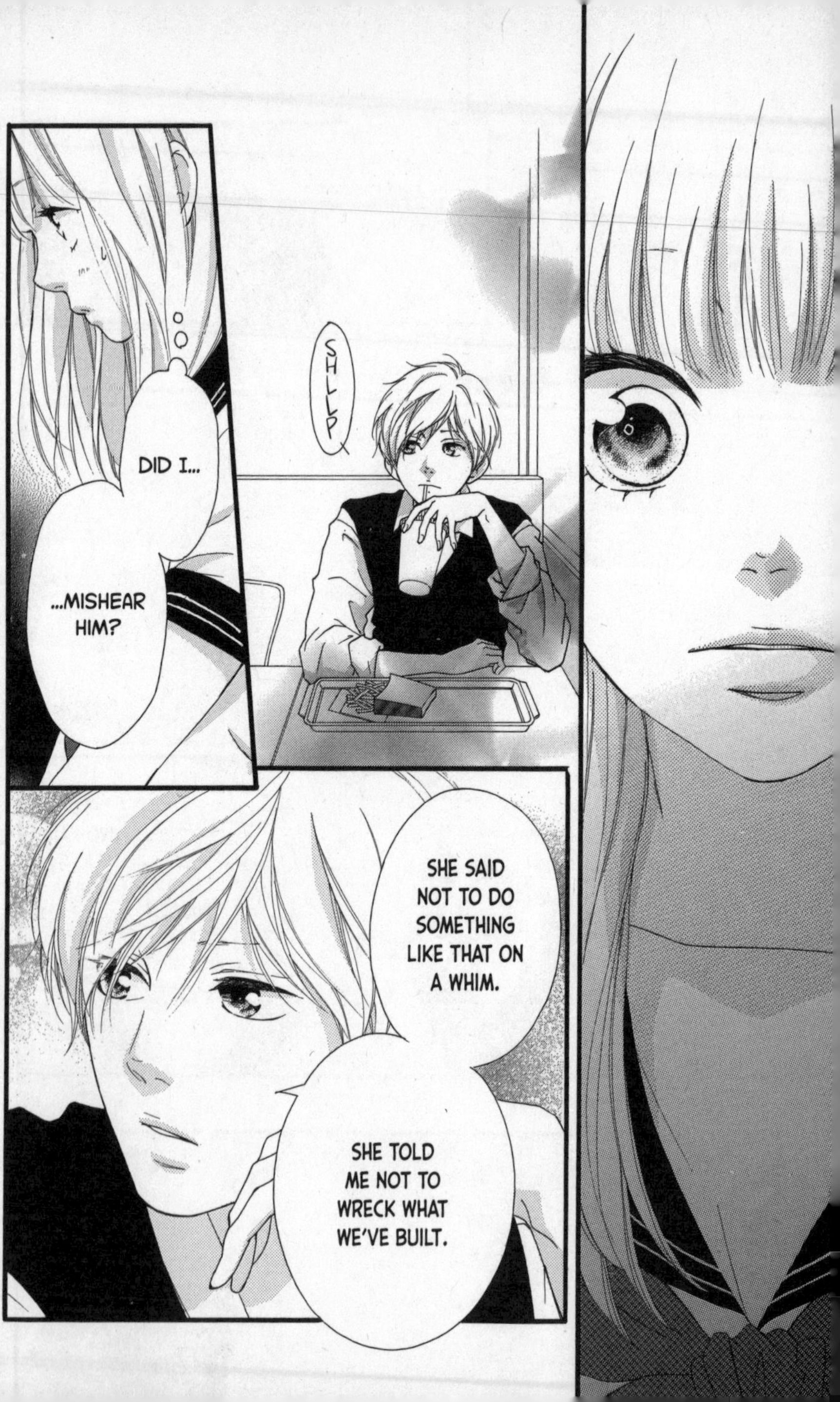
SHLLP
DID I...
...MISHEAR HIM?
SHE SAID NOT TO DO SOMETHING LIKE THAT ON A WHIM.
SHE TOLD ME NOT TO WRECK WHAT WE'VE BUILT.

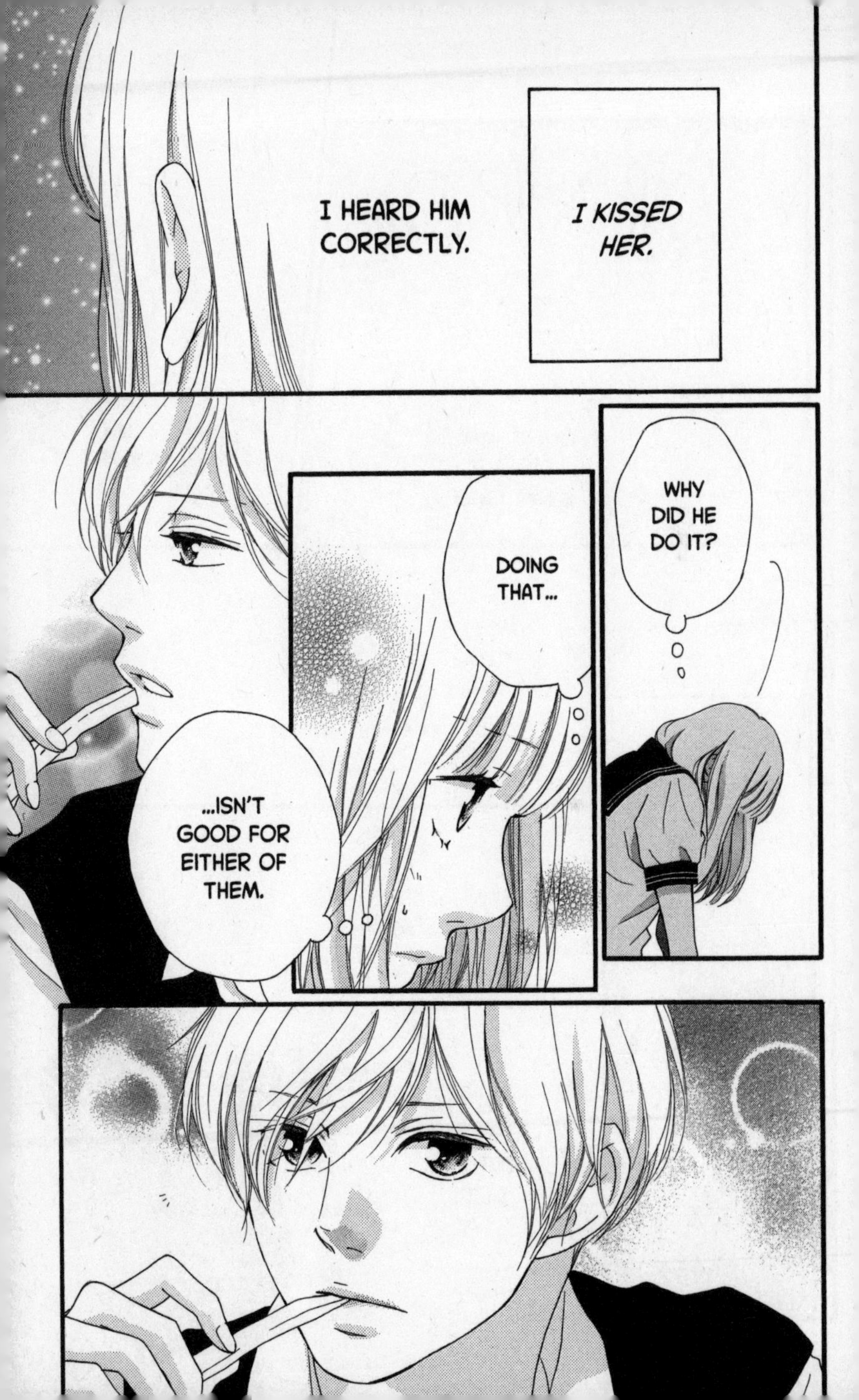
I KISSED HER.
I HEARD HIM CORRECTLY.
WHY DID HE DO IT?
DOING THAT...
...ISN'T GOOD FOR EITHER OF THEM.

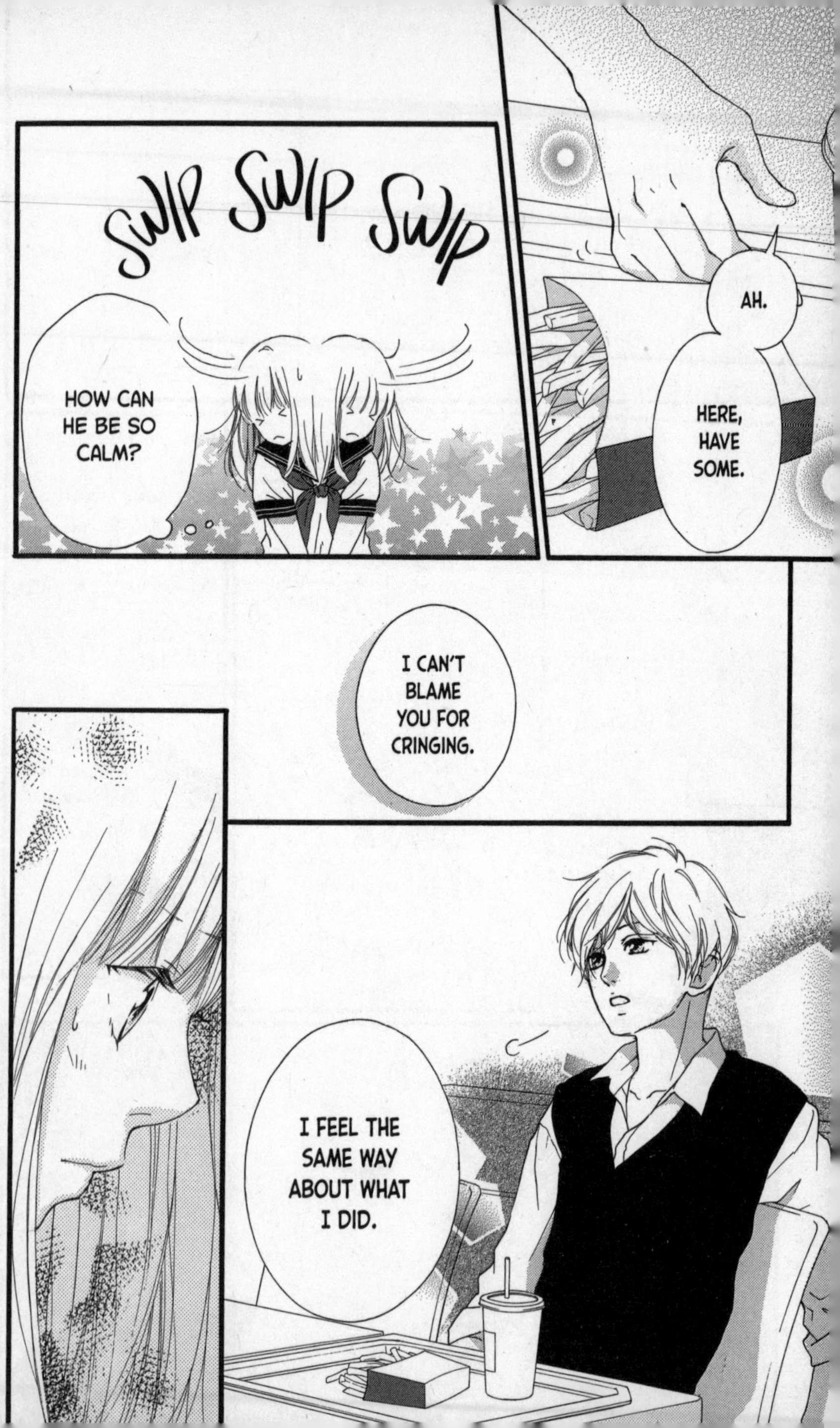

AH.
HERE, HAVE SOME.
SWIP SWIP SWIP
HOW CAN HE BE SO CALM?
I CAN'T BLAME YOU FOR CRINGING.
I FEEL THE SAME WAY ABOUT WHAT I DID.

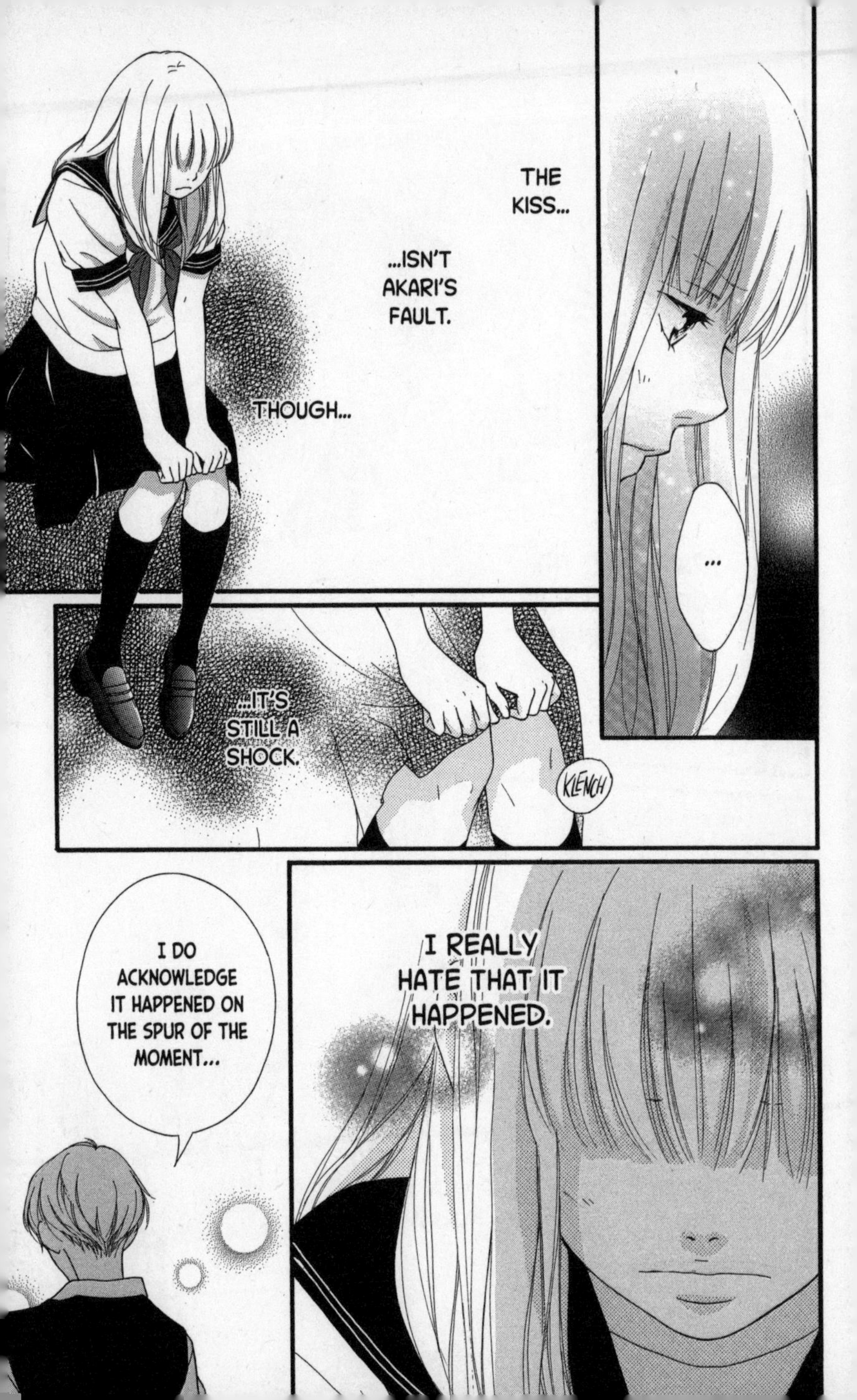
...
THE KISS...
...ISN'T AKARI'S FAULT.
THOUGH...
...IT'S STILL A SHOCK.
KLENCH
I REALLY HATE THAT IT HAPPENED.
I DO ACKNOWLEDGE IT HAPPENED ON THE SPUR OF THE MOMENT...

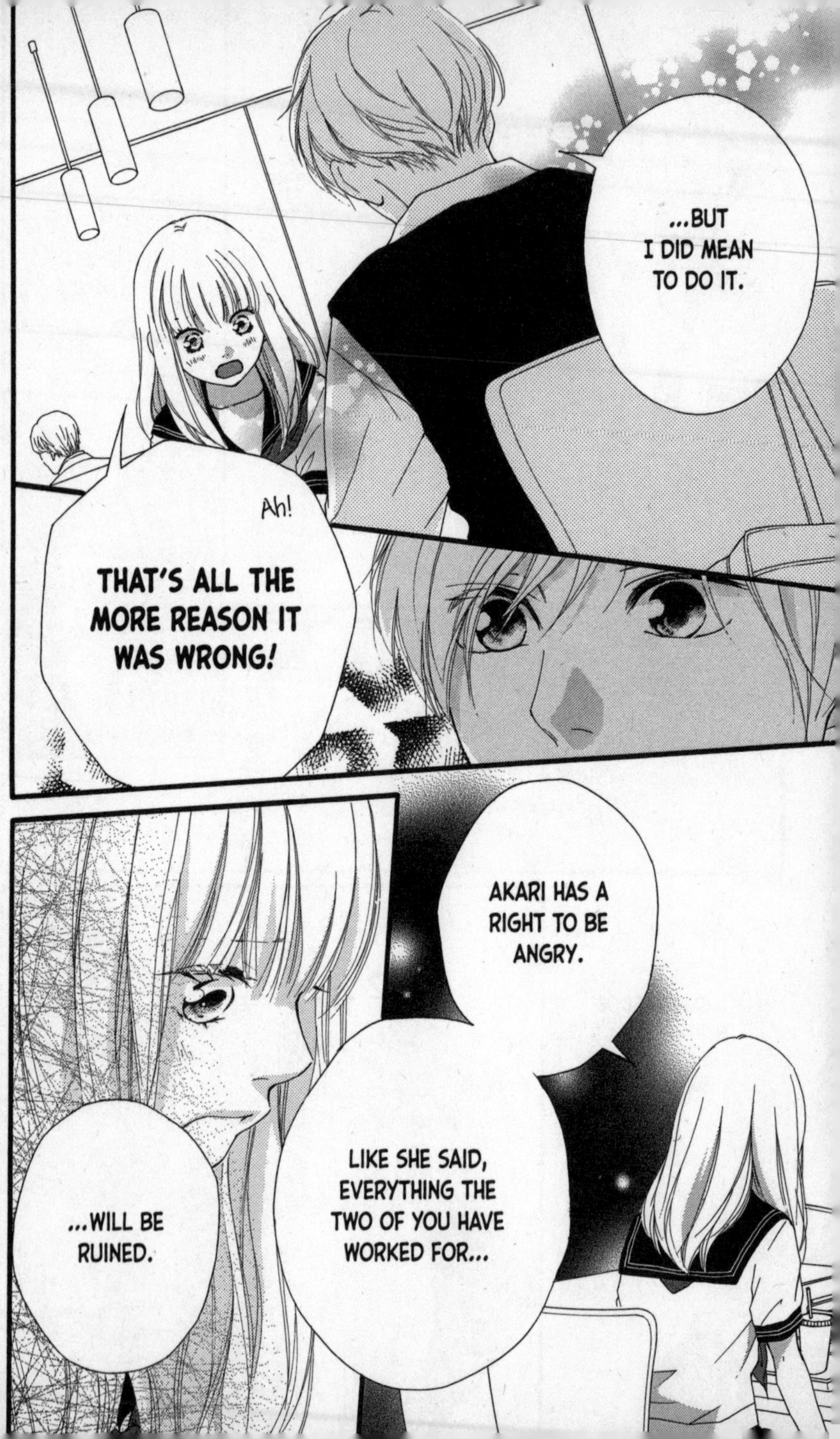
...BUT I DID MEAN TO DO IT.
Ah!
THAT'S ALL THE MORE REASON IT WAS WRONG!
AKARI HAS A RIGHT TO BE ANGRY.
LIKE SHE SAID, EVERYTHING THE TWO OF YOU HAVE WORKED FOR...
...WILL BE RUINED.

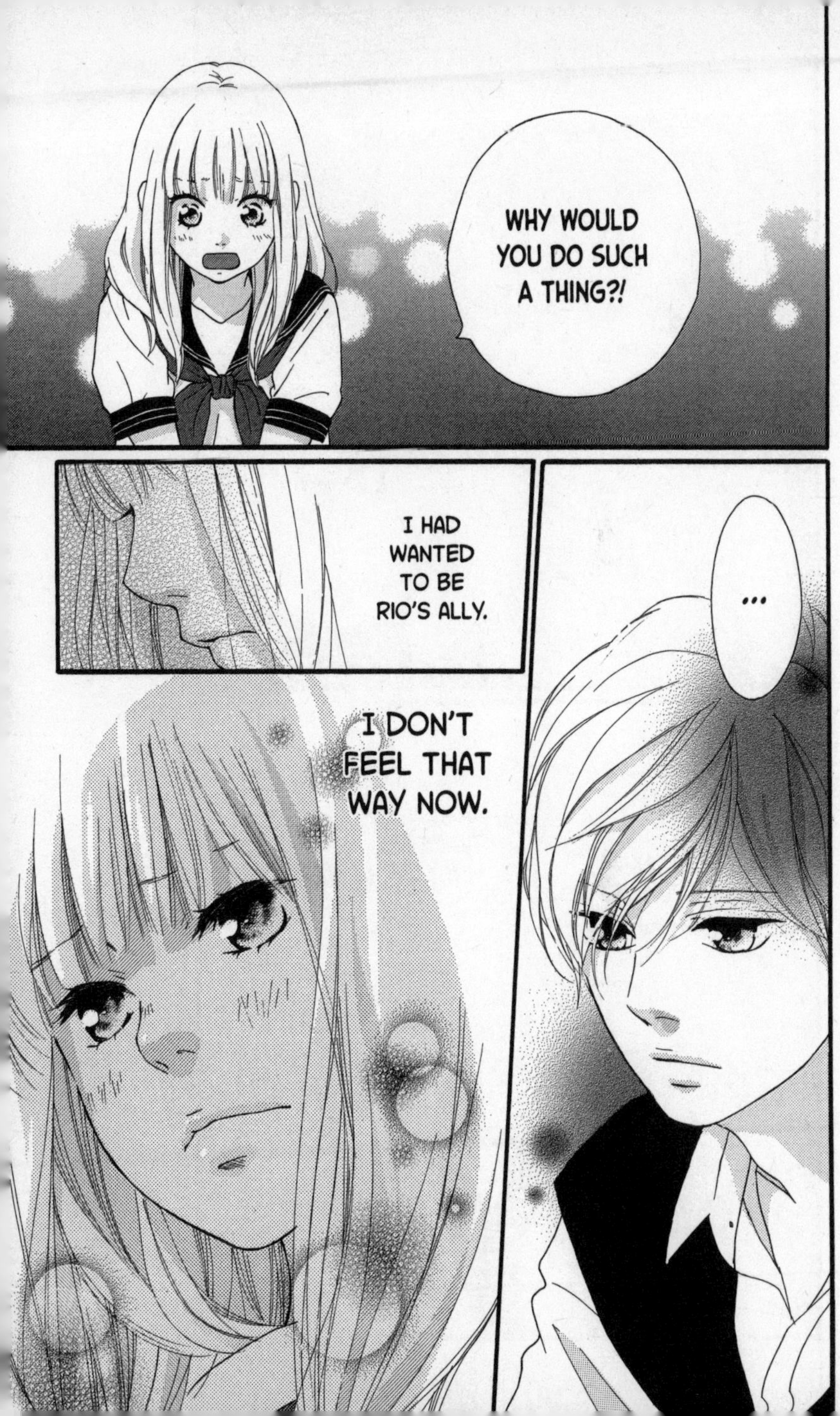
WHY WOULD YOU DO SUCH A THING?!
...
I HAD WANTED TO BE RIO'S ALLY.
I DON'T FEEL THAT WAY NOW.

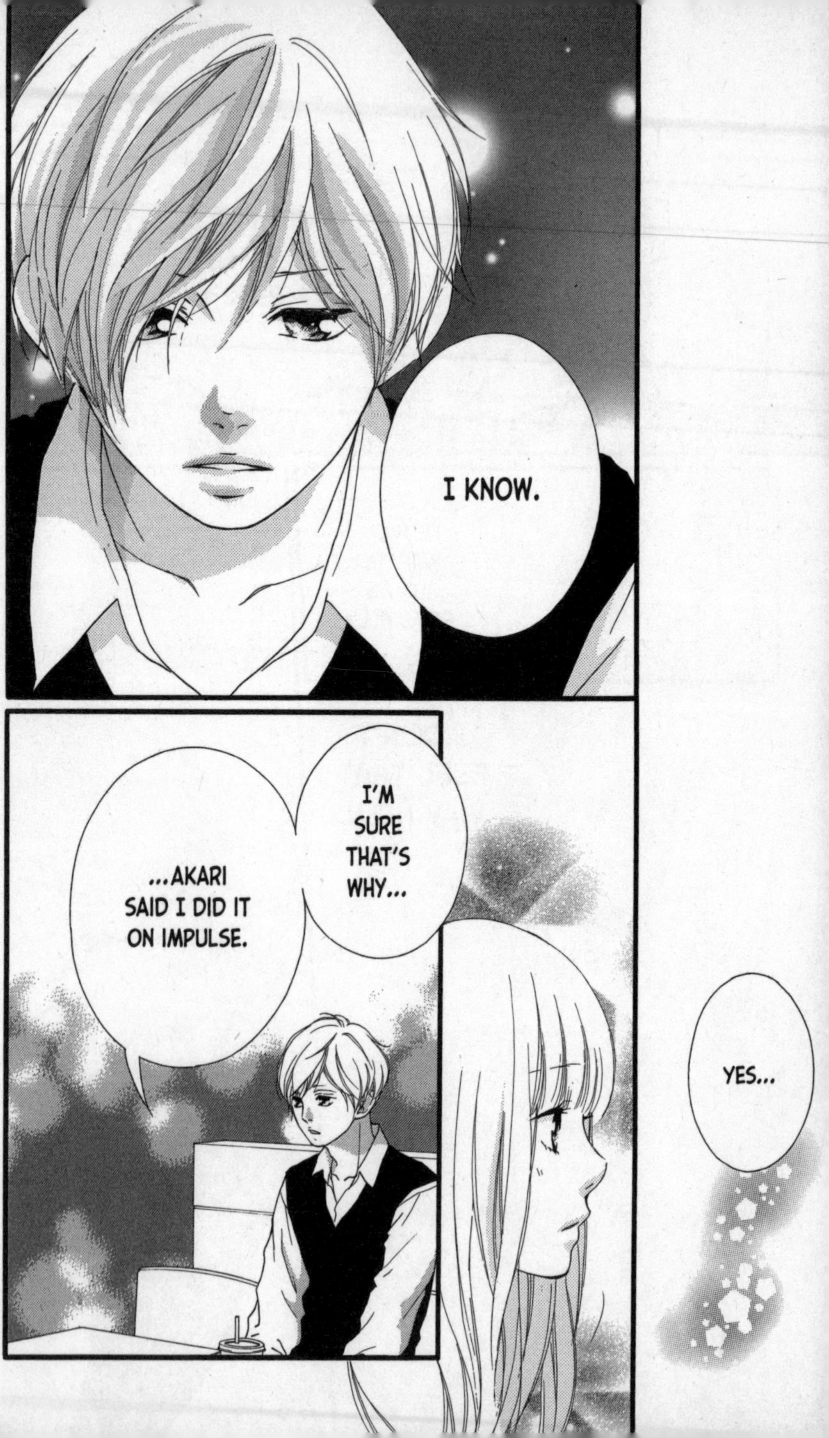
I KNOW.
I'M SURE THAT'S WHY...
...AKARI SAID I DID IT ON IMPULSE.
YES...

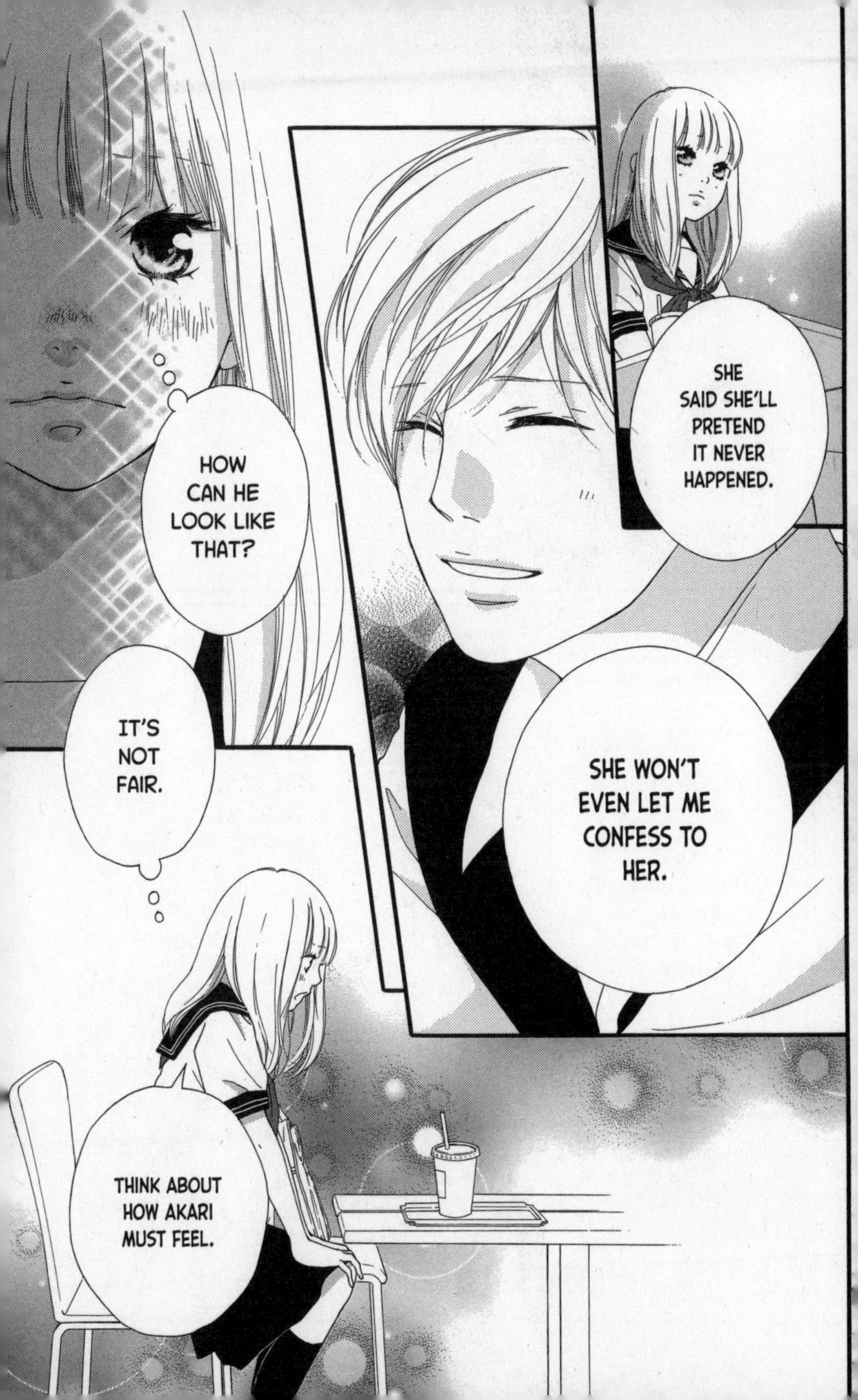
SHE SAID SHE'LL PRETEND IT NEVER HAPPENED.
SHE WON'T EVEN LET ME CONFESS TO HER.
HOW CAN HE LOOK LIKE THAT?
IT'S NOT FAIR.
THINK ABOUT HOW AKARI MUST FEEL.

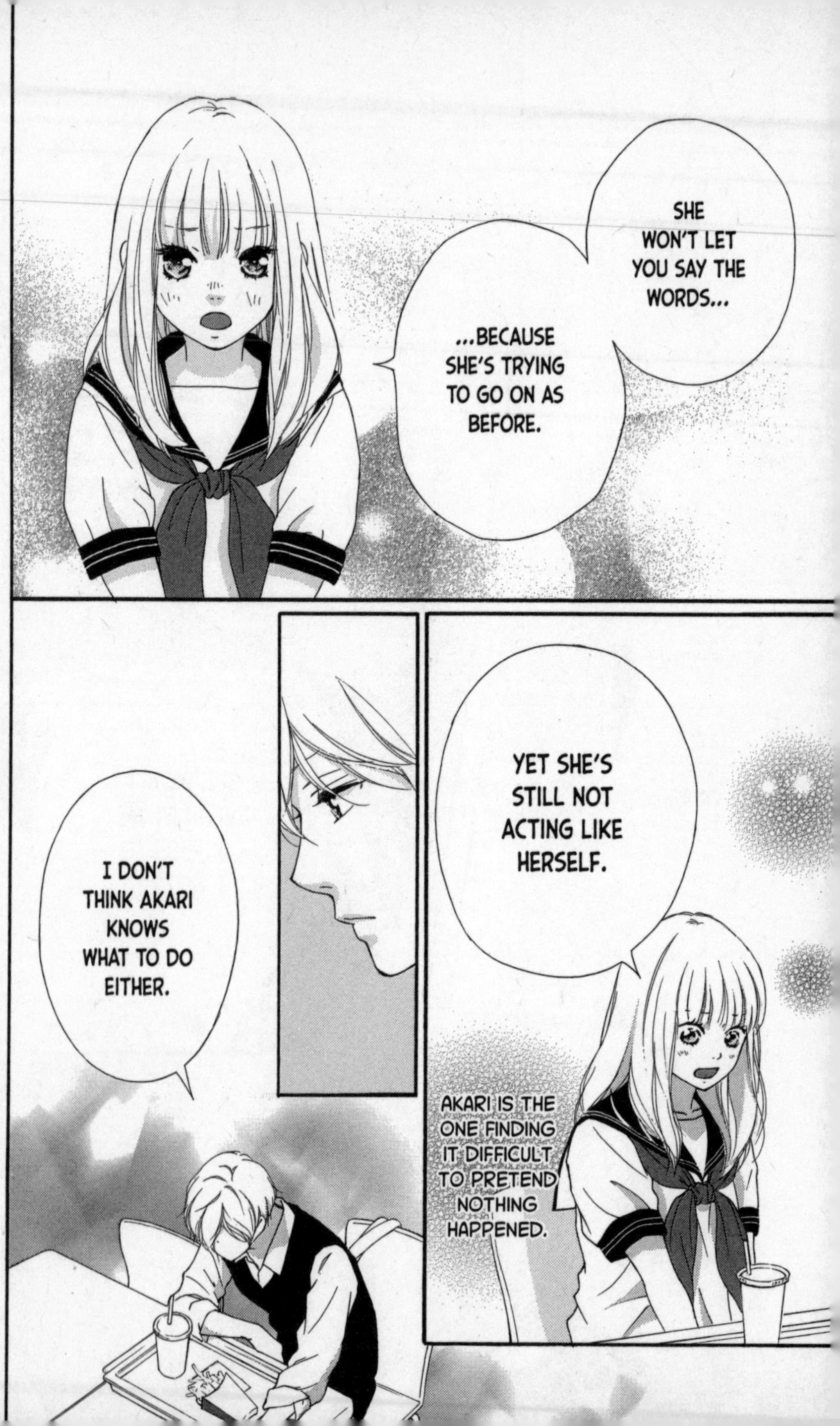
SHE WON'T LET YOU SAY THE WORDS...
...BECAUSE SHE'S TRYING TO GO ON AS BEFORE.
YET SHE'S STILL NOT ACTING LIKE HERSELF.
AKARI IS THE ONE FINDING IT DIFFICULT TO PRETEND NOTHING HAPPENED.
I DON'T THINK AKARI KNOWS WHAT TO DO EITHER.

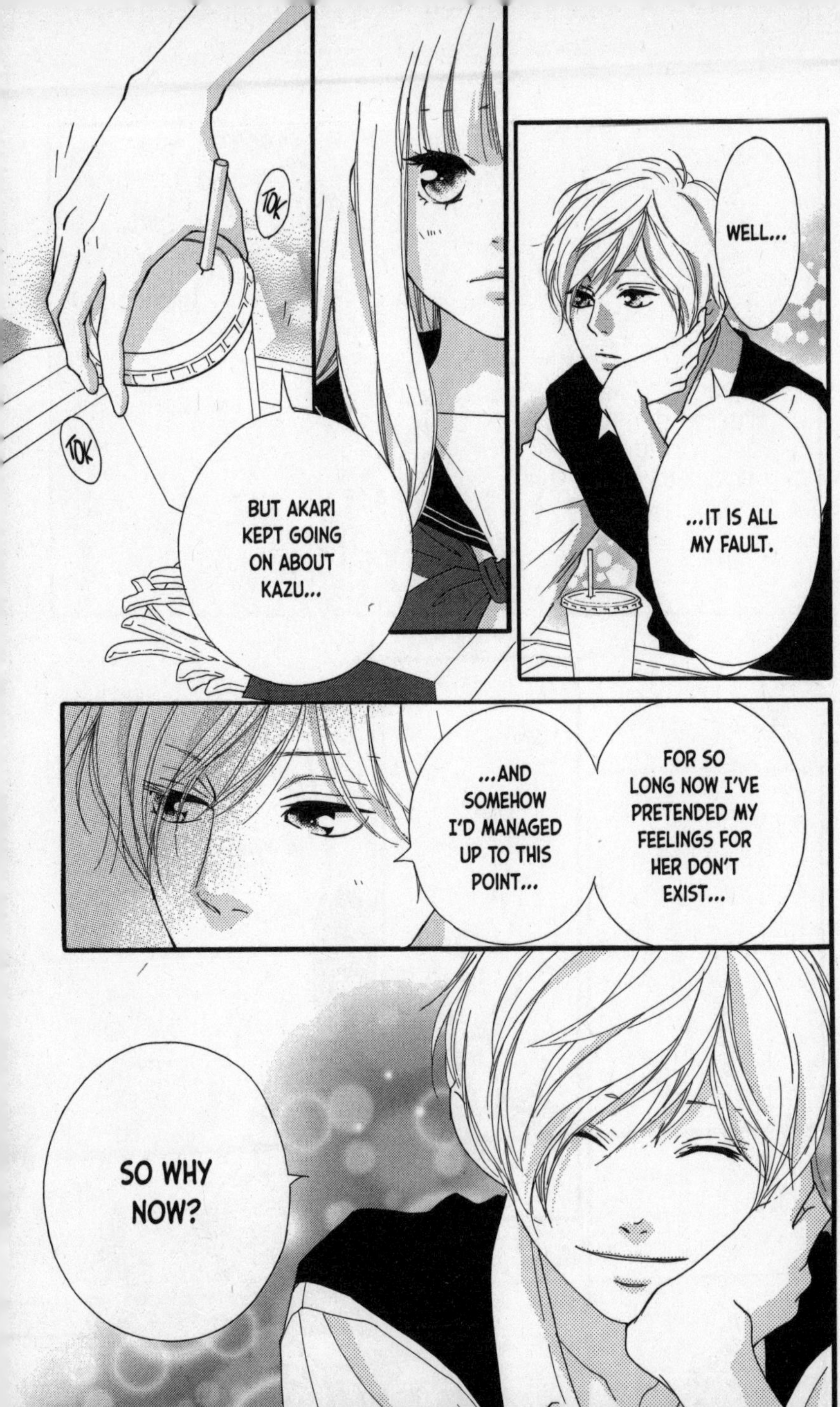
WELL...
...IT IS ALL MY FAULT.
TOK
TOK
BUT AKARI KEPT GOING ON ABOUT KAZU...
FOR SO LONG NOW I'VE PRETENDED MY FEELINGS FOR HER DON'T EXIST...
...AND SOMEHOW I'D MANAGED UP TO THIS POINT...
SO WHY NOW?

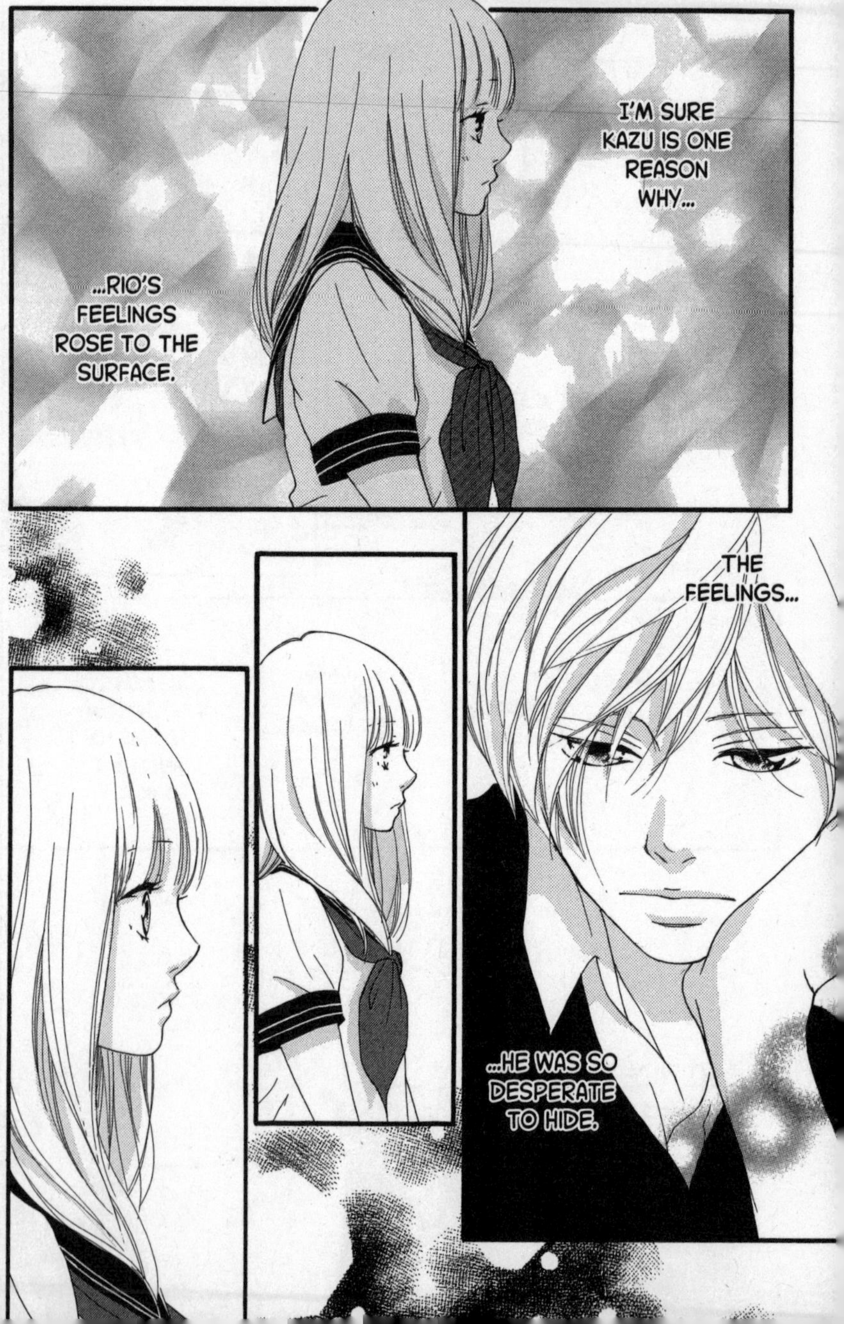
I'M SURE KAZU IS ONE REASON WHY...
...RIO'S FEELINGS ROSE TO THE SURFACE.
THE FEELINGS...
...HE WAS SO DESPERATE TO HIDE.

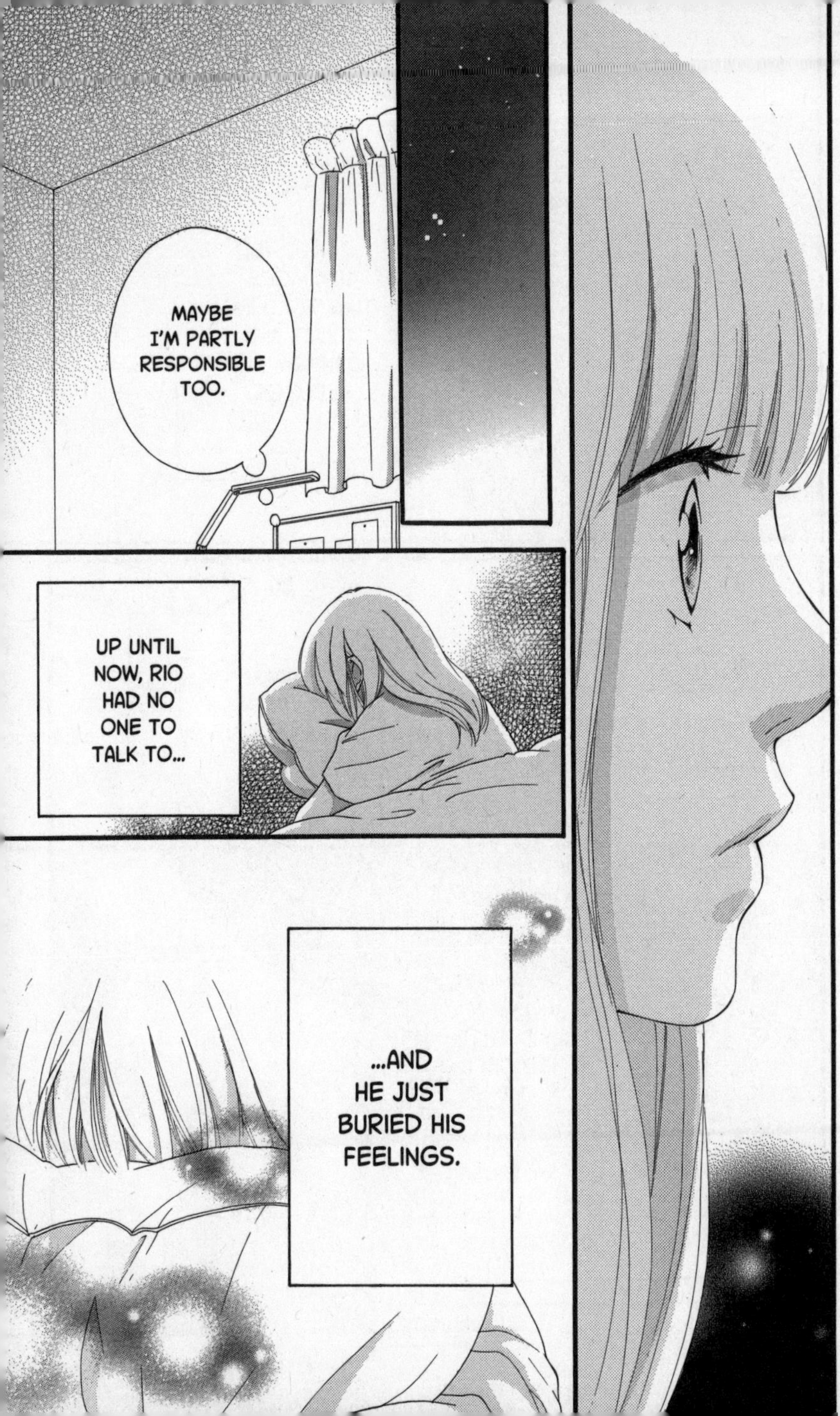
MAYBE I'M PARTLY RESPONSIBLE TOO.
UP UNTIL NOW, RIO HAD NO ONE TO TALK TO...
...AND HE JUST BURIED HIS FEELINGS.

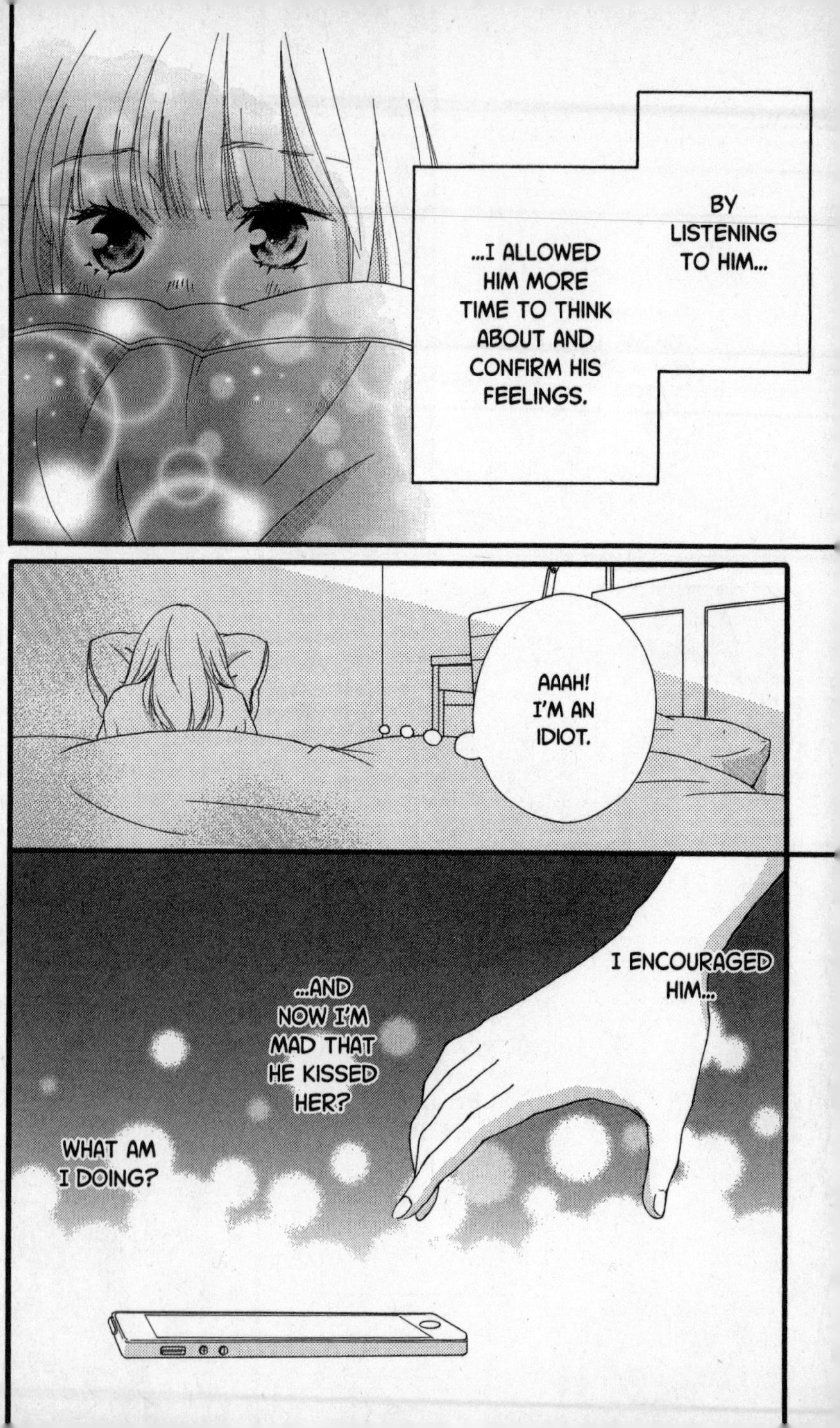
BY LISTENING TO HIM...
...I ALLOWED HIM MORE TIME TO THINK ABOUT AND CONFIRM HIS FEELINGS.
AAAH! I'M AN IDIOT.
I ENCOURAGED HIM...
...AND NOW I'M MAD THAT HE KISSED HER?
WHAT AM I DOING?

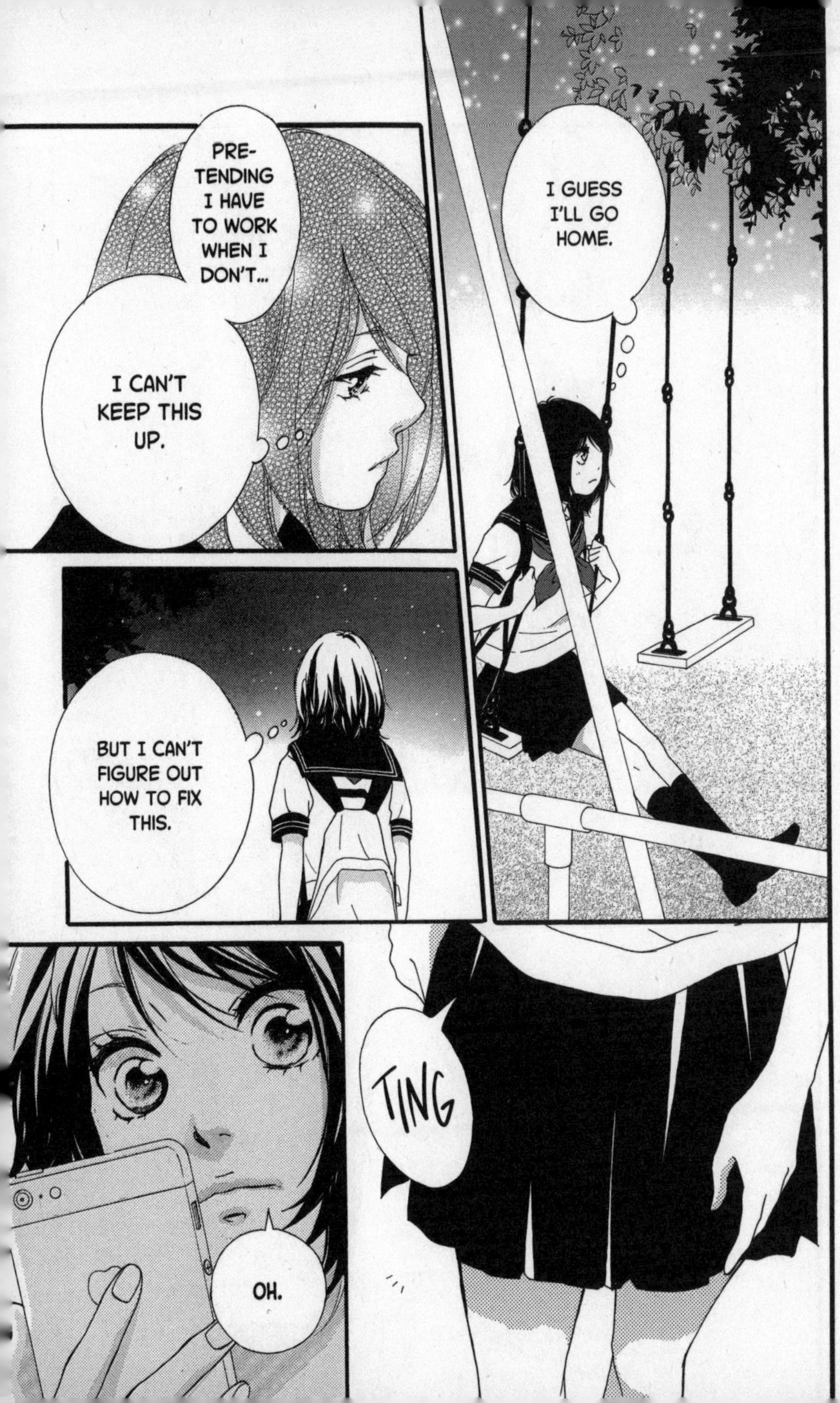
I GUESS I'LL GO HOME.
PRE-TENDING I HAVE TO WORK WHEN I DON'T...
I CAN'T KEEP THIS UP.
BUT I CAN'T FIGURE OUT HOW TO FIX THIS.
TING
OH.

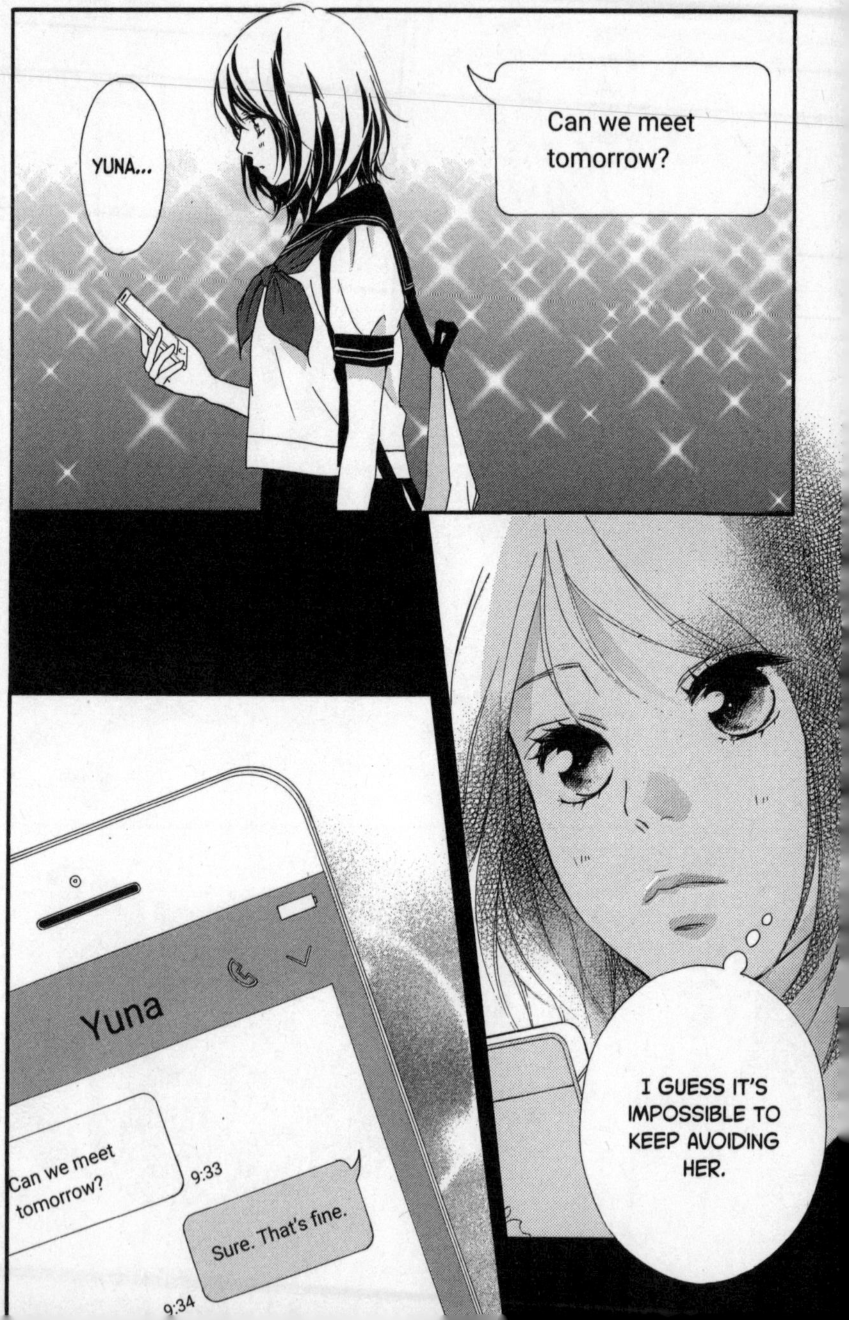
Can we meet tomorrow?
YUNA...
I GUESS IT'S IMPOSSIBLE TO KEEP AVOIDING HER.
Yuna
Can we meet tomorrow?
9:33
Sure. That's fine.
9:34

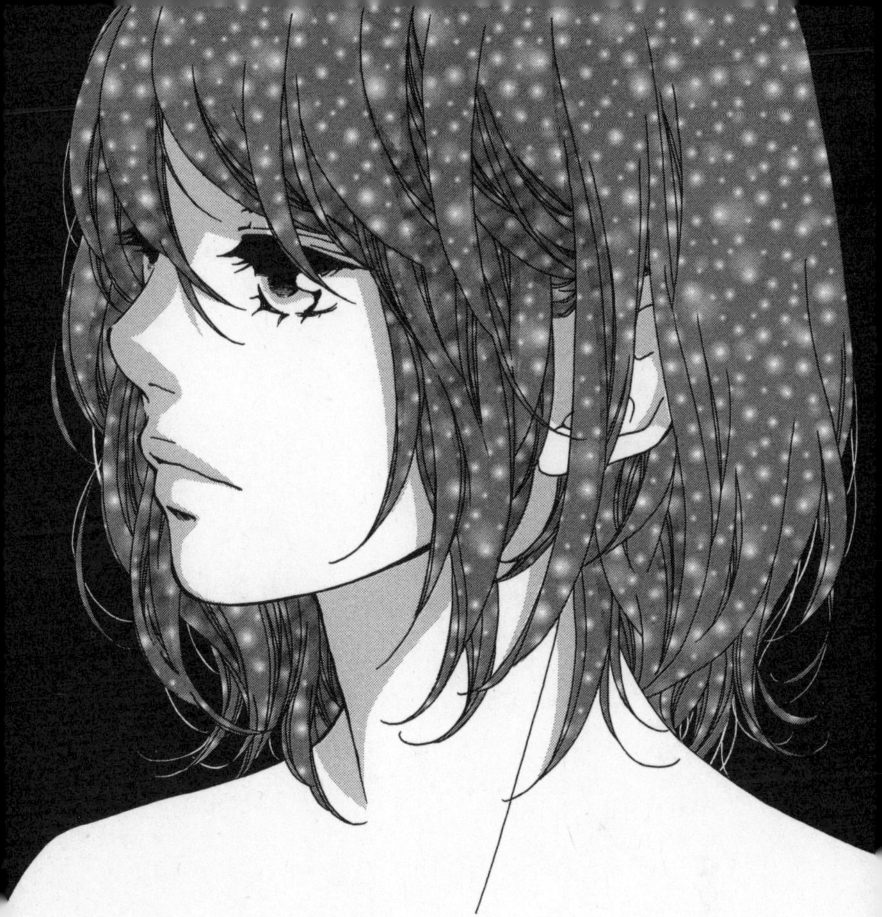

Love Me, Love Me Not

Piece 14

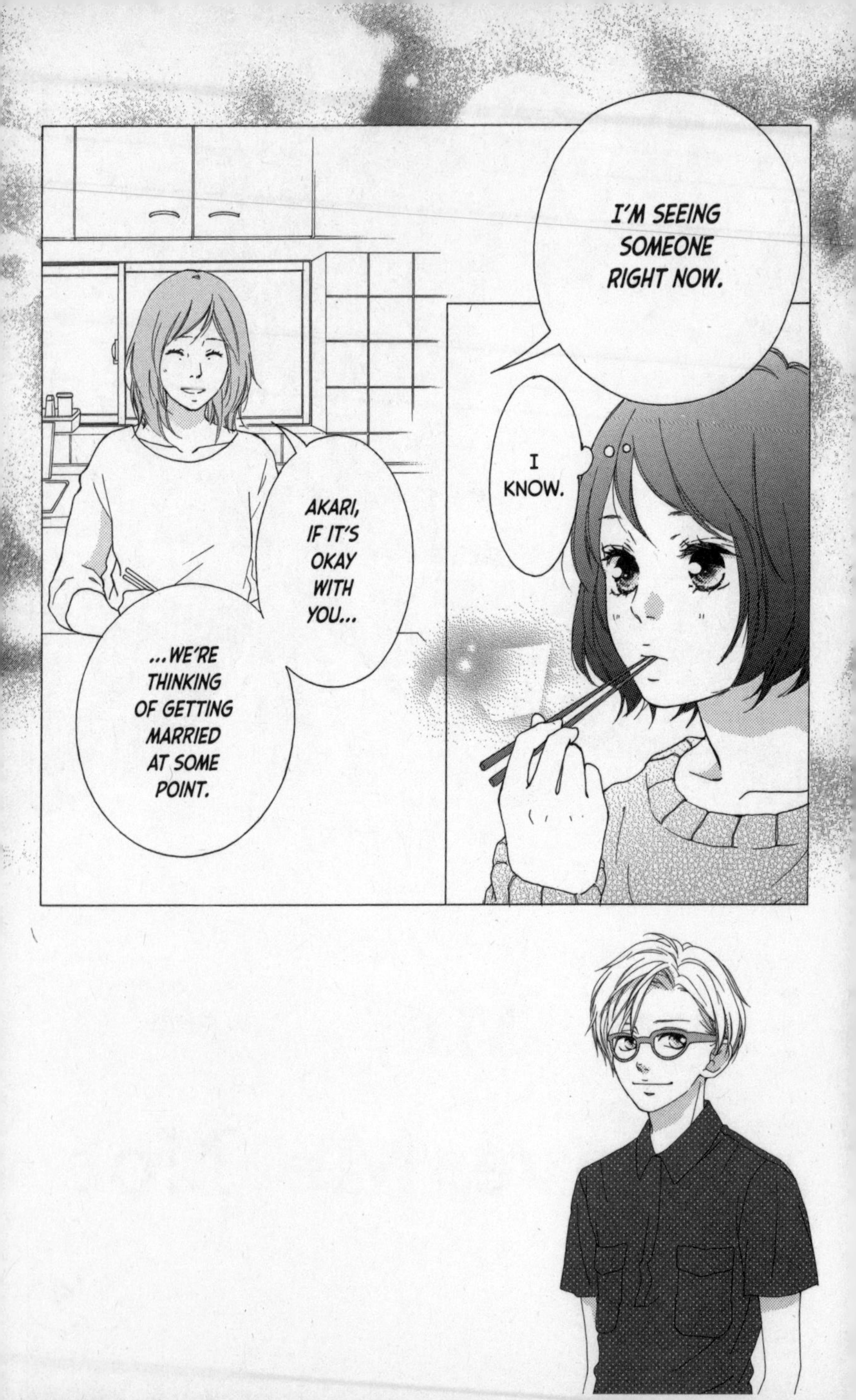
I'M SEEING SOMEONE RIGHT NOW.
I KNOW.
AKARI, IF IT'S OKAY WITH YOU...
...WE'RE THINKING OF GETTING MARRIED AT SOME POINT.

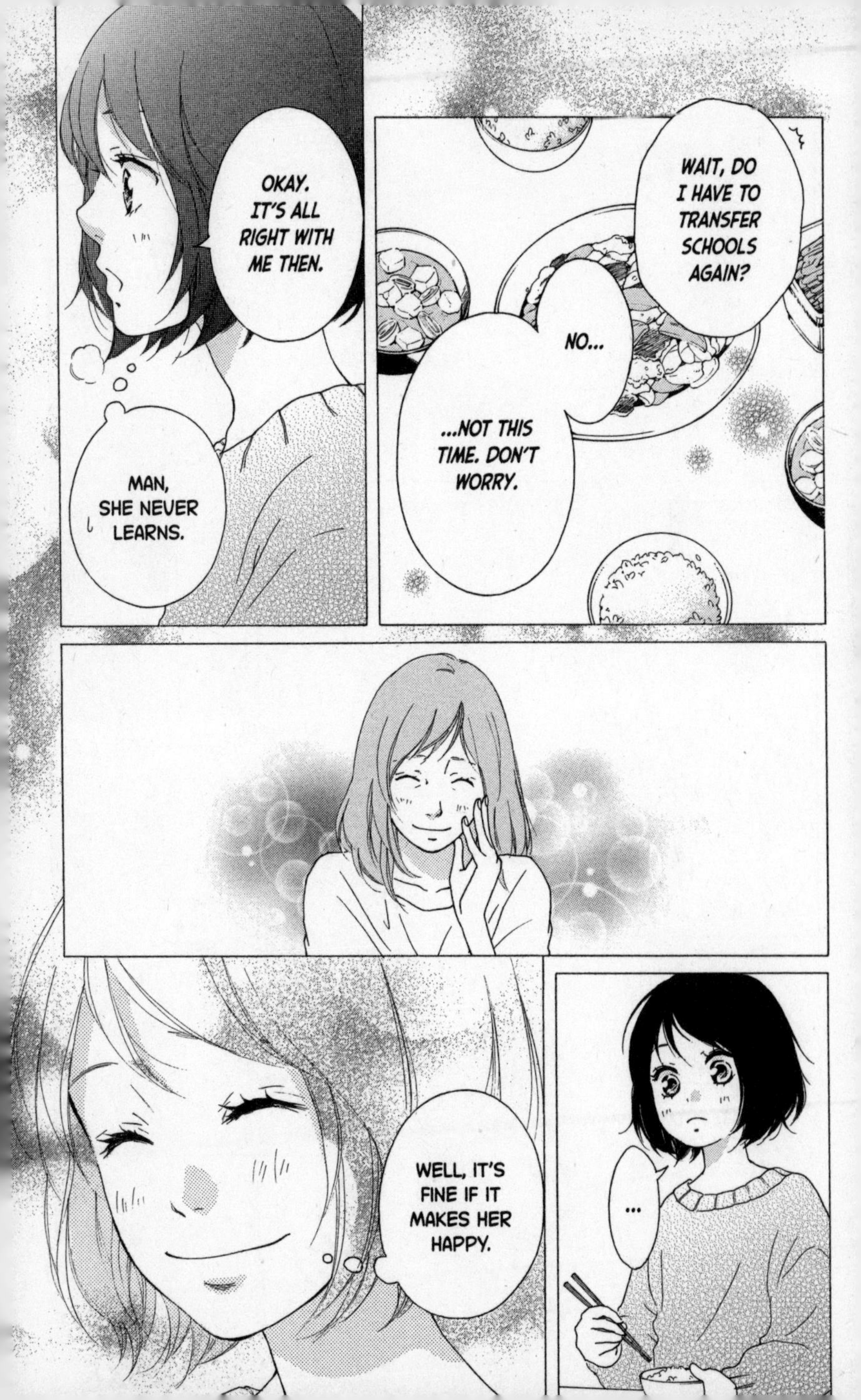
WAIT, DO I HAVE TO TRANSFER SCHOOLS AGAIN?
NO...
...NOT THIS TIME. DON'T WORRY.
OKAY. IT'S ALL RIGHT WITH ME THEN.
MAN, SHE NEVER LEARNS.
...
WELL, IT'S FINE IF IT MAKES HER HAPPY.

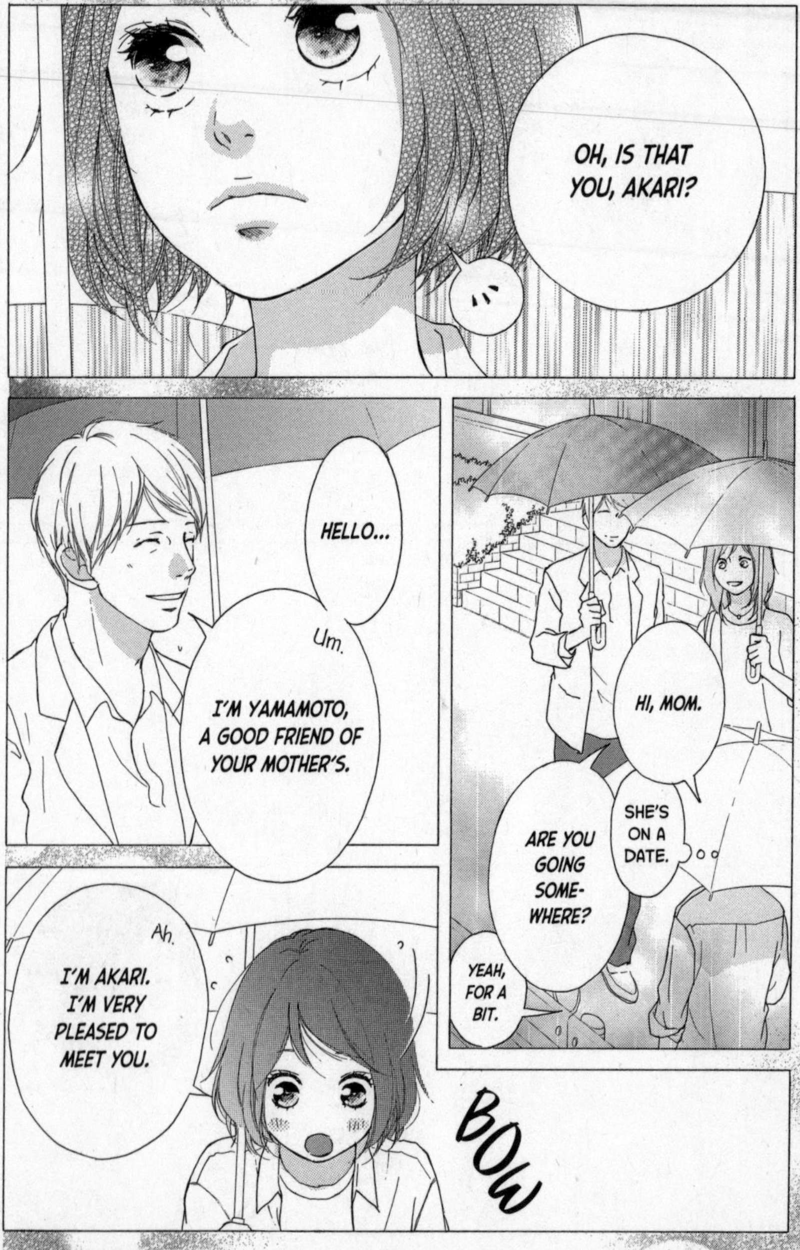
OH, IS THAT YOU, AKARI?
HI, MOM.
SHE'S ON A DATE...
ARE YOU GOING SOME-WHERE?
YEAH, FOR A BIT.
HELLO...
Um.
I'M YAMAMOTO, A GOOD FRIEND OF YOUR MOTHER'S.
BOW
Ah.
I'M AKARI. I'M VERY PLEASED TO MEET YOU.

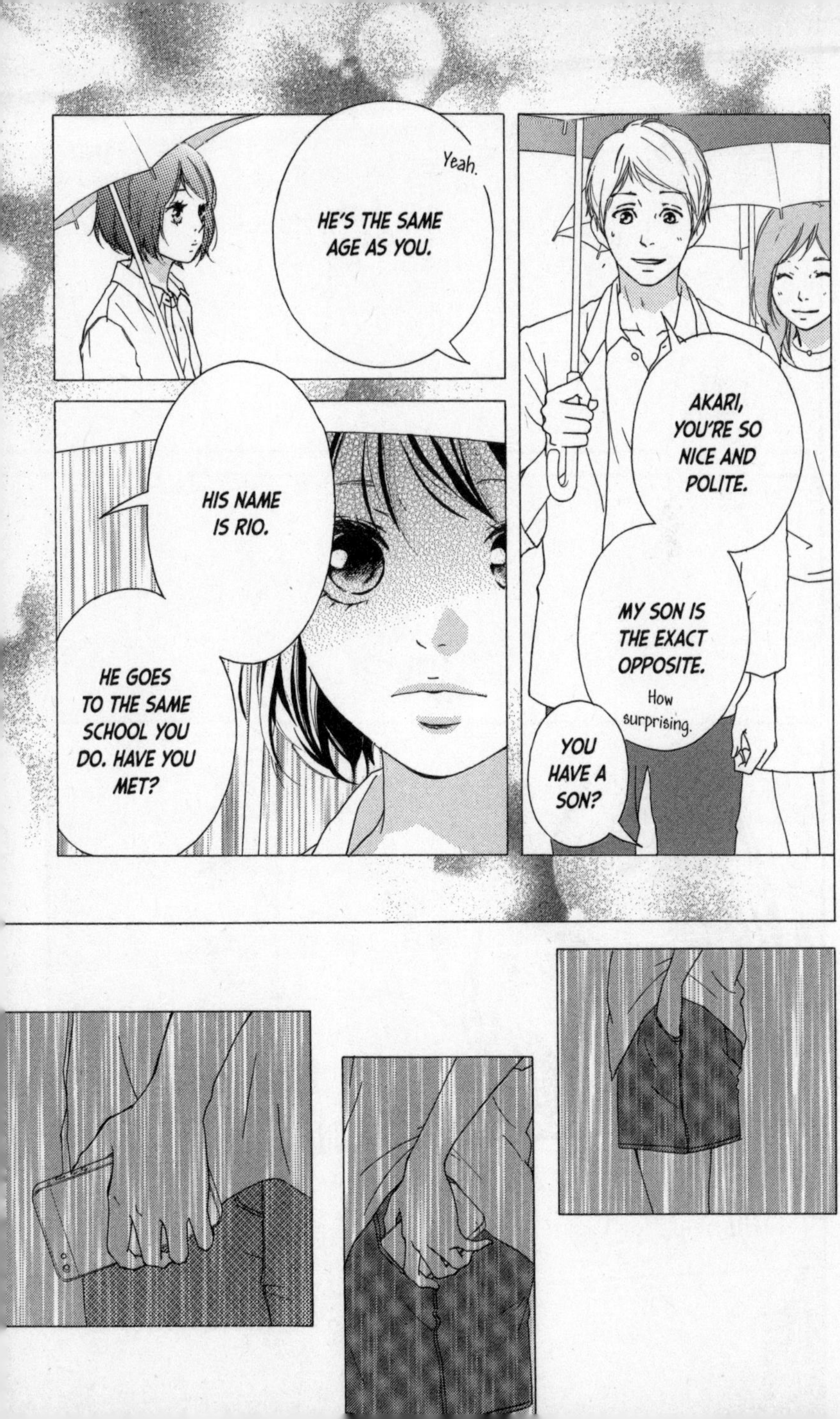
AKARI, YOU'RE SO NICE AND POLITE.
MY SON IS THE EXACT OPPOSITE.
How surprising.
YOU HAVE A SON?
Yeah.
HE'S THE SAME AGE AS YOU.
HIS NAME IS RIO.
HE GOES TO THE SAME SCHOOL YOU DO. HAVE YOU MET?

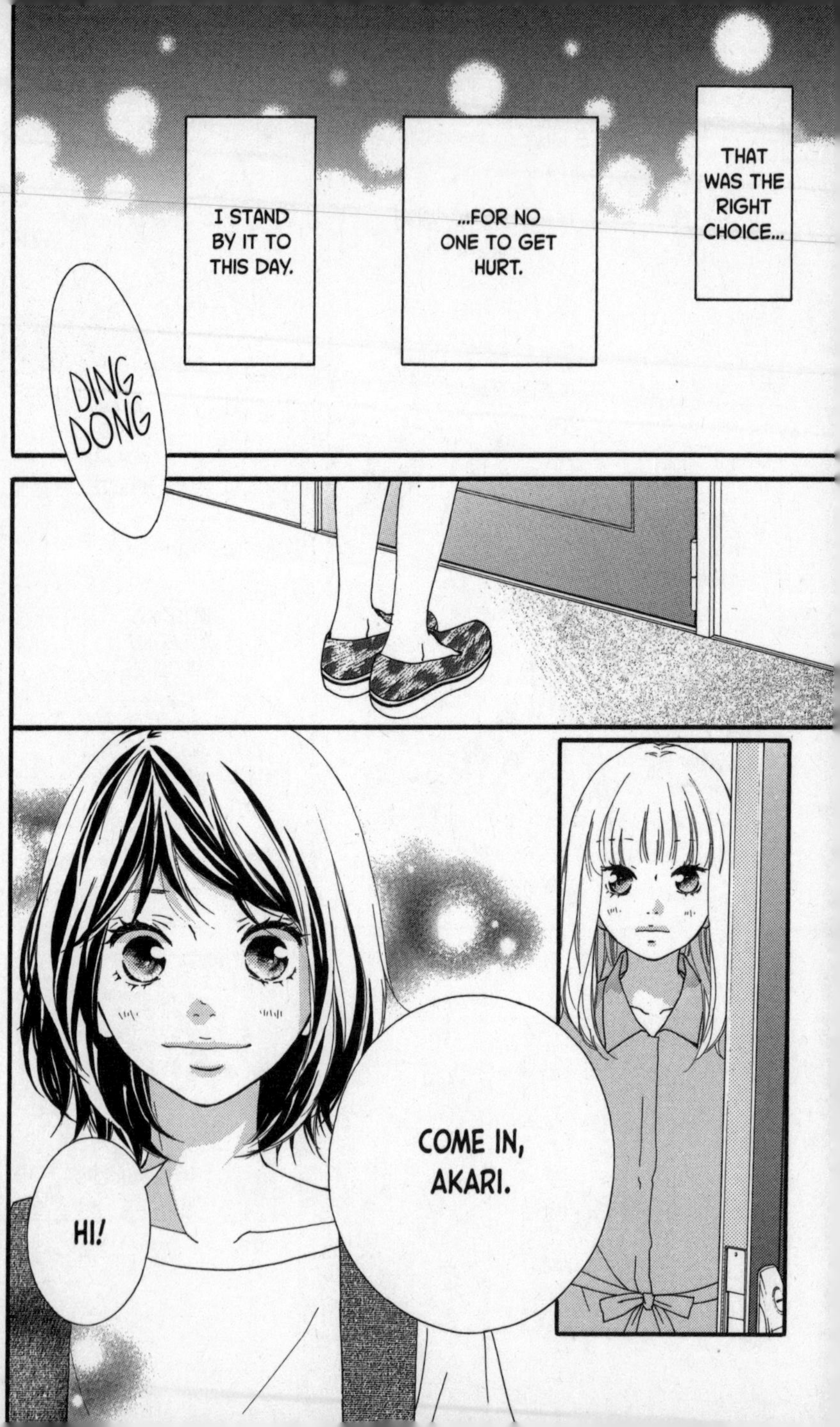
THAT WAS THE RIGHT CHOICE...
...FOR NO ONE TO GET HURT.
I STAND BY IT TO THIS DAY.
DING DONG
COME IN, AKARI.
HI!

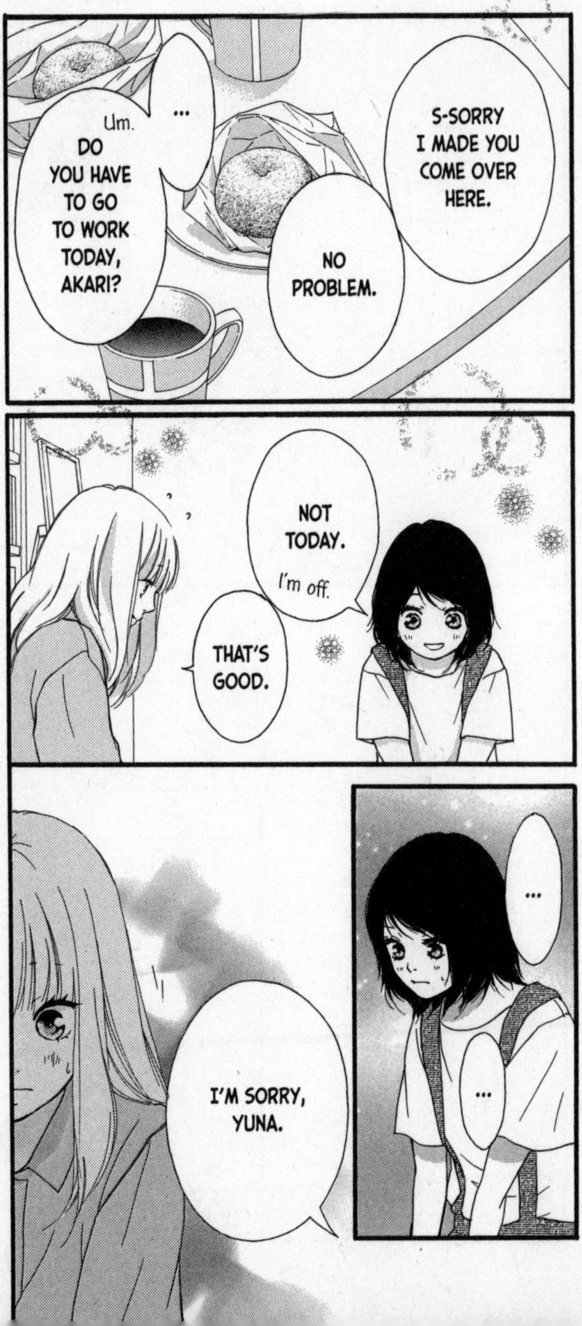
S-SORRY I MADE YOU COME OVER HERE.
NO PROBLEM.
...
Um. DO YOU HAVE TO GO TO WORK TODAY, AKARI?
NOT TODAY. I'm off.
THAT'S GOOD.
...
...
I'M SORRY, YUNA.

A little while ago, I slipped a disk. The reason for this first slipped disk in my life was a sneeze. I was sitting quietly on my chair working. At first I felt like my back cracked. It hurt, but that was it, so I kept on working. Then I took a break and tried to get up from my chair... "Oh, it kind of hurts... I can't stand up straight. What are these symptoms?" I looked them up and was astounded to discover it's probably a minor case of a slipped disc. The only thing I have going for me is my durability. I couldn't believe I slipped a disc with a sneeze! But at that time I was overconfident in my constitution. I thought, "Well, I'm sure it'll be better by tomorrow. It's me, after all!" The next day, I was far from better. If I moved super slowly, I could get around. And because of that, I had to miss the two events I'd been planning to go to in tiptop shape. *Sob sob sob*... I really had been looking forward to them.

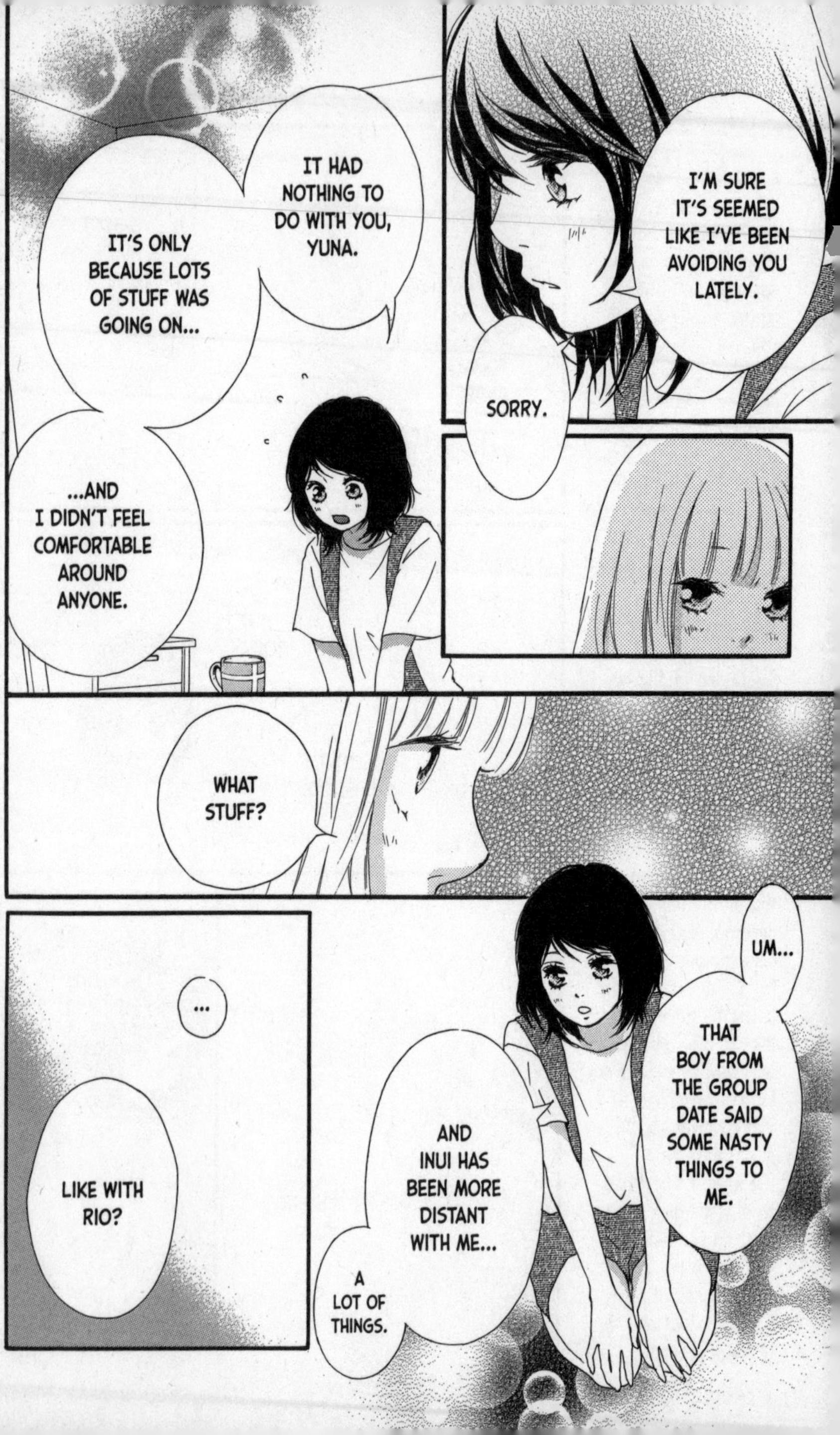
I'M SURE IT'S SEEMED LIKE I'VE BEEN AVOIDING YOU LATELY.
SORRY.
IT HAD NOTHING TO DO WITH YOU, YUNA.
IT'S ONLY BECAUSE LOTS OF STUFF WAS GOING ON...
...AND I DIDN'T FEEL COMFORTABLE AROUND ANYONE.
WHAT STUFF?
UM...
THAT BOY FROM THE GROUP DATE SAID SOME NASTY THINGS TO ME.
AND INUI HAS BEEN MORE DISTANT WITH ME...
A LOT OF THINGS.
...
LIKE WITH RIO?

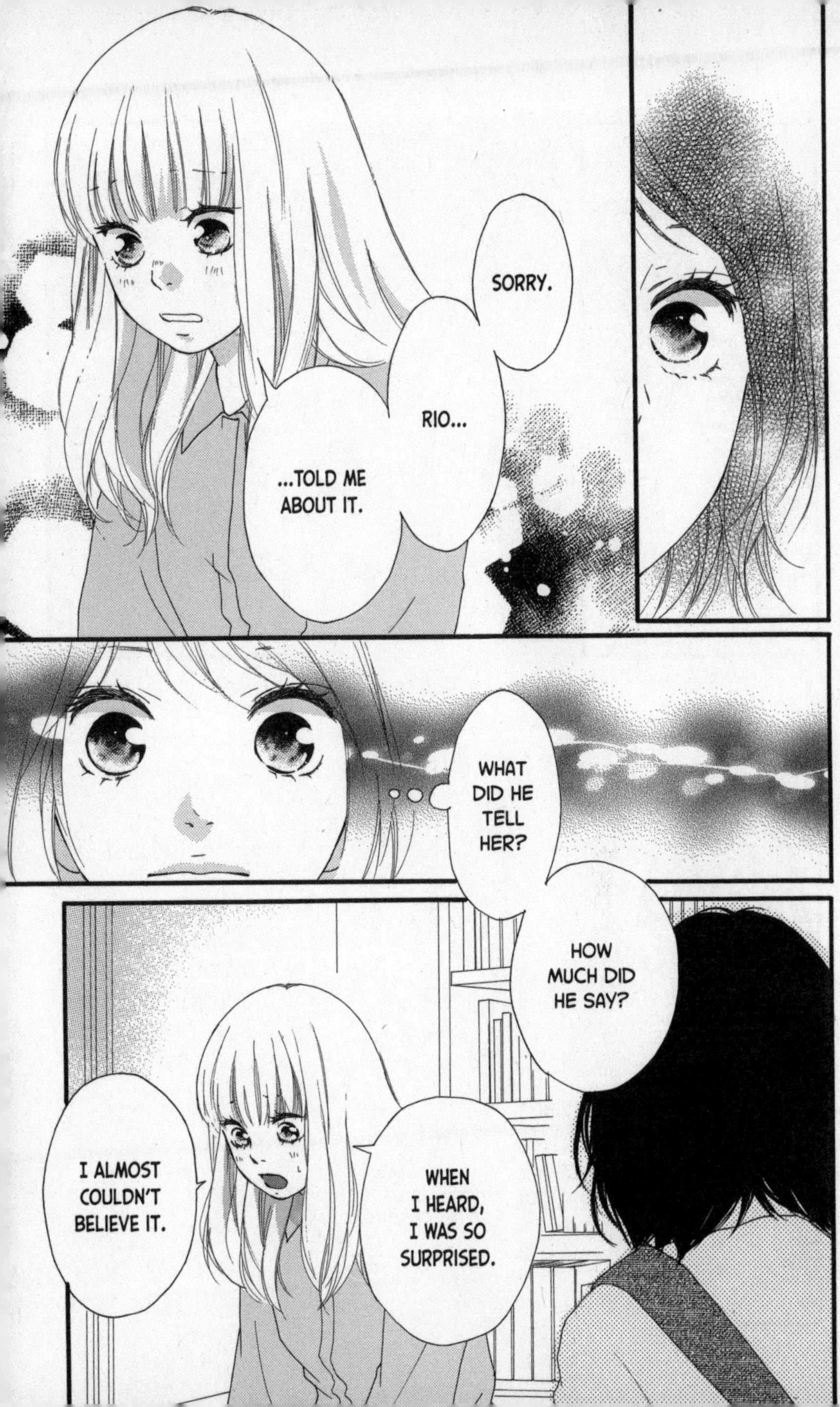
SORRY.
RIO...
...TOLD ME ABOUT IT.
WHAT DID HE TELL HER?
HOW MUCH DID HE SAY?
WHEN I HEARD, I WAS SO SURPRISED.
I ALMOST COULDN'T BELIEVE IT.

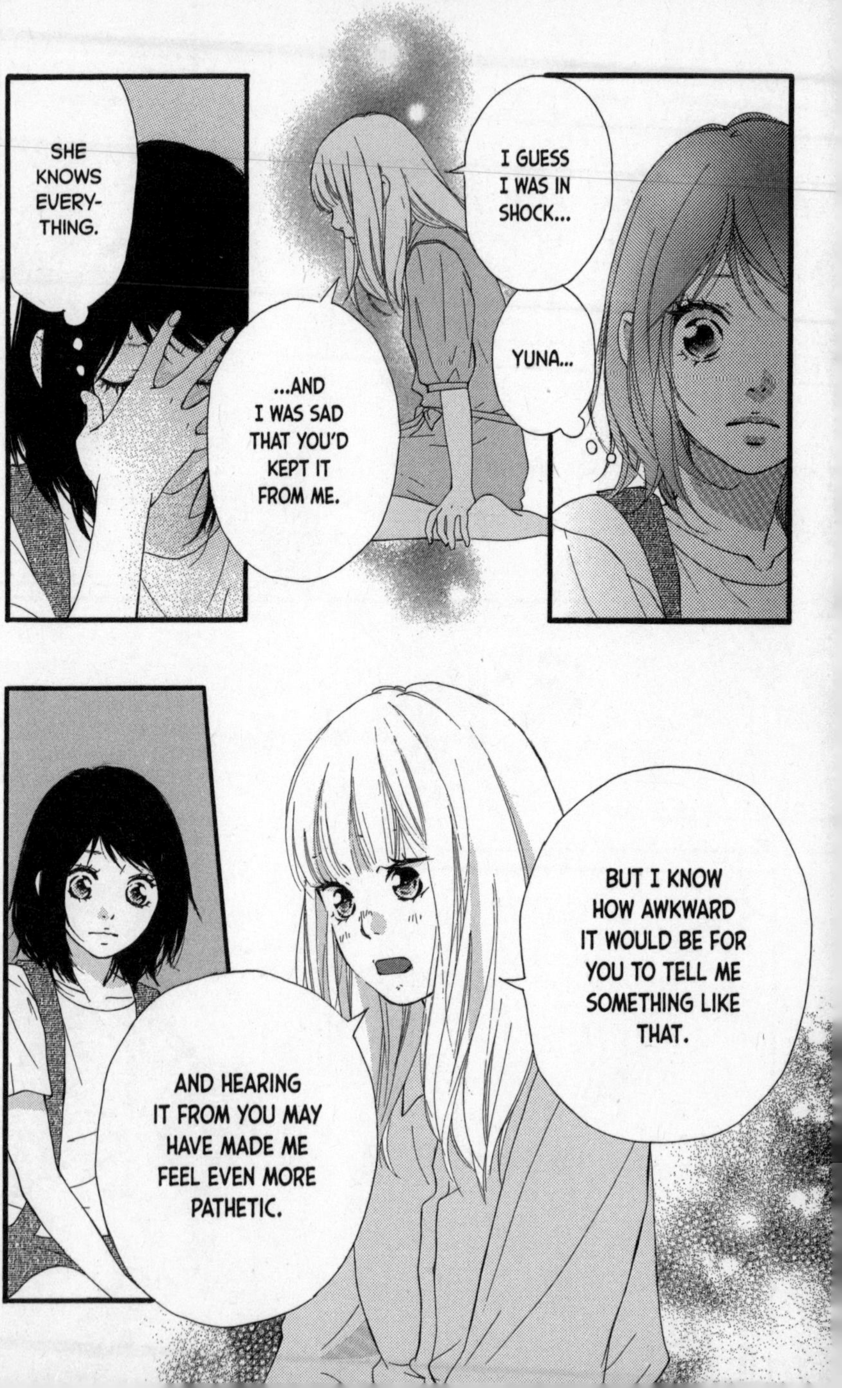
I GUESS I WAS IN SHOCK...
YUNA...
...AND I WAS SAD THAT YOU'D KEPT IT FROM ME.
SHE KNOWS EVERY-THING.
BUT I KNOW HOW AWKWARD IT WOULD BE FOR YOU TO TELL ME SOMETHING LIKE THAT.
AND HEARING IT FROM YOU MAY HAVE MADE ME FEEL EVEN MORE PATHETIC.

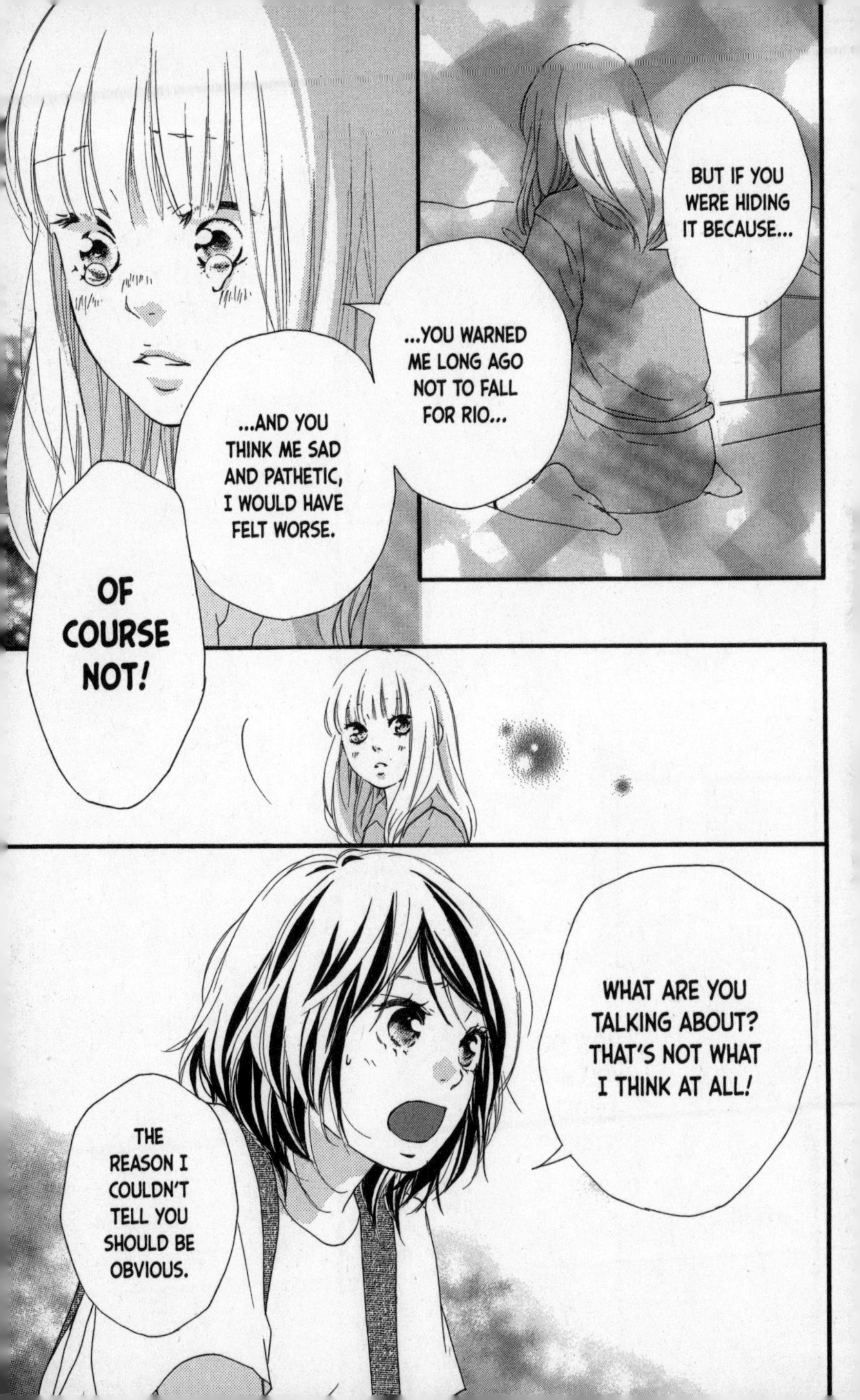
BUT IF YOU WERE HIDING IT BECAUSE...
...YOU WARNED ME LONG AGO NOT TO FALL FOR RIO...
...AND YOU THINK ME SAD AND PATHETIC, I WOULD HAVE FELT WORSE.
OF COURSE NOT!
WHAT ARE YOU TALKING ABOUT? THAT'S NOT WHAT I THINK AT ALL!
THE REASON I COULDN'T TELL YOU SHOULD BE OBVIOUS.

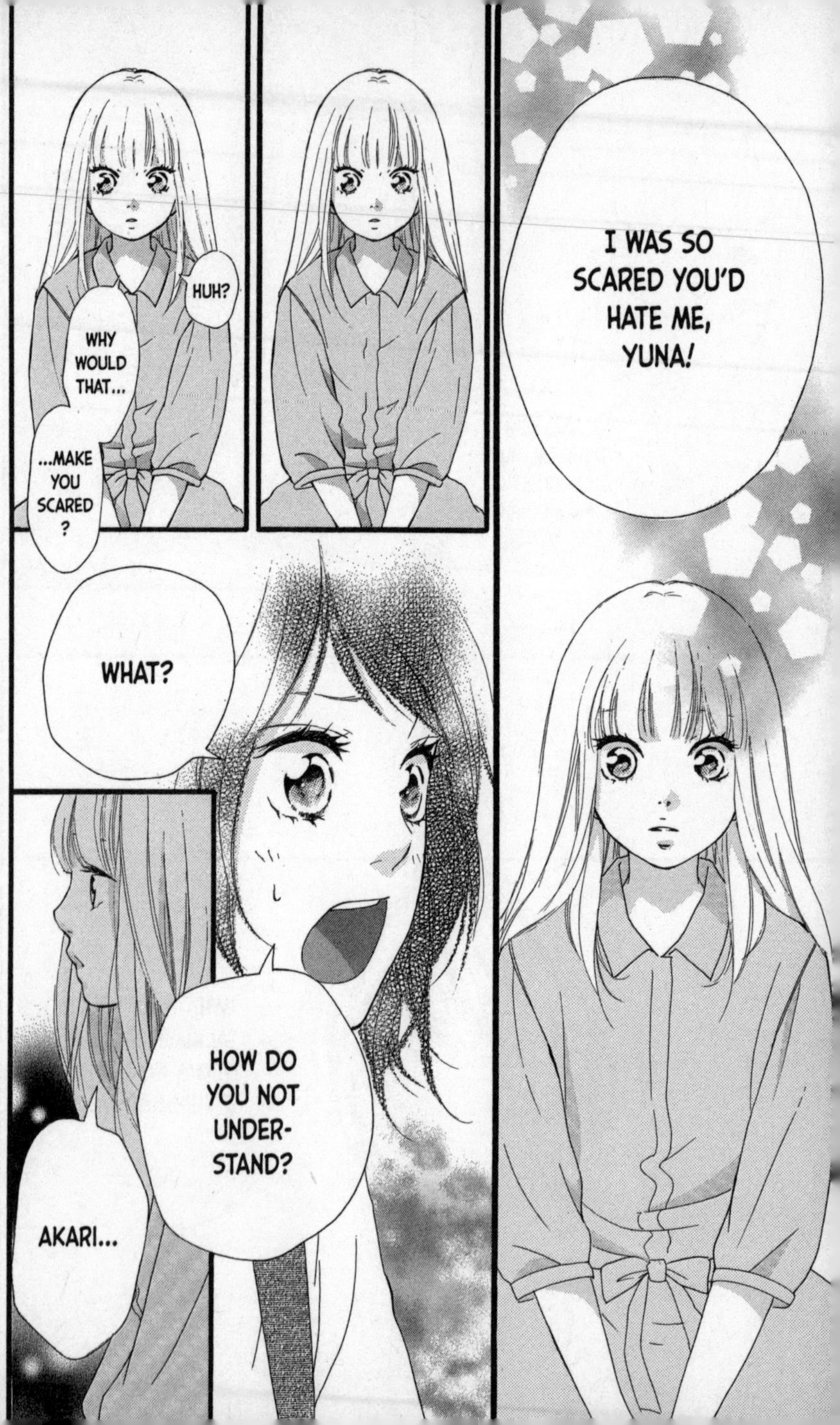
I WAS SO SCARED YOU'D HATE ME, YUNA!
HUH?
WHY WOULD THAT...
...MAKE YOU SCARED?
WHAT?
HOW DO YOU NOT UNDER-STAND?
AKARI...

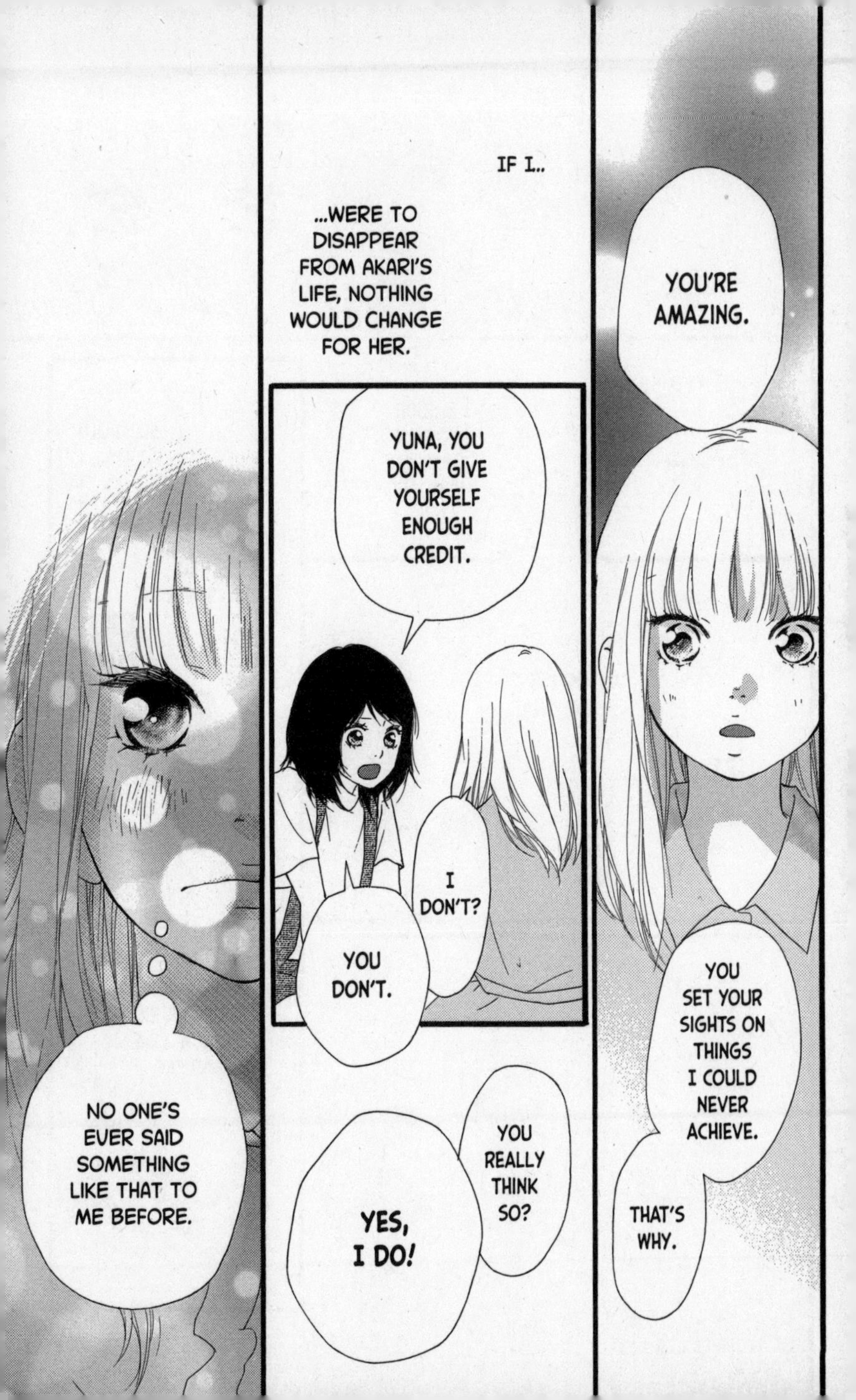
YOU'RE AMAZING.
YOU SET YOUR SIGHTS ON THINGS I COULD NEVER ACHIEVE.
THAT'S WHY.
IF I..
...WERE TO DISAPPEAR FROM AKARI'S LIFE, NOTHING WOULD CHANGE FOR HER.
YUNA, YOU DON'T GIVE YOURSELF ENOUGH CREDIT.
I DON'T?
YOU DON'T.
YOU REALLY THINK SO?
YES, I DO!
NO ONE'S EVER SAID SOMETHING LIKE THAT TO ME BEFORE.

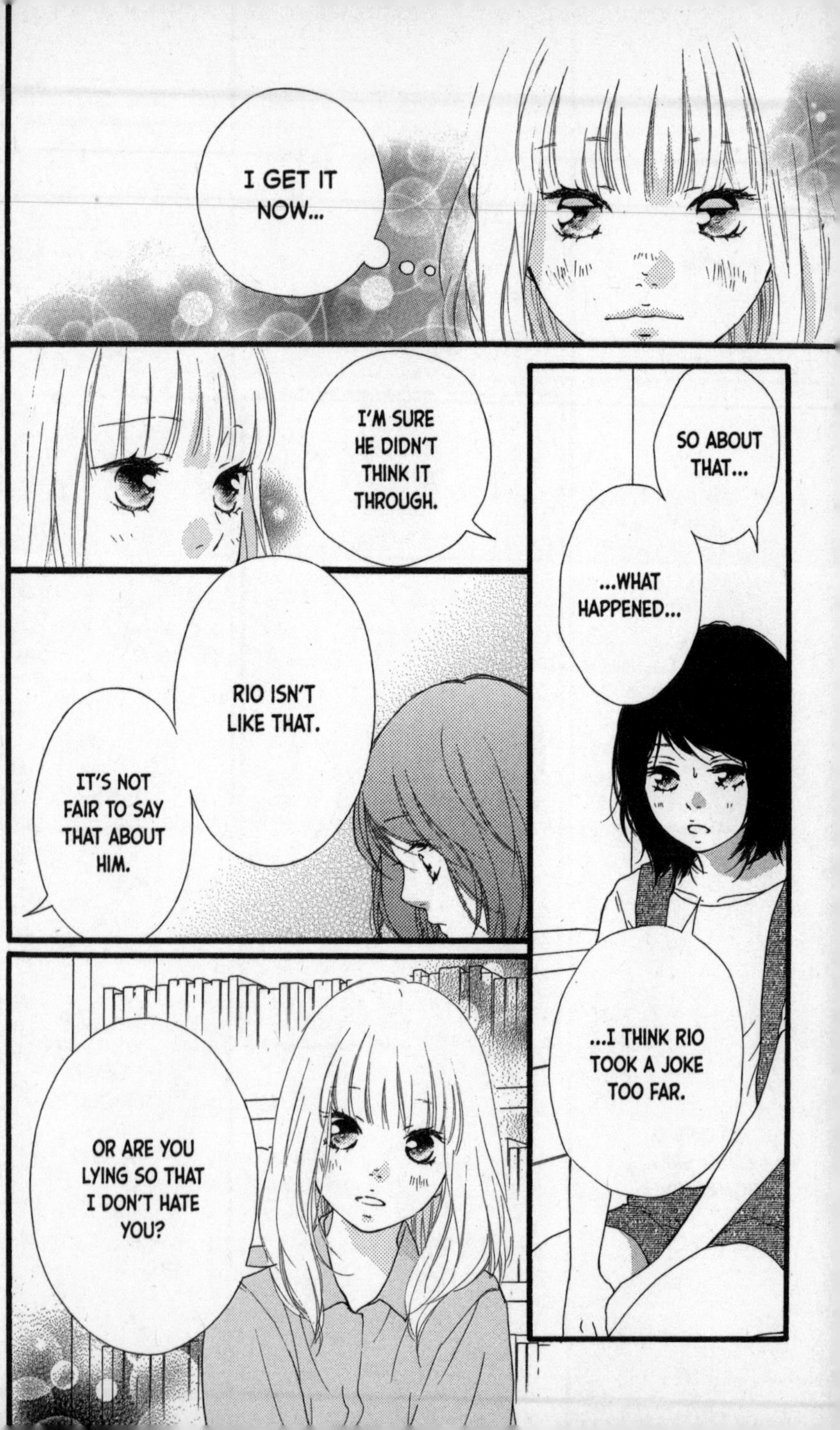
I GET IT NOW...
SO ABOUT THAT...
...WHAT HAPPENED...
...I THINK RIO TOOK A JOKE TOO FAR.
I'M SURE HE DIDN'T THINK IT THROUGH.
RIO ISN'T LIKE THAT.
IT'S NOT FAIR TO SAY THAT ABOUT HIM.
OR ARE YOU LYING SO THAT I DON'T HATE YOU?

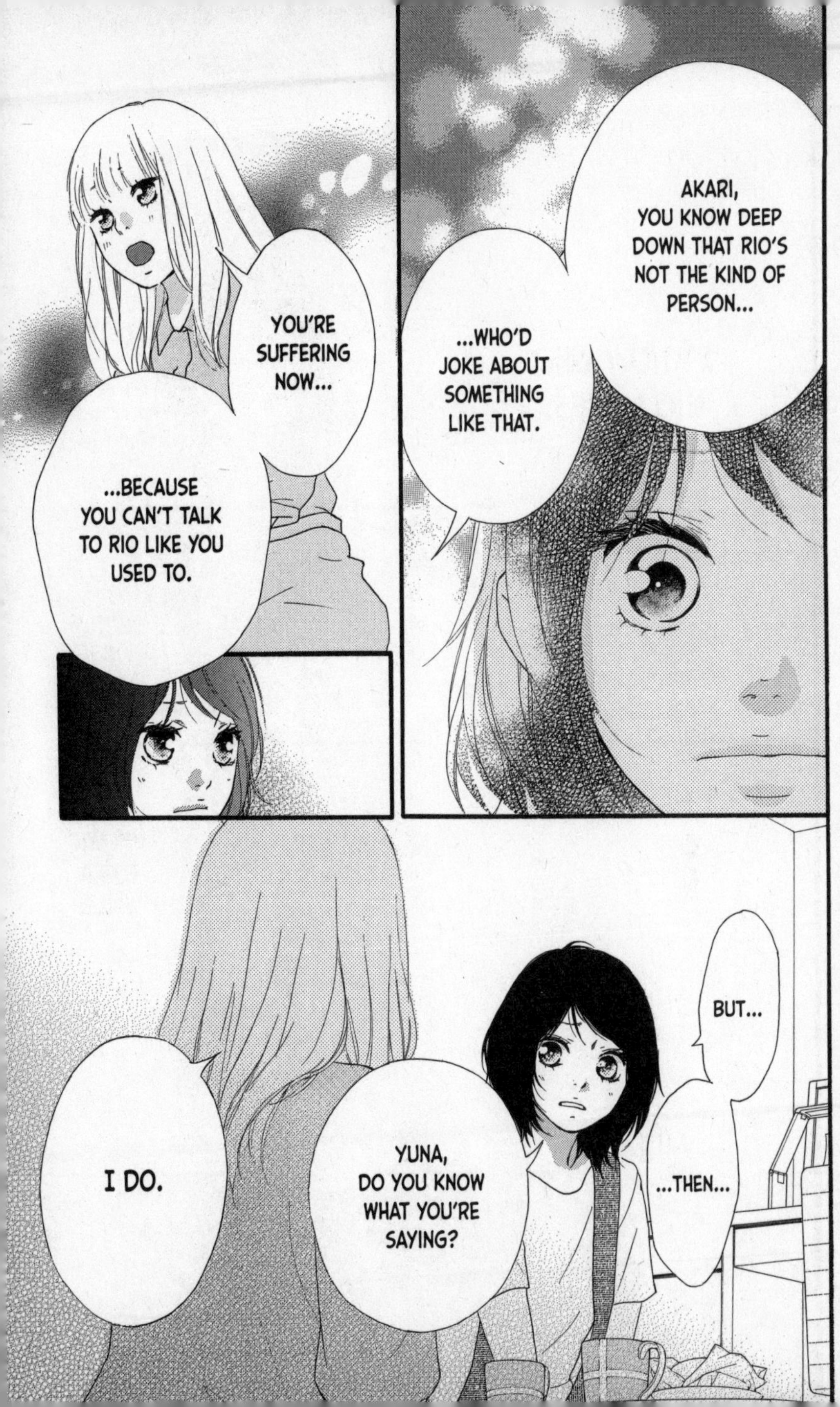
AKARI, YOU KNOW DEEP DOWN THAT RIO'S NOT THE KIND OF PERSON...
...WHO'D JOKE ABOUT SOMETHING LIKE THAT.
YOU'RE SUFFERING NOW...
...BECAUSE YOU CAN'T TALK TO RIO LIKE YOU USED TO.
BUT...
...THEN...
YUNA, DO YOU KNOW WHAT YOU'RE SAYING?
I DO.

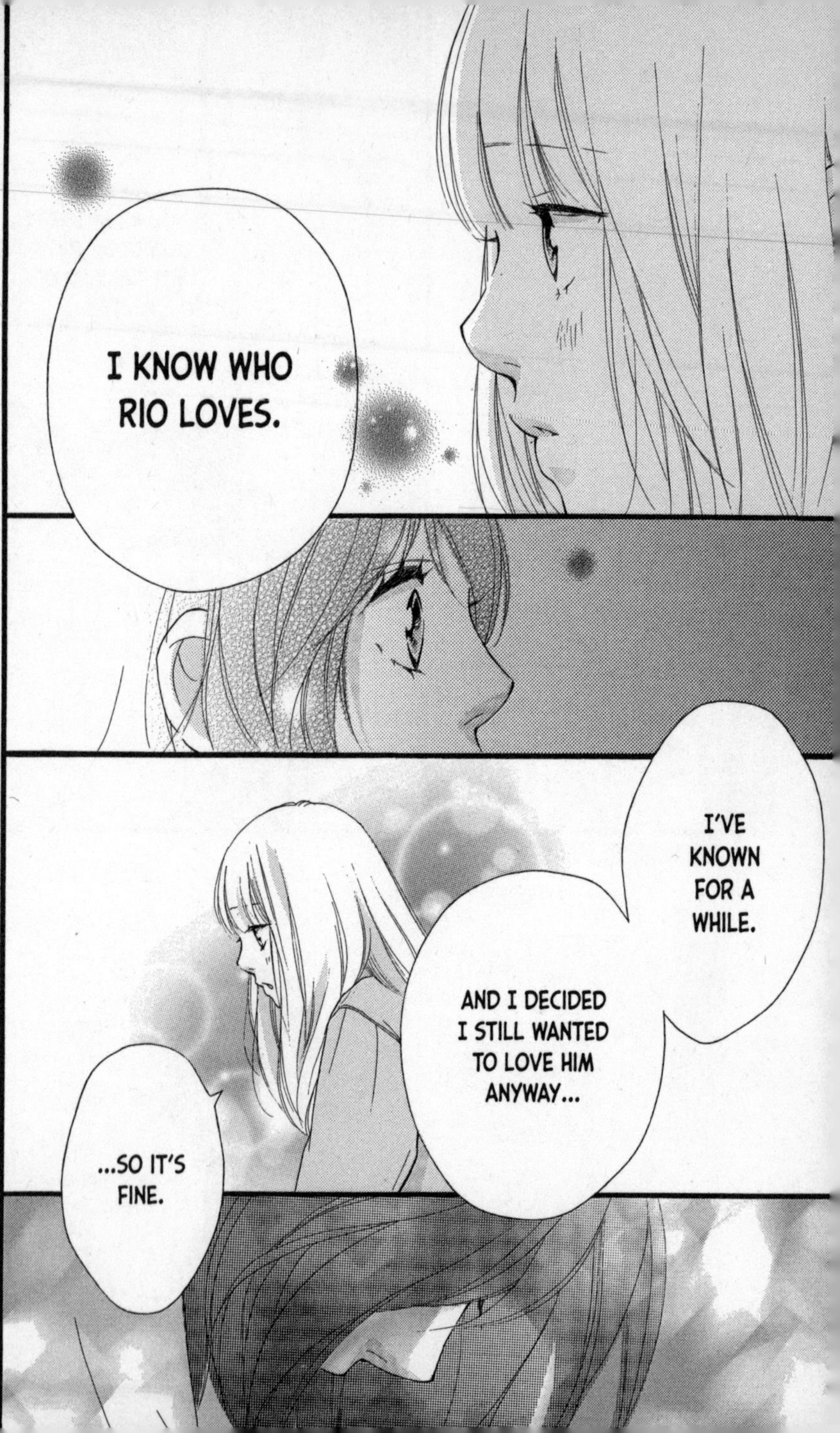
I KNOW WHO RIO LOVES.
I'VE KNOWN FOR A WHILE.
AND I DECIDED I STILL WANTED TO LOVE HIM ANYWAY...
...SO IT'S FINE.

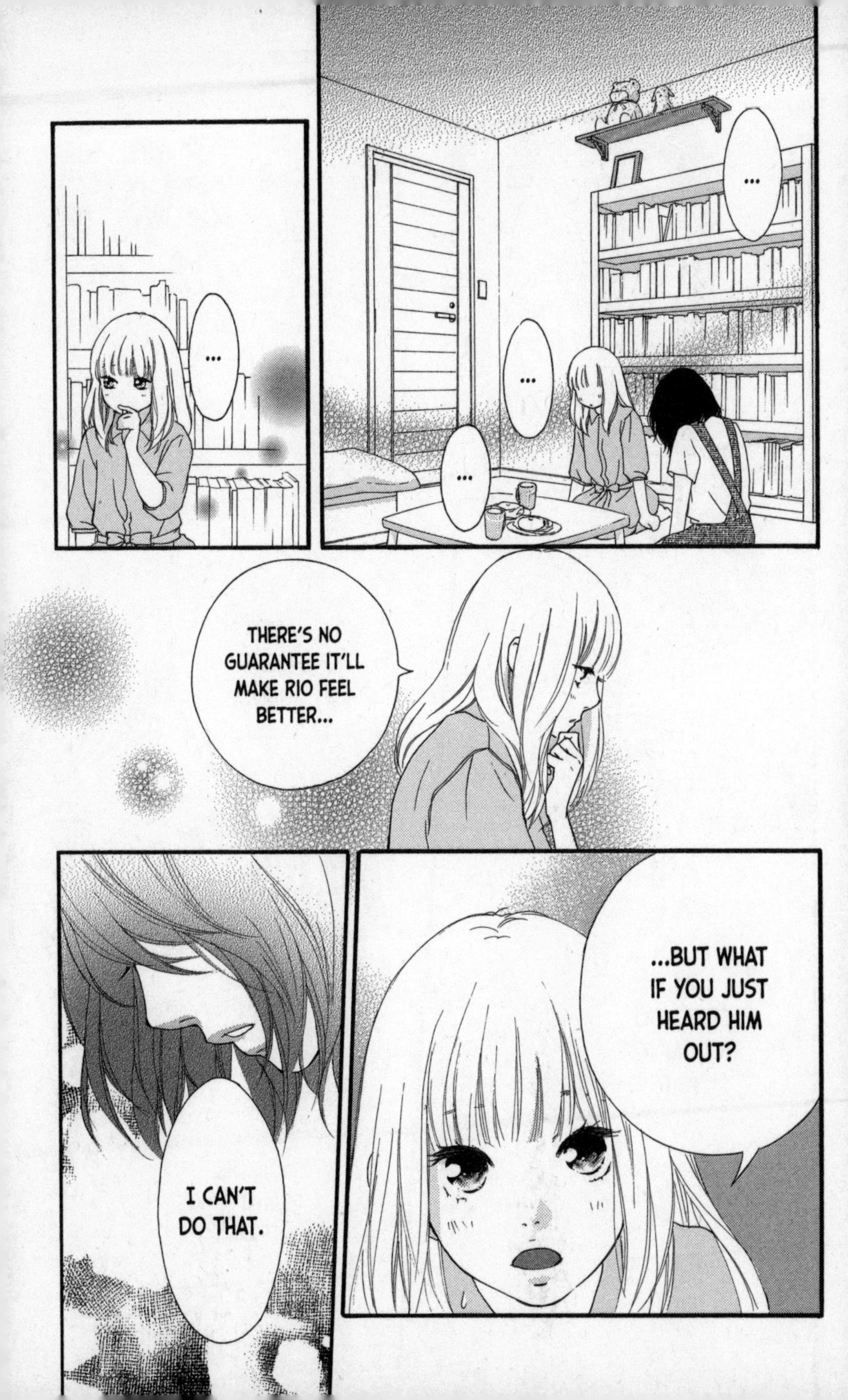
...
...
...
...
THERE'S NO GUARANTEE IT'LL MAKE RIO FEEL BETTER...
...BUT WHAT IF YOU JUST HEARD HIM OUT?
I CAN'T DO THAT.

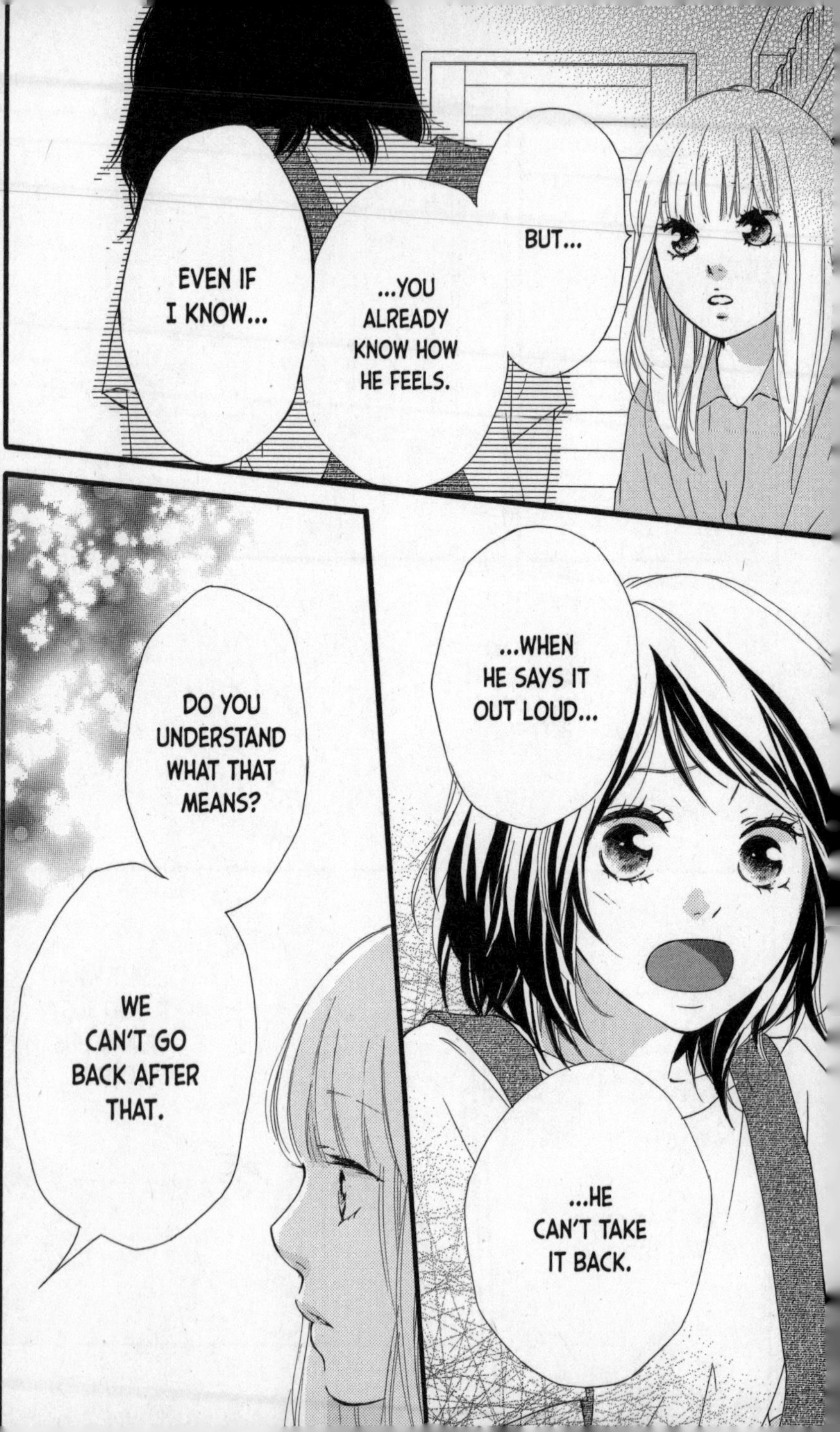
BUT...
...YOU ALREADY KNOW HOW HE FEELS.
EVEN IF I KNOW...
...WHEN HE SAYS IT OUT LOUD...
...HE CAN'T TAKE IT BACK.
DO YOU UNDERSTAND WHAT THAT MEANS?
WE CAN'T GO BACK AFTER THAT.

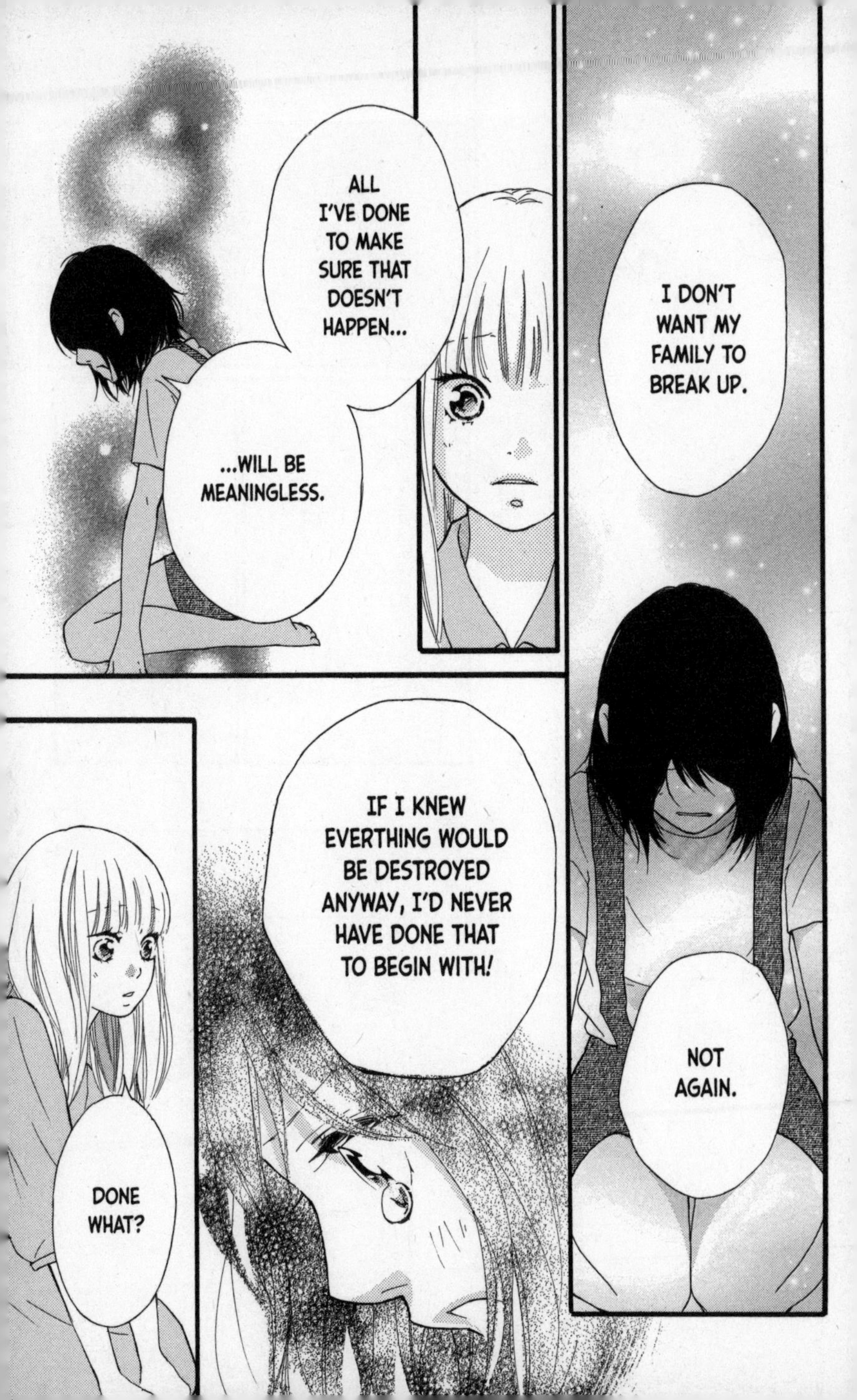
I DON'T WANT MY FAMILY TO BREAK UP.
NOT AGAIN.
ALL I'VE DONE TO MAKE SURE THAT DOESN'T HAPPEN...
...WILL BE MEANINGLESS.
IF I KNEW EVERTHING WOULD BE DESTROYED ANYWAY, I'D NEVER HAVE DONE THAT TO BEGIN WITH!
DONE WHAT?

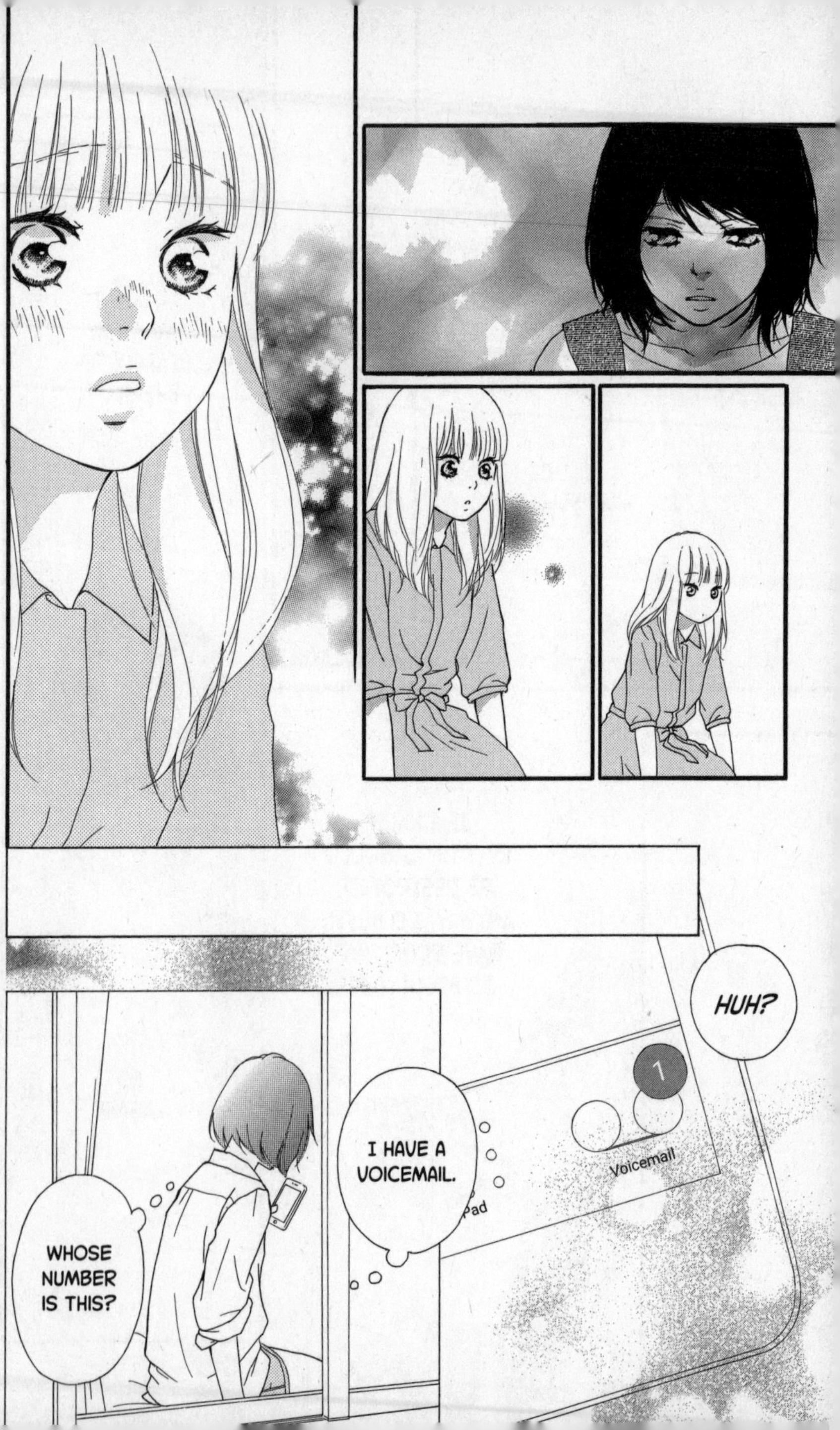
HUH?
Voicemail
I HAVE A VOICEMAIL.
WHOSE NUMBER IS THIS?

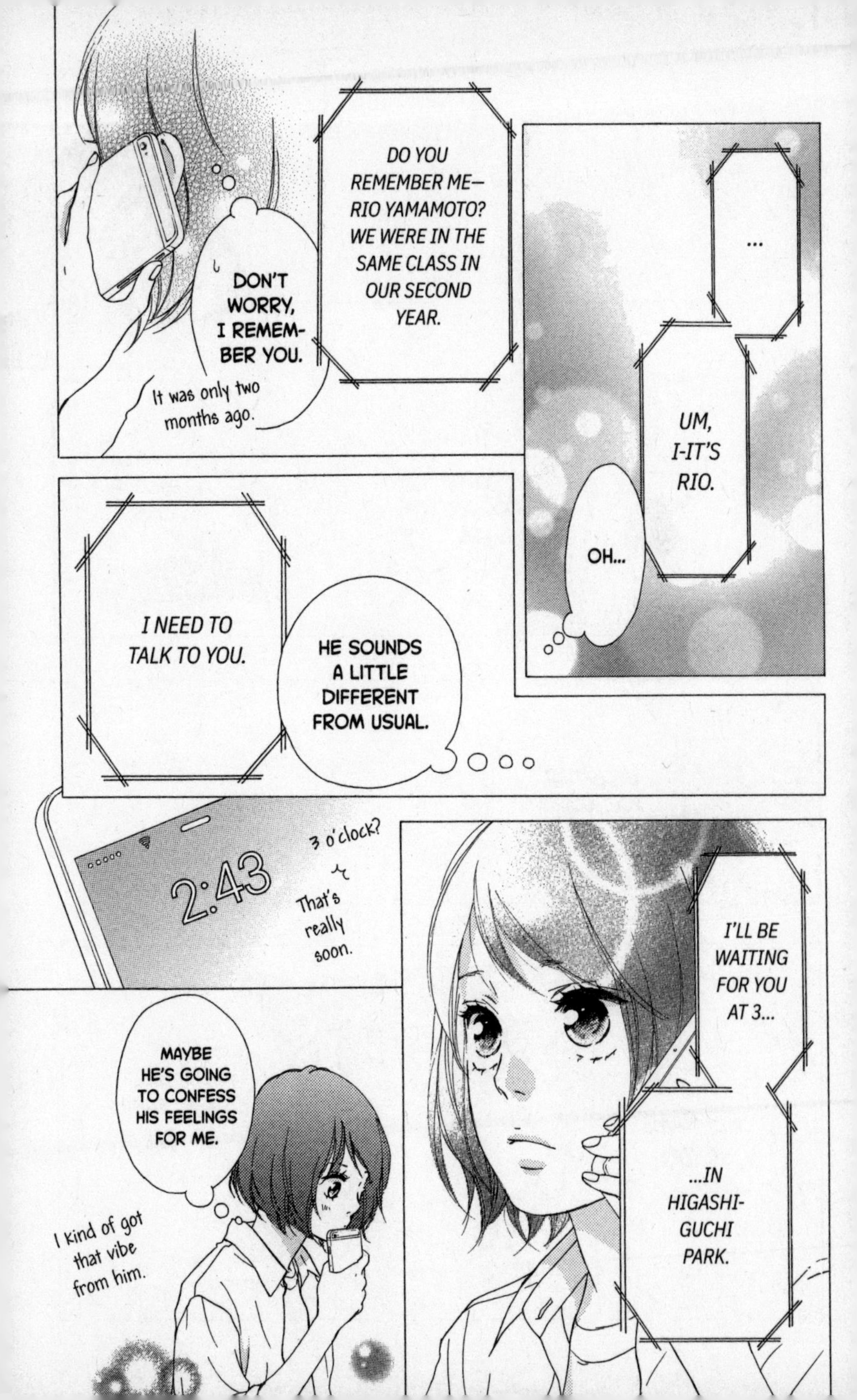
...
UM, I-IT'S RIO.
OH...
DO YOU REMEMBER ME— RIO YAMAMOTO? WE WERE IN THE SAME CLASS IN OUR SECOND YEAR.
DON'T WORRY, I REMEMBER YOU.
It was only two months ago.
I NEED TO TALK TO YOU.
HE SOUNDS A LITTLE DIFFERENT FROM USUAL.
I'LL BE WAITING FOR YOU AT 3...
...IN HIGASHI-GUCHI PARK.
2:43
3 o'clock?
That's really soon.
MAYBE HE'S GOING TO CONFESS HIS FEELINGS FOR ME.
I kind of got that vibe from him.

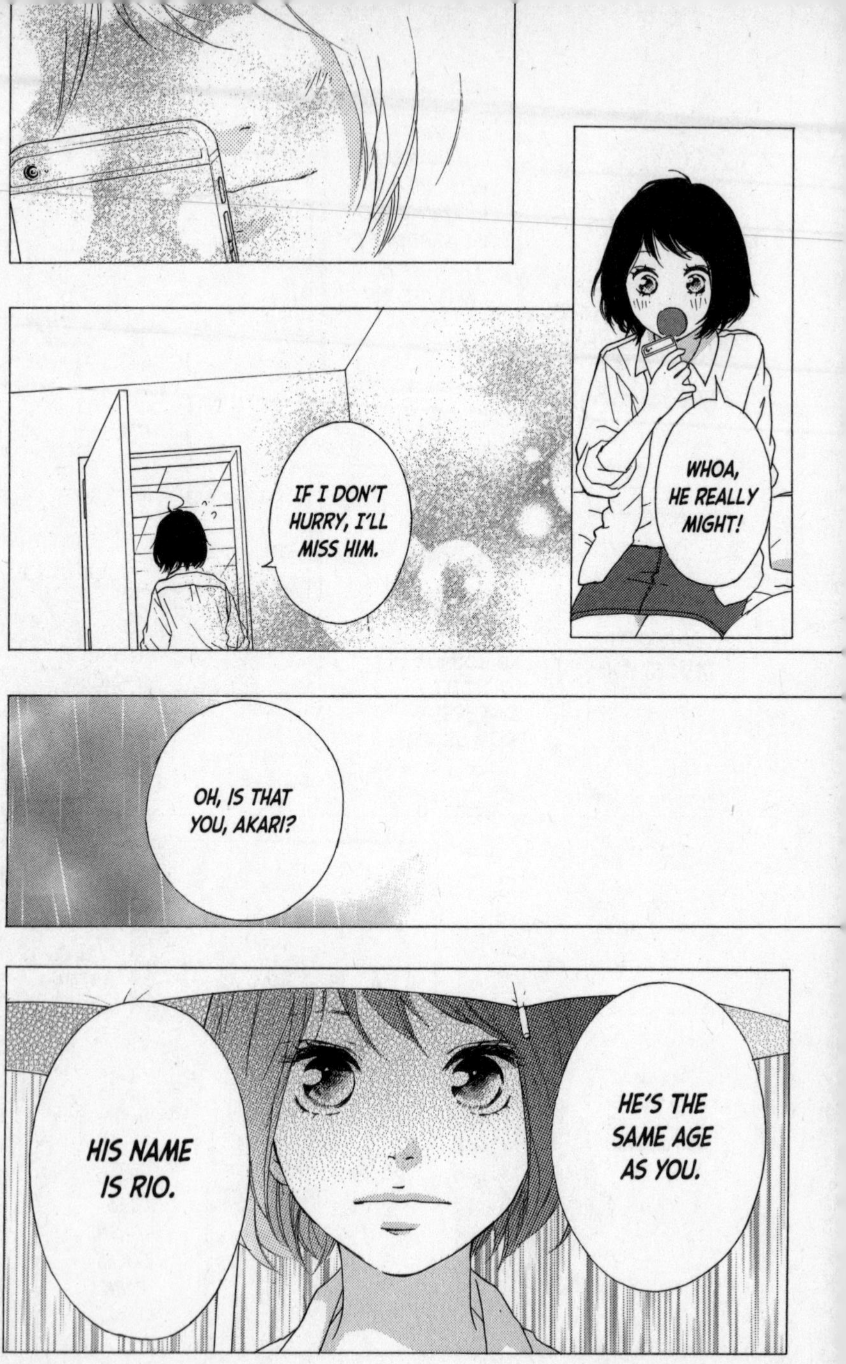
WHOA, HE REALLY MIGHT!
IF I DON'T HURRY, I'LL MISS HIM.
OH, IS THAT YOU, AKARI?
HE'S THE SAME AGE AS YOU.
HIS NAME IS RIO.

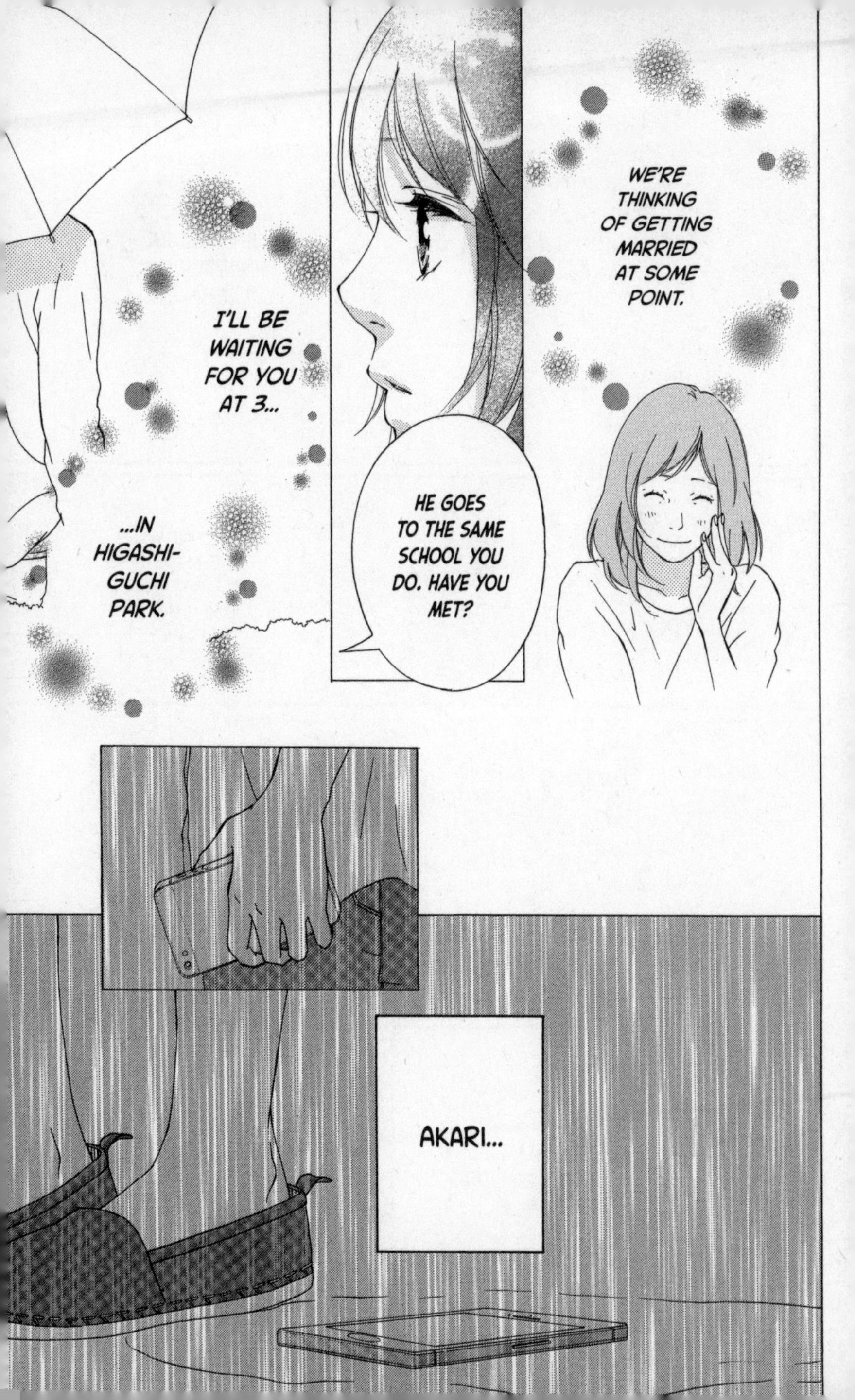
WE'RE THINKING OF GETTING MARRIED AT SOME POINT.
HE GOES TO THE SAME SCHOOL YOU DO. HAVE YOU MET?
I'LL BE WAITING FOR YOU AT 3...
...IN HIGASHI-GUCHI PARK.
AKARI...

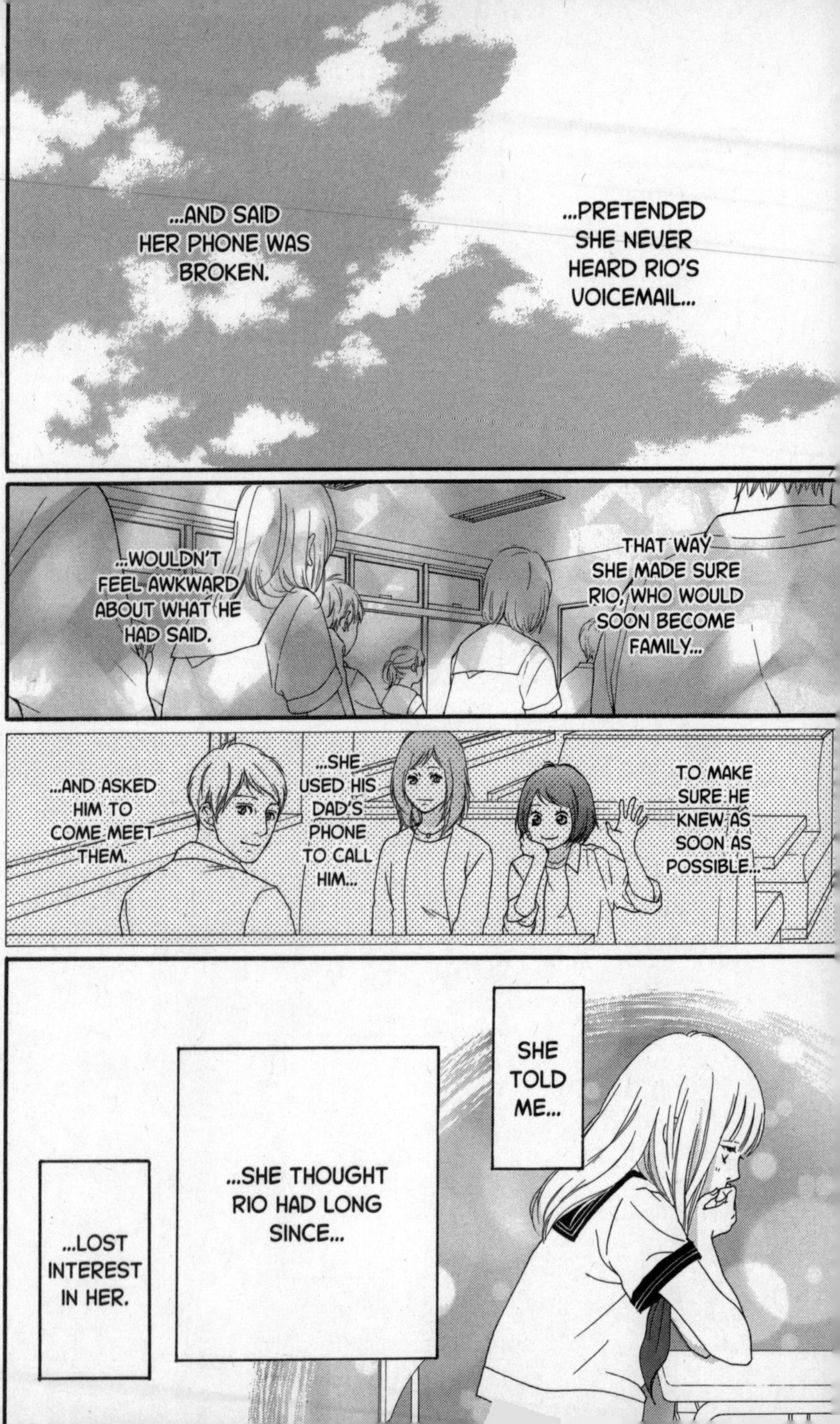
...PRETENDED SHE NEVER HEARD RIO'S VOICEMAIL...
...AND SAID HER PHONE WAS BROKEN.
THAT WAY SHE MADE SURE RIO, WHO WOULD SOON BECOME FAMILY...
...WOULDN'T FEEL AWKWARD ABOUT WHAT HE HAD SAID.
TO MAKE SURE HE KNEW AS SOON AS POSSIBLE...
...SHE USED HIS DAD'S PHONE TO CALL HIM...
...AND ASKED HIM TO COME MEET THEM.
SHE TOLD ME...
...SHE THOUGHT RIO HAD LONG SINCE...
...LOST INTEREST IN HER.

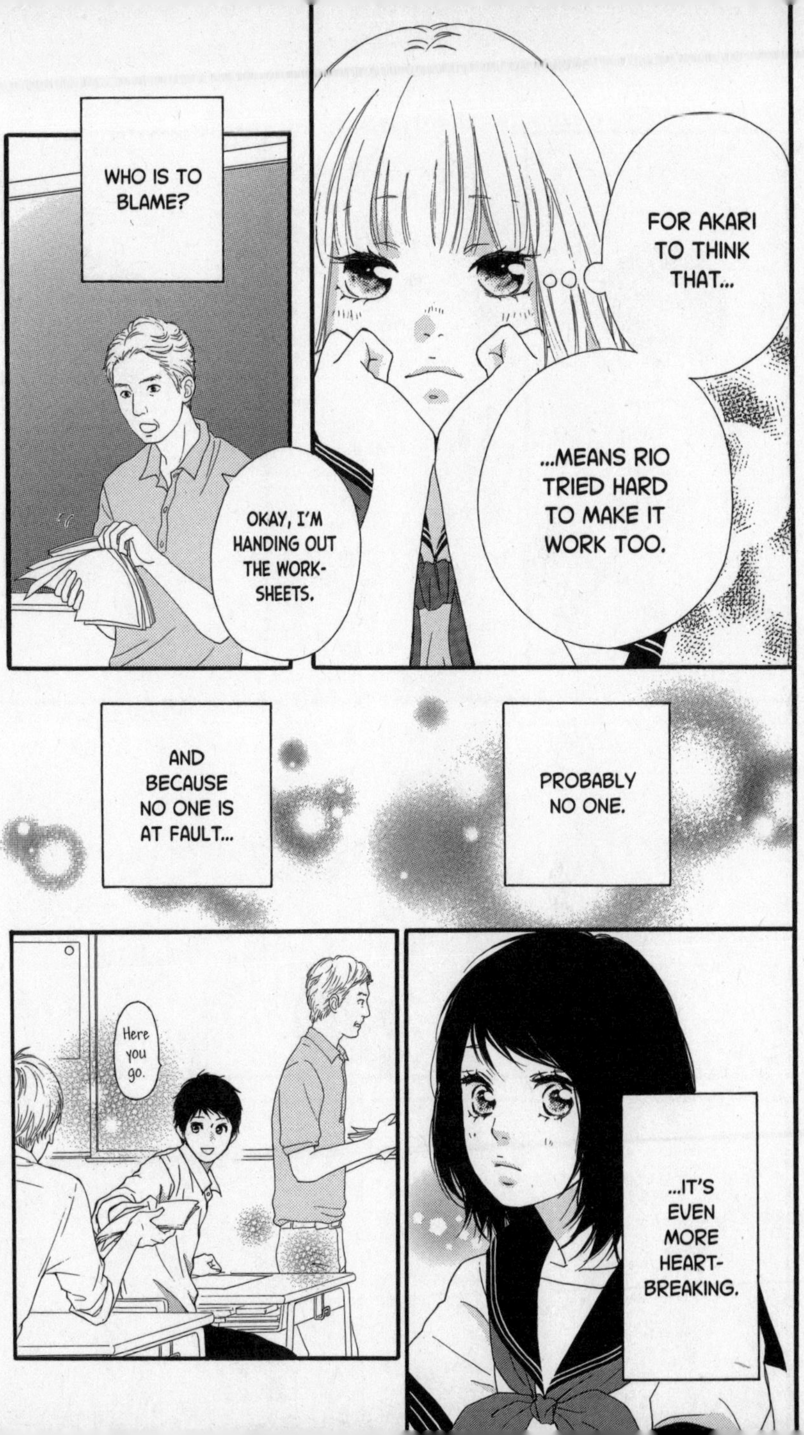
FOR AKARI TO THINK THAT...
...MEANS RIO TRIED HARD TO MAKE IT WORK TOO.
WHO IS TO BLAME?
OKAY, I'M HANDING OUT THE WORK-SHEETS.
PROBABLY NO ONE.
AND BECAUSE NO ONE IS AT FAULT...
...IT'S EVEN MORE HEART-BREAKING.
Here you go.

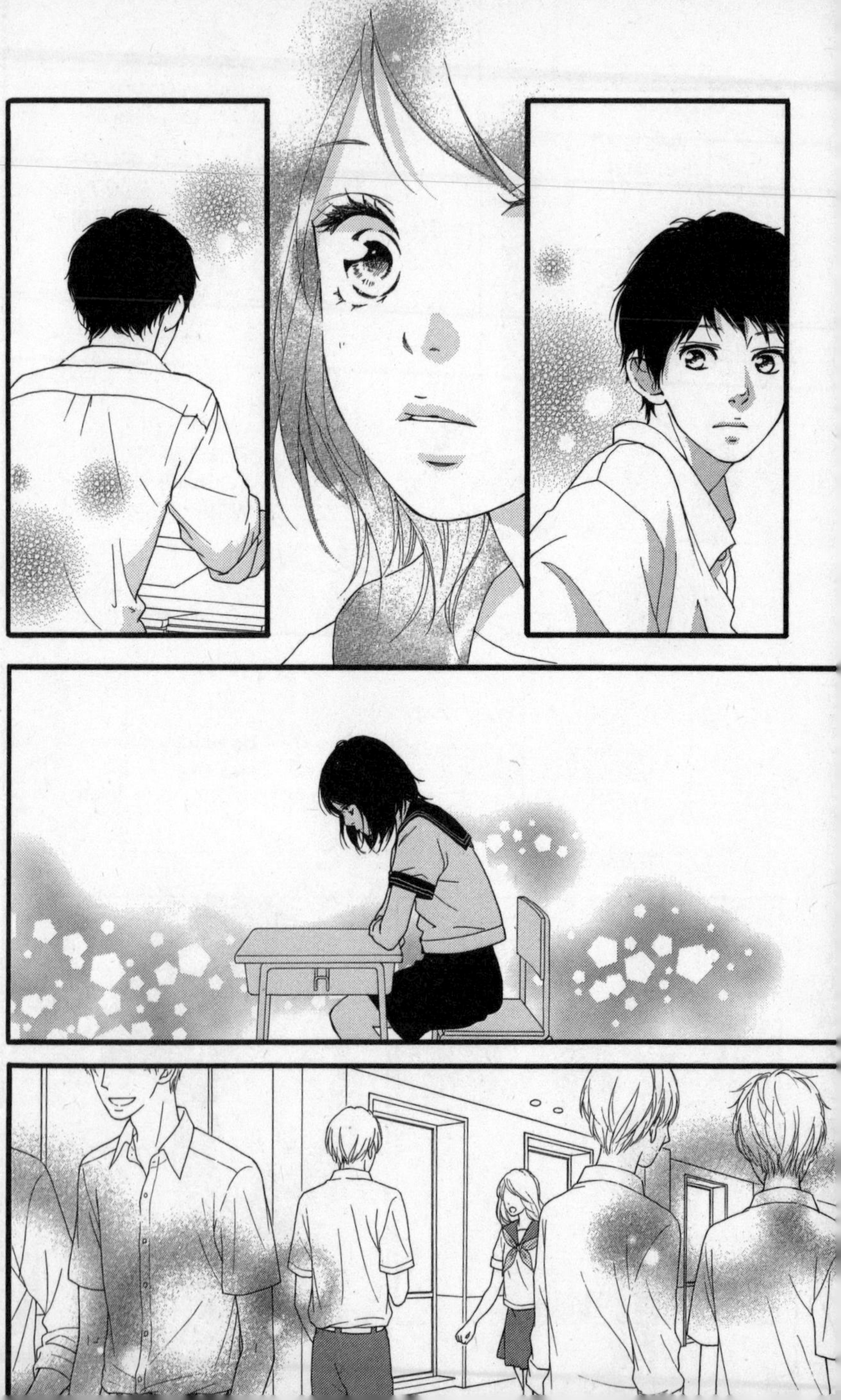

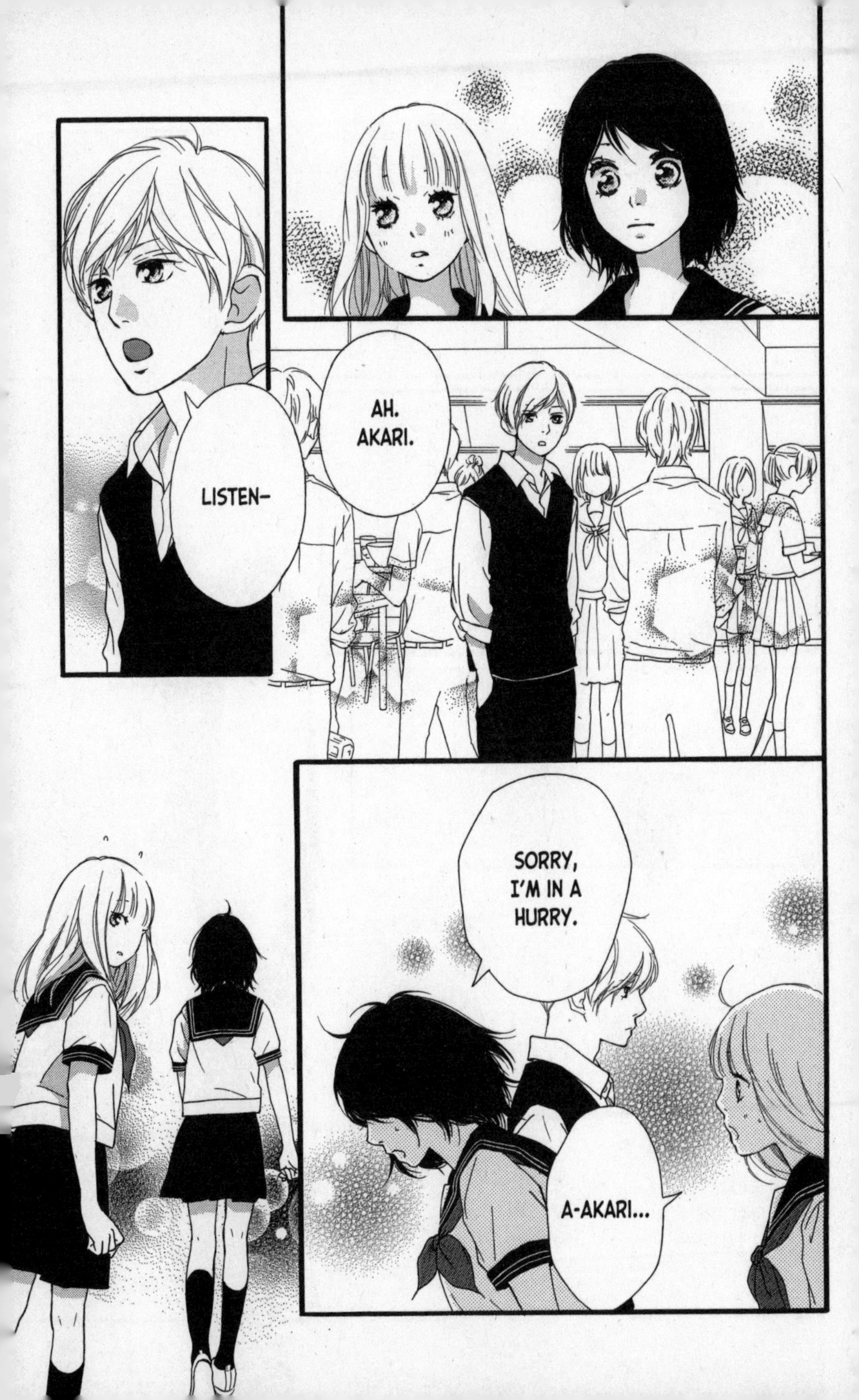
AH. AKARI.
LISTEN-
SORRY, I'M IN A HURRY.
A-AKARI...

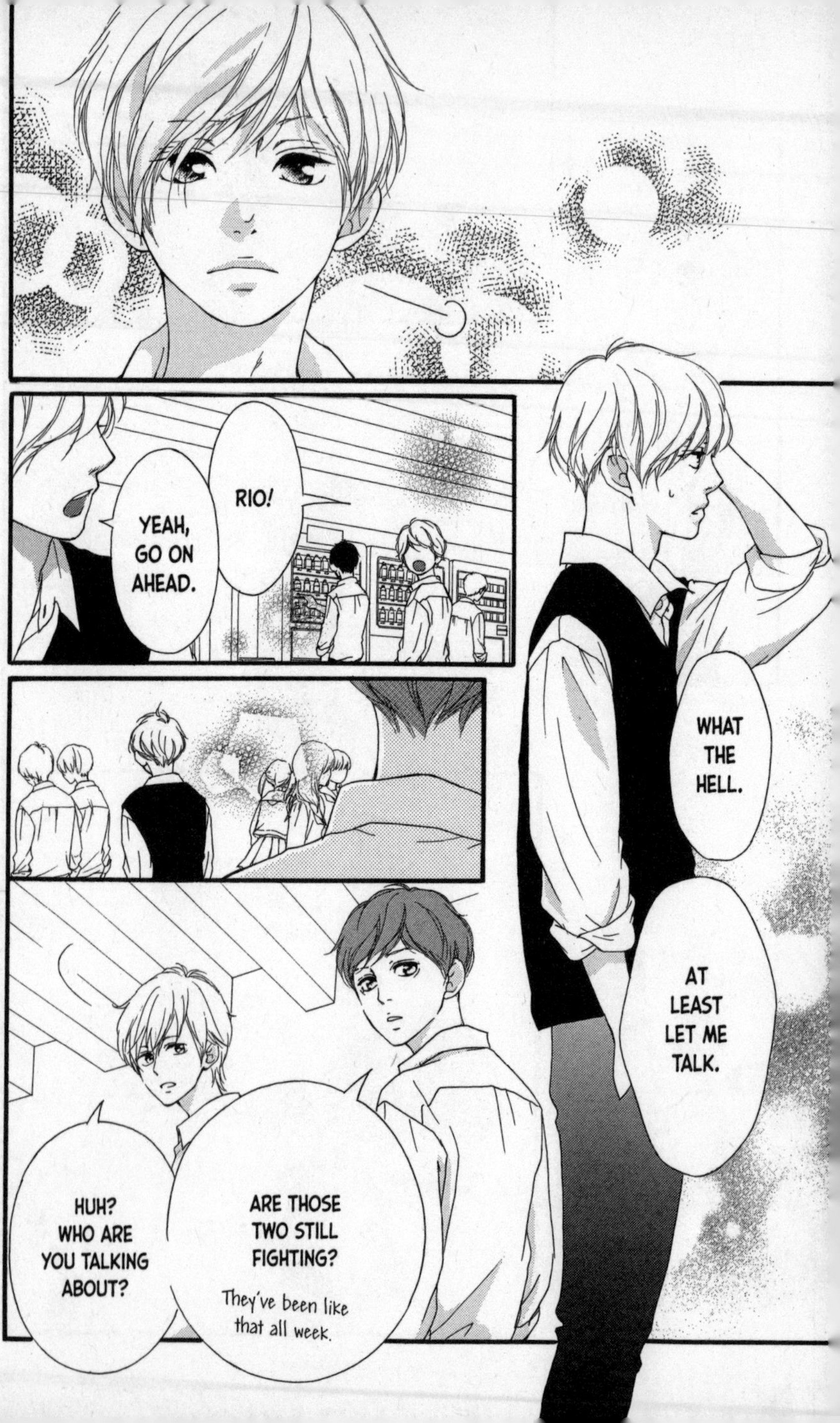
WHAT THE HELL.
AT LEAST LET ME TALK.
RIO!
YEAH, GO ON AHEAD.
ARE THOSE TWO STILL FIGHTING?
They've been like that all week.
HUH? WHO ARE YOU TALKING ABOUT?

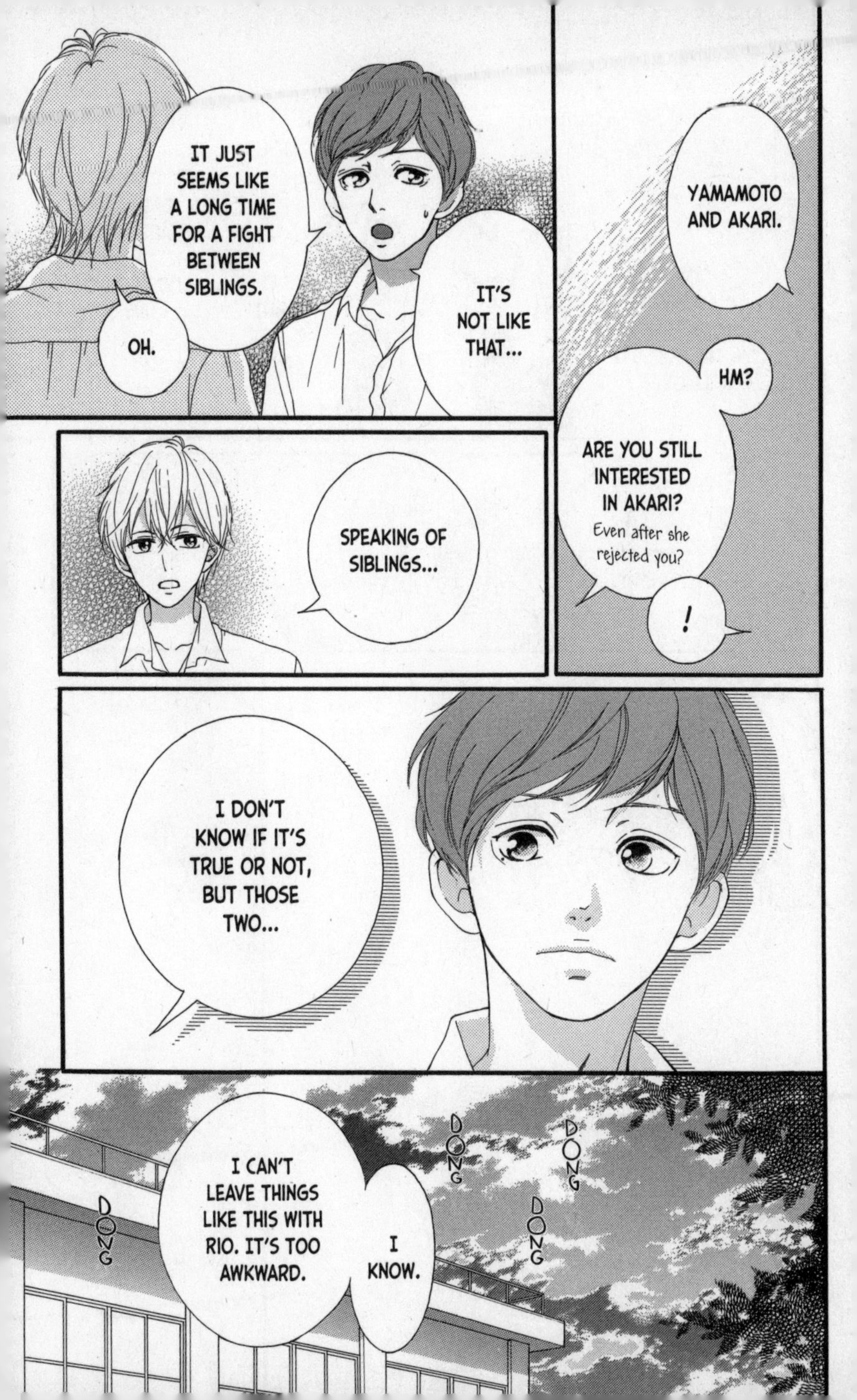
YAMAMOTO AND AKARI.
HM?
ARE YOU STILL INTERESTED IN AKARI? Even after she rejected you?
!
IT'S NOT LIKE THAT...
IT JUST SEEMS LIKE A LONG TIME FOR A FIGHT BETWEEN SIBLINGS.
OH.
SPEAKING OF SIBLINGS...
I DON'T KNOW IF IT'S TRUE OR NOT, BUT THOSE TWO...
DONG
DONG
DONG
I KNOW.
I CAN'T LEAVE THINGS LIKE THIS WITH RIO. IT'S TOO AWKWARD.
DONG

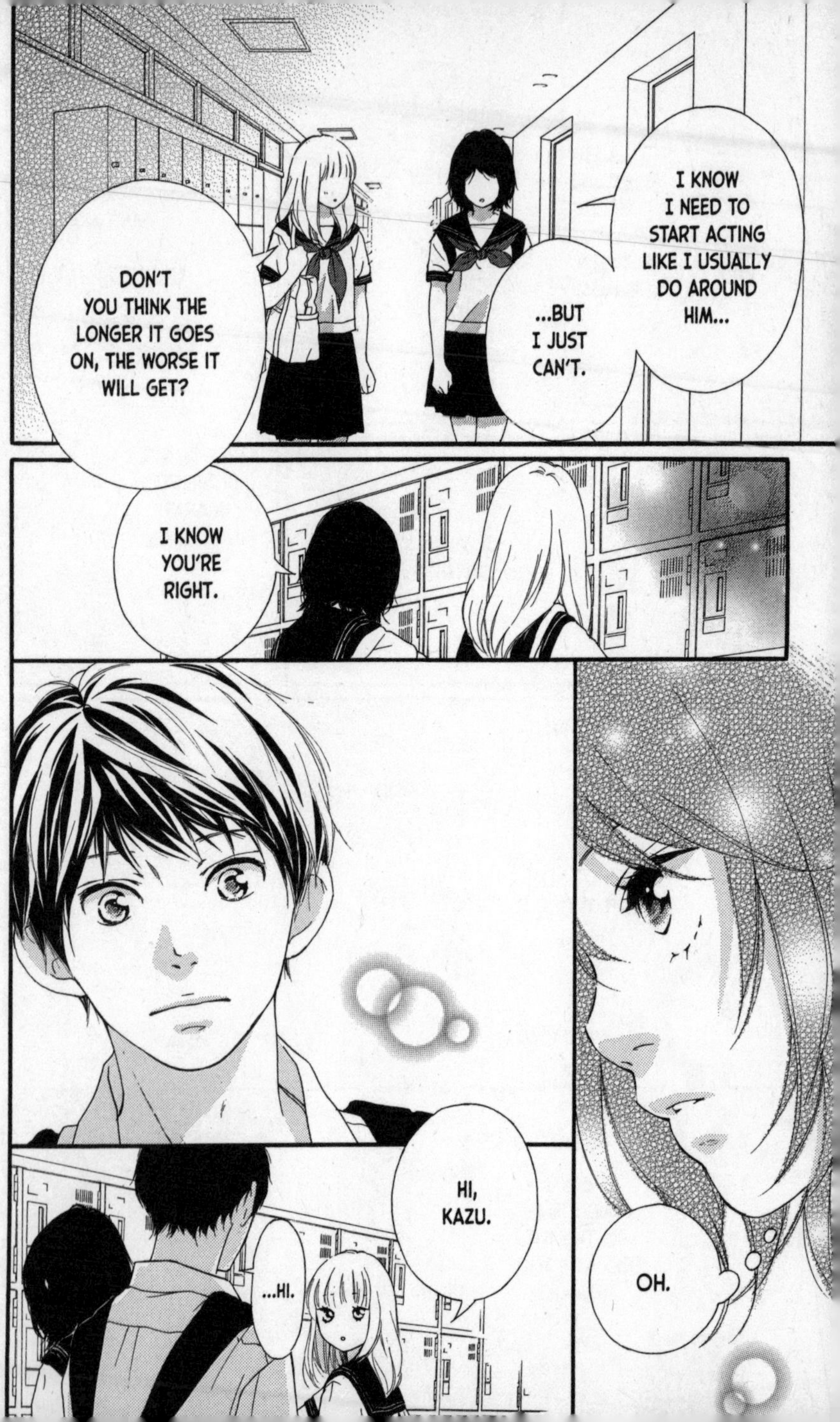
I KNOW I NEED TO START ACTING LIKE I USUALLY DO AROUND HIM...
...BUT I JUST CAN'T.
DON'T YOU THINK THE LONGER IT GOES ON, THE WORSE IT WILL GET?
I KNOW YOU'RE RIGHT.
OH.
HI, KAZU.
...HI.

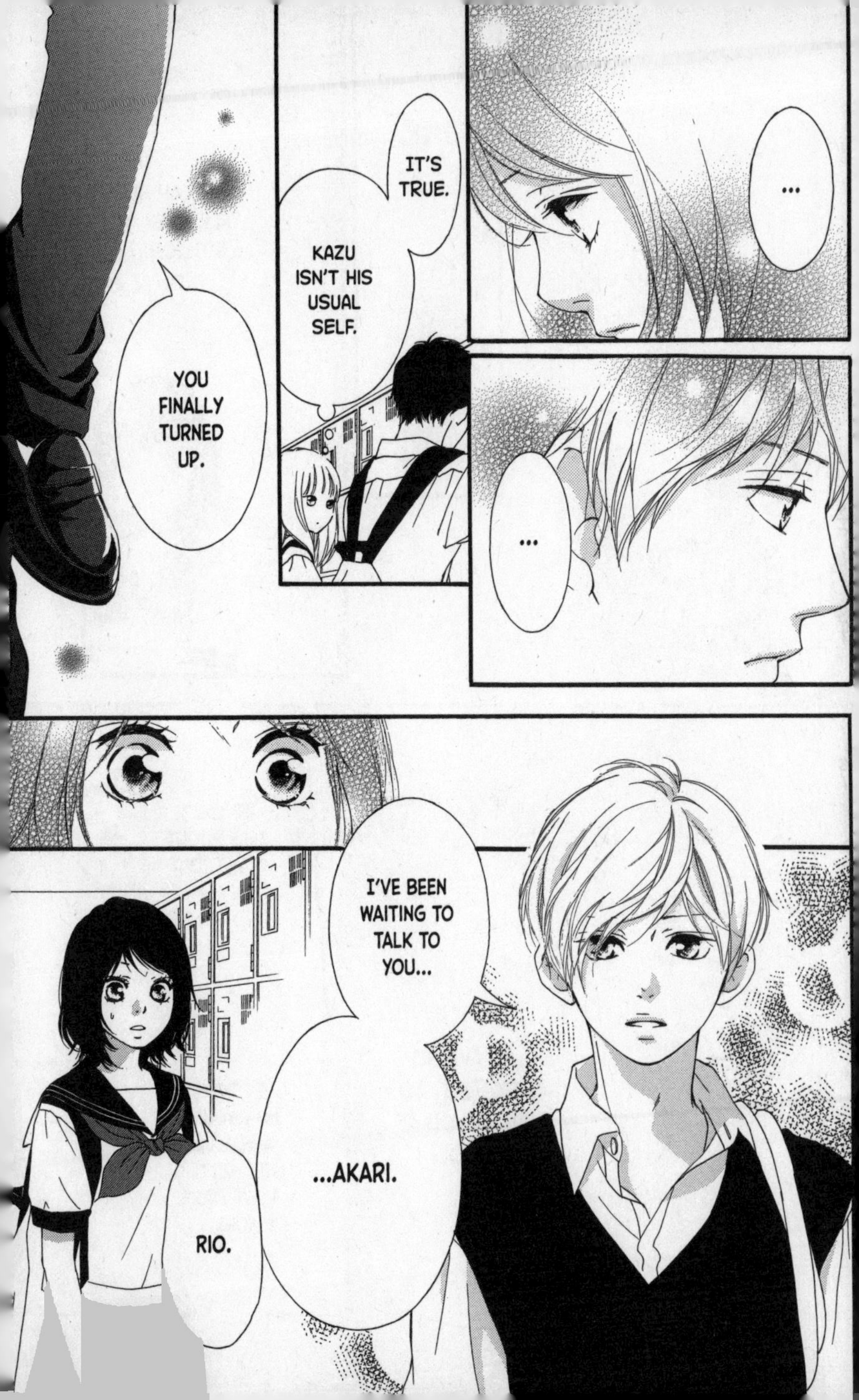
...
...
IT'S TRUE.
KAZU ISN'T HIS USUAL SELF.
YOU FINALLY TURNED UP.
I'VE BEEN WAITING TO TALK TO YOU...
...AKARI.
RIO.

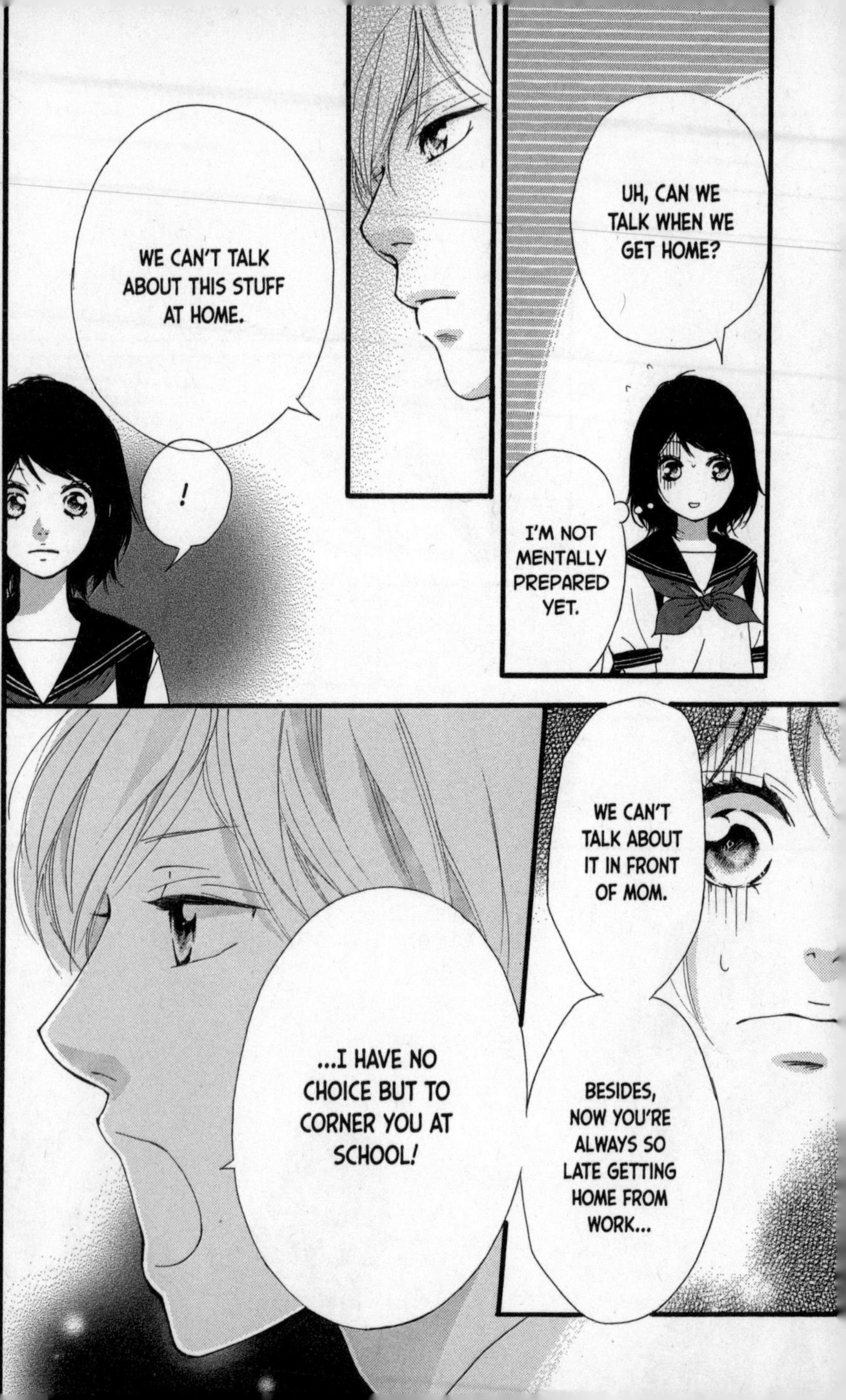
UH, CAN WE TALK WHEN WE GET HOME?
I'M NOT MENTALLY PREPARED YET.
WE CAN'T TALK ABOUT THIS STUFF AT HOME.
!
WE CAN'T TALK ABOUT IT IN FRONT OF MOM.
BESIDES, NOW YOU'RE ALWAYS SO LATE GETTING HOME FROM WORK...
...I HAVE NO CHOICE BUT TO CORNER YOU AT SCHOOL!

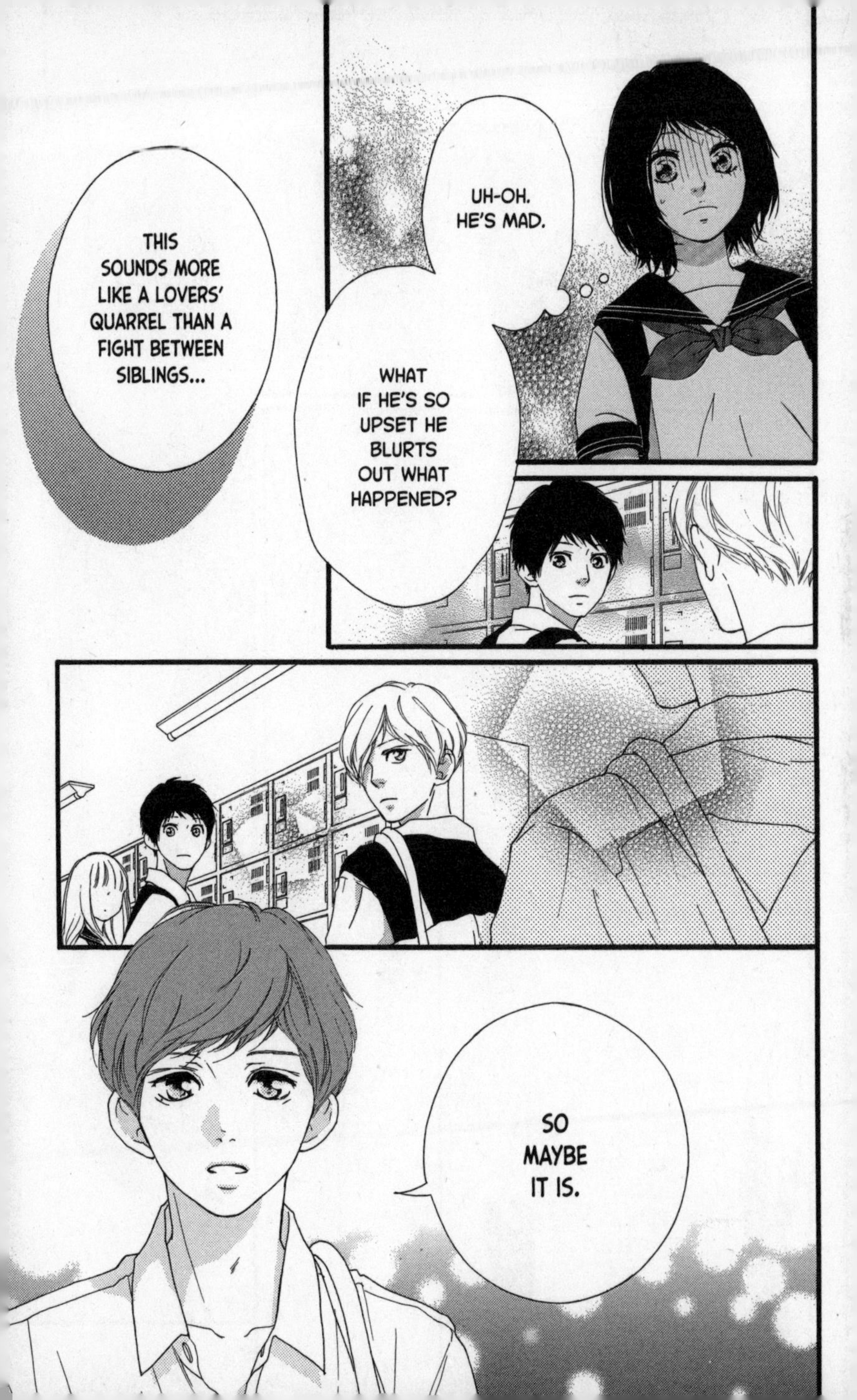
UH-OH. HE'S MAD.
WHAT IF HE'S SO UPSET HE BLURTS OUT WHAT HAPPENED?
THIS SOUNDS MORE LIKE A LOVERS' QUARREL THAN A FIGHT BETWEEN SIBLINGS...
SO MAYBE IT IS.

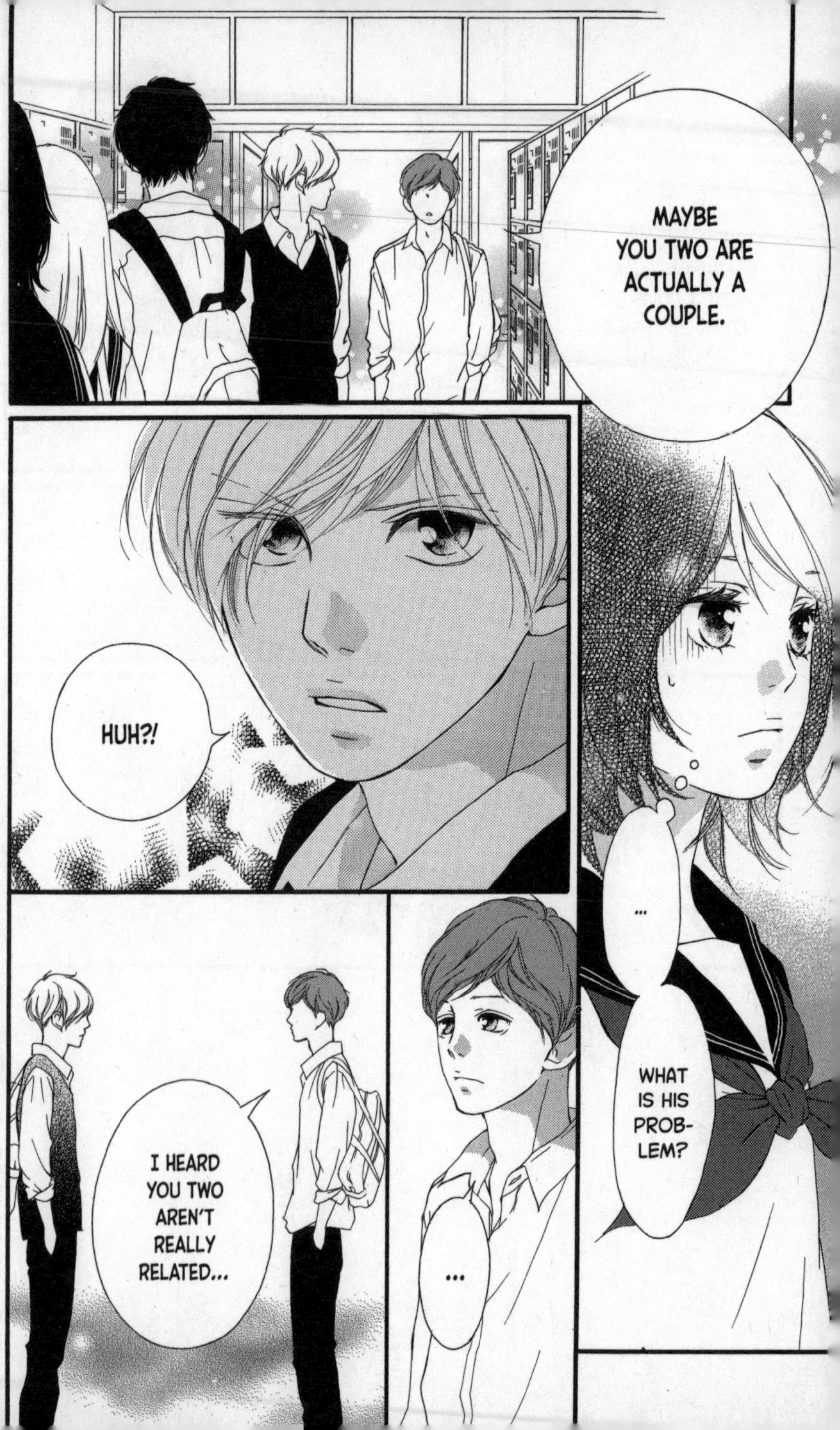
MAYBE YOU TWO ARE ACTUALLY A COUPLE.
...
WHAT IS HIS PROB-LEM?
HUH?!
...
I HEARD YOU TWO AREN'T REALLY RELATED...

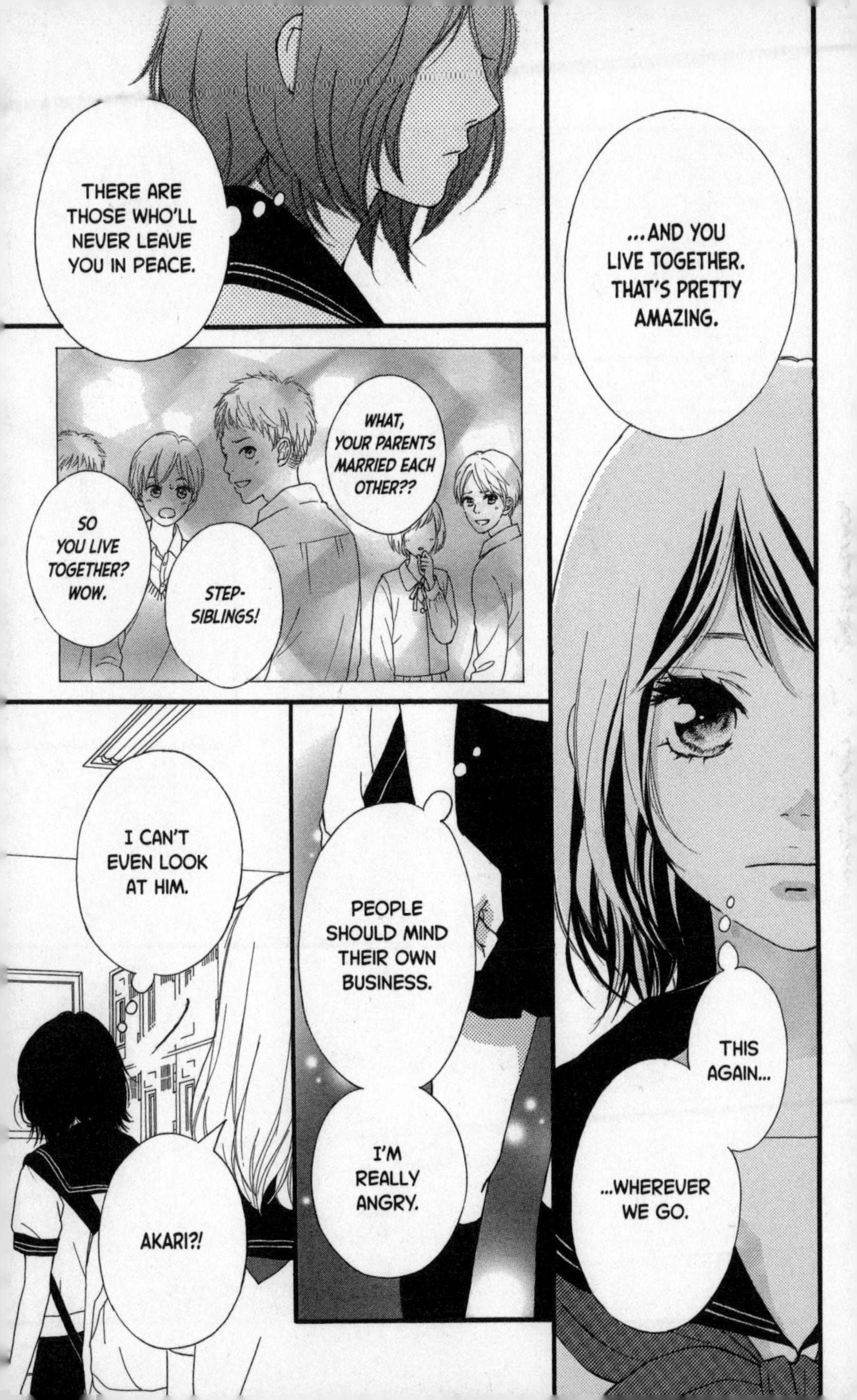
...AND YOU LIVE TOGETHER. THAT'S PRETTY AMAZING.
THIS AGAIN...
...WHEREVER WE GO.
THERE ARE THOSE WHO'LL NEVER LEAVE YOU IN PEACE.
WHAT, YOUR PARENTS MARRIED EACH OTHER??
STEP-SIBLINGS!
SO YOU LIVE TOGETHER? WOW.
PEOPLE SHOULD MIND THEIR OWN BUSINESS.
I'M REALLY ANGRY.
I CAN'T EVEN LOOK AT HIM.
AKARI?!

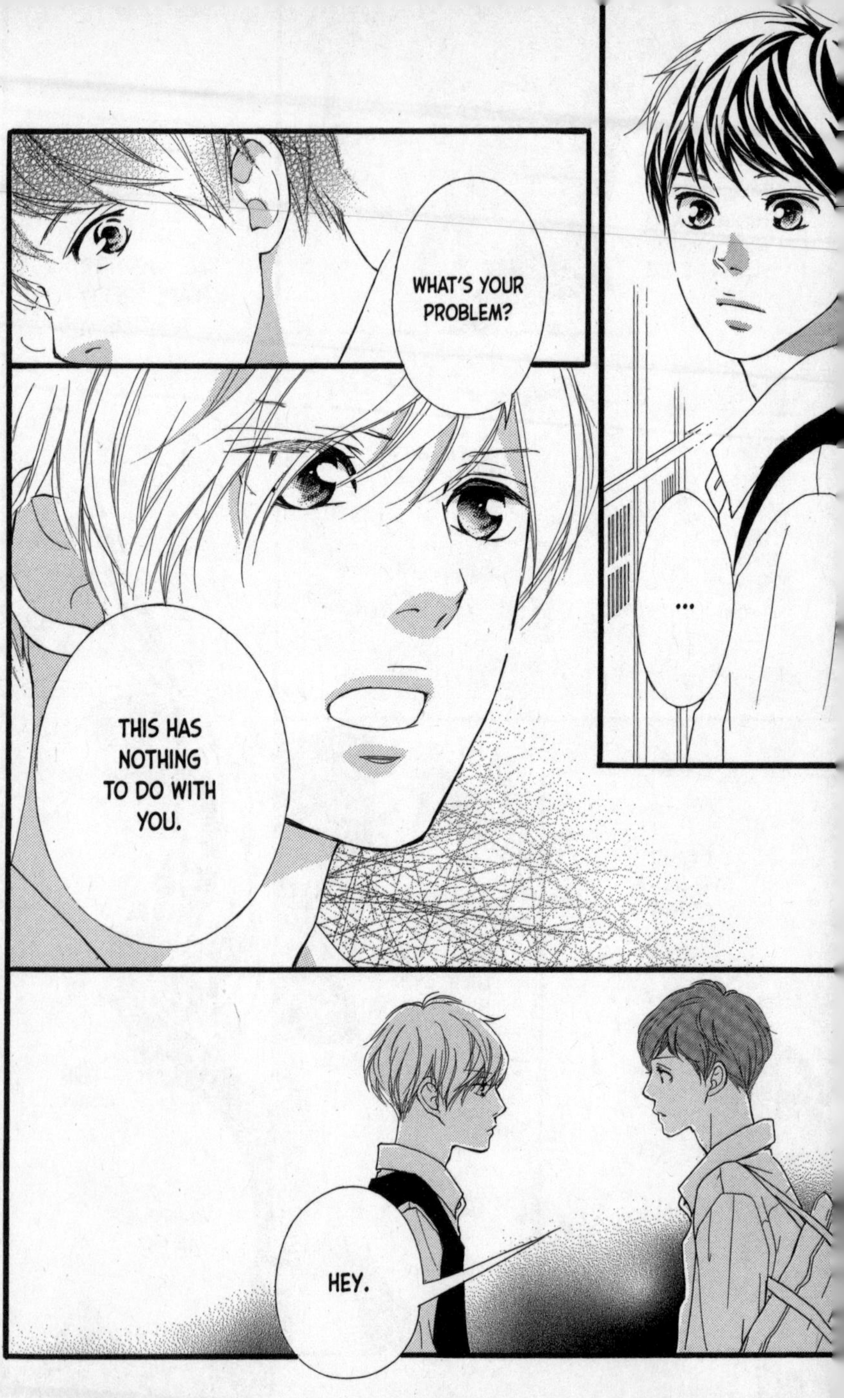
...
WHAT'S YOUR PROBLEM?
THIS HAS NOTHING TO DO WITH YOU.
HEY.

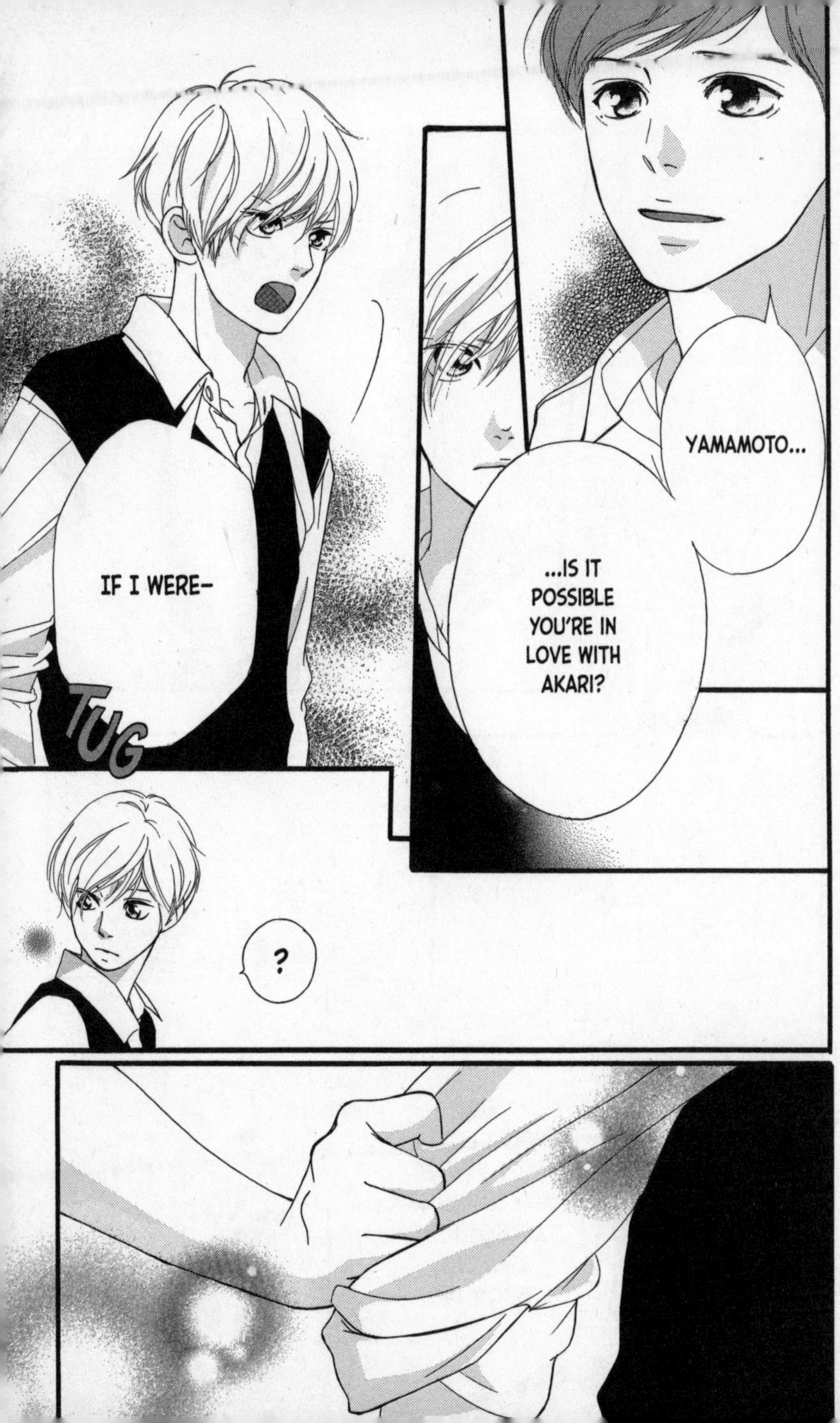
YAMAMOTO...
...IS IT POSSIBLE YOU'RE IN LOVE WITH AKARI?
IF I WERE-
TUG
?

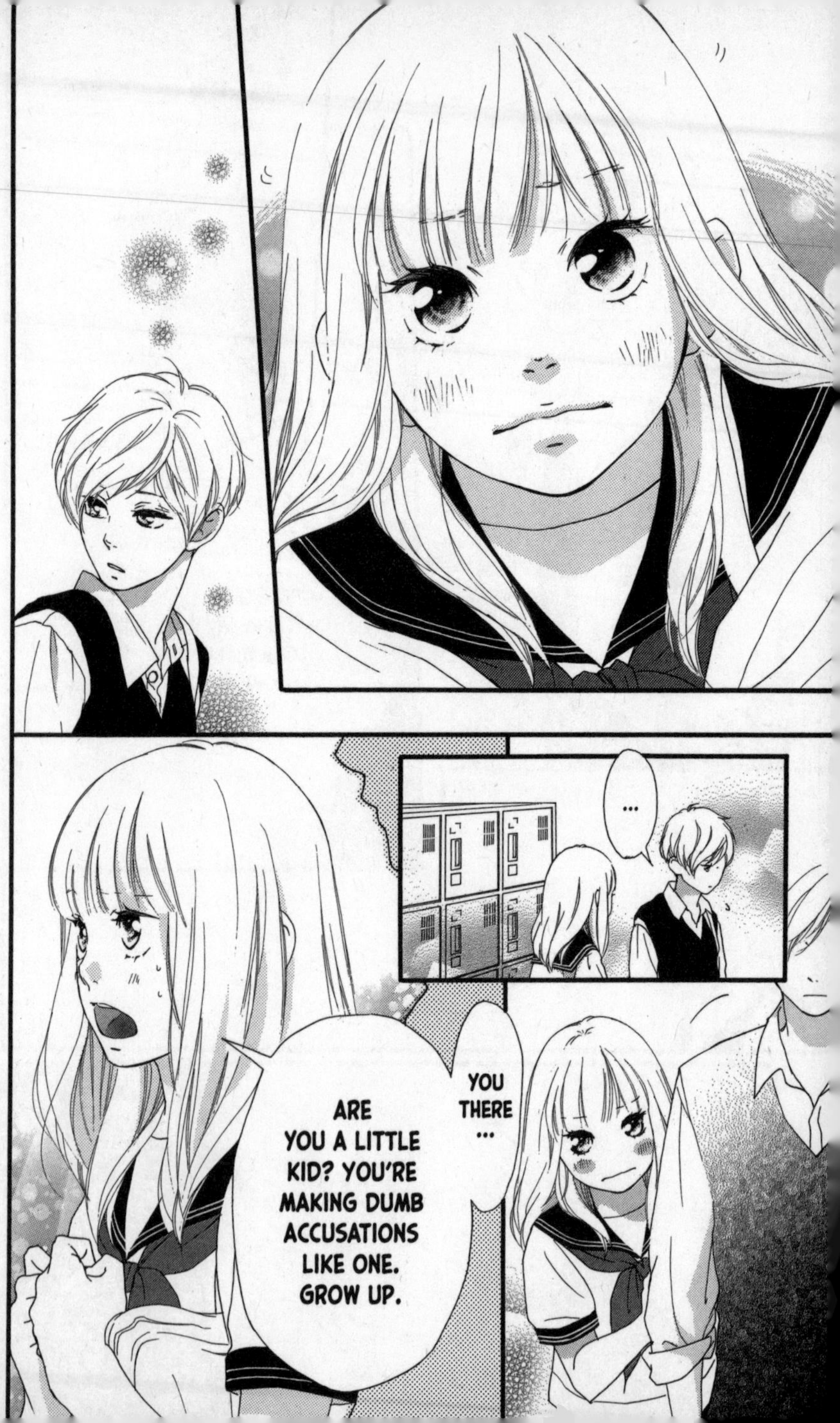
...
YOU THERE...
ARE YOU A LITTLE KID? YOU'RE MAKING DUMB ACCUSATIONS LIKE ONE. GROW UP.

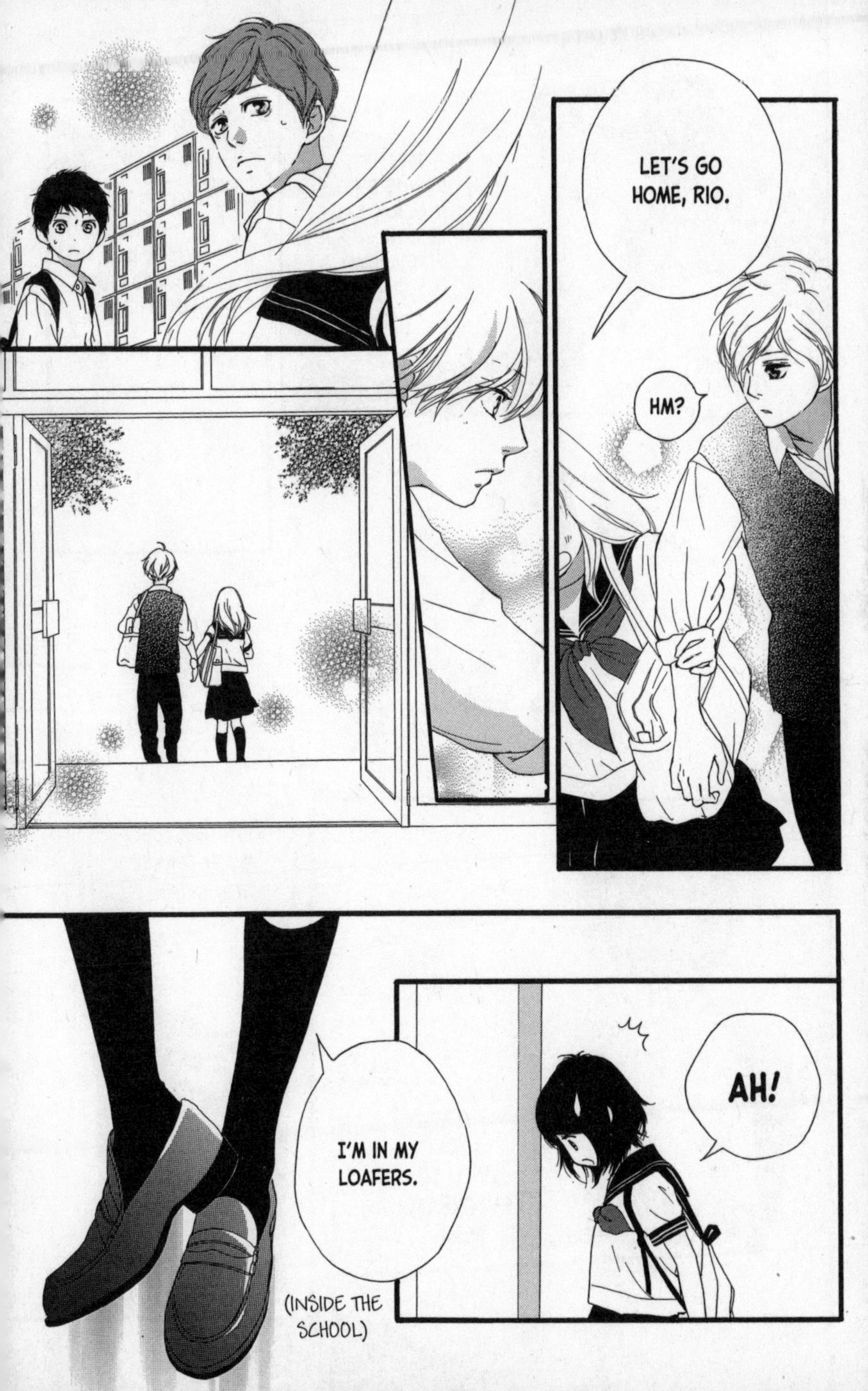
LET'S GO HOME, RIO.
HM?
AH!
I'M IN MY LOAFERS.
(INSIDE THE SCHOOL)

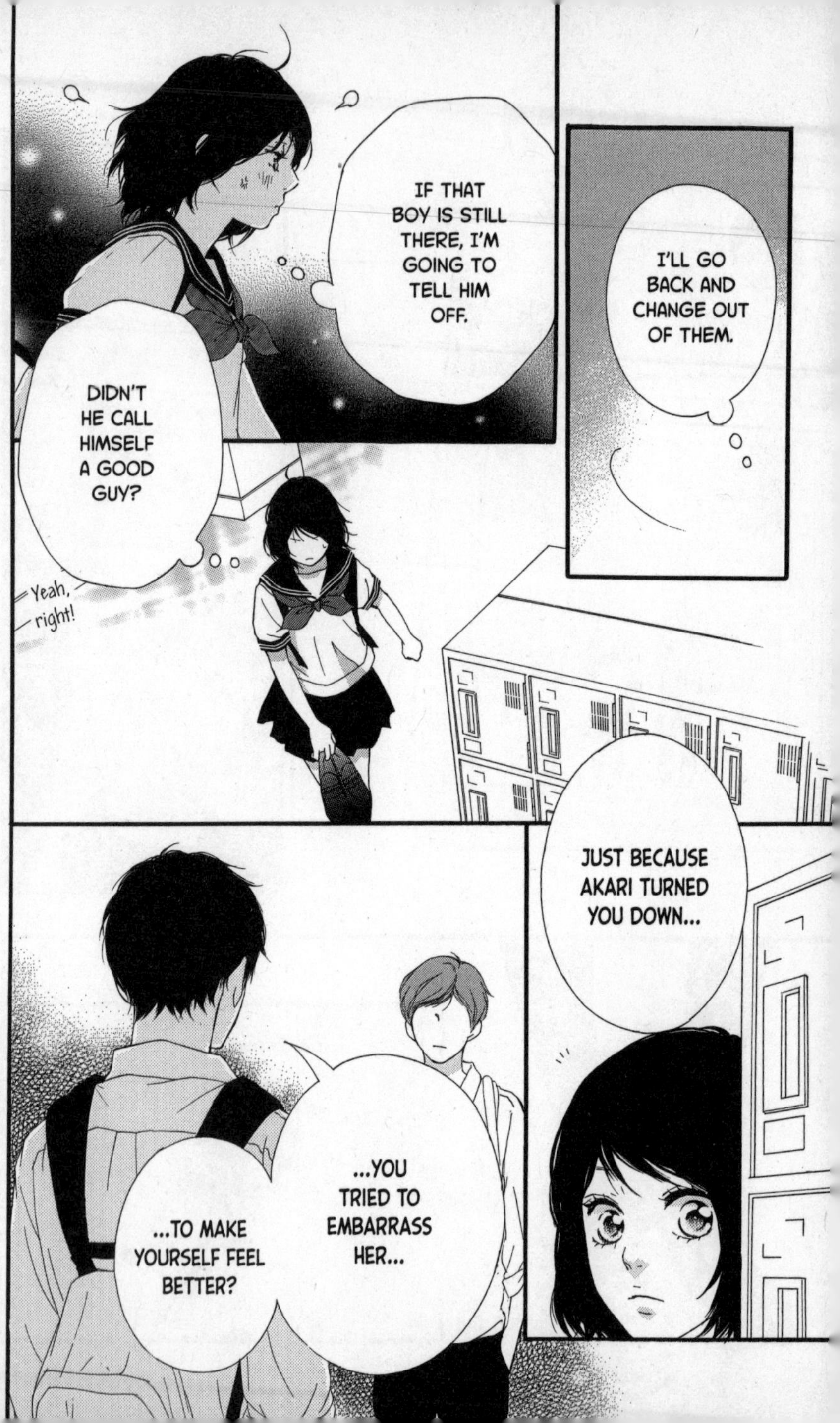

I'LL GO BACK AND CHANGE OUT OF THEM.
IF THAT BOY IS STILL THERE, I'M GOING TO TELL HIM OFF.
DIDN'T HE CALL HIMSELF A GOOD GUY?
Yeah, right!
JUST BECAUSE AKARI TURNED YOU DOWN...
...YOU TRIED TO EMBARRASS HER...
...TO MAKE YOURSELF FEEL BETTER?

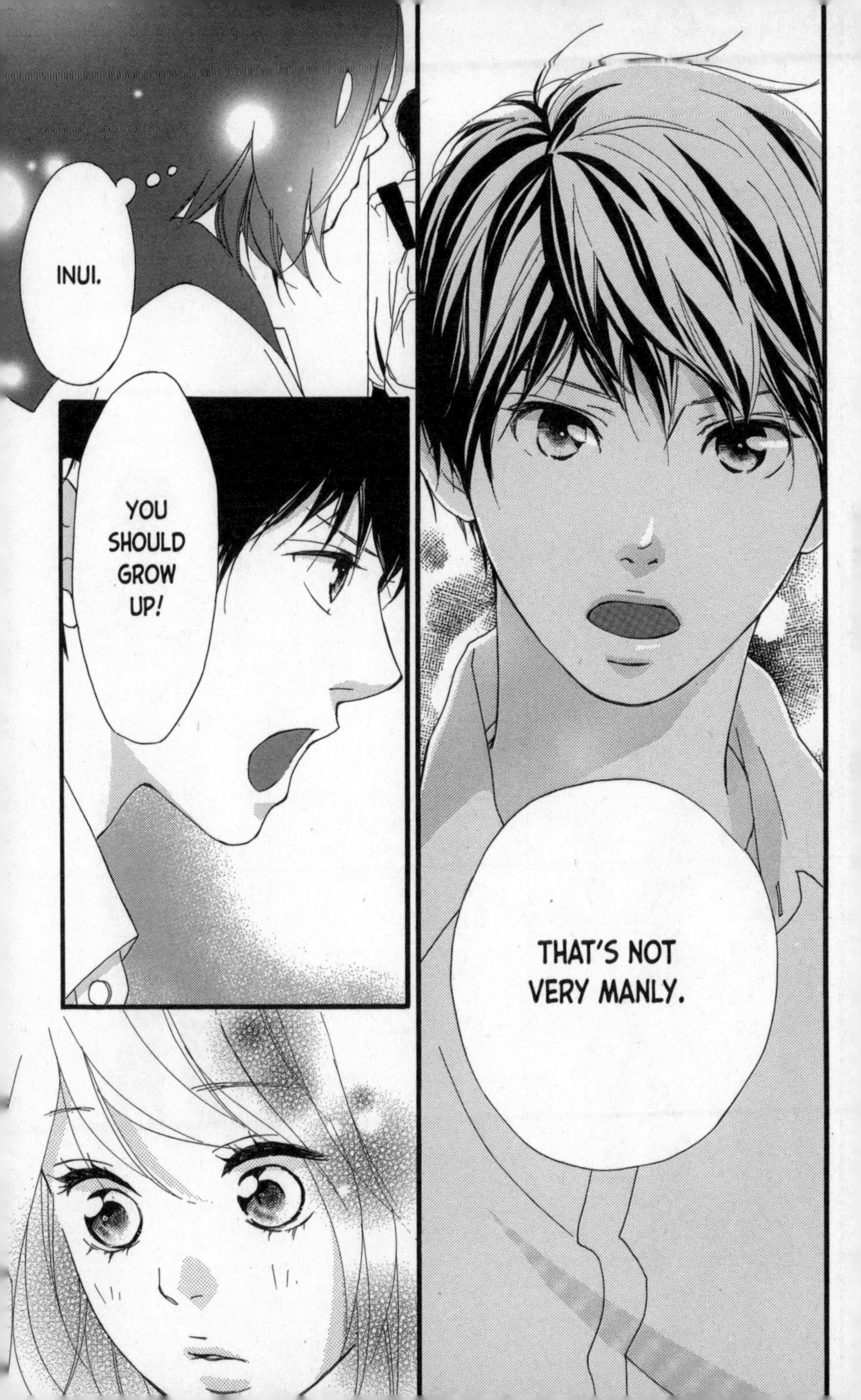
THAT'S NOT VERY MANLY.
INUI.
YOU SHOULD GROW UP!

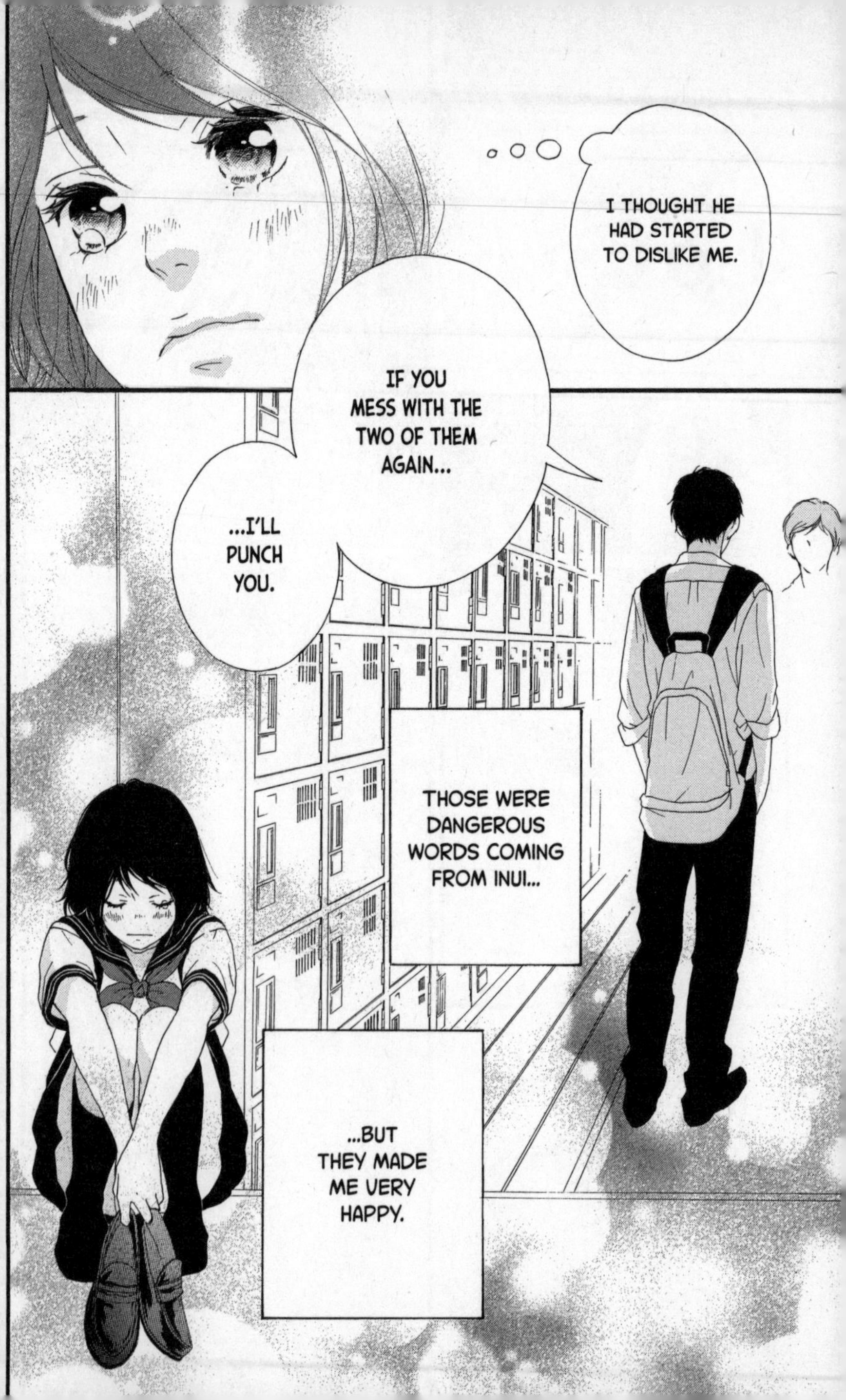
I THOUGHT HE HAD STARTED TO DISLIKE ME.
IF YOU MESS WITH THE TWO OF THEM AGAIN...
...I'LL PUNCH YOU.
THOSE WERE DANGEROUS WORDS COMING FROM INUI...
...BUT THEY MADE ME VERY HAPPY.

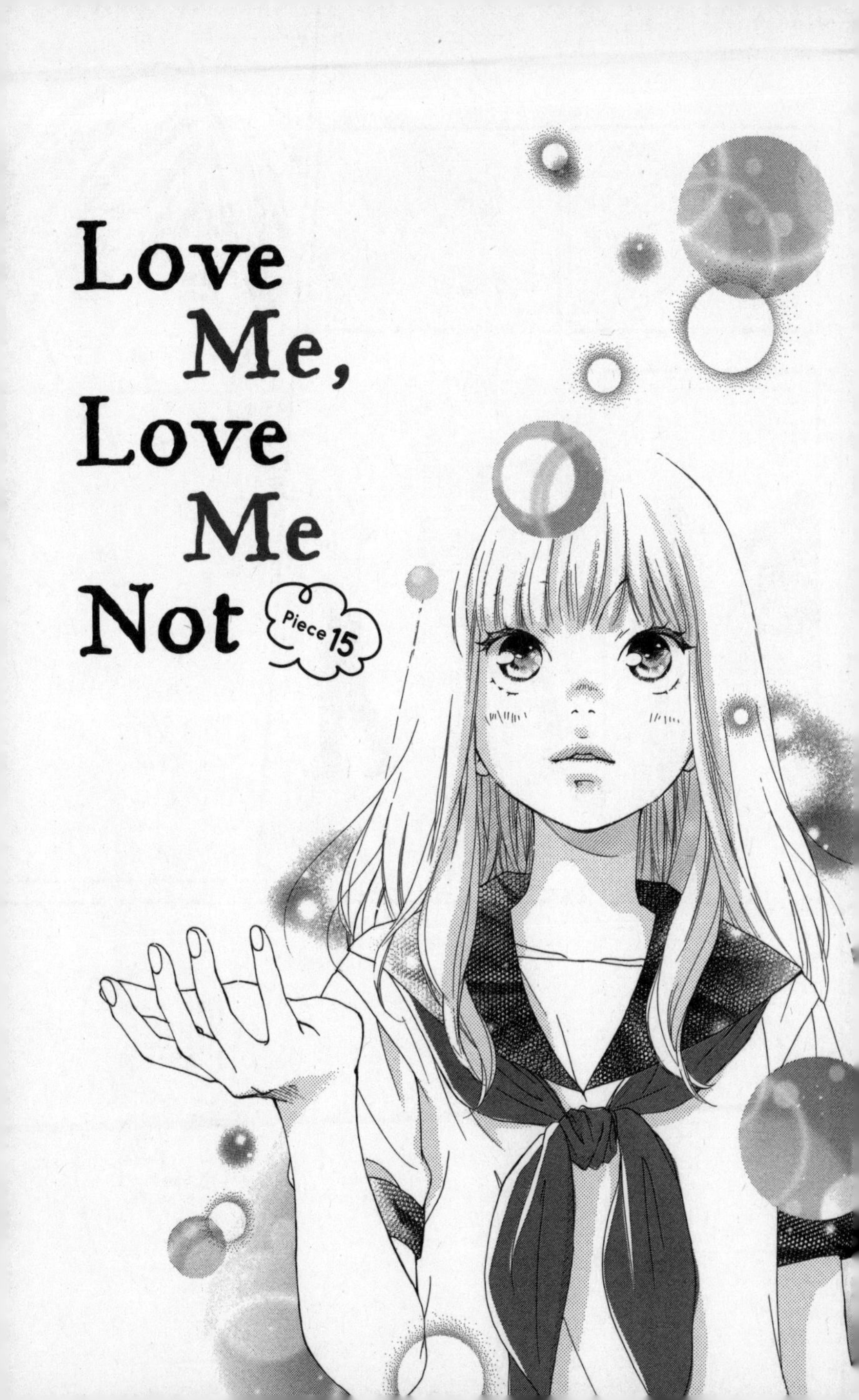
Love Me, Love Me Not
Piece 15

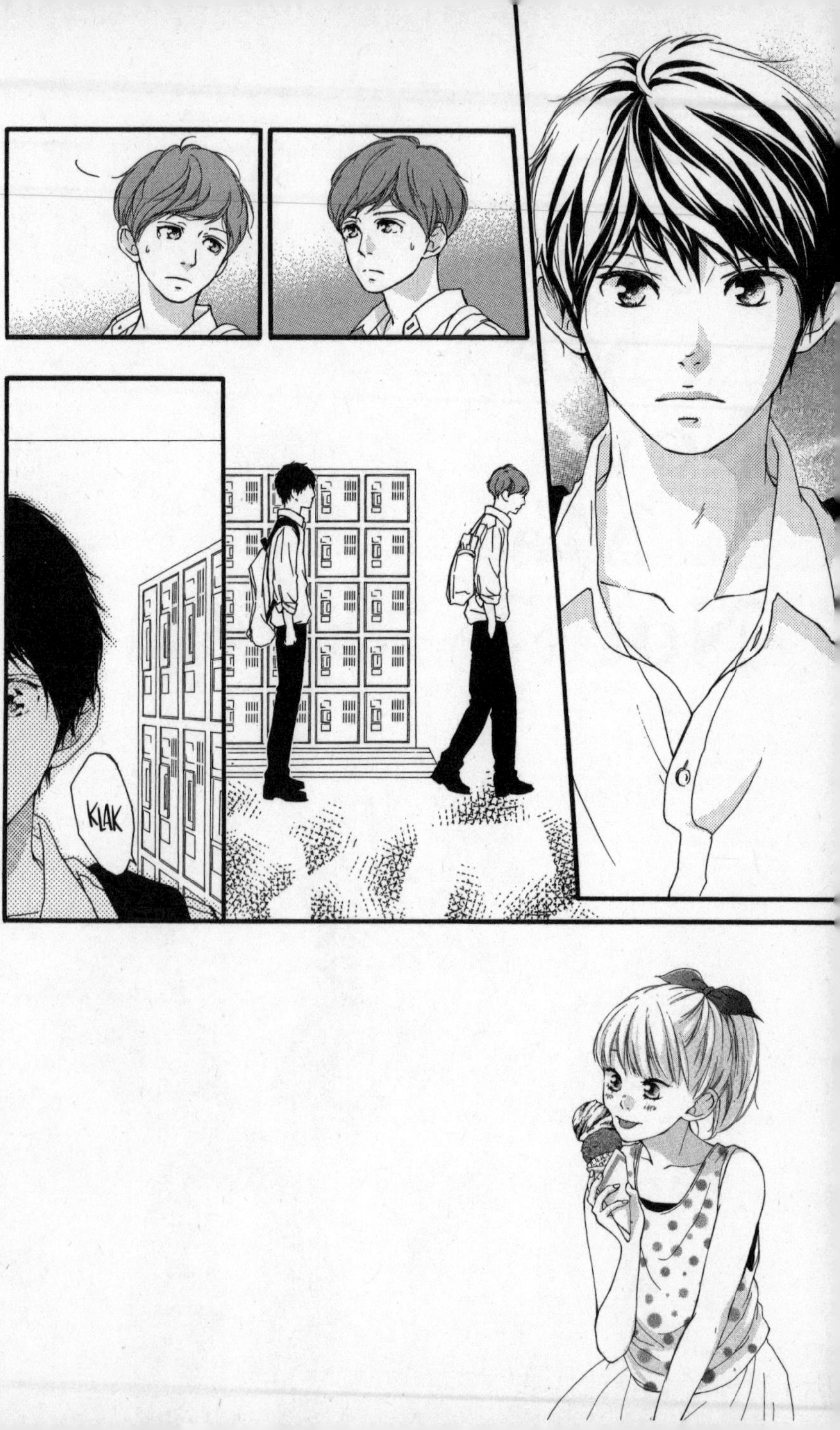
KLAK

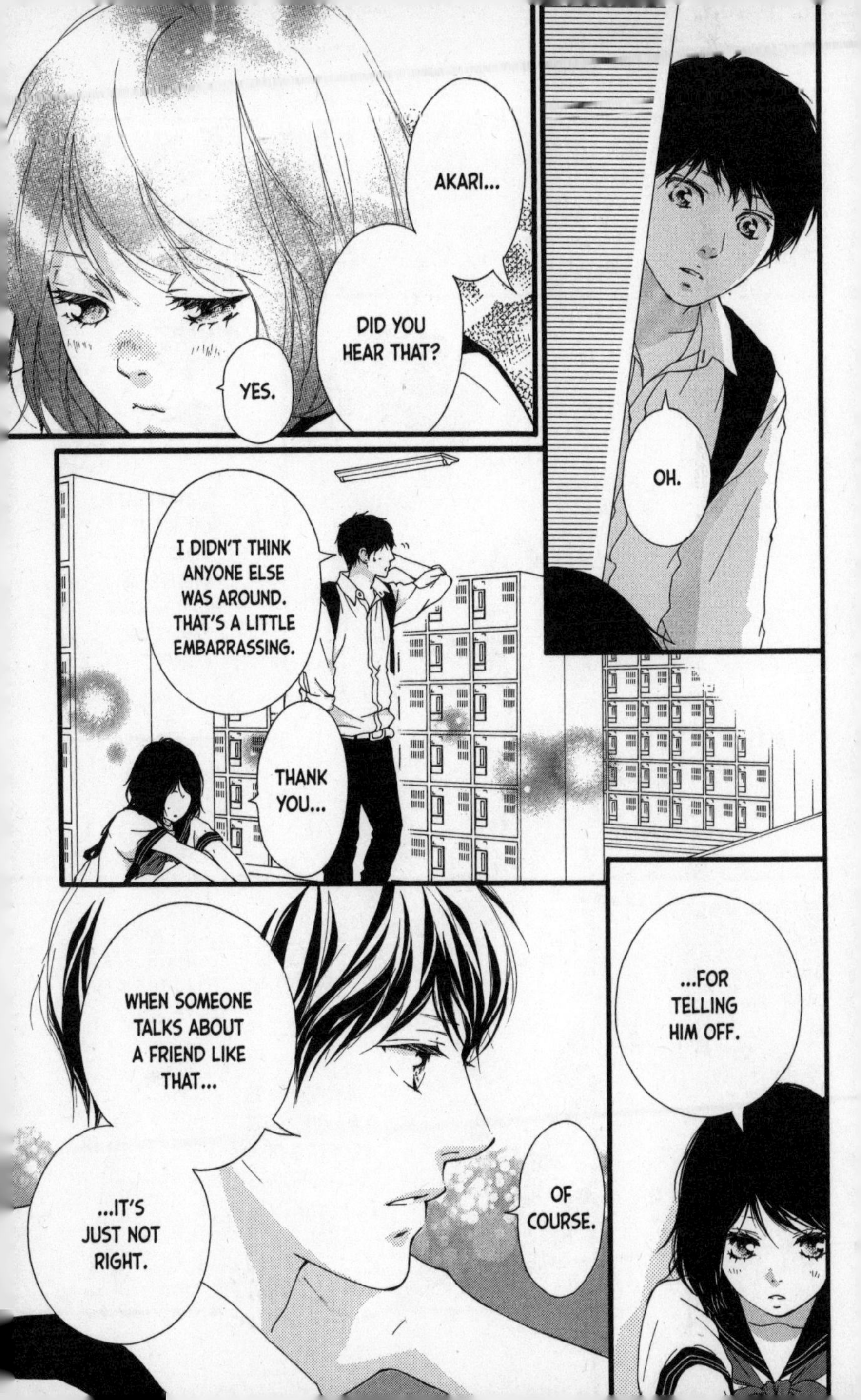
OH.
AKARI...
DID YOU HEAR THAT?
YES.
I DIDN'T THINK ANYONE ELSE WAS AROUND. THAT'S A LITTLE EMBARRASSING.
THANK YOU...
...FOR TELLING HIM OFF.
OF COURSE.
WHEN SOMEONE TALKS ABOUT A FRIEND LIKE THAT...
...IT'S JUST NOT RIGHT.

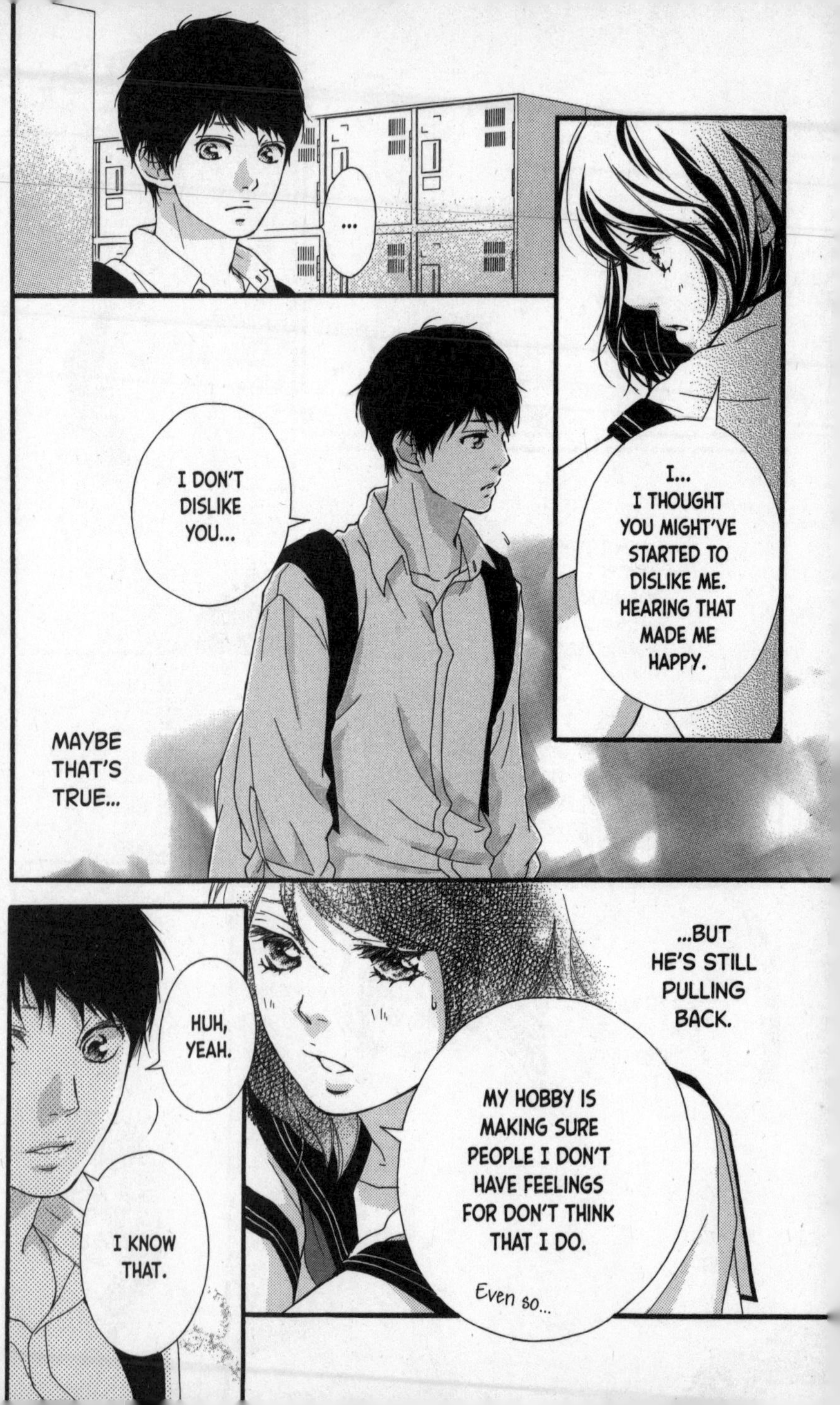
I... I THOUGHT YOU MIGHT'VE STARTED TO DISLIKE ME. HEARING THAT MADE ME HAPPY.
...
I DON'T DISLIKE YOU...
MAYBE THAT'S TRUE...
...BUT HE'S STILL PULLING BACK.
MY HOBBY IS MAKING SURE PEOPLE I DON'T HAVE FEELINGS FOR DON'T THINK THAT I DO.
Even so...
HUH, YEAH.
I KNOW THAT.

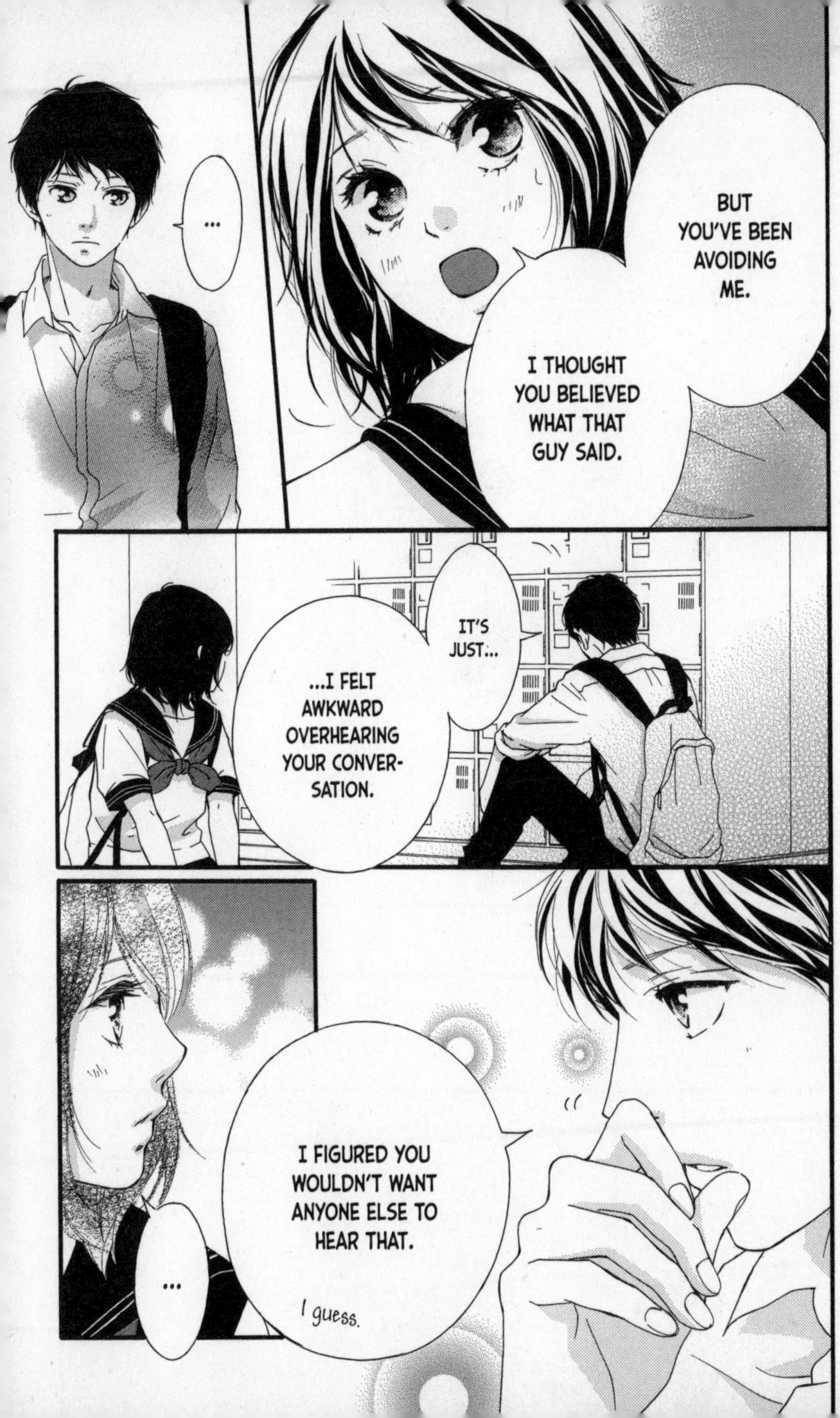
BUT YOU'VE BEEN AVOIDING ME.
I THOUGHT YOU BELIEVED WHAT THAT GUY SAID.
...
IT'S JUST...
...I FELT AWKWARD OVERHEARING YOUR CONVERSATION.
I FIGURED YOU WOULDN'T WANT ANYONE ELSE TO HEAR THAT.
I guess.
...

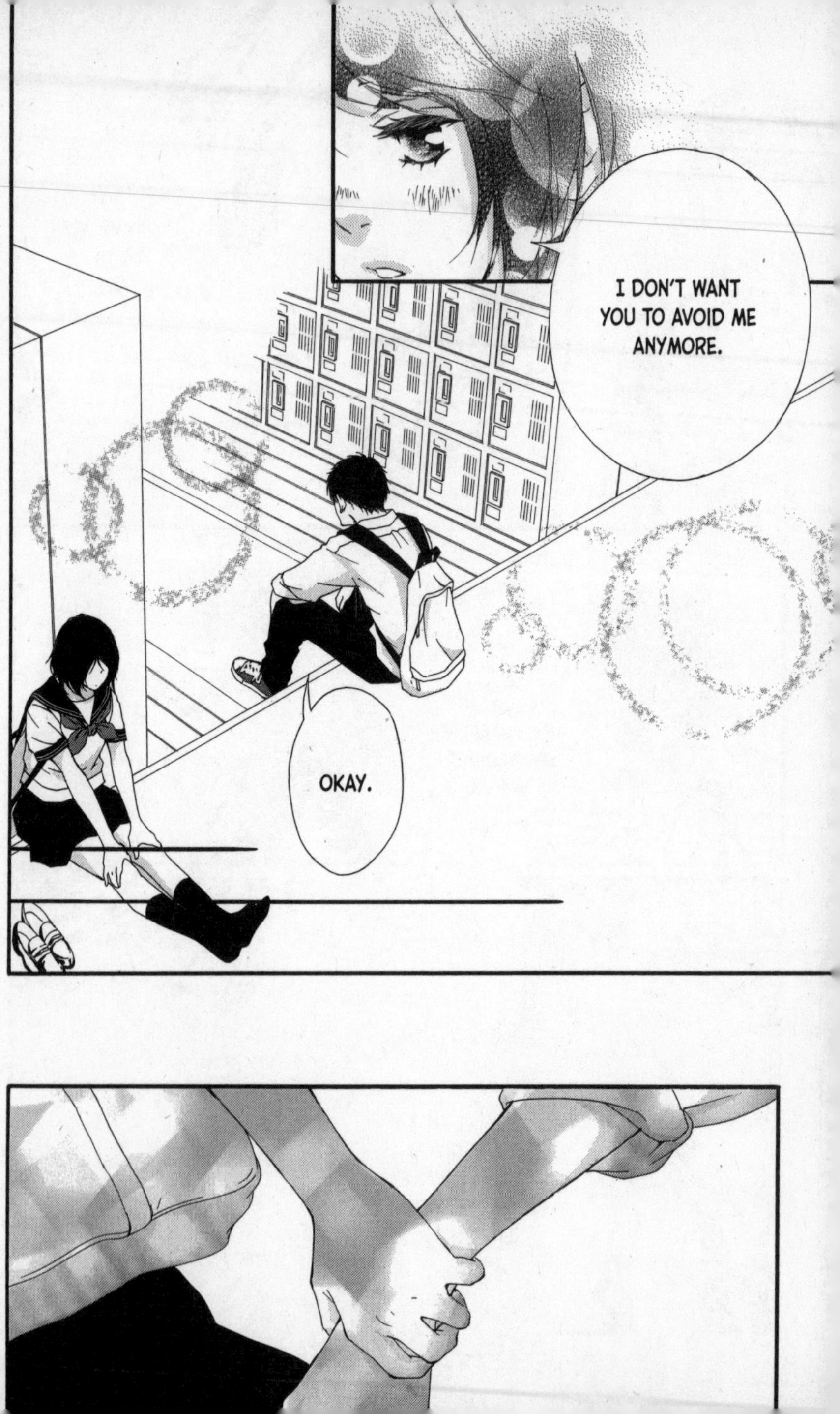
I DON'T WANT YOU TO AVOID ME ANYMORE.
OKAY.

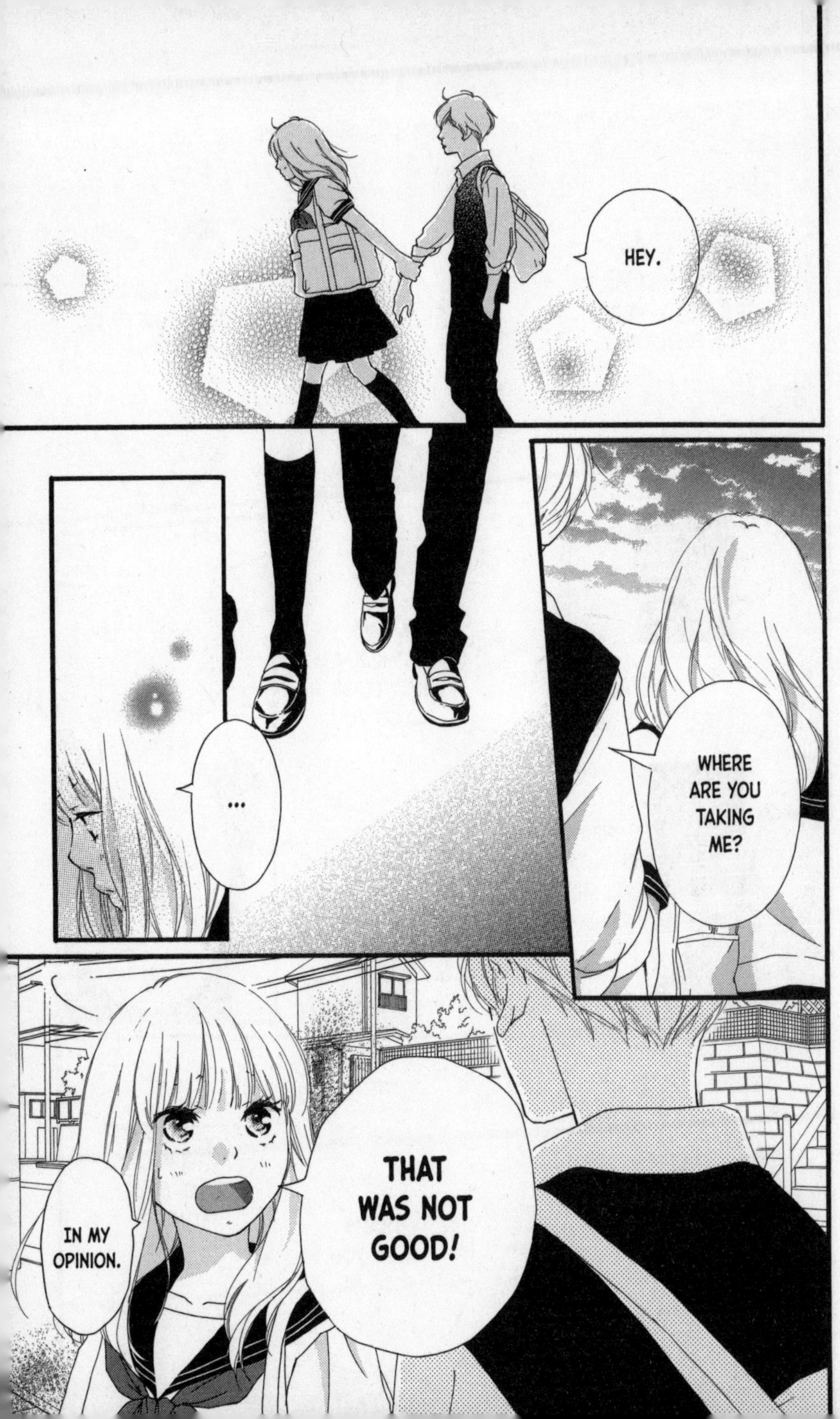
HEY.
WHERE ARE YOU TAKING ME?
...
THAT WAS NOT GOOD!
IN MY OPINION.

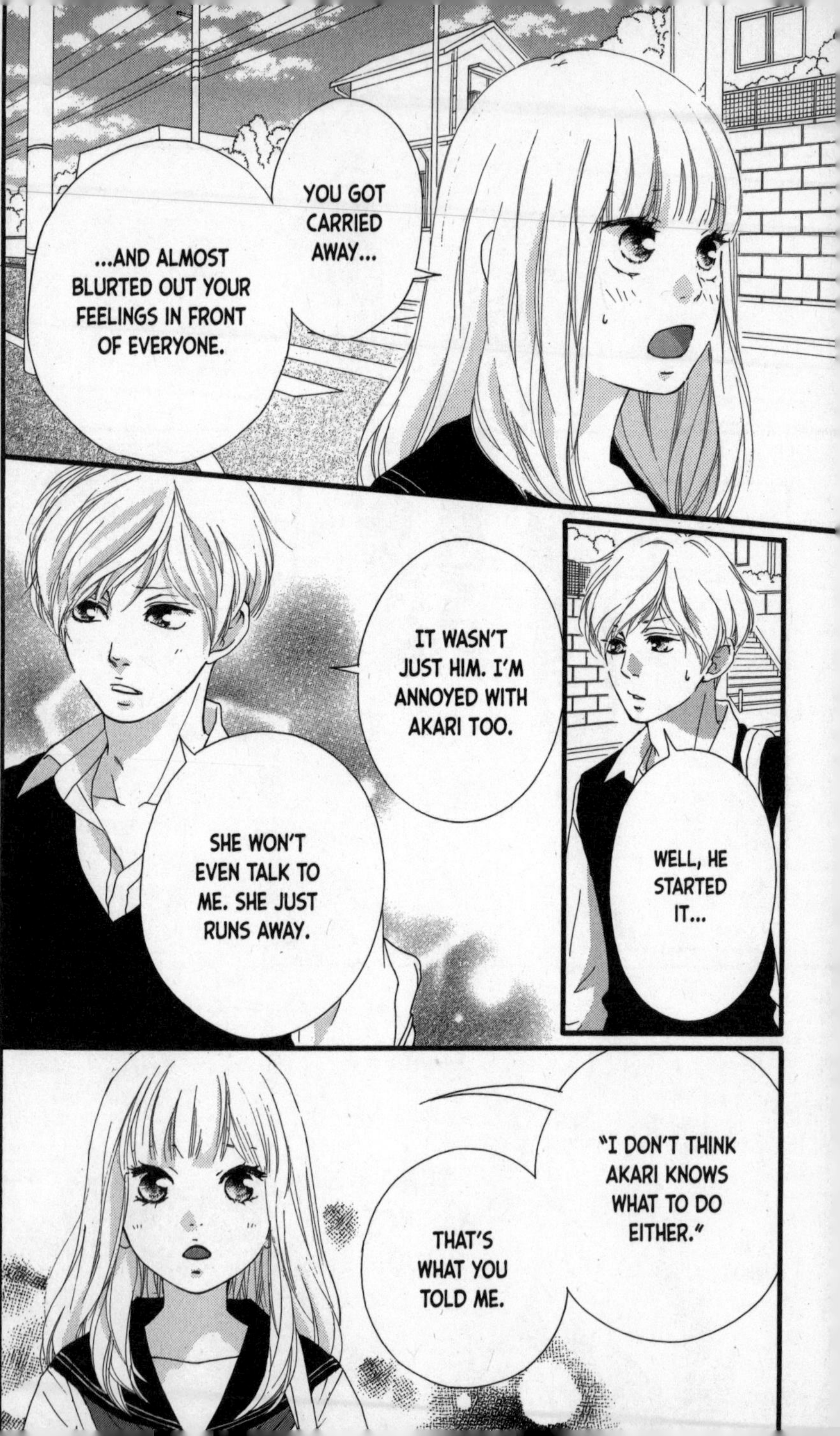
YOU GOT CARRIED AWAY...
...AND ALMOST BLURTED OUT YOUR FEELINGS IN FRONT OF EVERYONE.
WELL, HE STARTED IT...
IT WASN'T JUST HIM. I'M ANNOYED WITH AKARI TOO.
SHE WON'T EVEN TALK TO ME. SHE JUST RUNS AWAY.
"I DON'T THINK AKARI KNOWS WHAT TO DO EITHER."
THAT'S WHAT YOU TOLD ME.

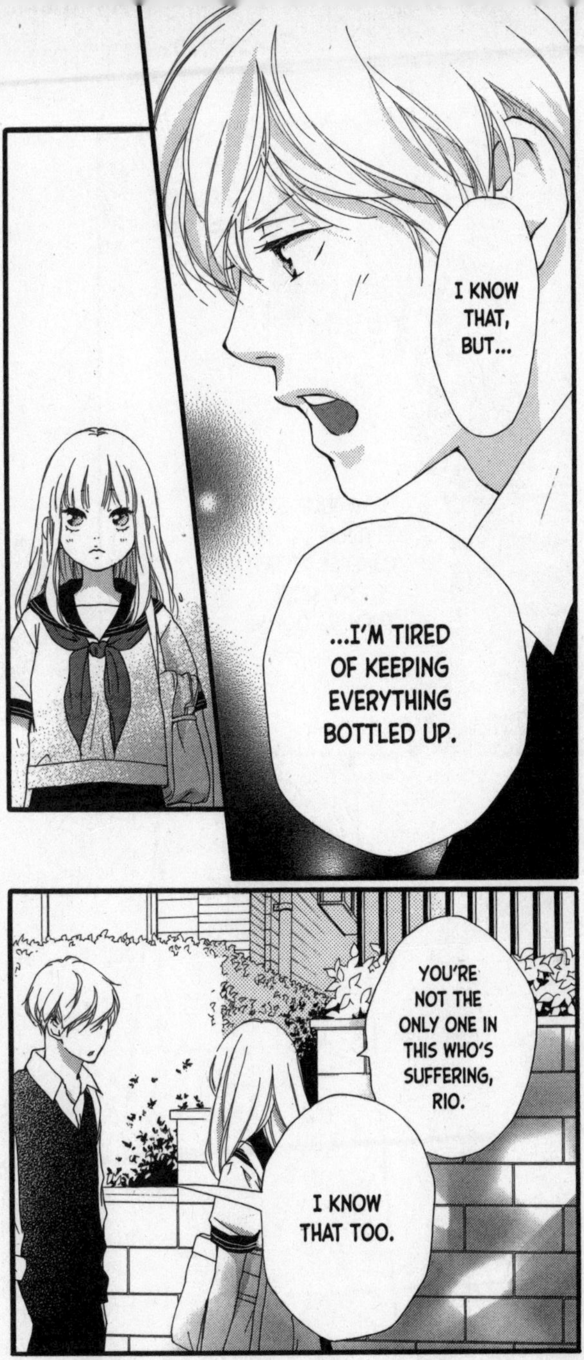
I KNOW THAT, BUT...
...I'M TIRED OF KEEPING EVERYTHING BOTTLED UP.
YOU'RE NOT THE ONLY ONE IN THIS WHO'S SUFFERING, RIO.
I KNOW THAT TOO.

I noticed something different when I took a cola out of the refrigerator one day. It wasn't chilled like it should be. I touched the other things in the fridge, and sure enough, it wasn't cooling properly. Same with the freezer. It's summer right now. I can't have my fridge goofing off... So I pulled the plug and waited a bit before plugging it back in and fiddling with the temperature controls. I shook it a little and tried all sorts of things, but the fridge continued to goof off. I finally called customer support and arranged to have someone come out. He couldn't come that day, but he was available the next day. In all honesty, there isn't much food to speak of in my fridge (it's drinks and condiments mostly), so I thought it was okay. But the level of awkwardness I felt when it fixed itself right before the repairman arrived...!

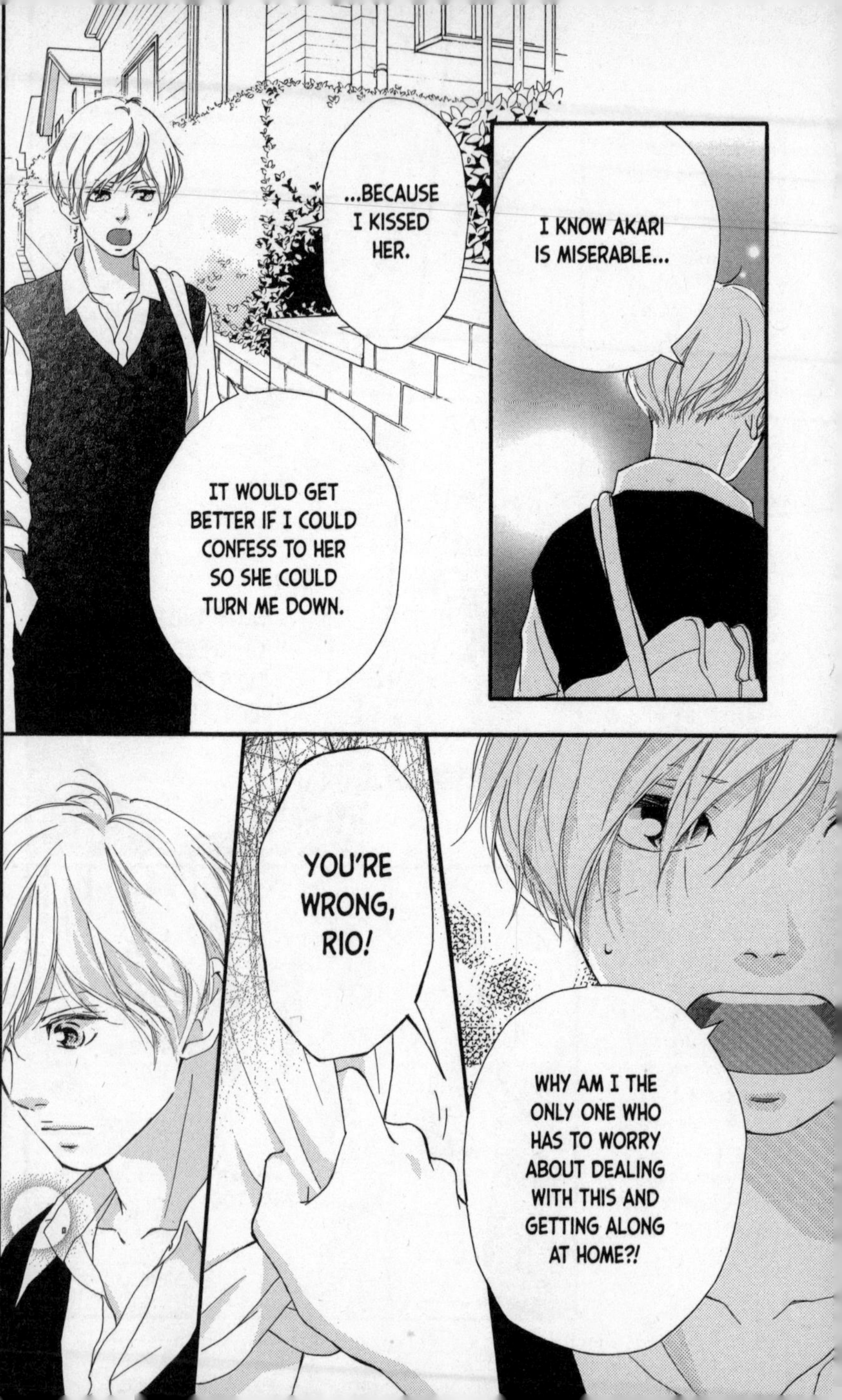
I KNOW AKARI IS MISERABLE...
...BECAUSE I KISSED HER.
IT WOULD GET BETTER IF I COULD CONFESS TO HER SO SHE COULD TURN ME DOWN.
WHY AM I THE ONLY ONE WHO HAS TO WORRY ABOUT DEALING WITH THIS AND GETTING ALONG AT HOME?!
YOU'RE WRONG, RIO!

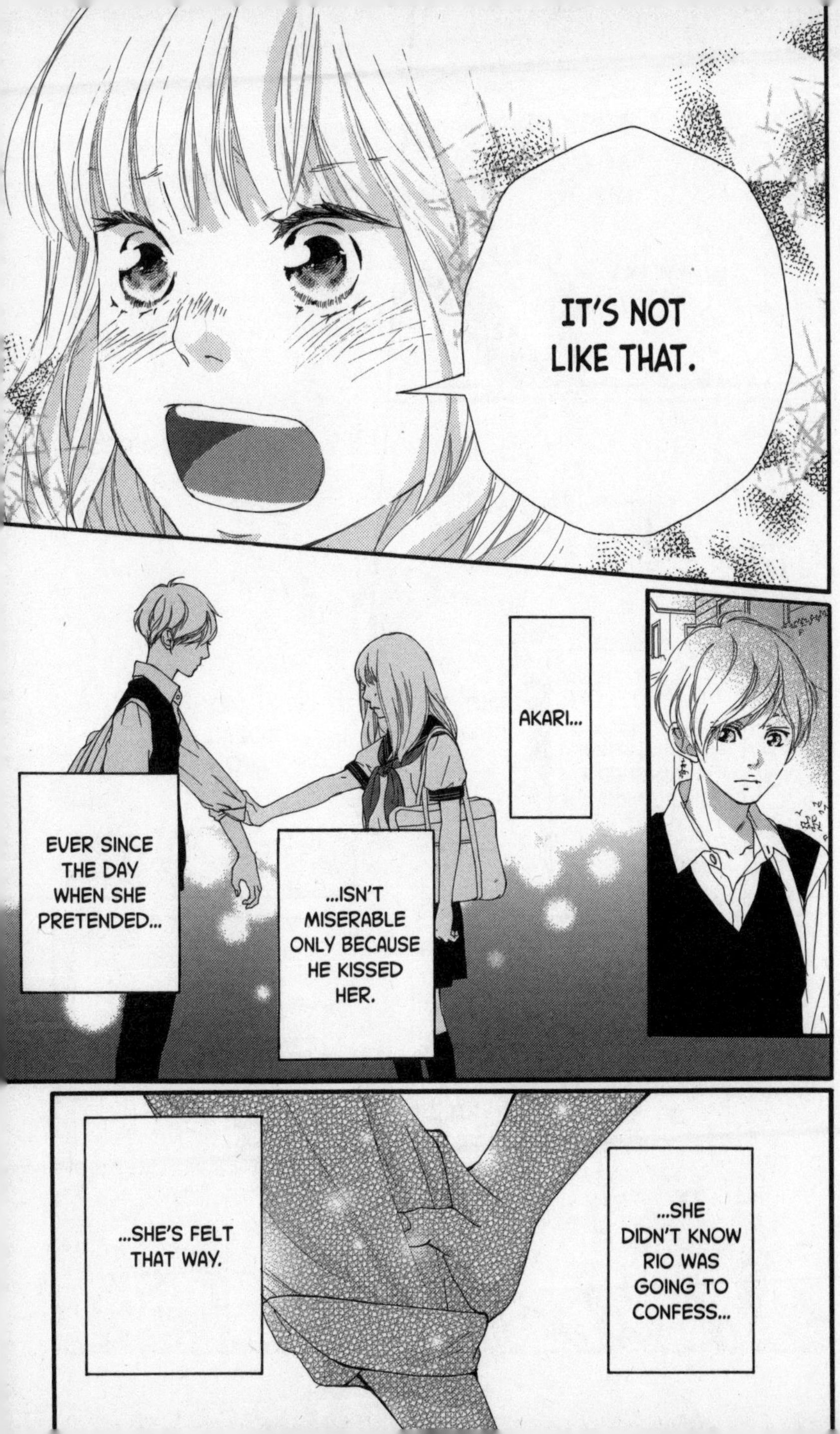
IT'S NOT LIKE THAT.
AKARI...
...ISN'T MISERABLE ONLY BECAUSE HE KISSED HER.
EVER SINCE THE DAY WHEN SHE PRETENDED...
...SHE DIDN'T KNOW RIO WAS GOING TO CONFESS...
...SHE'S FELT THAT WAY.

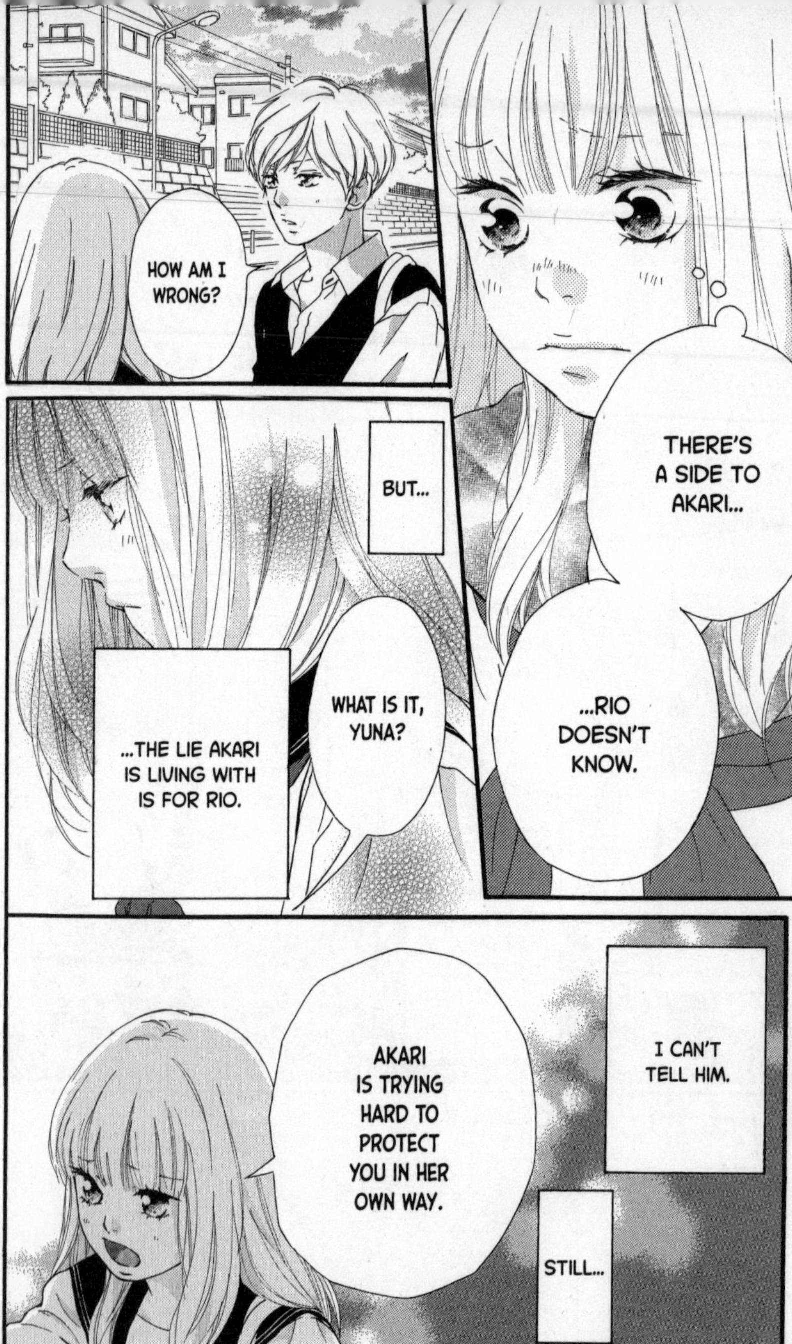
THERE'S A SIDE TO AKARI...
...RIO DOESN'T KNOW.
HOW AM I WRONG?
BUT...
WHAT IS IT, YUNA?
...THE LIE AKARI IS LIVING WITH IS FOR RIO.
I CAN'T TELL HIM.
STILL...
AKARI IS TRYING HARD TO PROTECT YOU IN HER OWN WAY.

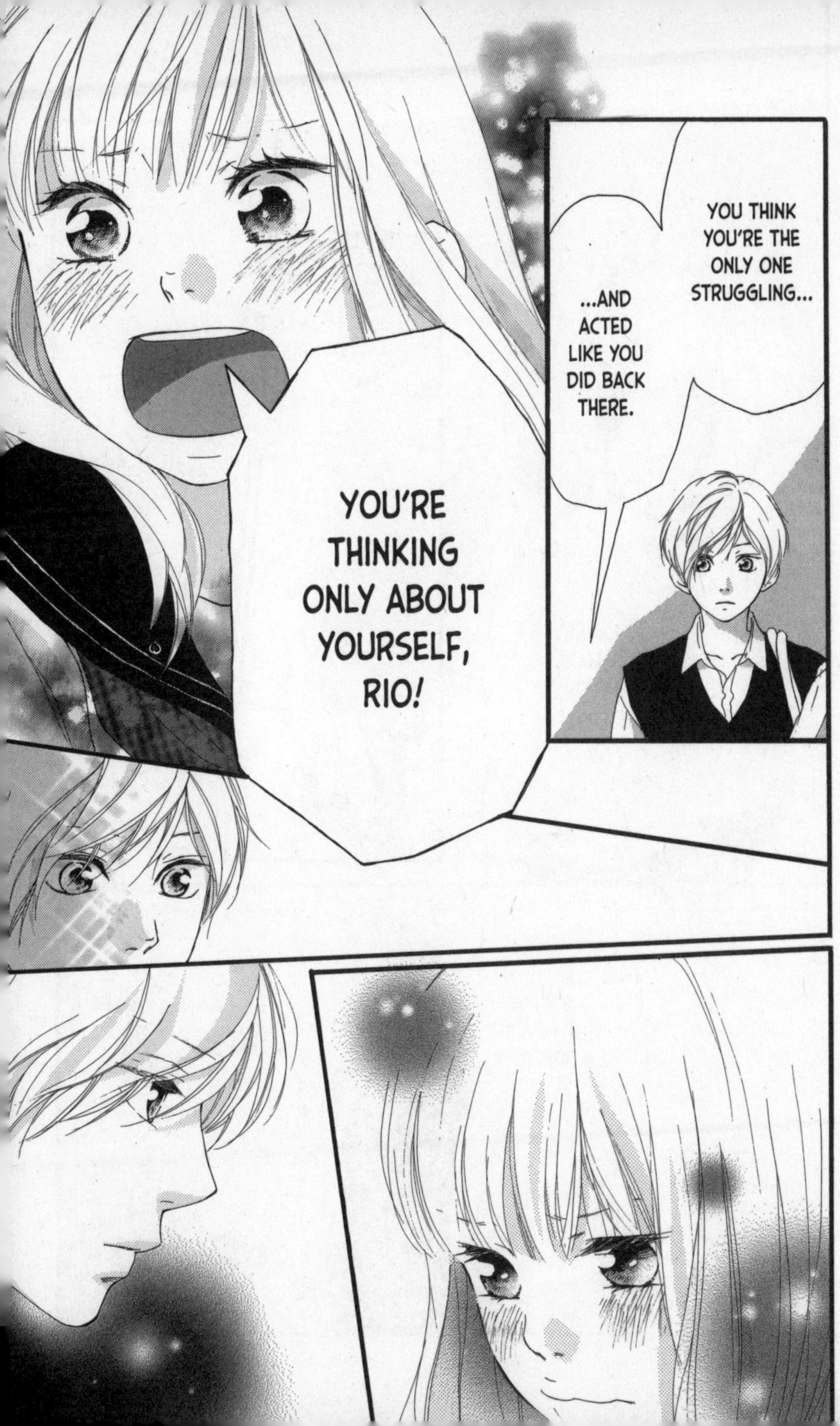
YOU THINK YOU'RE THE ONLY ONE STRUGGLING...
...AND ACTED LIKE YOU DID BACK THERE.
YOU'RE THINKING ONLY ABOUT YOURSELF, RIO!

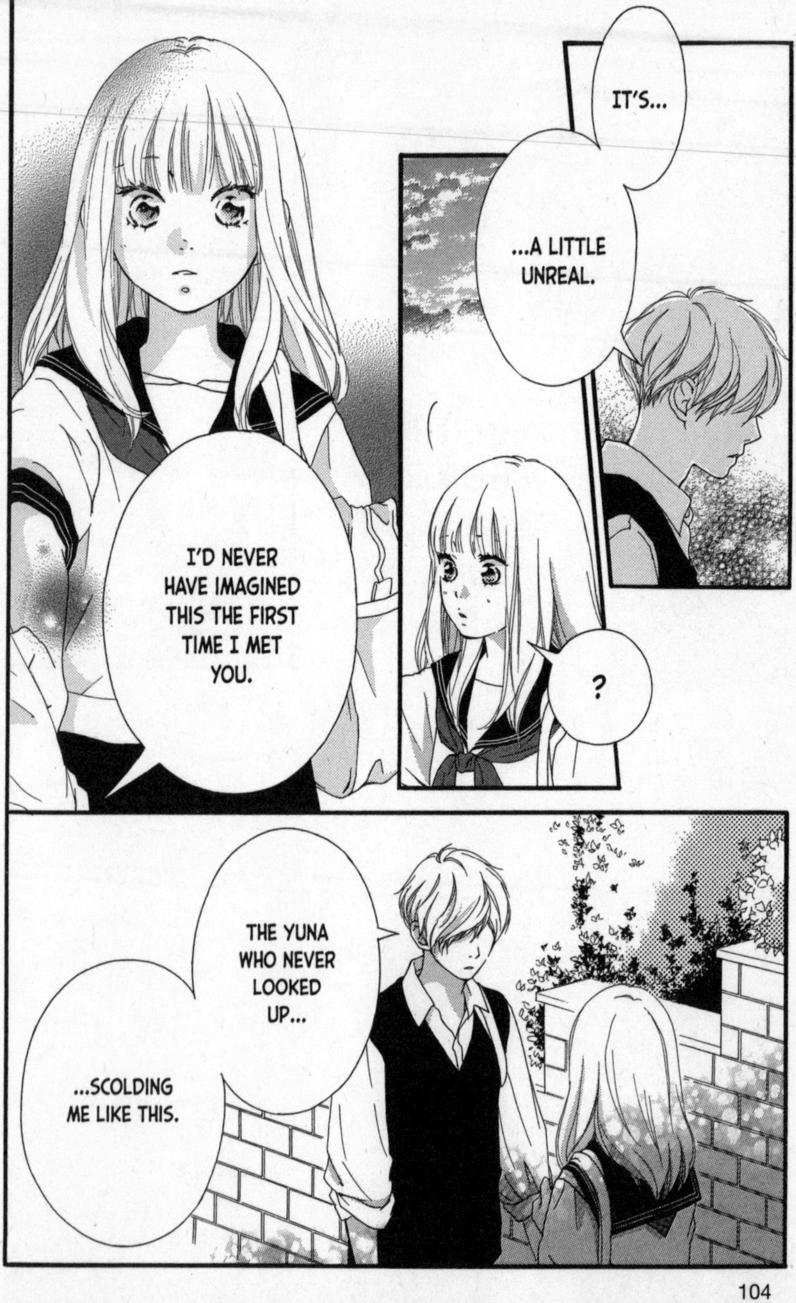
IT'S...
...A LITTLE UNREAL.
?
I'D NEVER HAVE IMAGINED THIS THE FIRST TIME I MET YOU.
THE YUNA WHO NEVER LOOKED UP...
...SCOLDING ME LIKE THIS.

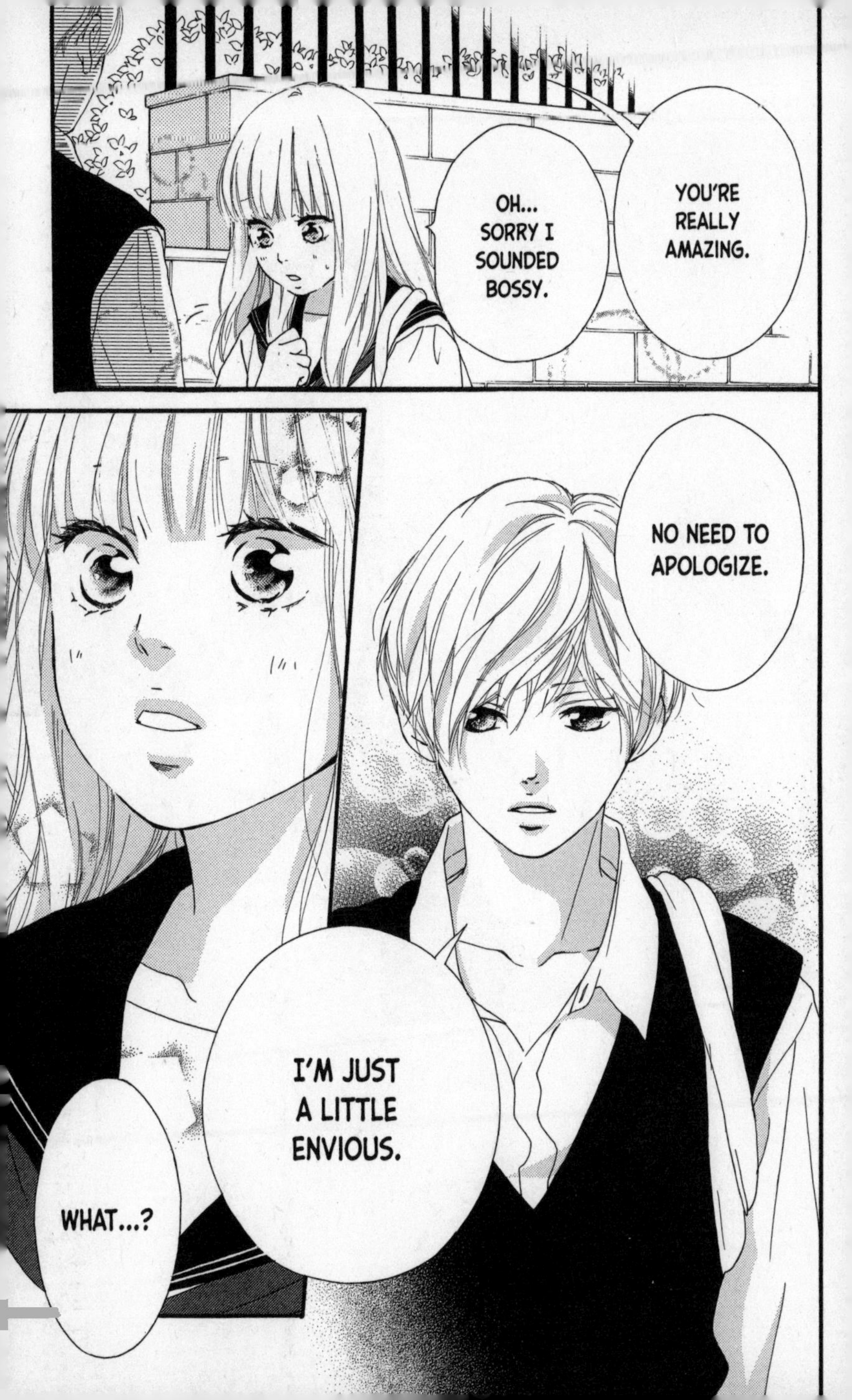
YOU'RE REALLY AMAZING.
OH... SORRY I SOUNDED BOSSY.
NO NEED TO APOLOGIZE.
I'M JUST A LITTLE ENVIOUS.
WHAT...?

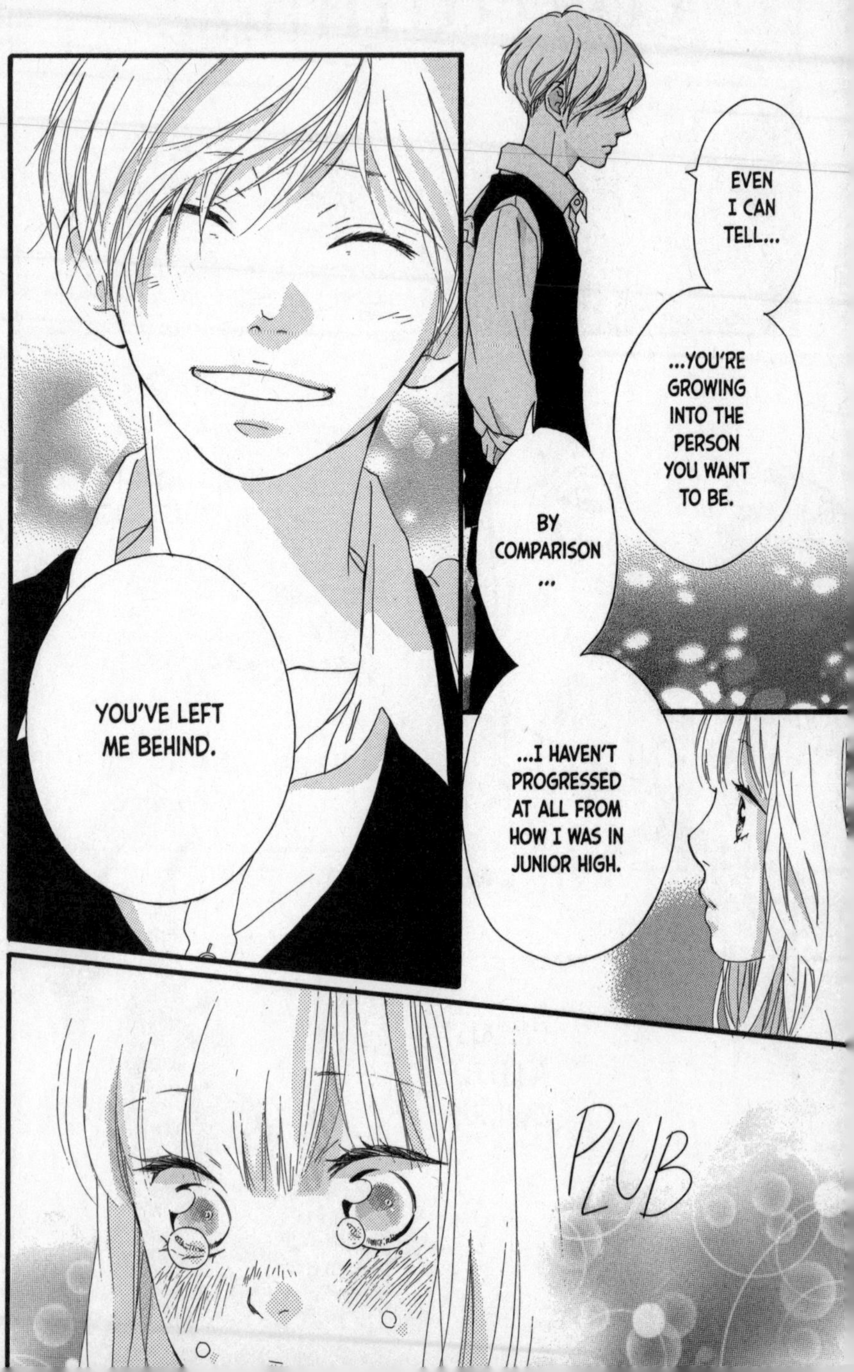
EVEN I CAN TELL...
...YOU'RE GROWING INTO THE PERSON YOU WANT TO BE.
BY COMPARISON ...
...I HAVEN'T PROGRESSED AT ALL FROM HOW I WAS IN JUNIOR HIGH.
YOU'VE LEFT ME BEHIND.
PLUB

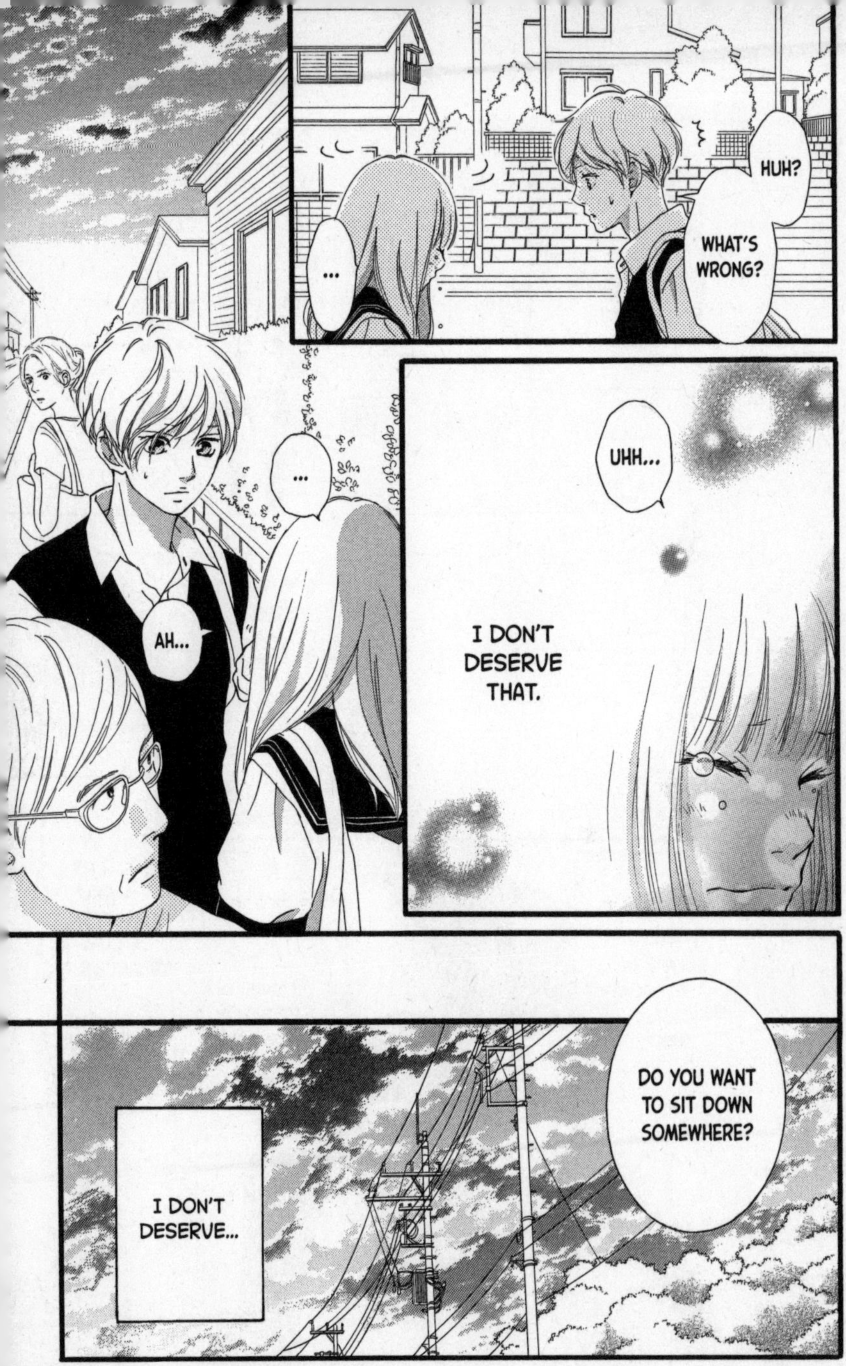
HUH?
WHAT'S WRONG?
...
UHH...
I DON'T DESERVE THAT.
...
AH...
DO YOU WANT TO SIT DOWN SOMEWHERE?
I DON'T DESERVE...

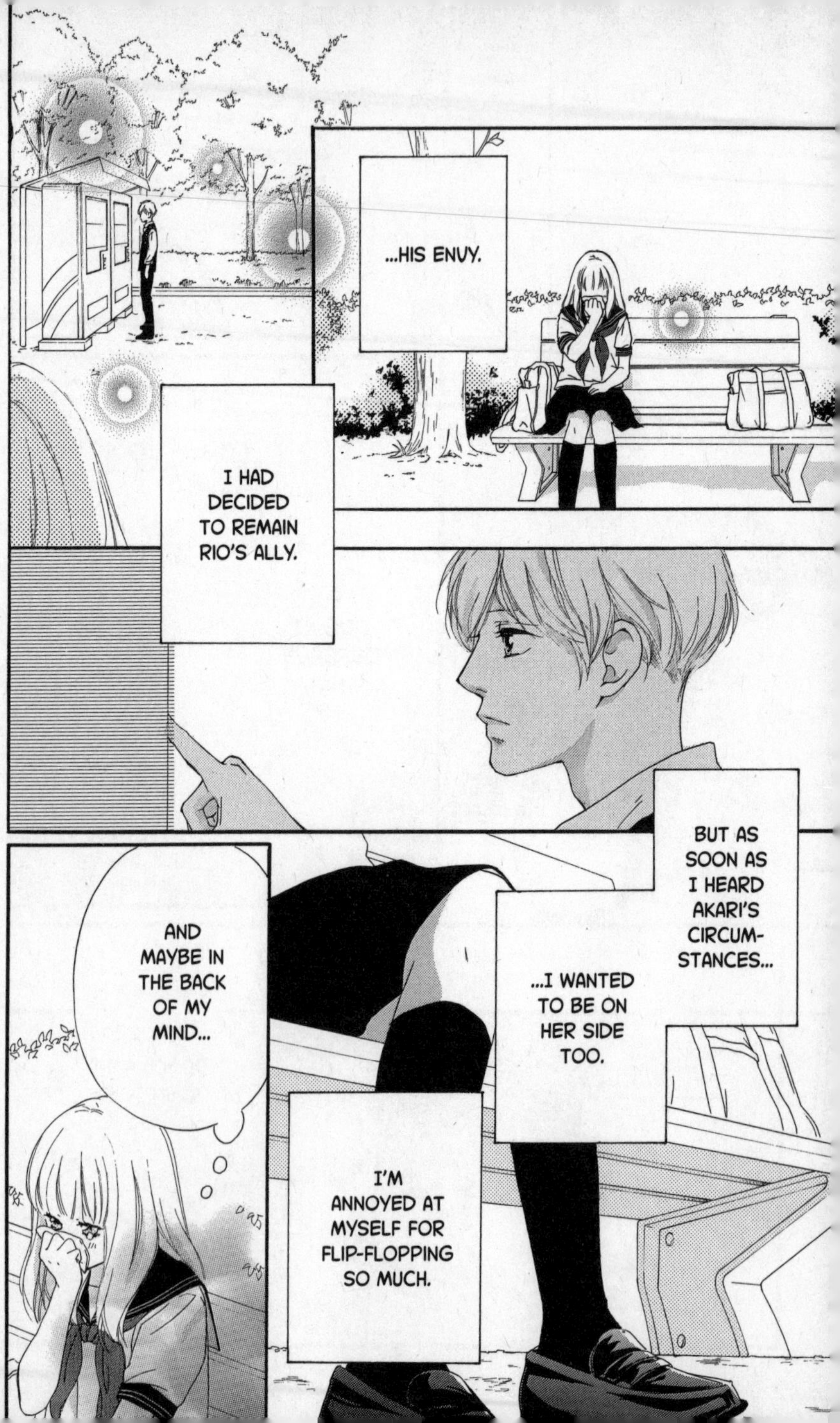
...HIS ENVY.
I HAD DECIDED TO REMAIN RIO'S ALLY.
BUT AS SOON AS I HEARD AKARI'S CIRCUM-STANCES...
...I WANTED TO BE ON HER SIDE TOO.
I'M ANNOYED AT MYSELF FOR FLIP-FLOPPING SO MUCH.
AND MAYBE IN THE BACK OF MY MIND...

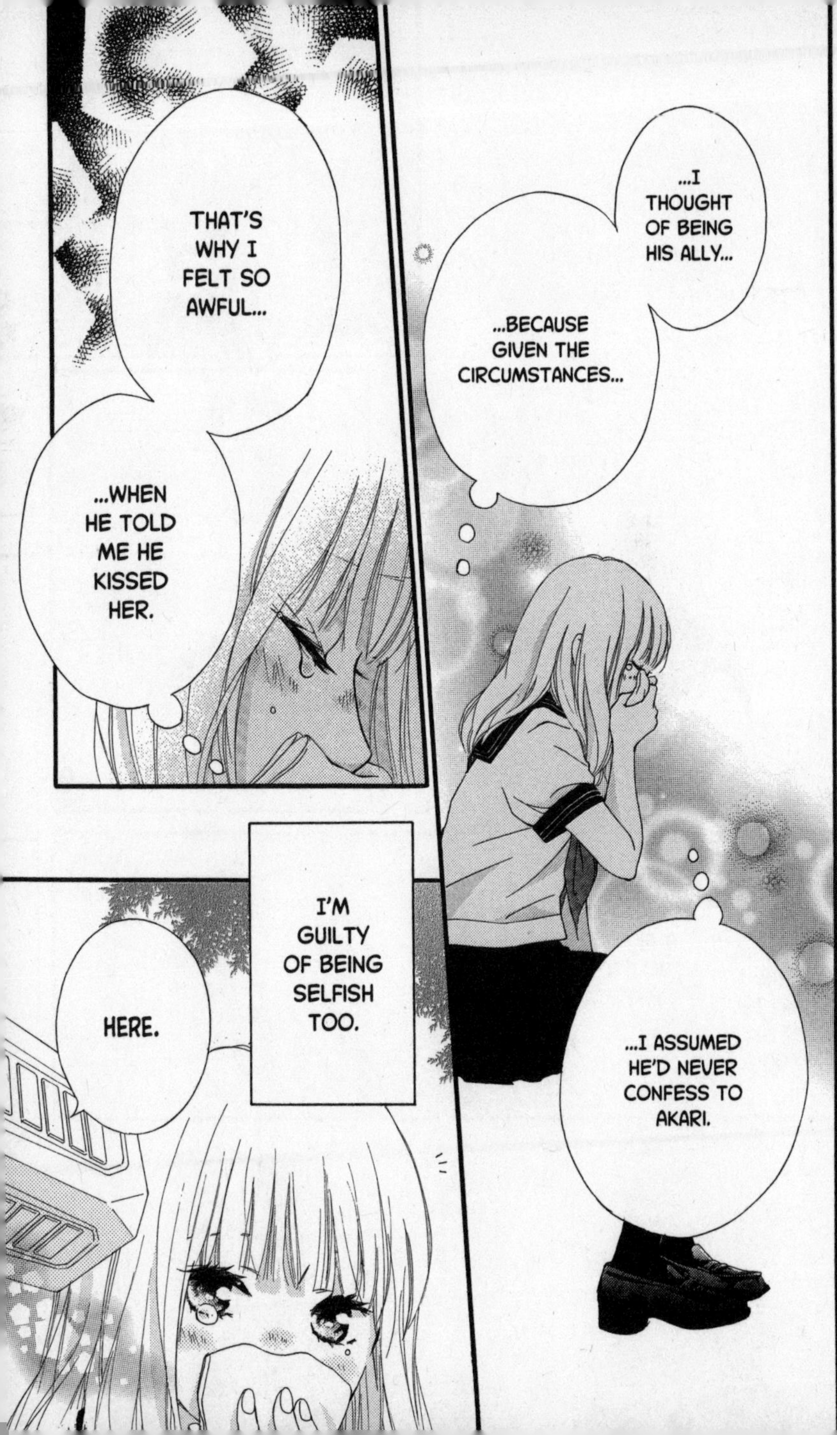

...I THOUGHT OF BEING HIS ALLY...
...BECAUSE GIVEN THE CIRCUMSTANCES...
...I ASSUMED HE'D NEVER CONFESS TO AKARI.
THAT'S WHY I FELT SO AWFUL...
...WHEN HE TOLD ME HE KISSED HER.
I'M GUILTY OF BEING SELFISH TOO.
HERE.

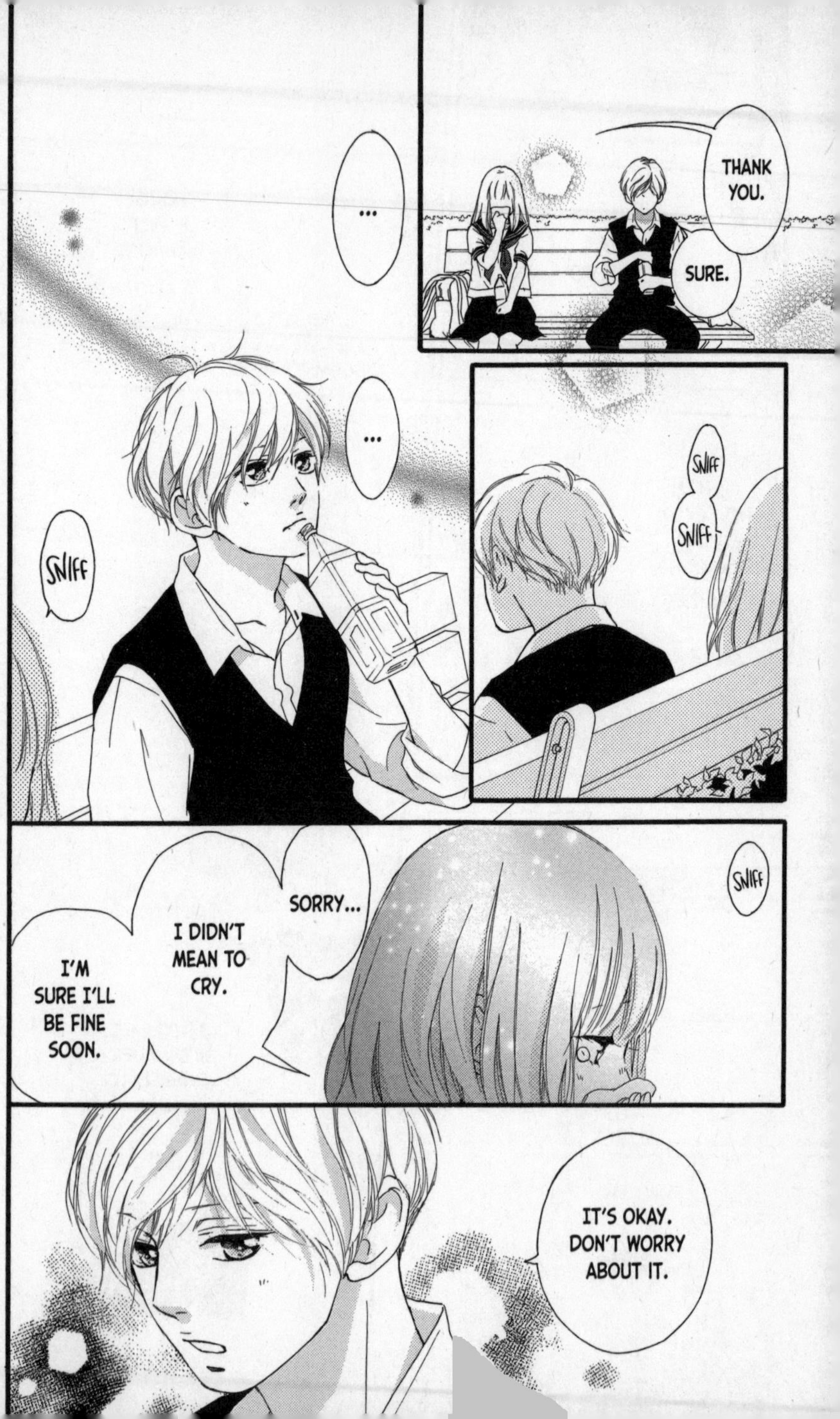
THANK YOU.
SURE.
SNIFF
SNIFF
...
...
SNIFF
SNIFF
SORRY...
I DIDN'T MEAN TO CRY.
I'M SURE I'LL BE FINE SOON.
IT'S OKAY. DON'T WORRY ABOUT IT.

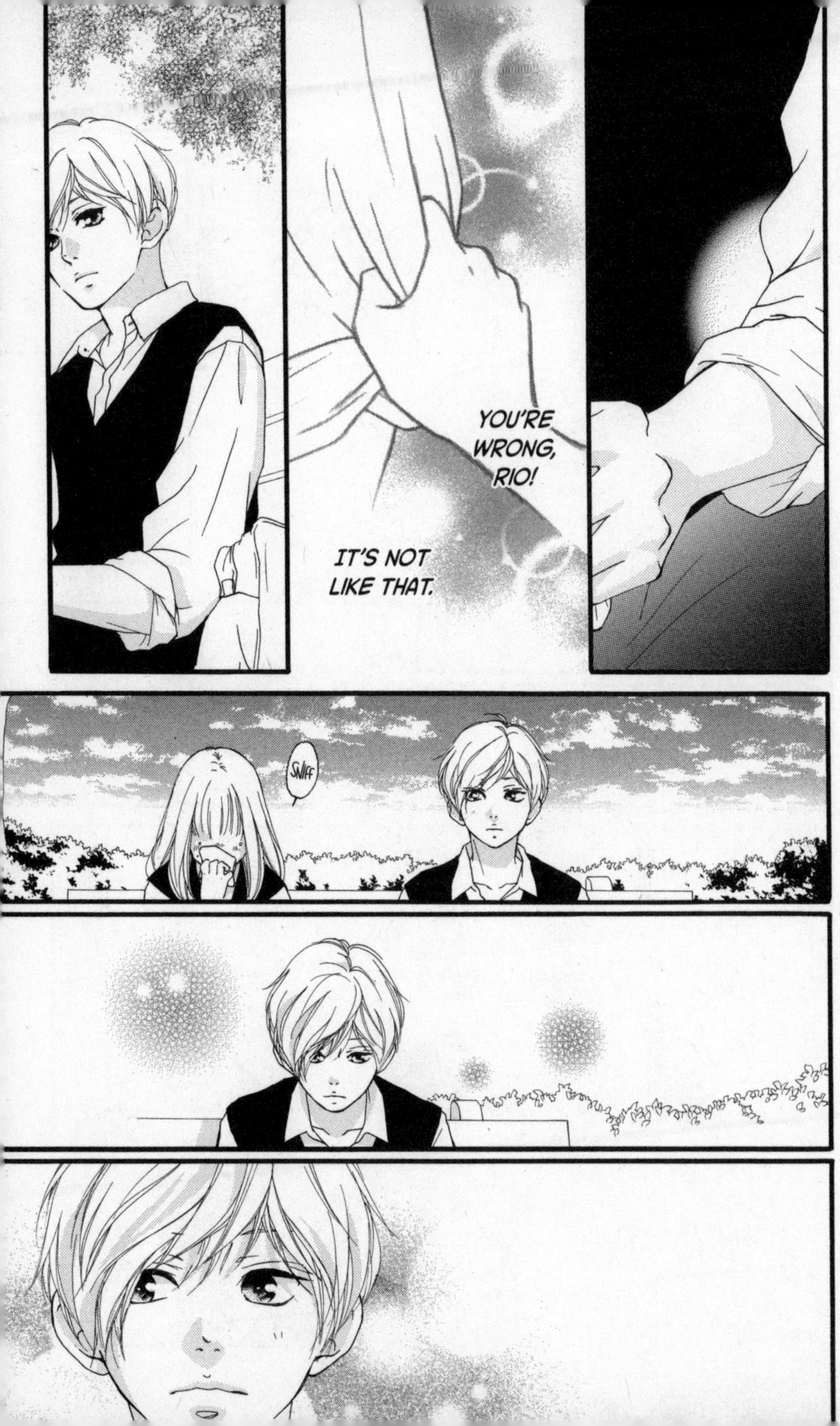
YOU'RE WRONG, RIO!
IT'S NOT LIKE THAT.
SNIFF

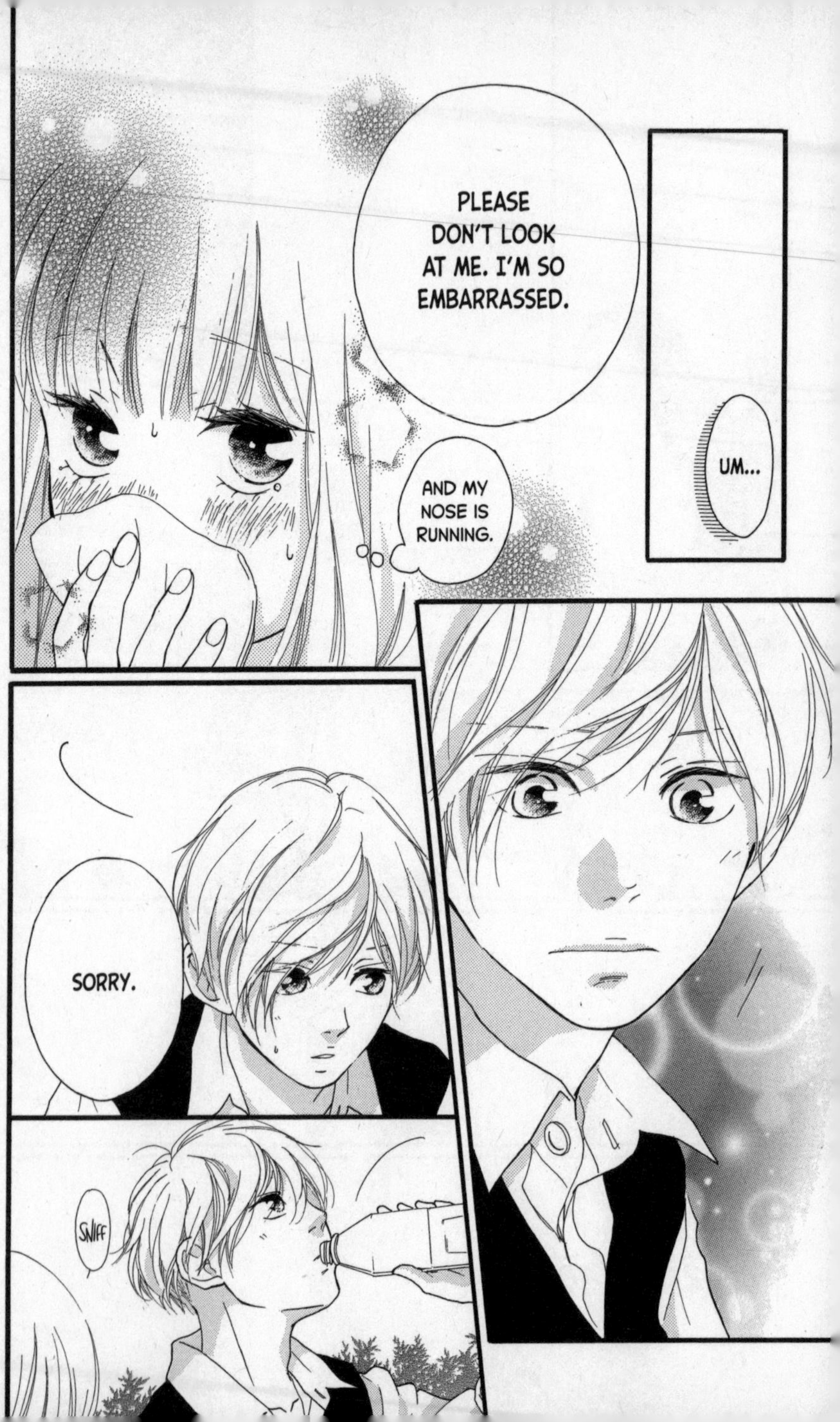
UM...
PLEASE DON'T LOOK AT ME. I'M SO EMBARRASSED.
AND MY NOSE IS RUNNING.
SORRY.
SNIFF

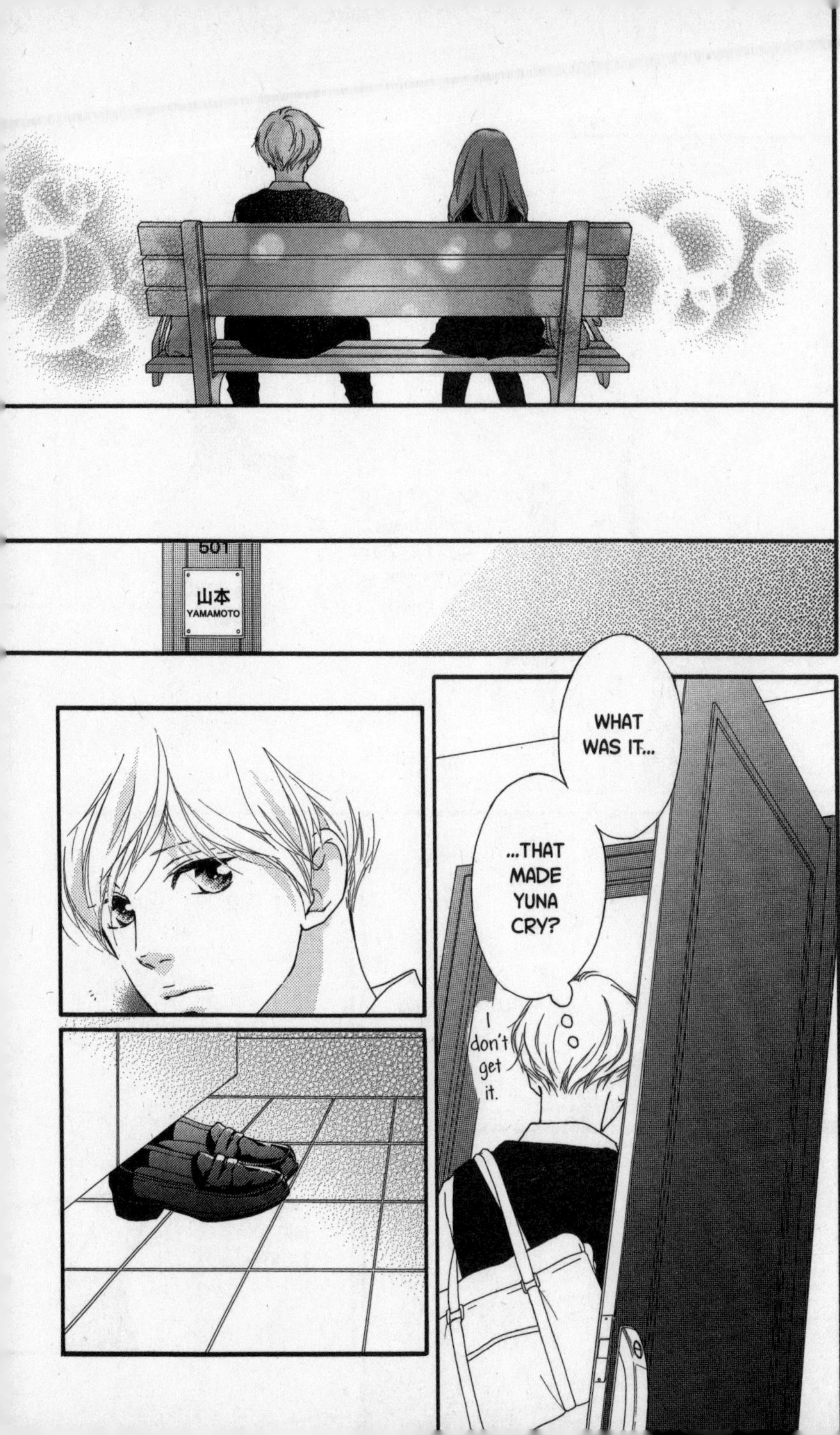
501
山本
YAMAMOTO
WHAT WAS IT...
...THAT MADE YUNA CRY?
I don't get it.

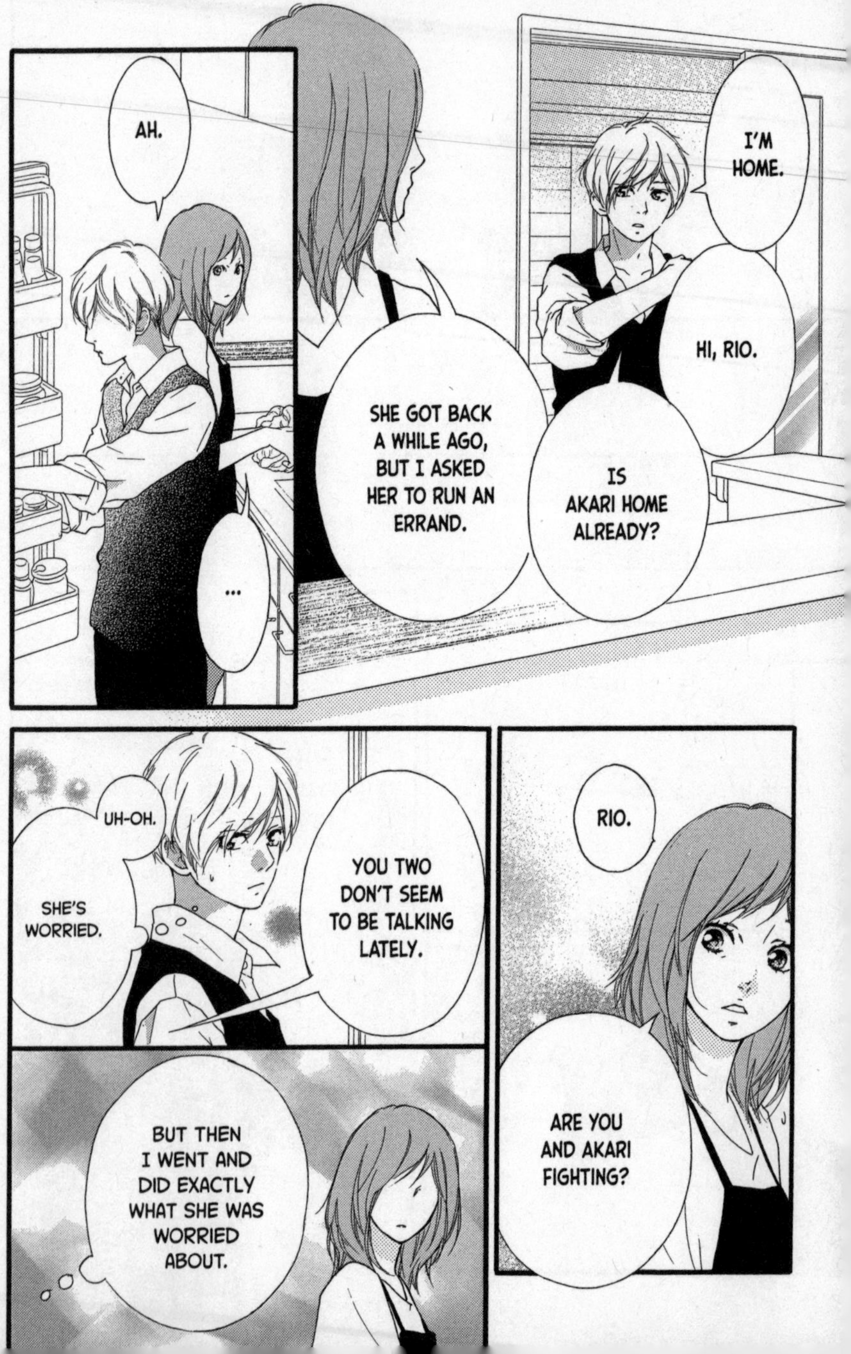
I'M HOME.
HI, RIO.
IS AKARI HOME ALREADY?
SHE GOT BACK A WHILE AGO, BUT I ASKED HER TO RUN AN ERRAND.
AH.
...
RIO.
ARE YOU AND AKARI FIGHTING?
YOU TWO DON'T SEEM TO BE TALKING LATELY.
UH-OH.
SHE'S WORRIED.
BUT THEN I WENT AND DID EXACTLY WHAT SHE WAS WORRIED ABOUT.

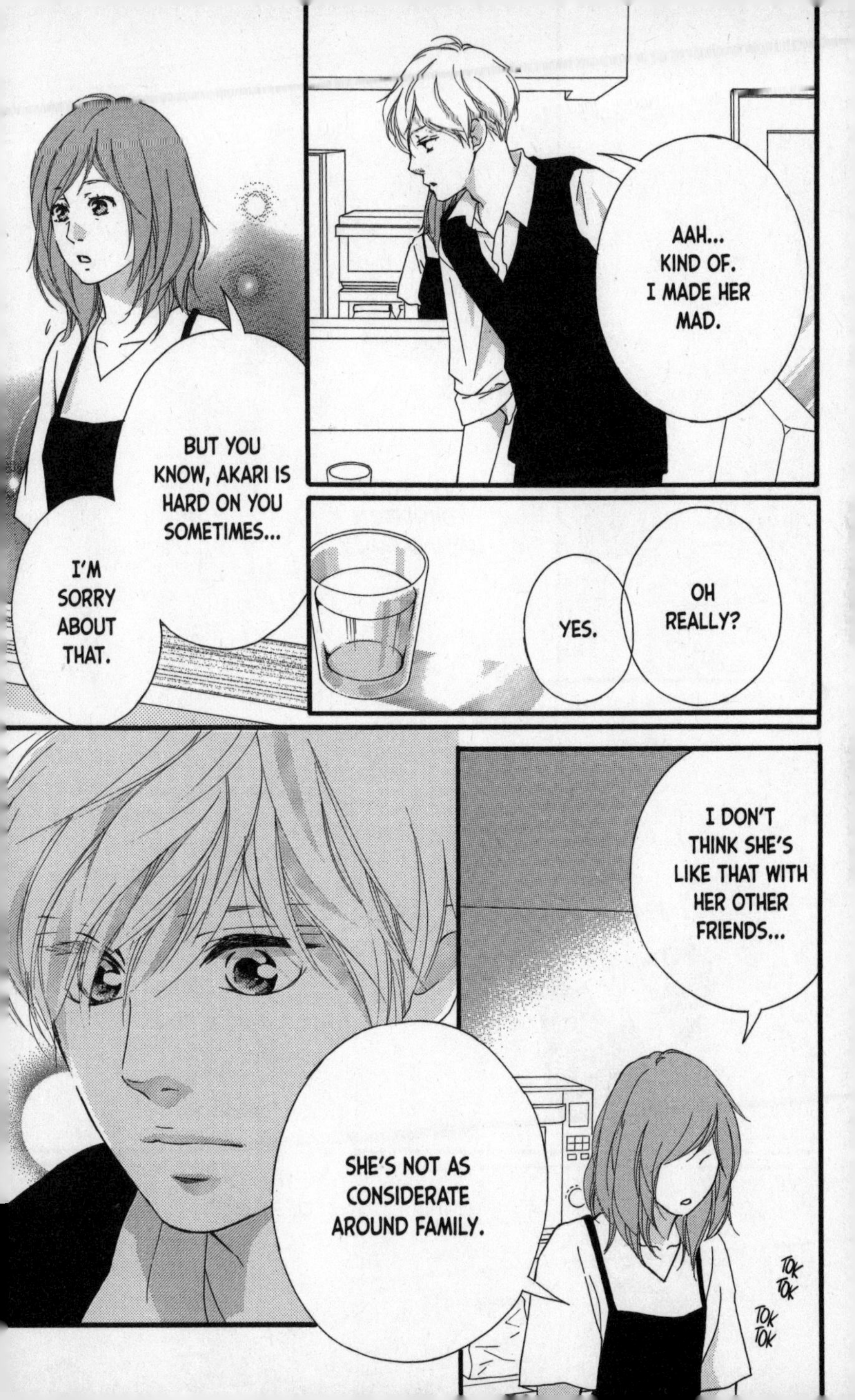
AAH... KIND OF. I MADE HER MAD.
OH REALLY?
YES.
BUT YOU KNOW, AKARI IS HARD ON YOU SOMETIMES...
I'M SORRY ABOUT THAT.
I DON'T THINK SHE'S LIKE THAT WITH HER OTHER FRIENDS...
SHE'S NOT AS CONSIDERATE AROUND FAMILY.
TOK TOK
TOK TOK

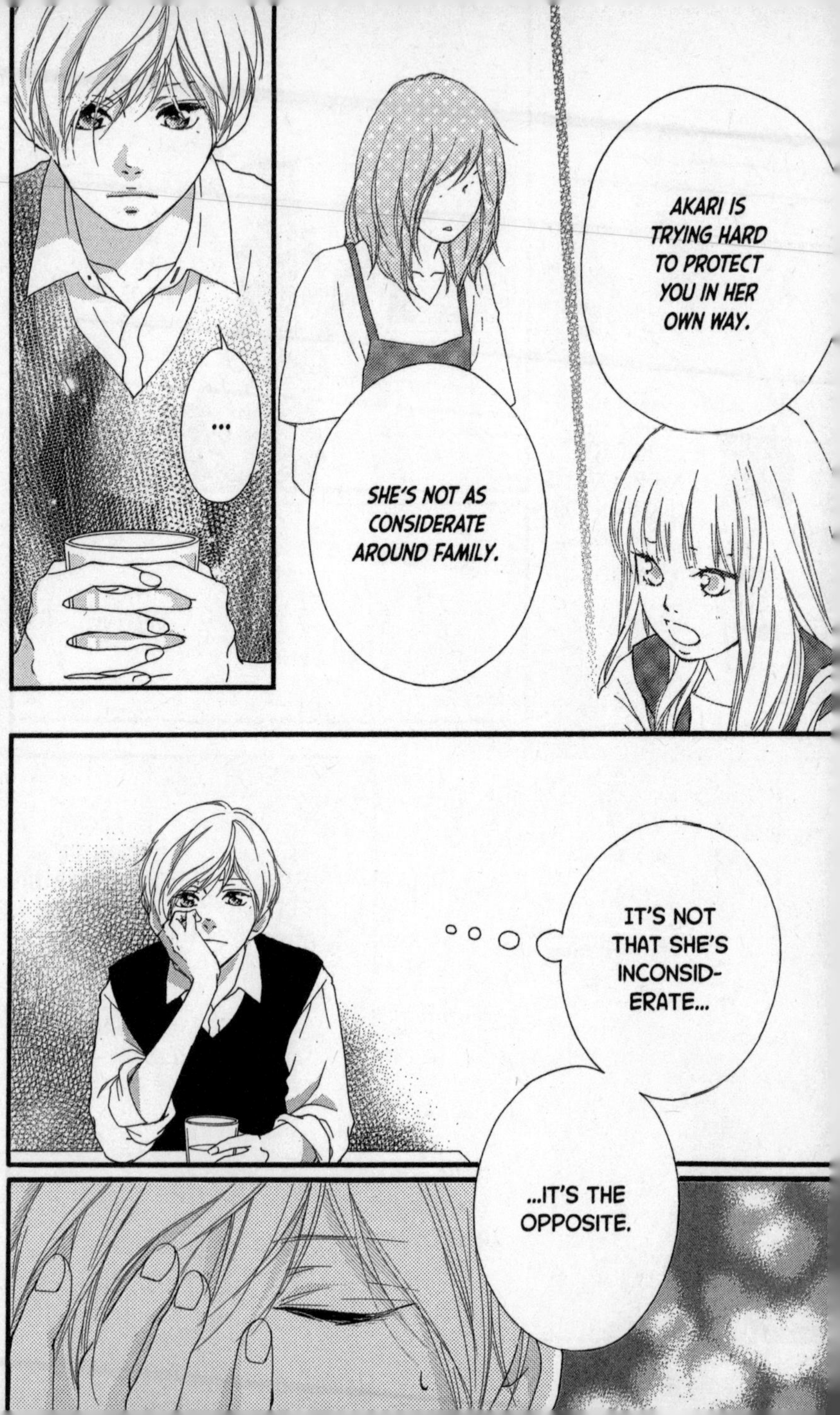
AKARI IS TRYING HARD TO PROTECT YOU IN HER OWN WAY.
SHE'S NOT AS CONSIDERATE AROUND FAMILY.
...
IT'S NOT THAT SHE'S INCONSID-ERATE...
...IT'S THE OPPOSITE.

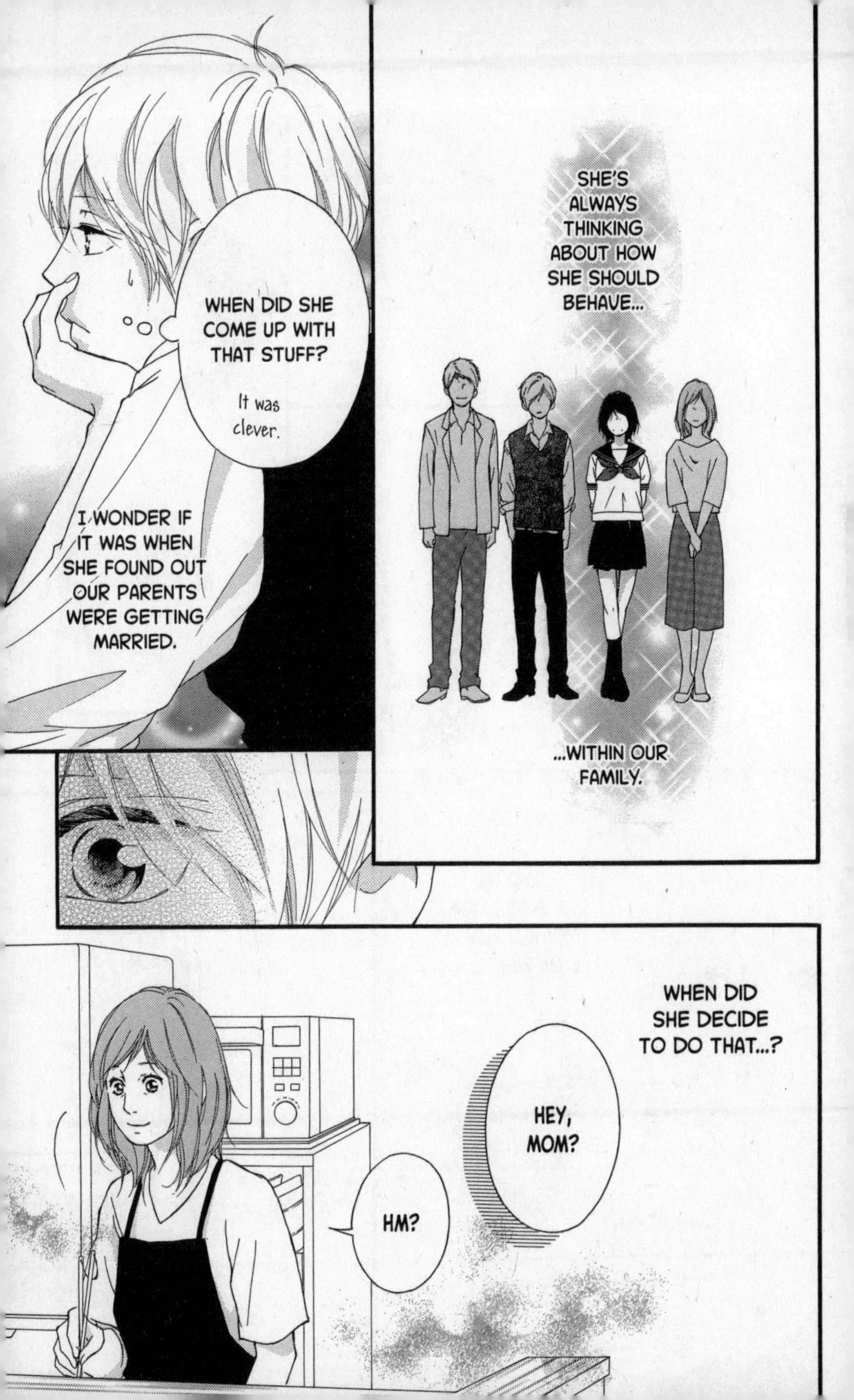
SHE'S ALWAYS THINKING ABOUT HOW SHE SHOULD BEHAVE...
...WITHIN OUR FAMILY.
WHEN DID SHE COME UP WITH THAT STUFF?
It was clever.
I WONDER IF IT WAS WHEN SHE FOUND OUT OUR PARENTS WERE GETTING MARRIED.
WHEN DID SHE DECIDE TO DO THAT...?
HEY, MOM?
HM?

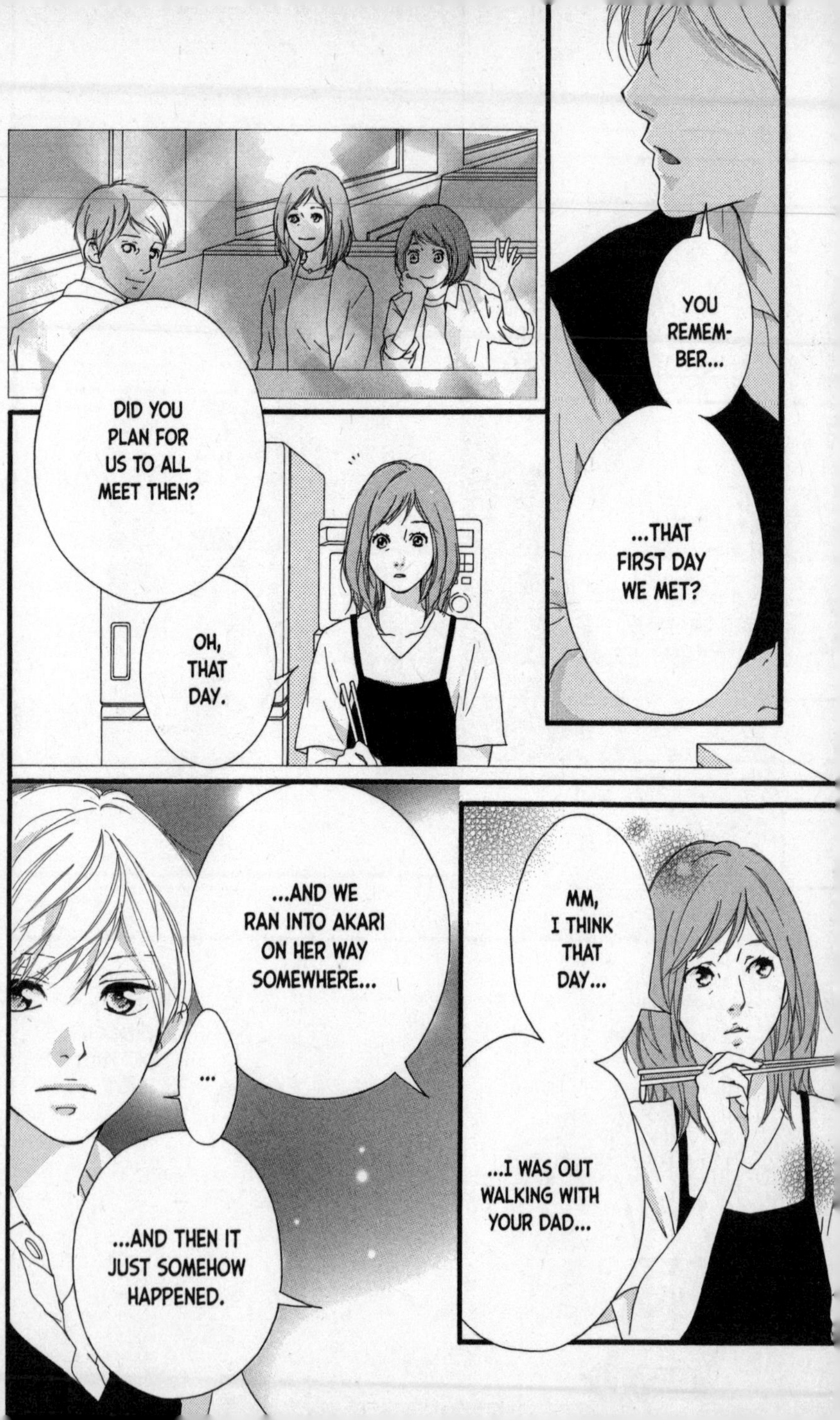
YOU REMEMBER...
...THAT FIRST DAY WE MET?
OH, THAT DAY.
DID YOU PLAN FOR US TO ALL MEET THEN?
MM, I THINK THAT DAY...
...I WAS OUT WALKING WITH YOUR DAD...
...AND WE RAN INTO AKARI ON HER WAY SOMEWHERE...
...
...AND THEN IT JUST SOMEHOW HAPPENED.

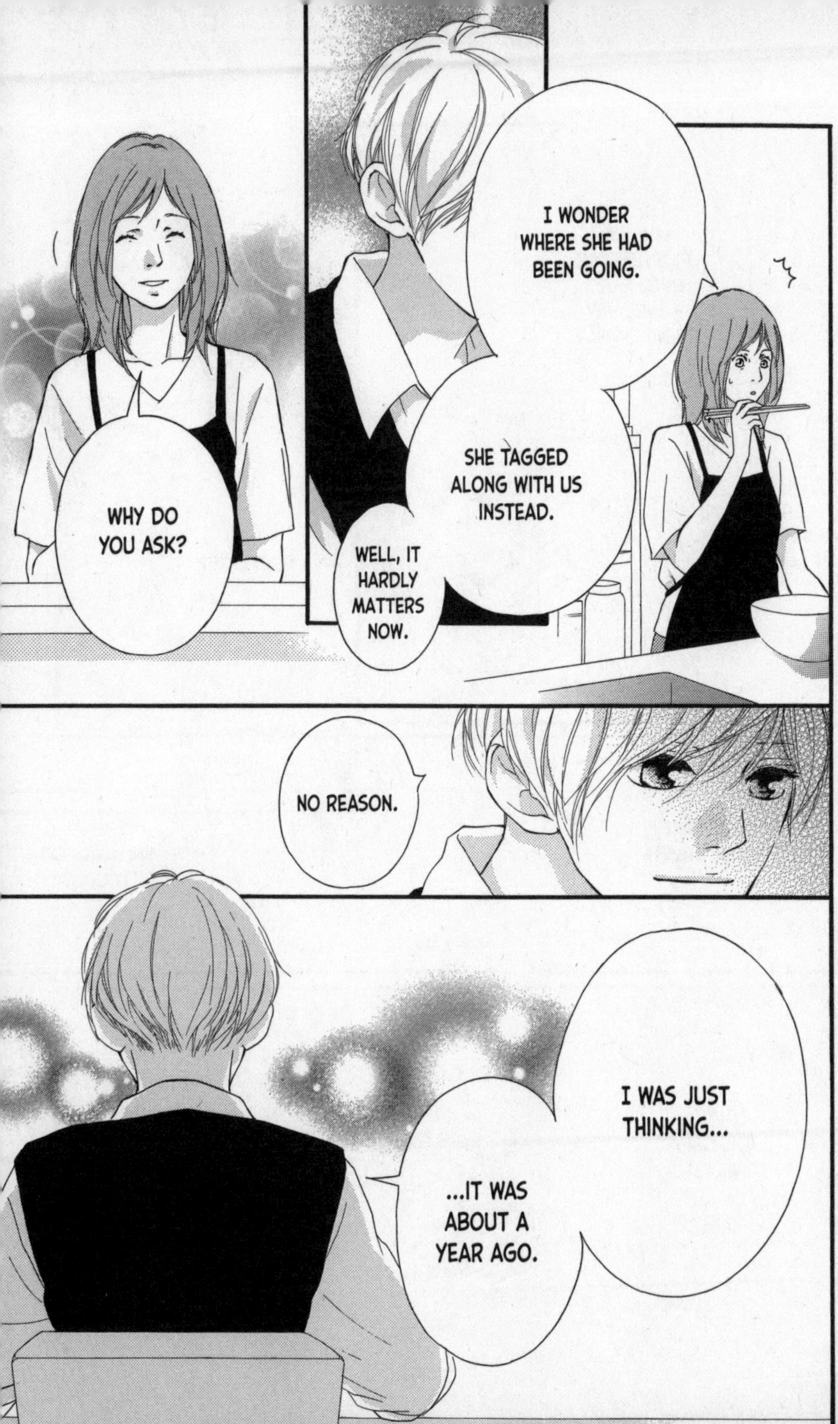
I WONDER WHERE SHE HAD BEEN GOING.
SHE TAGGED ALONG WITH US INSTEAD.
WELL, IT HARDLY MATTERS NOW.
WHY DO YOU ASK?
NO REASON.
I WAS JUST THINKING...
...IT WAS ABOUT A YEAR AGO.

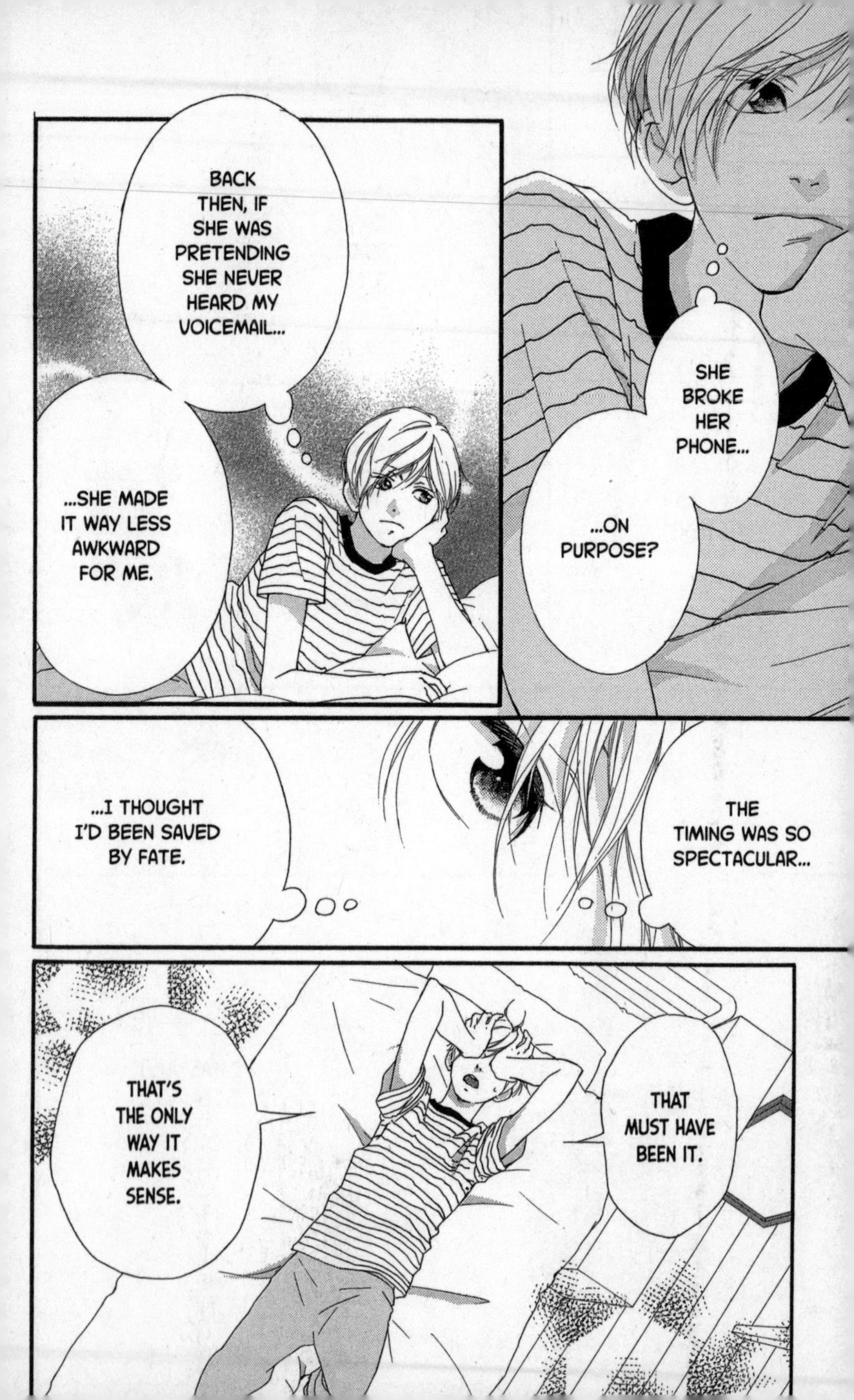
SHE BROKE HER PHONE...
...ON PURPOSE?
BACK THEN, IF SHE WAS PRETENDING SHE NEVER HEARD MY VOICEMAIL...
...SHE MADE IT WAY LESS AWKWARD FOR ME.
THE TIMING WAS SO SPECTACULAR...
...I THOUGHT I'D BEEN SAVED BY FATE.
THAT MUST HAVE BEEN IT.
THAT'S THE ONLY WAY IT MAKES SENSE.

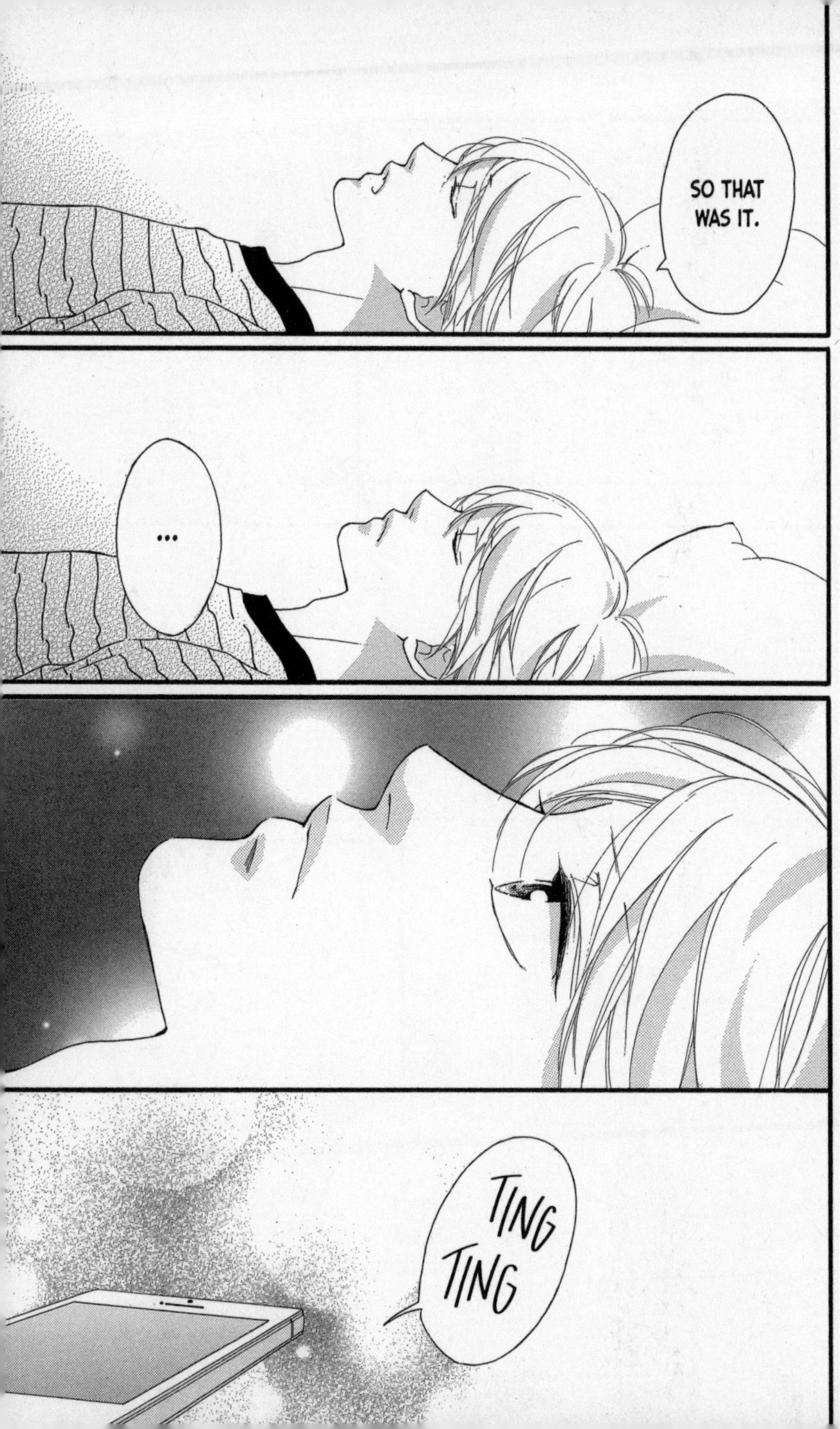
SO THAT WAS IT.
...
TING TING

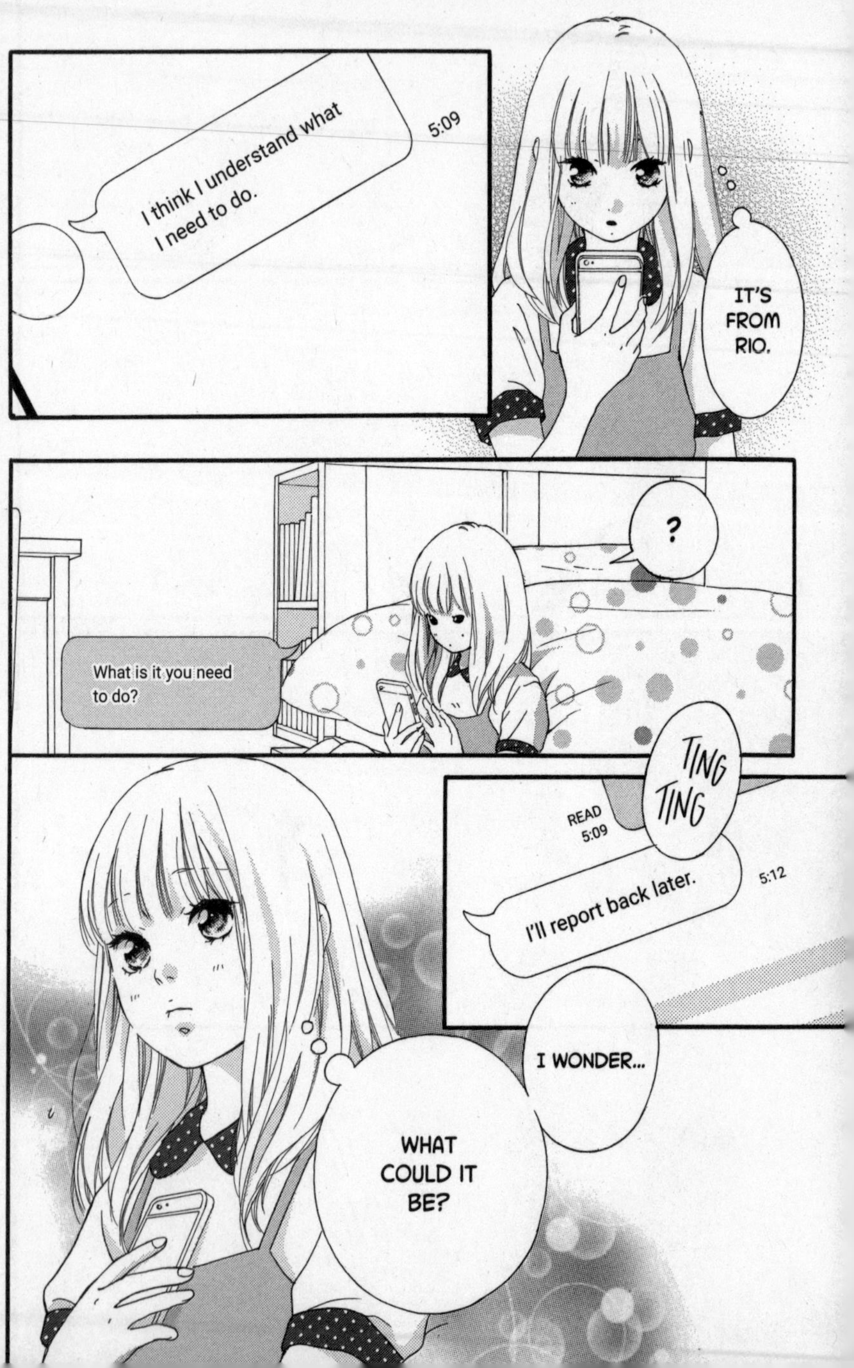
IT'S FROM RIO.
I think I understand what I need to do.
5:09
?
What is it you need to do?
TING TING
READ 5:09
I'll report back later.
5:12
I WONDER...
WHAT COULD IT BE?

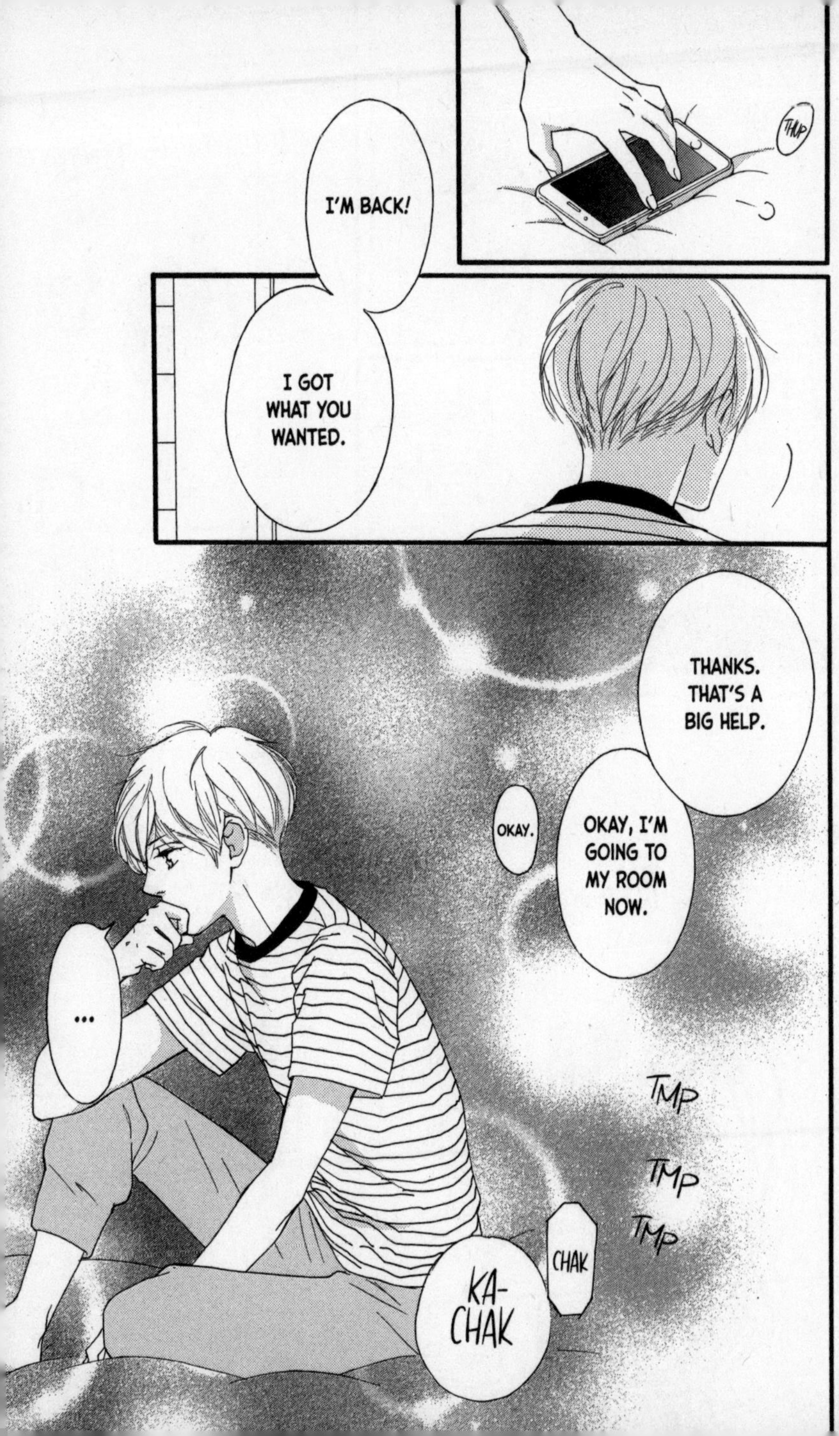
THMP
I'M BACK!
I GOT WHAT YOU WANTED.
THANKS. THAT'S A BIG HELP.
OKAY, I'M GOING TO MY ROOM NOW.
OKAY.
...
TMP
TMP
TMP
CHAK
KA-CHAK

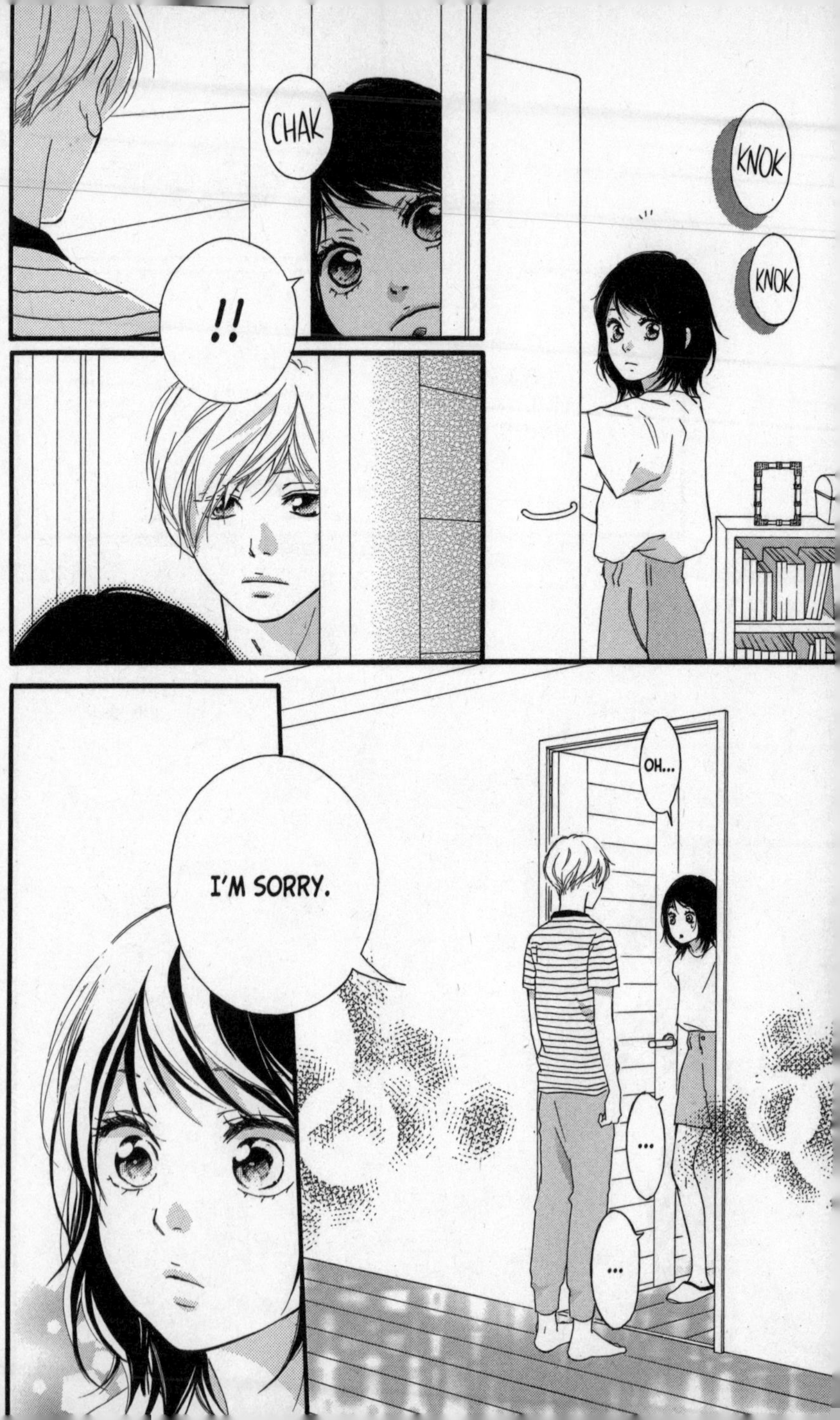
KNOK
KNOK
CHAK
!!
OH...
...
...
I'M SORRY.

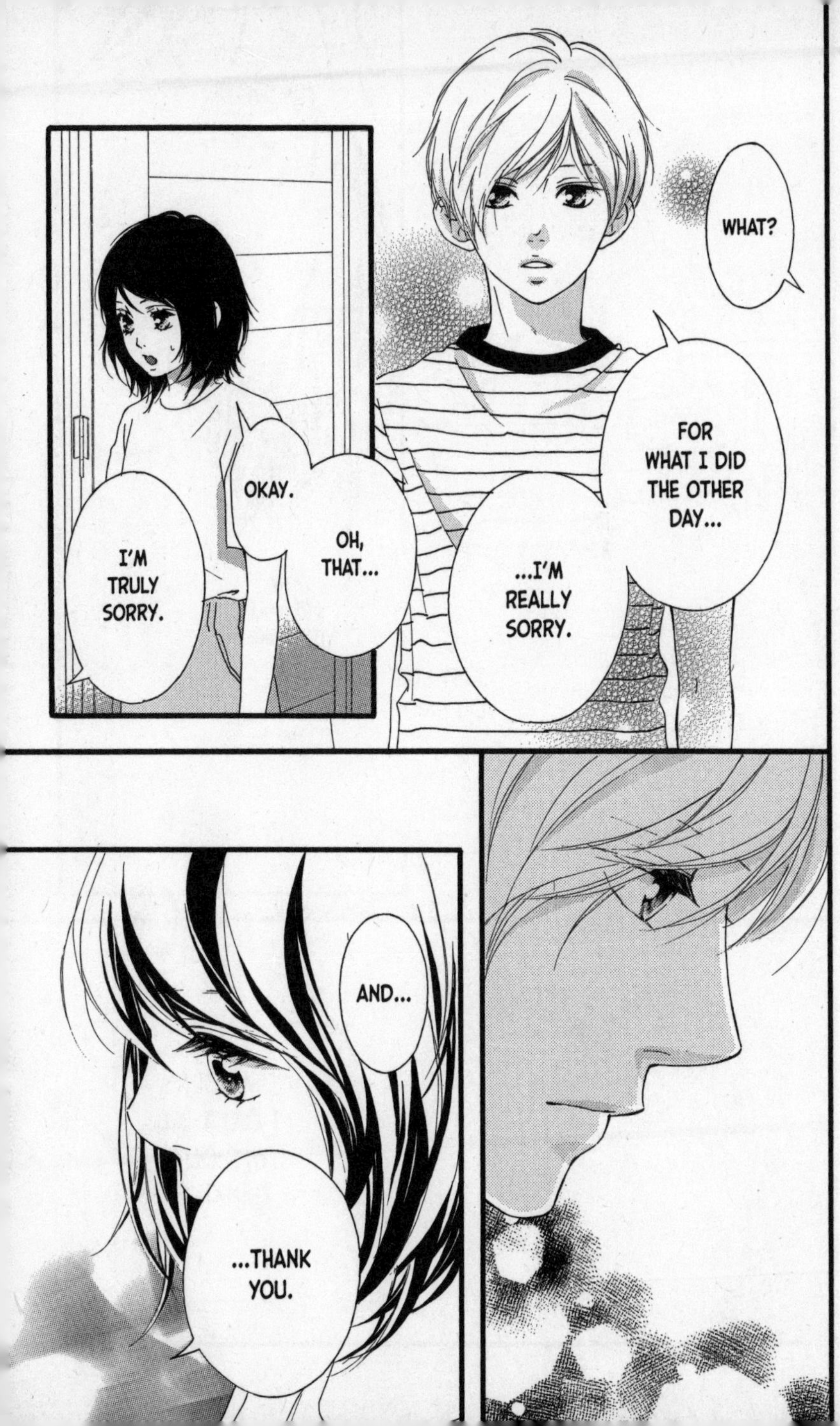
WHAT?
FOR WHAT I DID THE OTHER DAY...
...I'M REALLY SORRY.
OH, THAT...
OKAY.
I'M TRULY SORRY.
AND...
...THANK YOU.

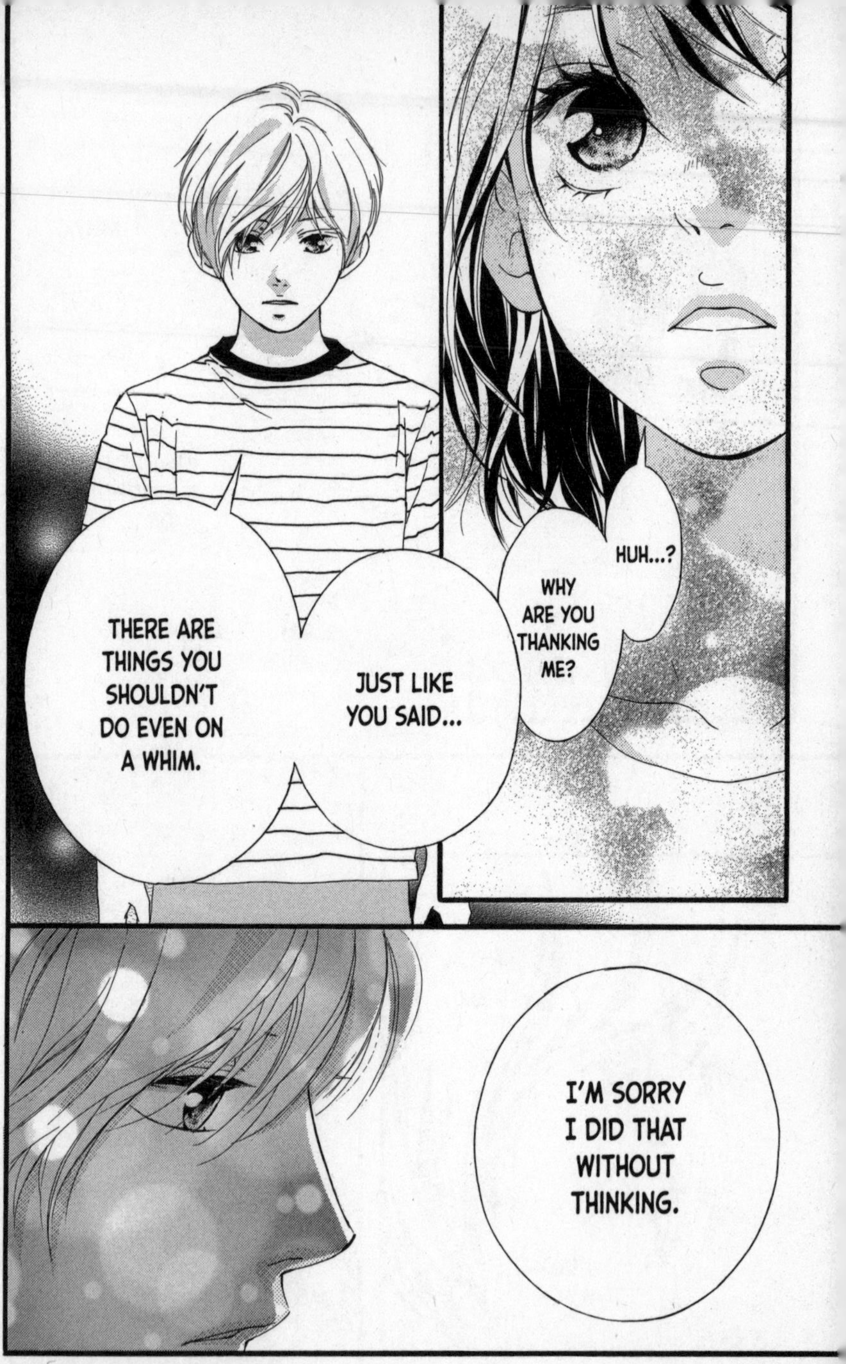
HUH...?
WHY ARE YOU THANKING ME?
JUST LIKE YOU SAID...
THERE ARE THINGS YOU SHOULDN'T DO EVEN ON A WHIM.
I'M SORRY I DID THAT WITHOUT THINKING.

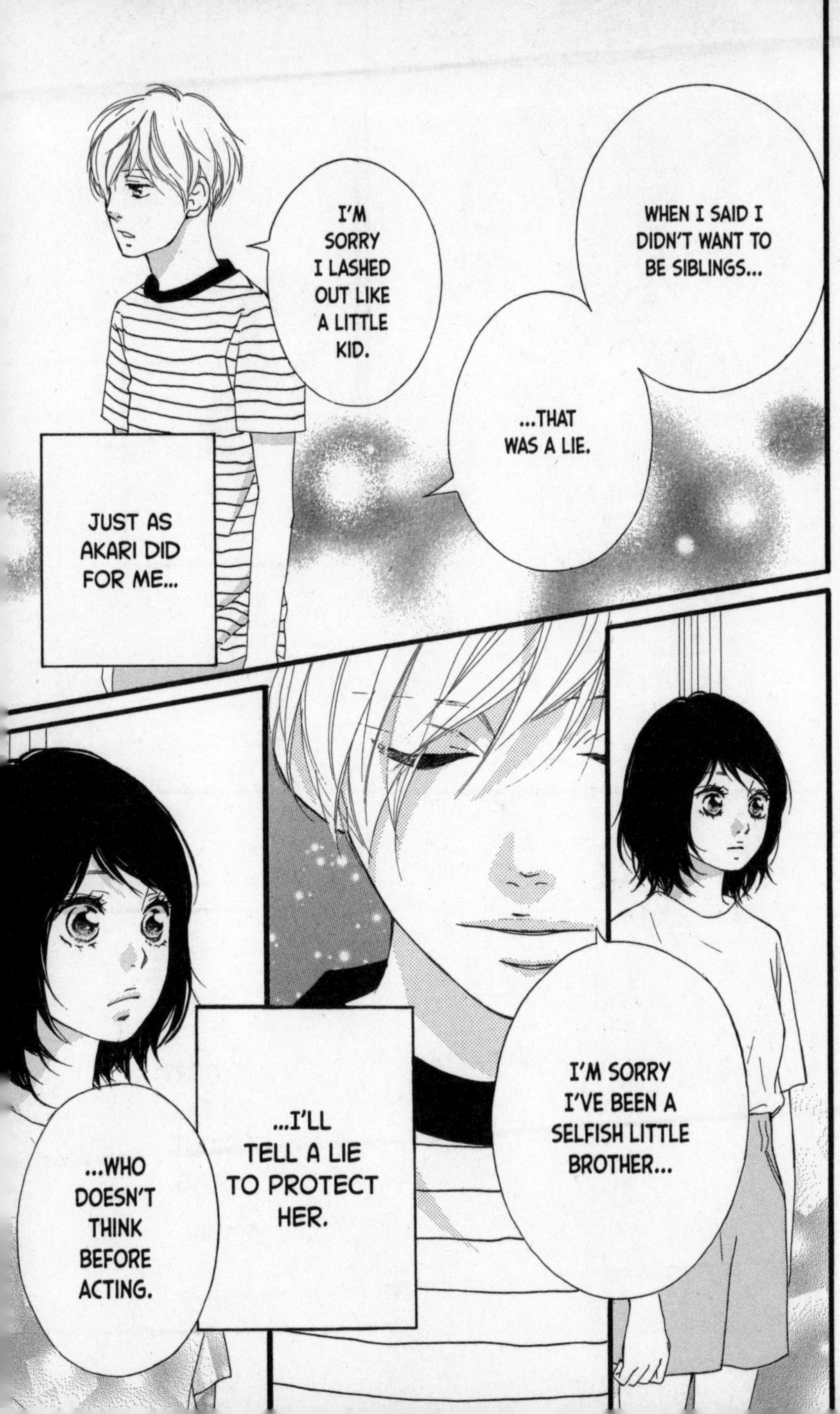

WHEN I SAID I DIDN'T WANT TO BE SIBLINGS...
...THAT WAS A LIE.
I'M SORRY I LASHED OUT LIKE A LITTLE KID.
JUST AS AKARI DID FOR ME...
I'M SORRY I'VE BEEN A SELFISH LITTLE BROTHER...
...I'LL TELL A LIE TO PROTECT HER.
...WHO DOESN'T THINK BEFORE ACTING.

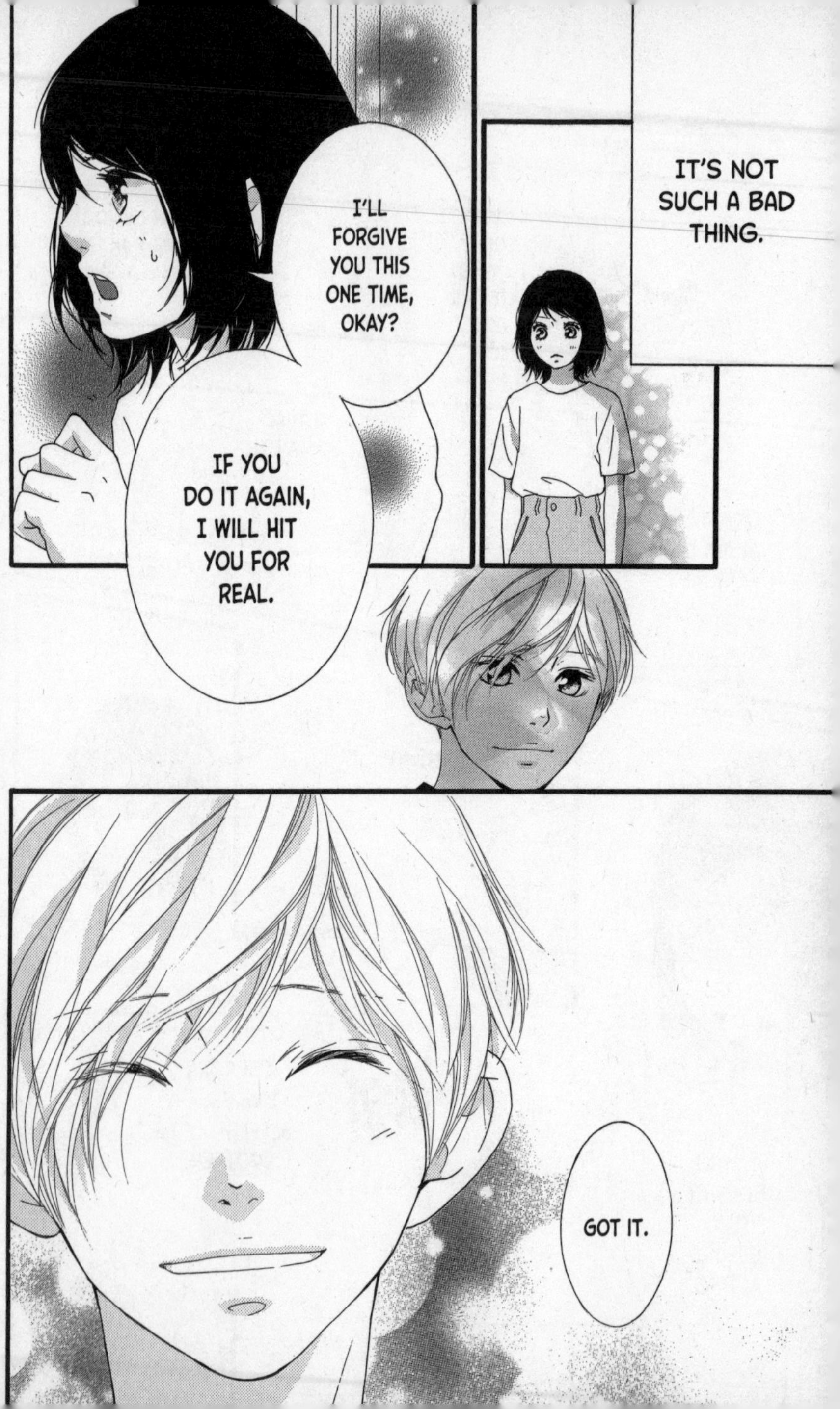
IT'S NOT SUCH A BAD THING.
I'LL FORGIVE YOU THIS ONE TIME, OKAY?
IF YOU DO IT AGAIN, I WILL HIT YOU FOR REAL.
GOT IT.

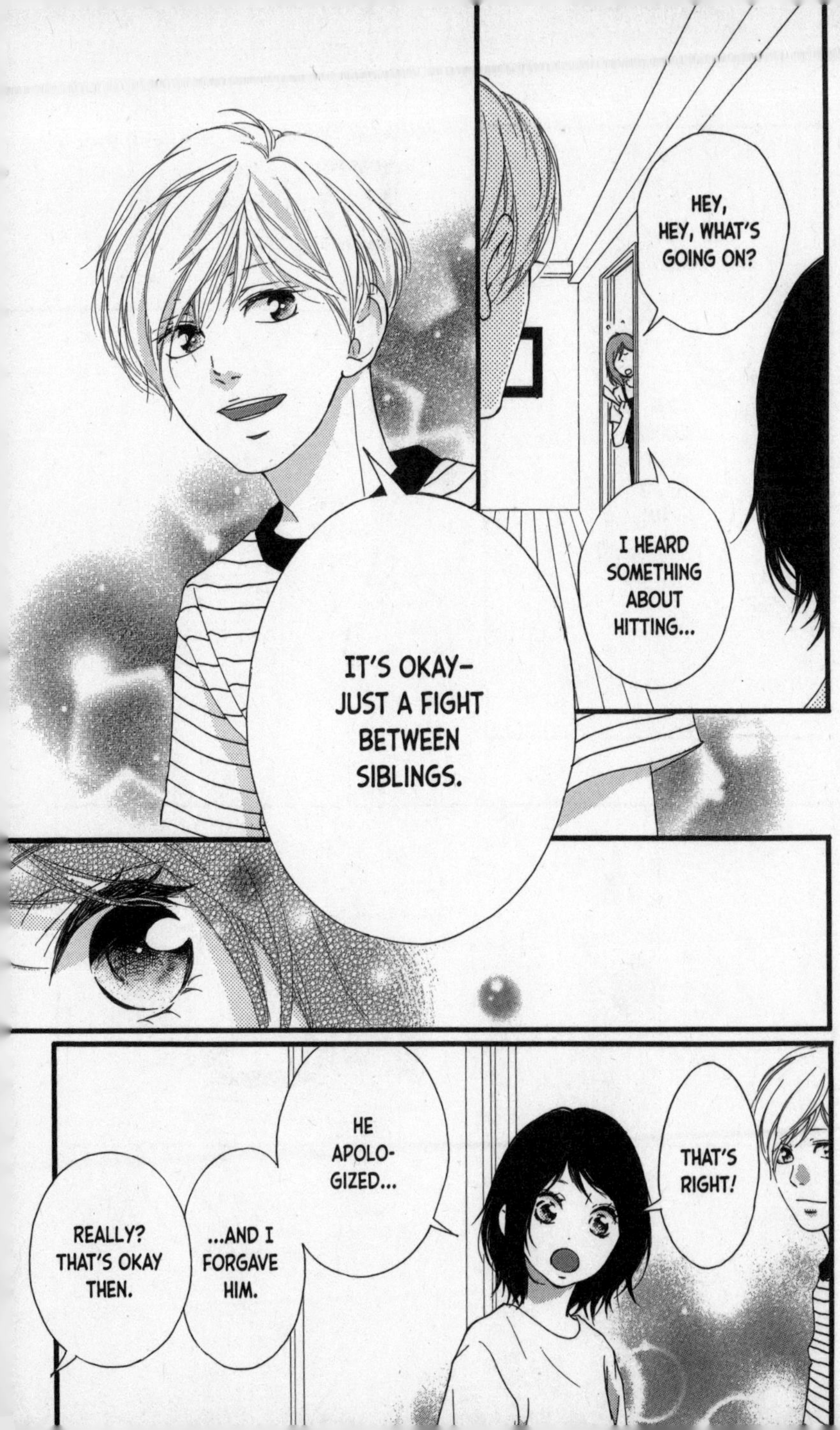
HEY, HEY, WHAT'S GOING ON?
I HEARD SOMETHING ABOUT HITTING...
IT'S OKAY—JUST A FIGHT BETWEEN SIBLINGS.
THAT'S RIGHT!
HE APOLO-GIZED...
...AND I FORGAVE HIM.
REALLY? THAT'S OKAY THEN.

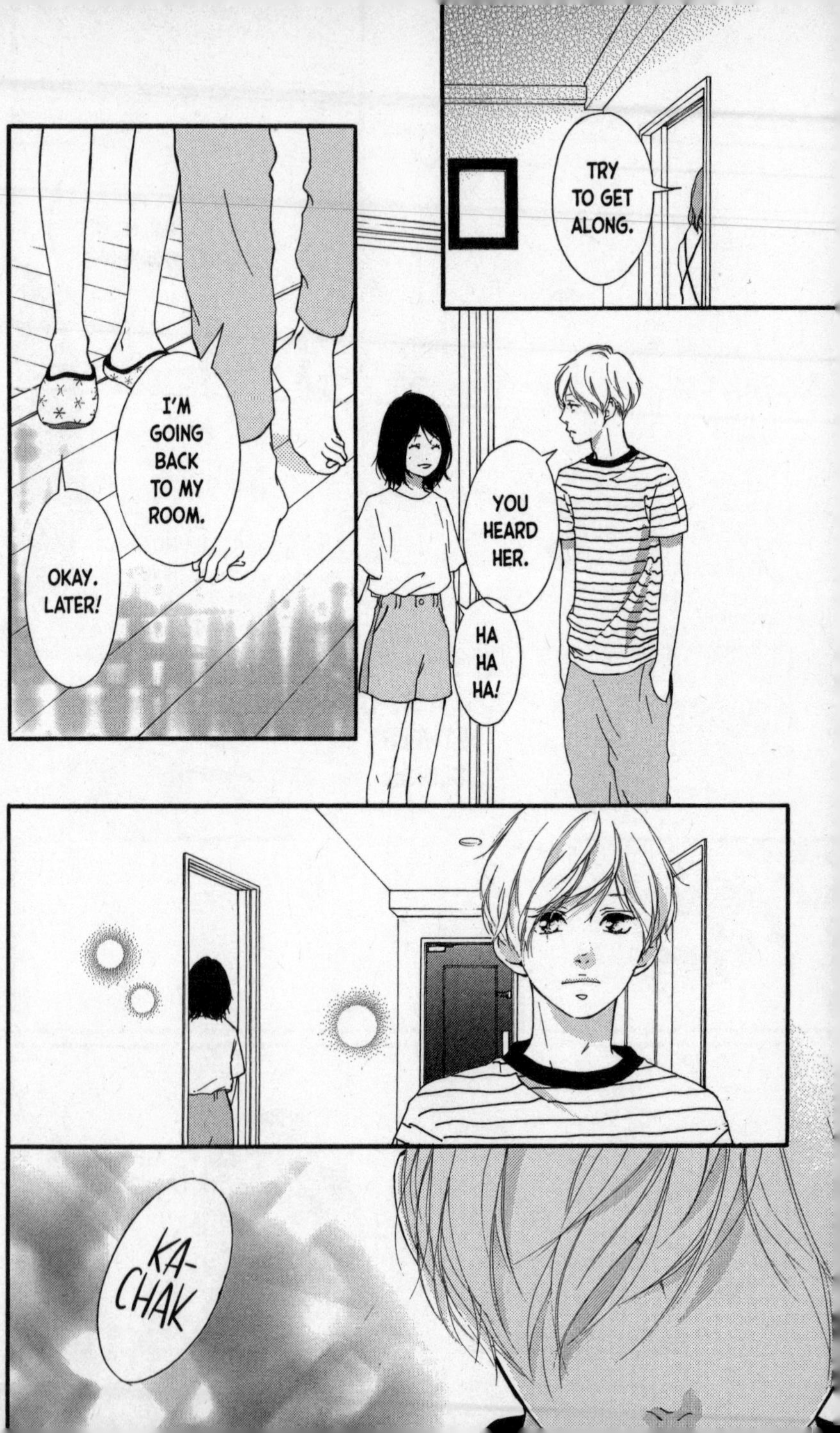
TRY TO GET ALONG.
YOU HEARD HER.
HA HA HA!
I'M GOING BACK TO MY ROOM.
OKAY. LATER!
KA-CHAK

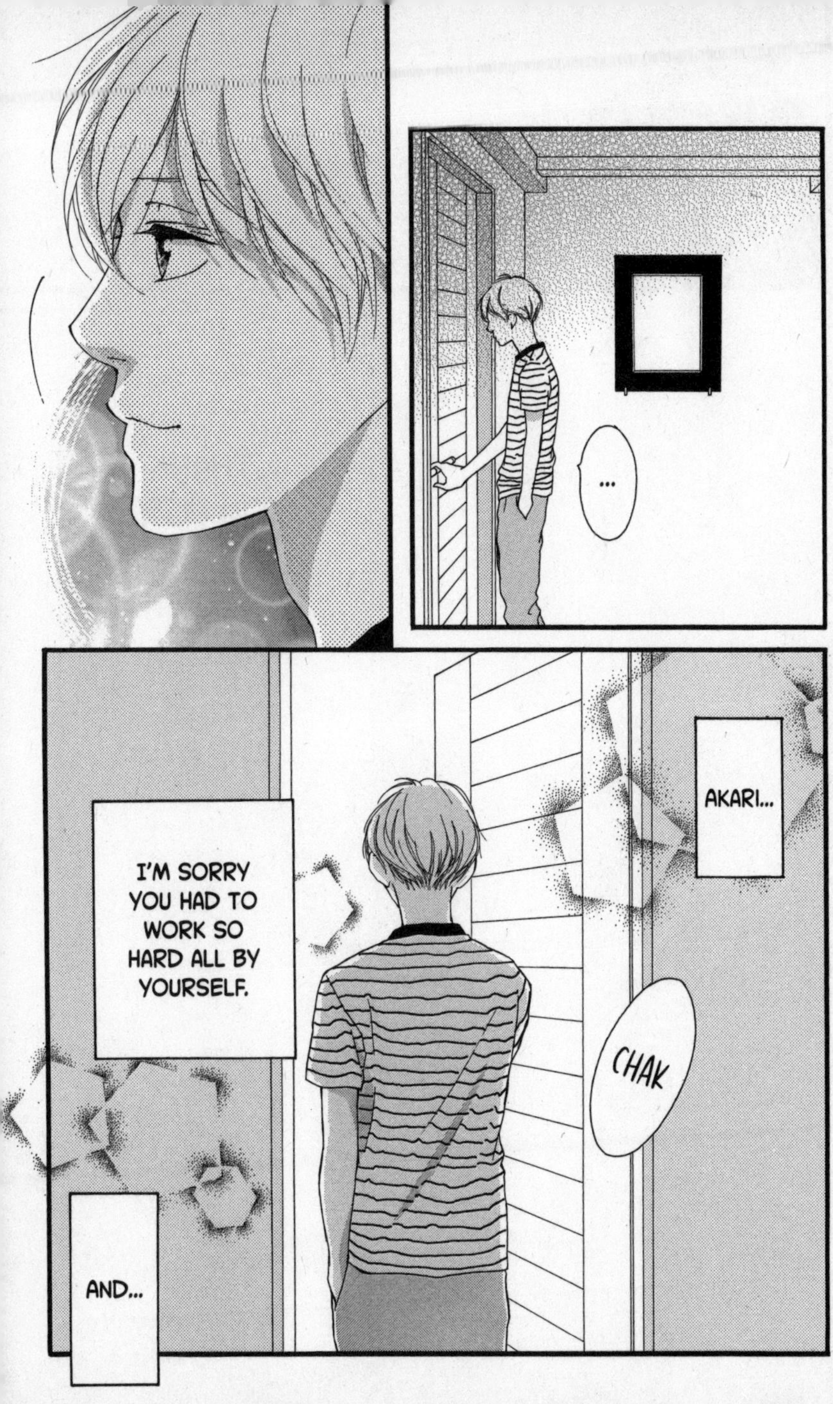
...
AKARI...
CHAK
I'M SORRY YOU HAD TO WORK SO HARD ALL BY YOURSELF.
AND...

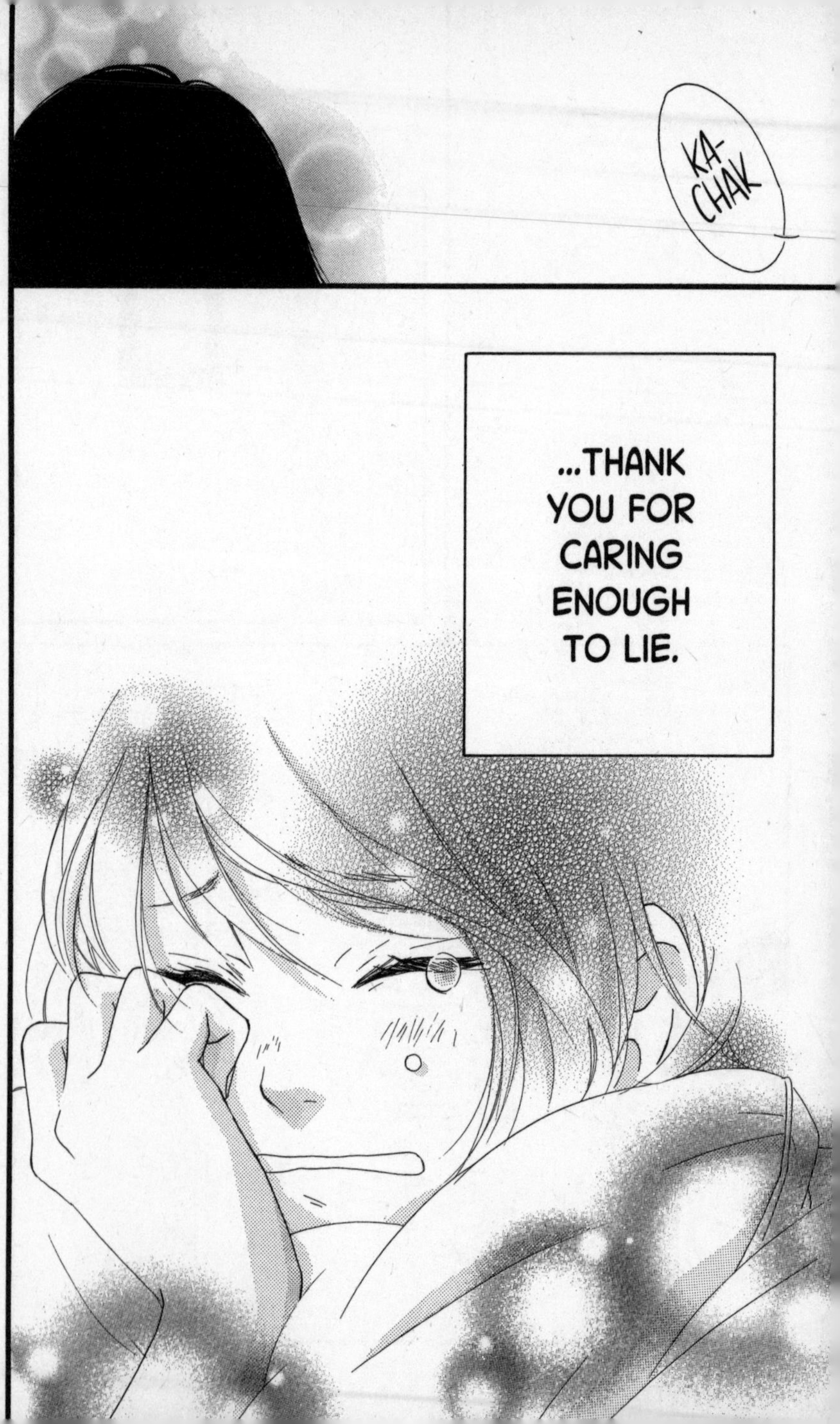
KA-
CHAK
...THANK YOU FOR CARING ENOUGH TO LIE.

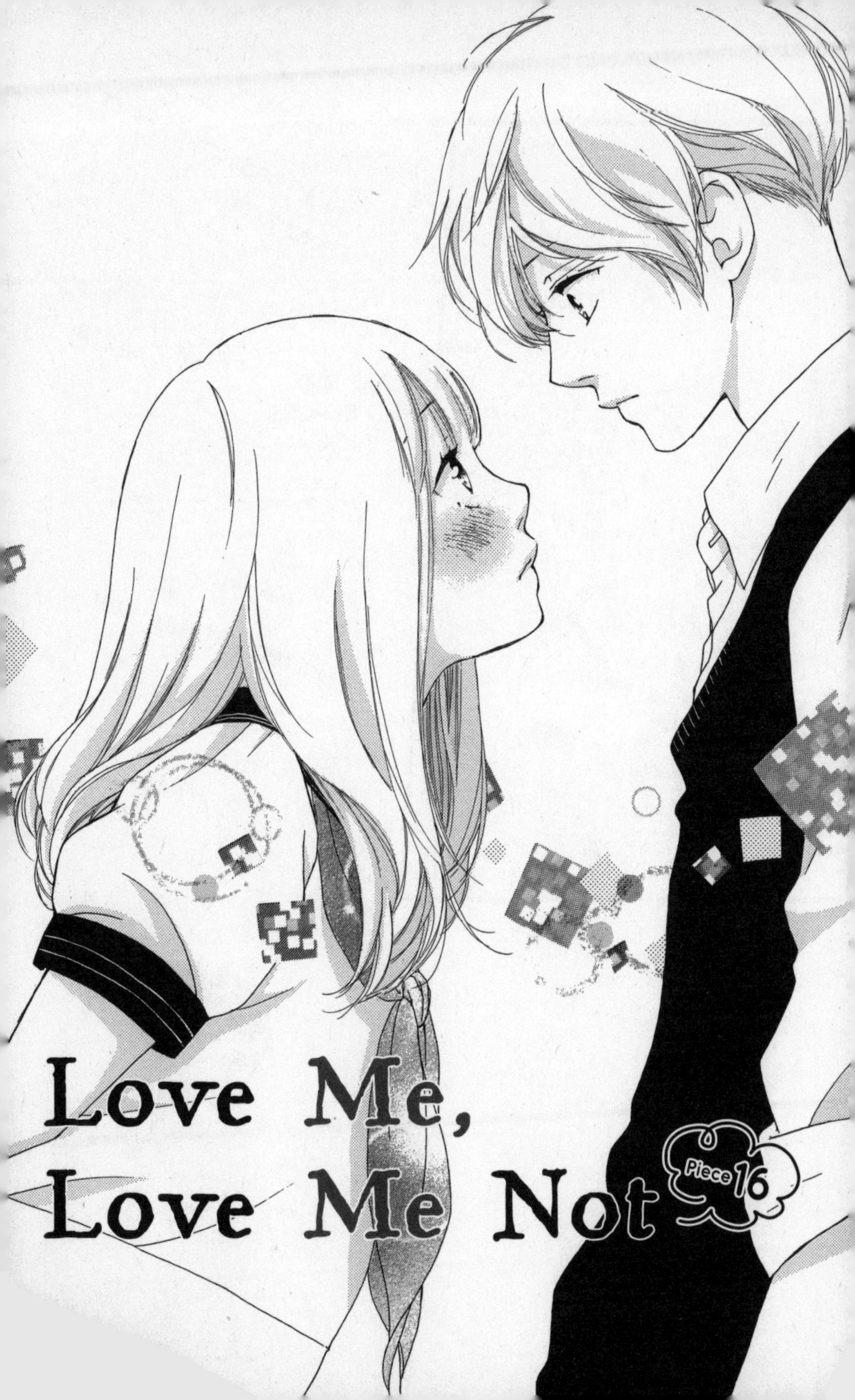
Love Me,
Love Me Not
Piece 16

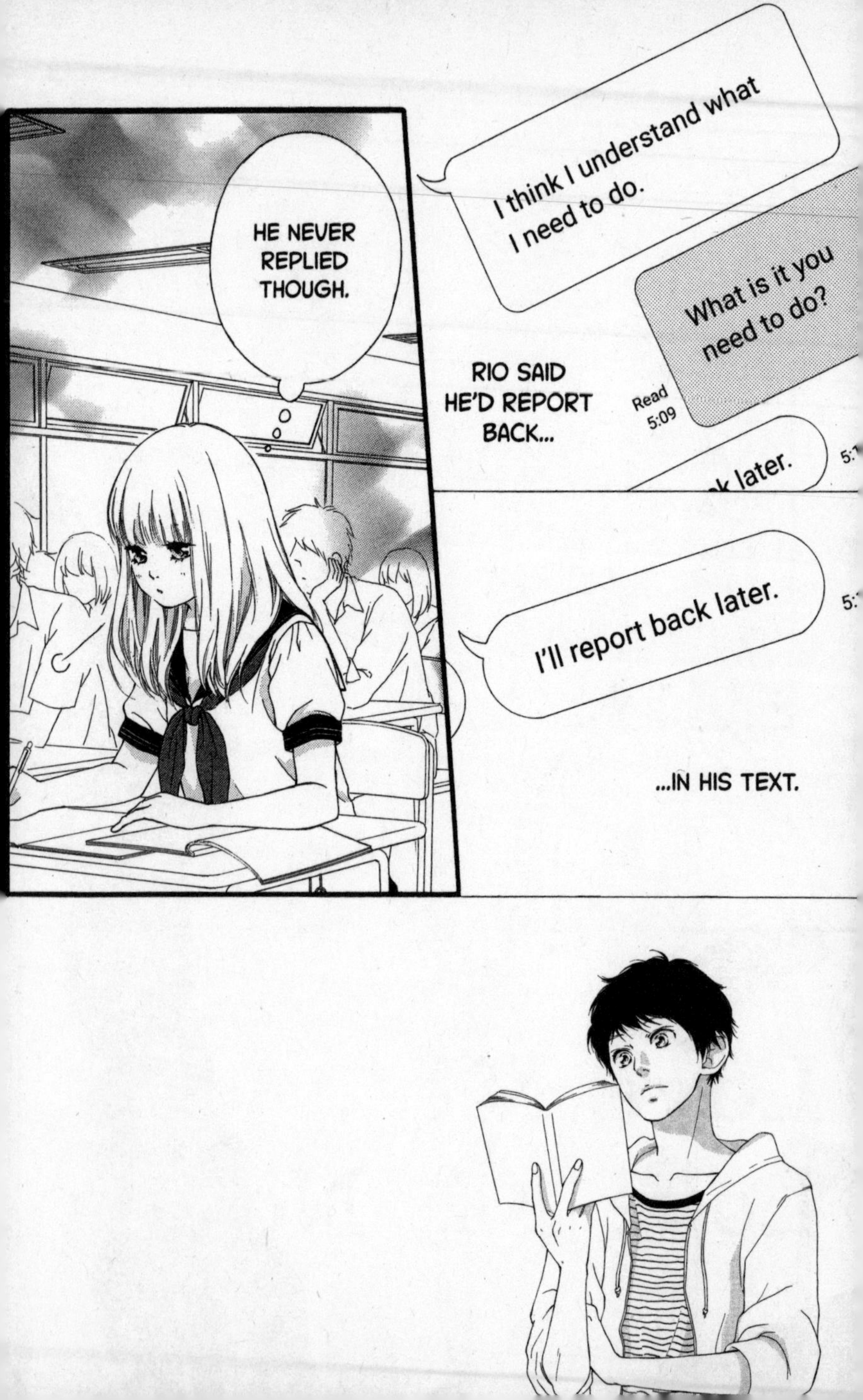
I think I understand what I need to do.
What is it you need to do?
Read 5:09
RIO SAID HE'D REPORT BACK...
I'll report back later.
...IN HIS TEXT.
HE NEVER REPLIED THOUGH.

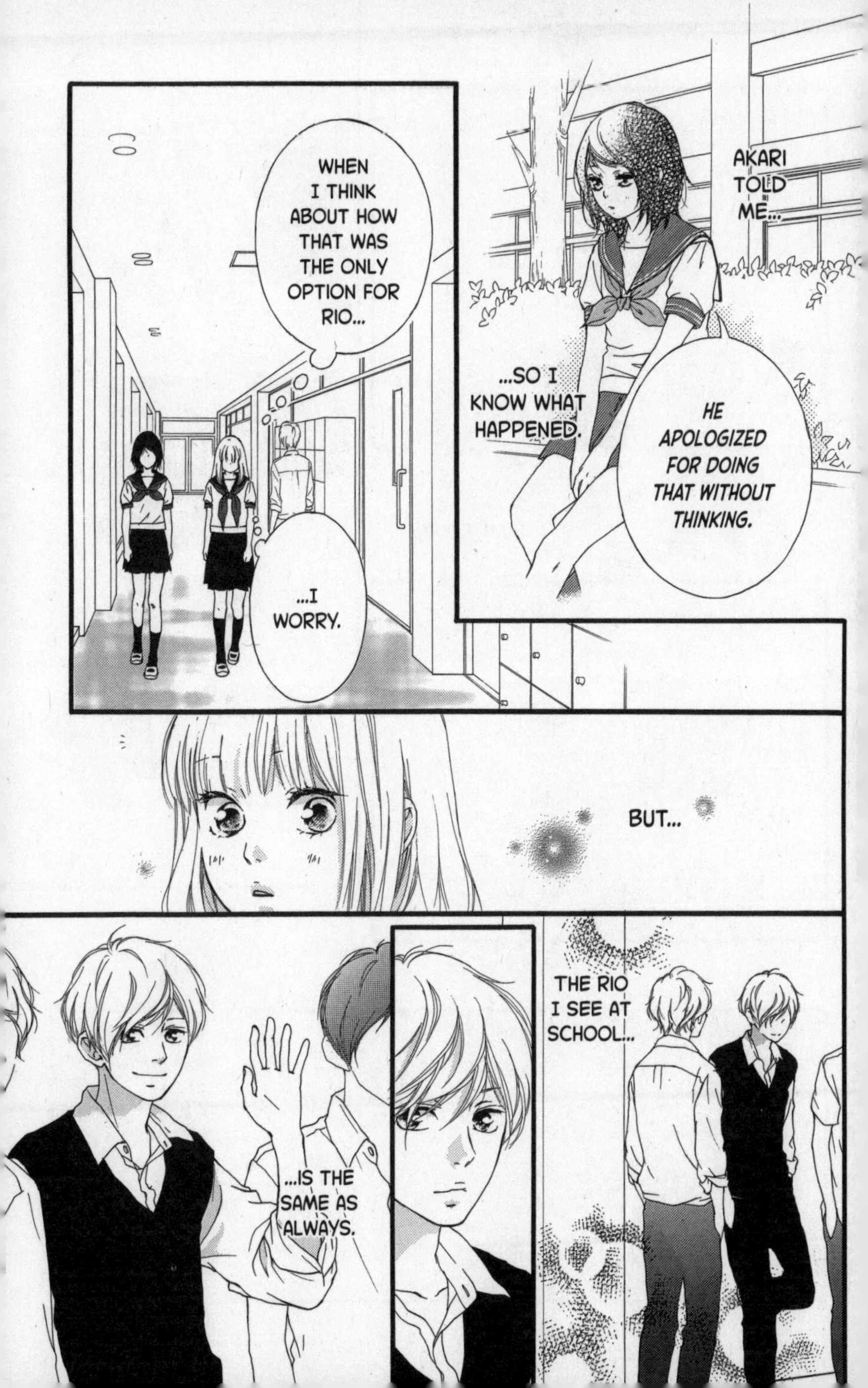
AKARI TOLD ME...
...SO I KNOW WHAT HAPPENED.
HE APOLOGIZED FOR DOING THAT WITHOUT THINKING.
WHEN I THINK ABOUT HOW THAT WAS THE ONLY OPTION FOR RIO...
...I WORRY.
BUT...
THE RIO I SEE AT SCHOOL...
...IS THE SAME AS ALWAYS.

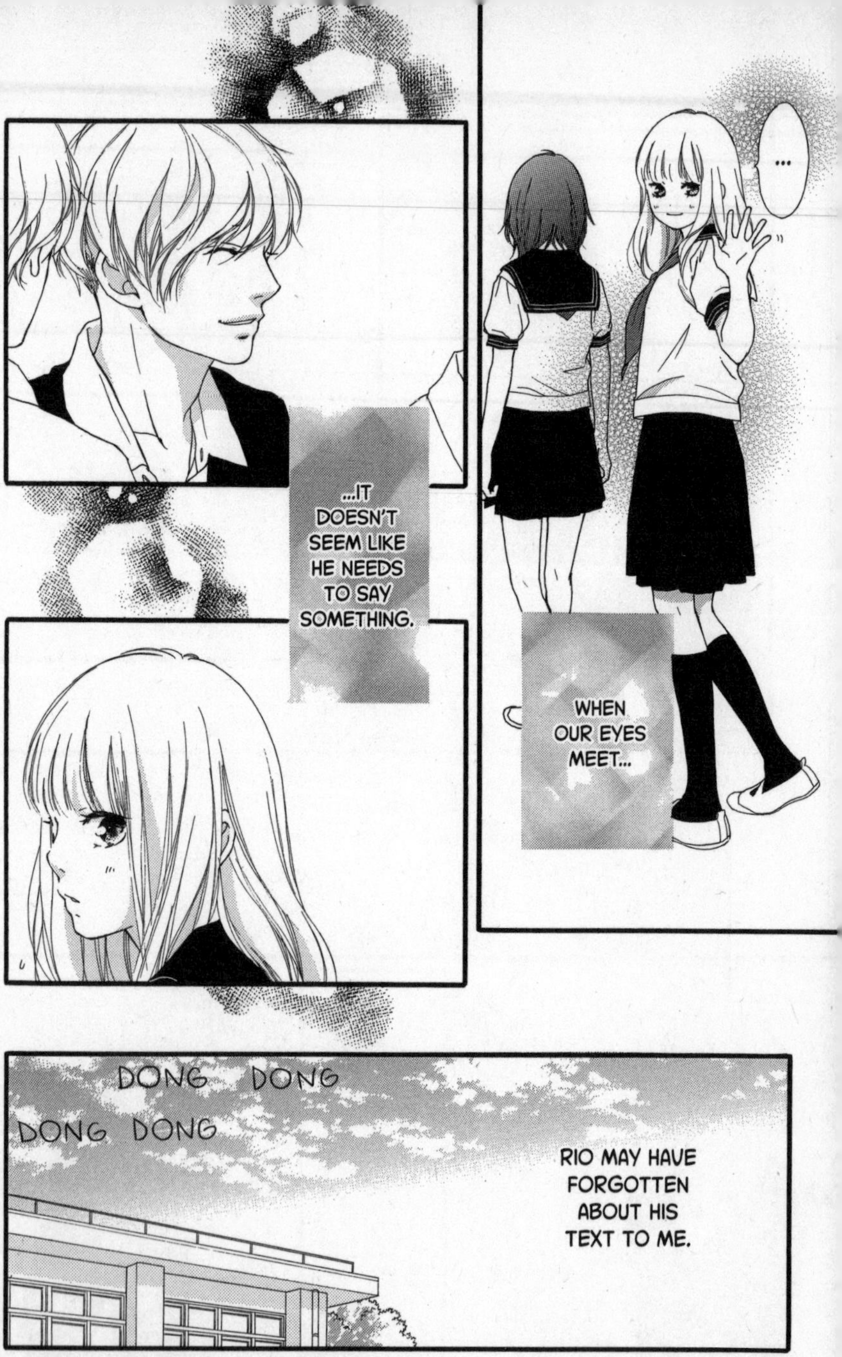
...
WHEN OUR EYES MEET...
...IT DOESN'T SEEM LIKE HE NEEDS TO SAY SOMETHING.
DONG DONG
DONG DONG
RIO MAY HAVE FORGOTTEN ABOUT HIS TEXT TO ME.

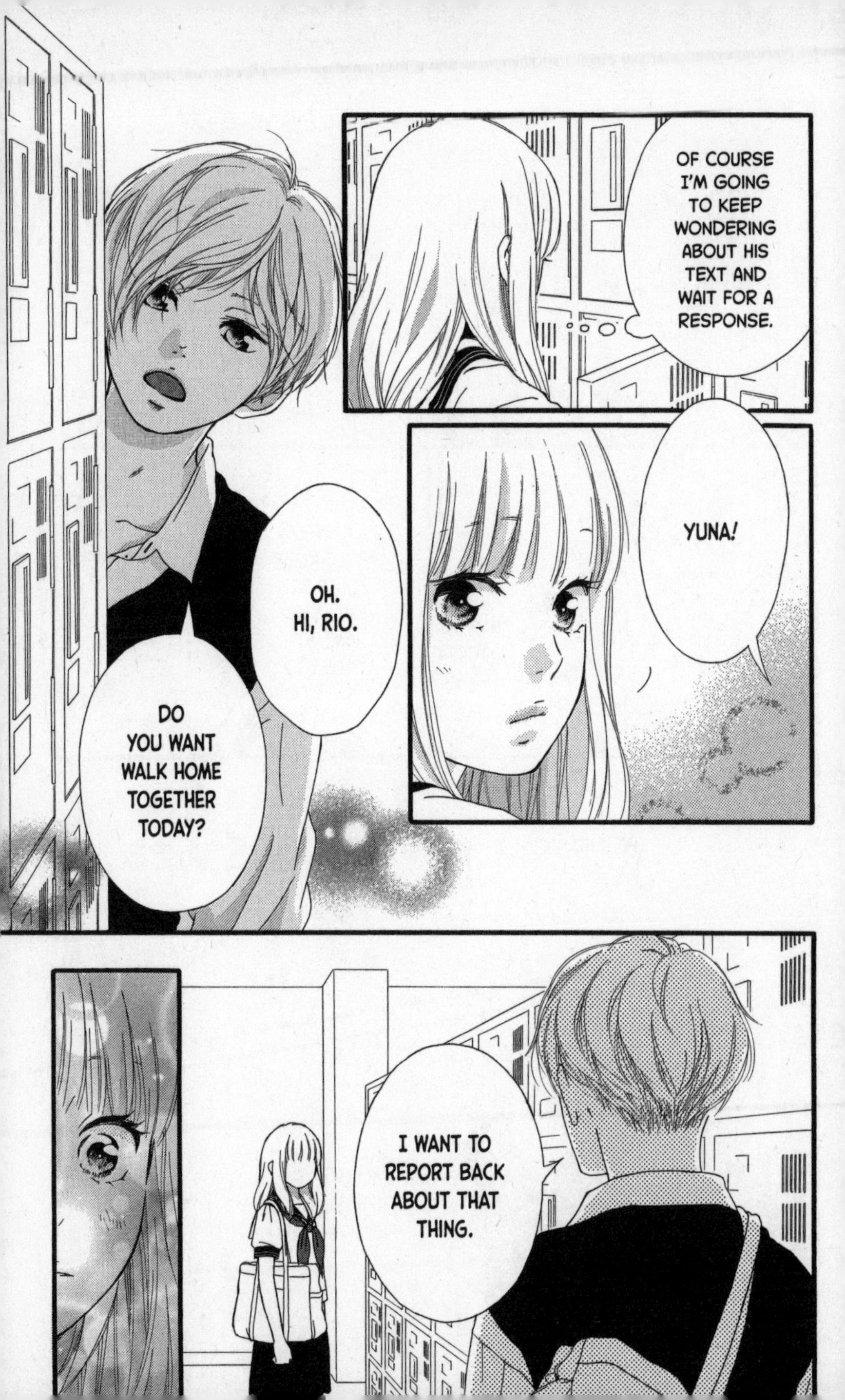
OF COURSE I'M GOING TO KEEP WONDERING ABOUT HIS TEXT AND WAIT FOR A RESPONSE.
YUNA!
OH. HI, RIO.
DO YOU WANT WALK HOME TOGETHER TODAY?
I WANT TO REPORT BACK ABOUT THAT THING.

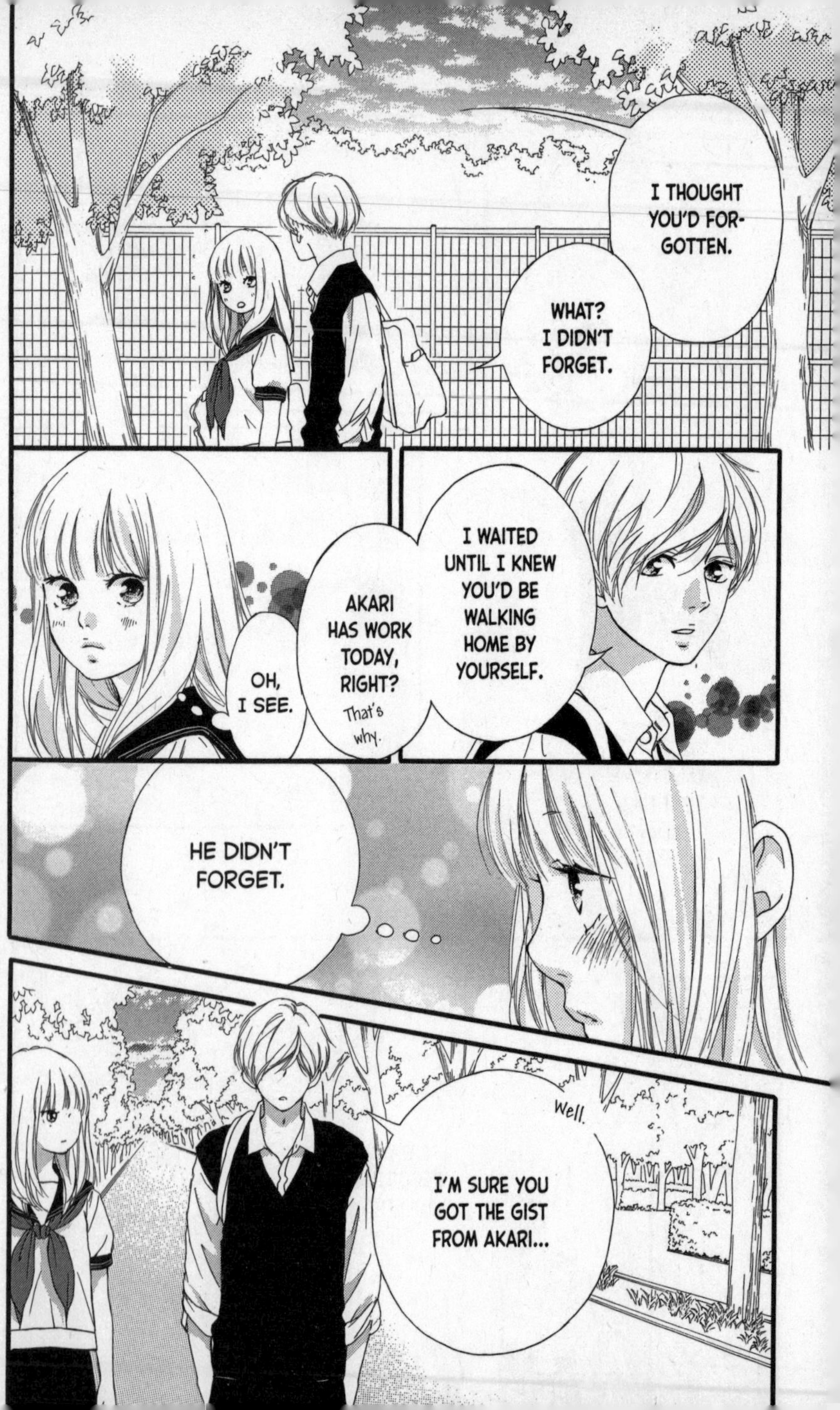
I THOUGHT YOU'D FOR-GOTTEN.
WHAT? I DIDN'T FORGET.
I WAITED UNTIL I KNEW YOU'D BE WALKING HOME BY YOURSELF.
AKARI HAS WORK TODAY, RIGHT? That's why.
OH, I SEE.
HE DIDN'T FORGET.
Well.
I'M SURE YOU GOT THE GIST FROM AKARI...

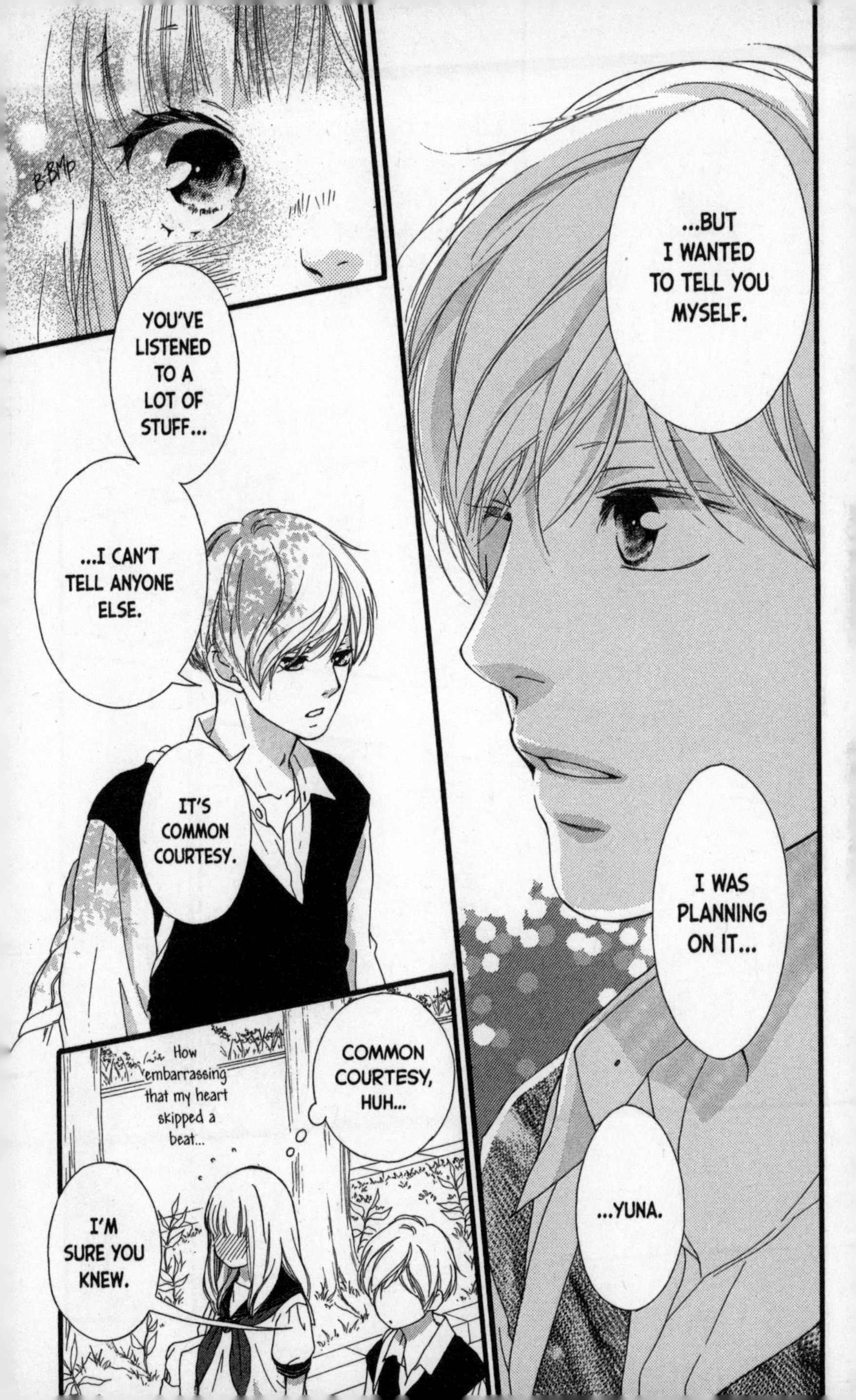
...BUT I WANTED TO TELL YOU MYSELF.
I WAS PLANNING ON IT...
...YUNA.
B-BMP
YOU'VE LISTENED TO A LOT OF STUFF...
...I CAN'T TELL ANYONE ELSE.
IT'S COMMON COURTESY.
COMMON COURTESY, HUH...
How embarrassing that my heart skipped a beat...
I'M SURE YOU KNEW.

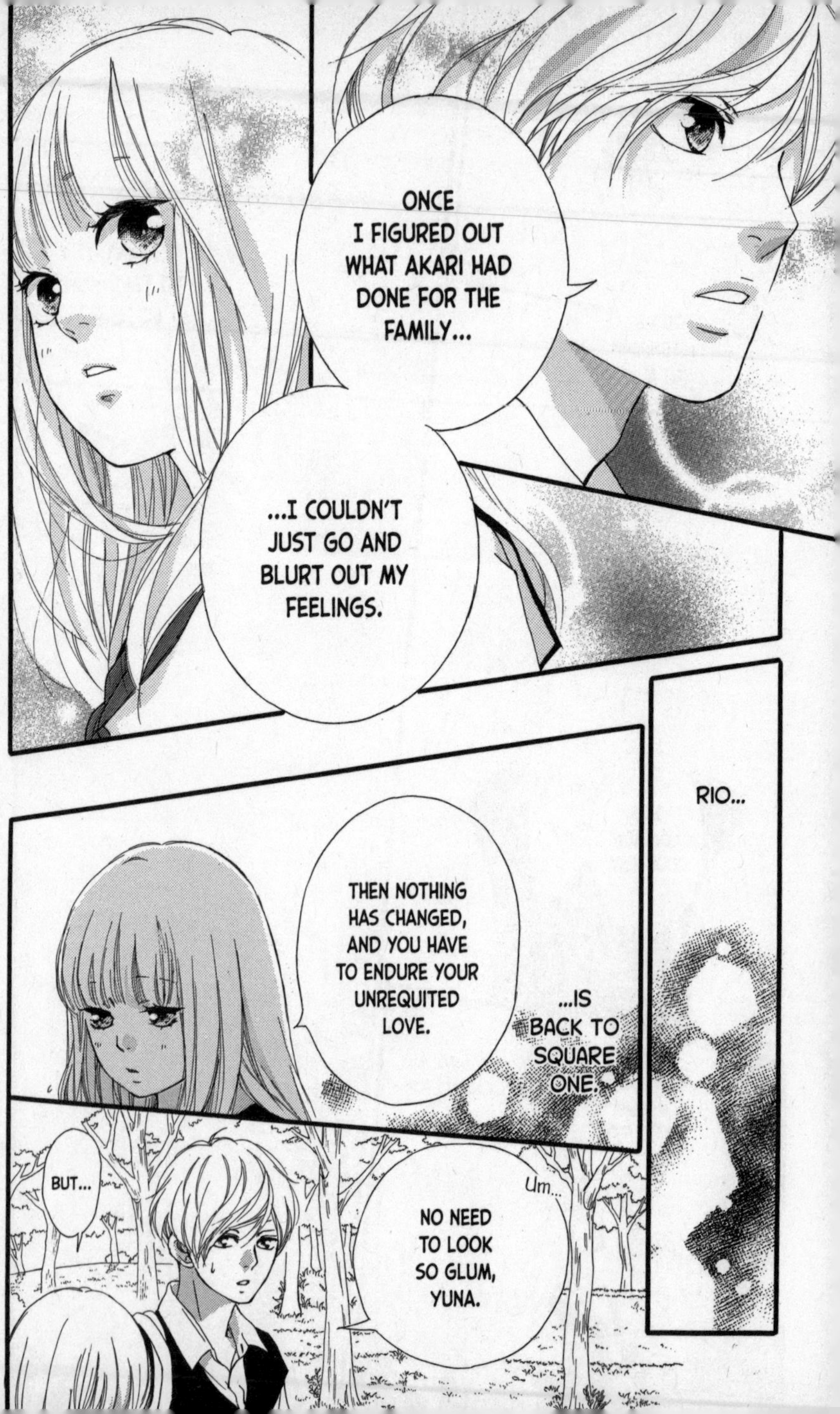
ONCE I FIGURED OUT WHAT AKARI HAD DONE FOR THE FAMILY...
...I COULDN'T JUST GO AND BLURT OUT MY FEELINGS.
RIO...
...IS BACK TO SQUARE ONE.
THEN NOTHING HAS CHANGED, AND YOU HAVE TO ENDURE YOUR UNREQUITED LOVE.
Um...
NO NEED TO LOOK SO GLUM, YUNA.
BUT...

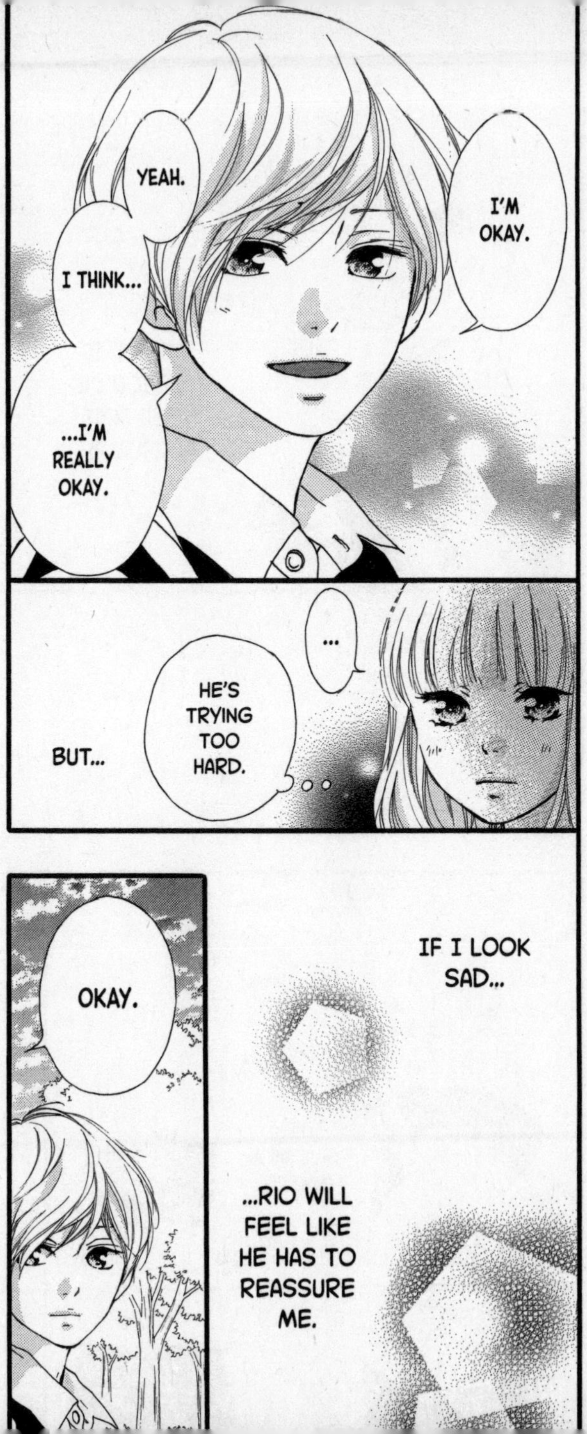
I'M OKAY.
YEAH.
I THINK...
...I'M REALLY OKAY.
...
HE'S TRYING TOO HARD.
BUT...
IF I LOOK SAD...
...RIO WILL FEEL LIKE HE HAS TO REASSURE ME.
OKAY.

I rarely check my mailbox, especially when I'm in the middle of a deadline. I don't leave the house very often, so the mail just accumulates. Even when I do go out, if I'm carrying a lot of things, I pretend I've forgotten the mailbox exists and just go inside. The other day I went out to check my mail for the first time in a while, and sure enough it was stuffed! Among the many flyers there was a notice for a fire safety equipment inspection that was to be carried out in several days' time. I was super-pumped because usually I don't get to the notice beforehand, and it turns into an "Oh, it's today! Thank goodness I'm awake." (If I'm not home, they come in with a spare key. And if I'm asleep, we both feel awkward. It's happened before...) It's a bit of a gamble every time, so I was very happy I found out early this time. This year I won!

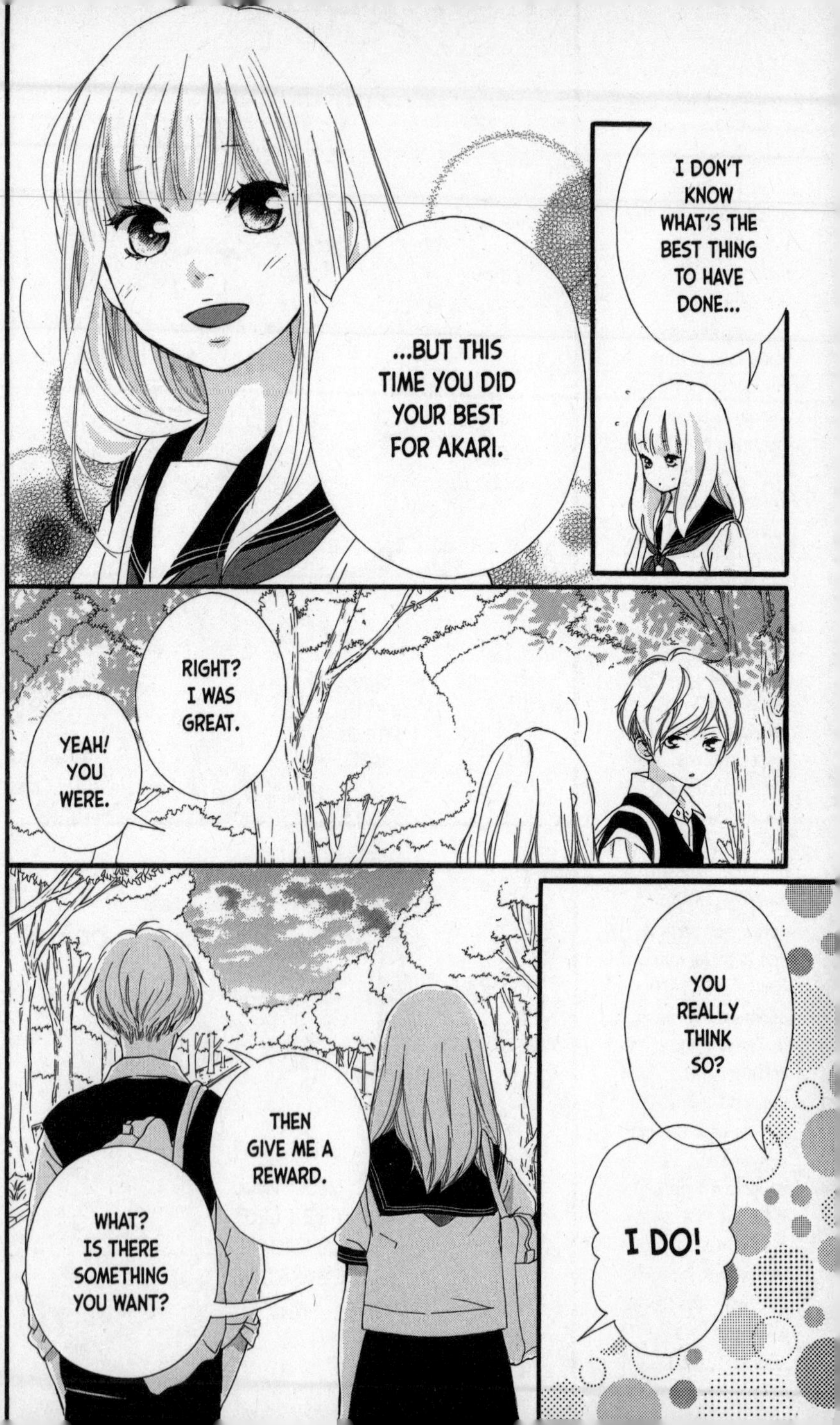
I DON'T KNOW WHAT'S THE BEST THING TO HAVE DONE...
...BUT THIS TIME YOU DID YOUR BEST FOR AKARI.
RIGHT? I WAS GREAT.
YEAH! YOU WERE.
YOU REALLY THINK SO?
I DO!
THEN GIVE ME A REWARD.
WHAT? IS THERE SOMETHING YOU WANT?

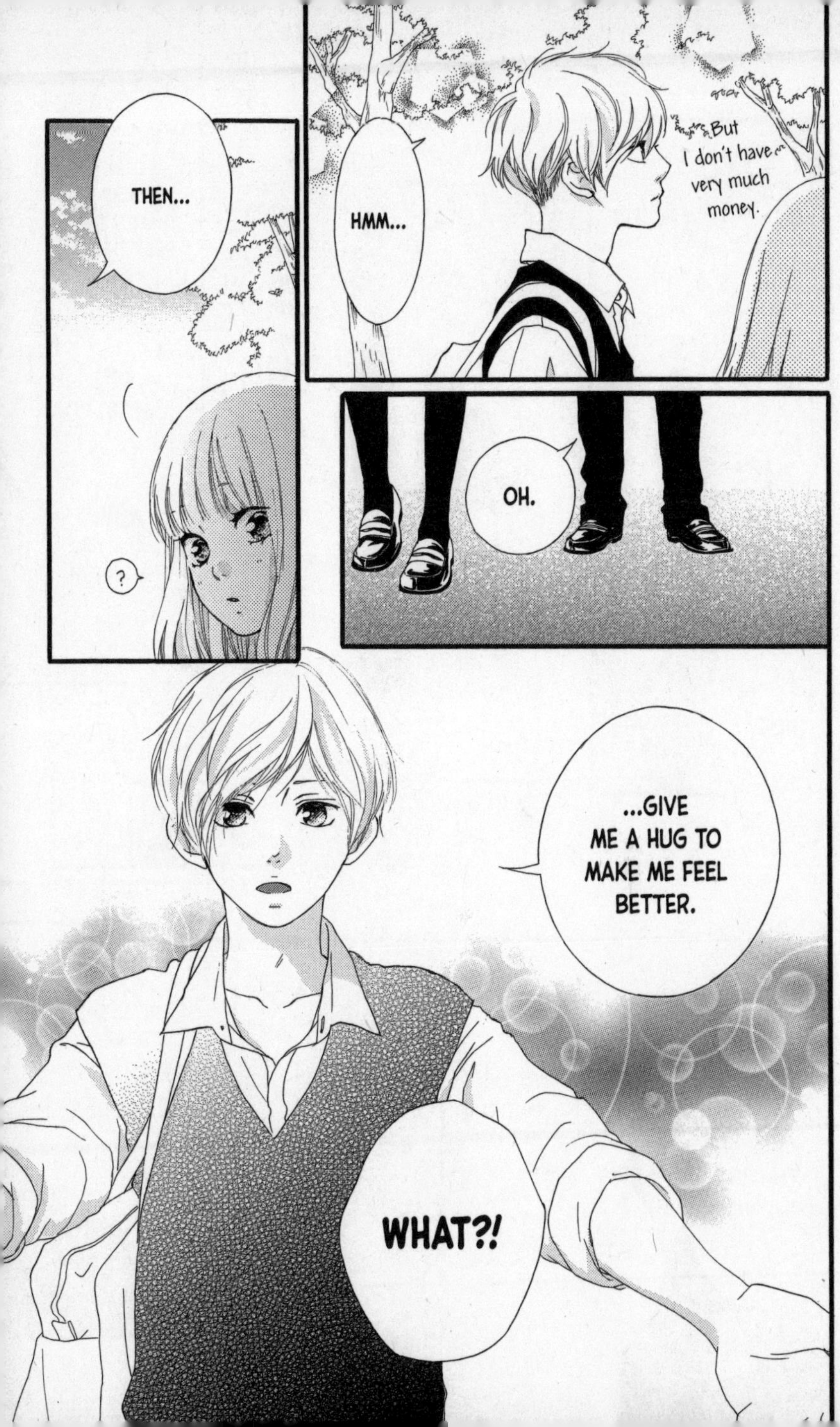
But I don't have very much money.
HMM...
OH.
THEN...
?
...GIVE ME A HUG TO MAKE ME FEEL BETTER.
WHAT?!

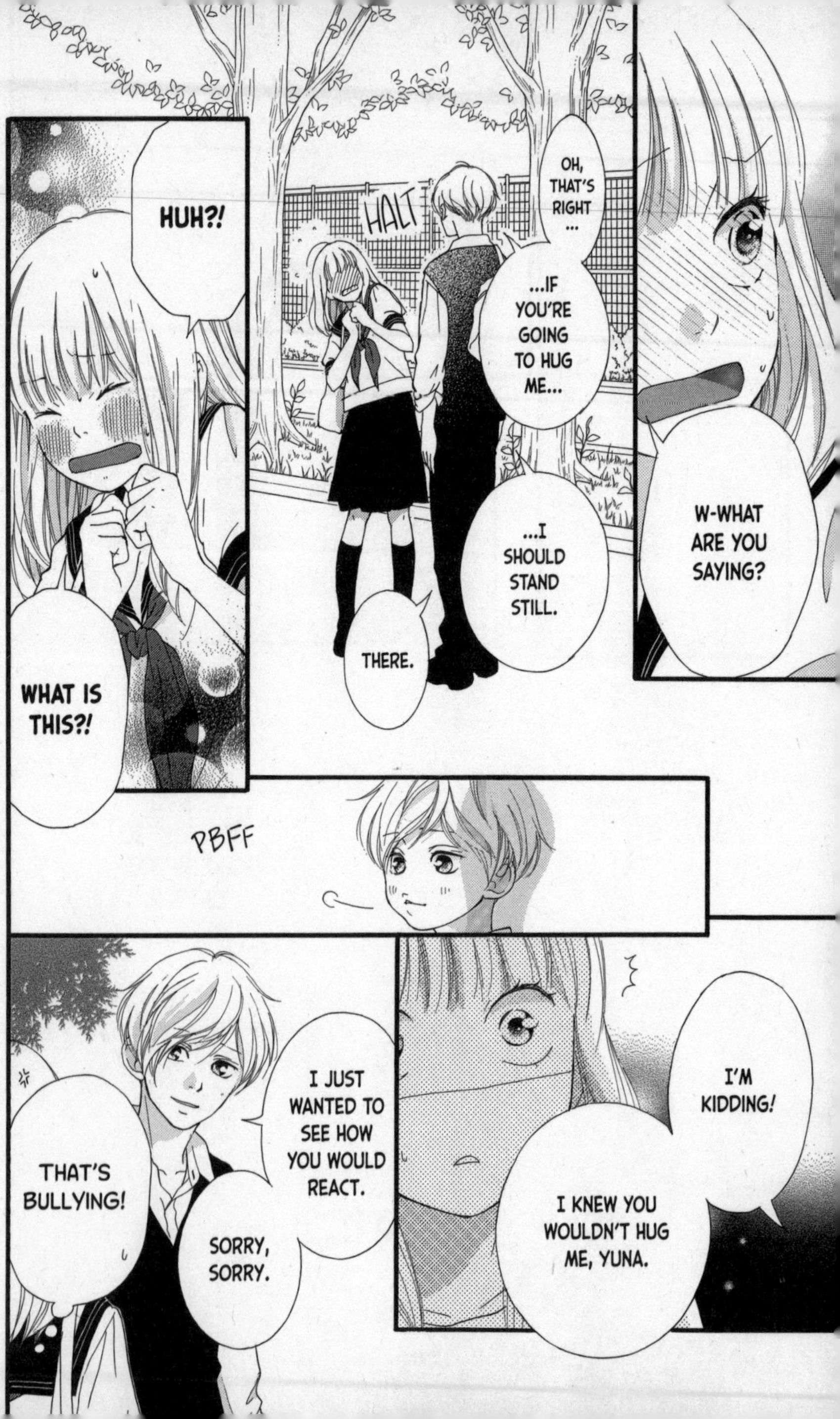
W-WHAT ARE YOU SAYING?
OH, THAT'S RIGHT ...
...IF YOU'RE GOING TO HUG ME...
...I SHOULD STAND STILL.
HALT
THERE.
HUH?!
WHAT IS THIS?!
PBFF
I'M KIDDING!
I KNEW YOU WOULDN'T HUG ME, YUNA.
I JUST WANTED TO SEE HOW YOU WOULD REACT.
SORRY, SORRY.
THAT'S BULLYING!

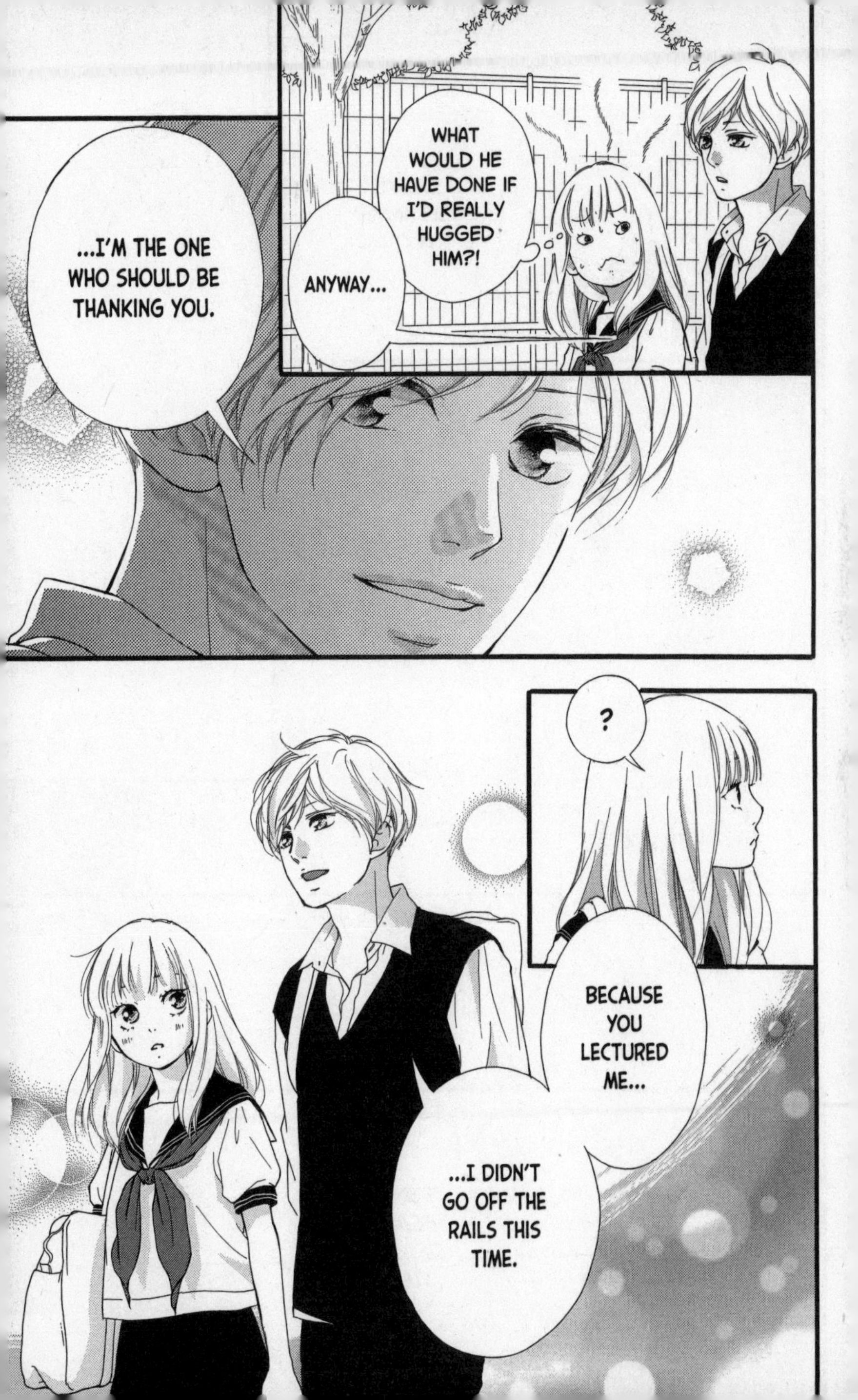
WHAT WOULD HE HAVE DONE IF I'D REALLY HUGGED HIM?!
ANYWAY...
...I'M THE ONE WHO SHOULD BE THANKING YOU.
?
BECAUSE YOU LECTURED ME...
...I DIDN'T GO OFF THE RAILS THIS TIME.

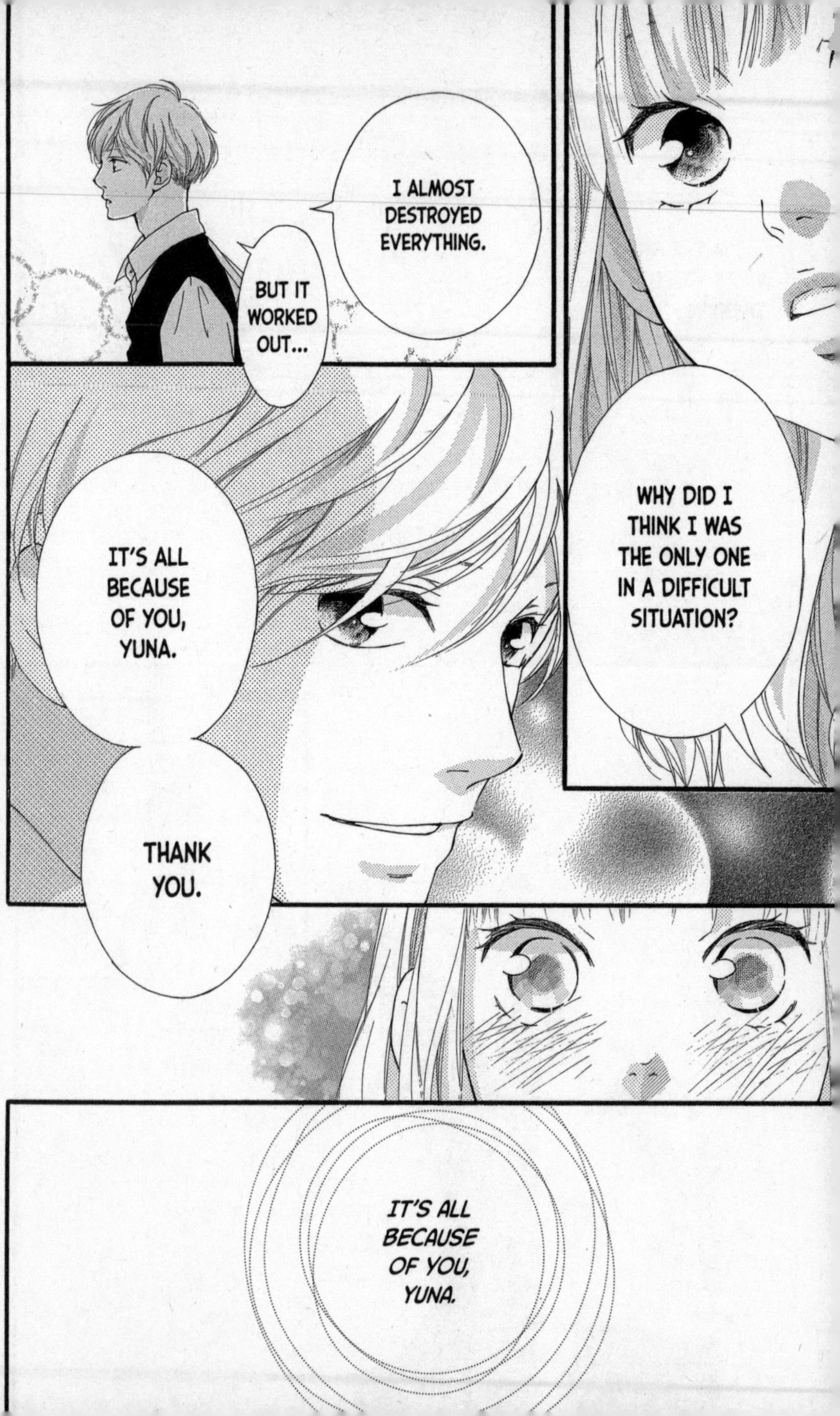
WHY DID I THINK I WAS THE ONLY ONE IN A DIFFICULT SITUATION?
I ALMOST DESTROYED EVERYTHING.
BUT IT WORKED OUT...
IT'S ALL BECAUSE OF YOU, YUNA.
THANK YOU.
IT'S ALL BECAUSE OF YOU, YUNA.

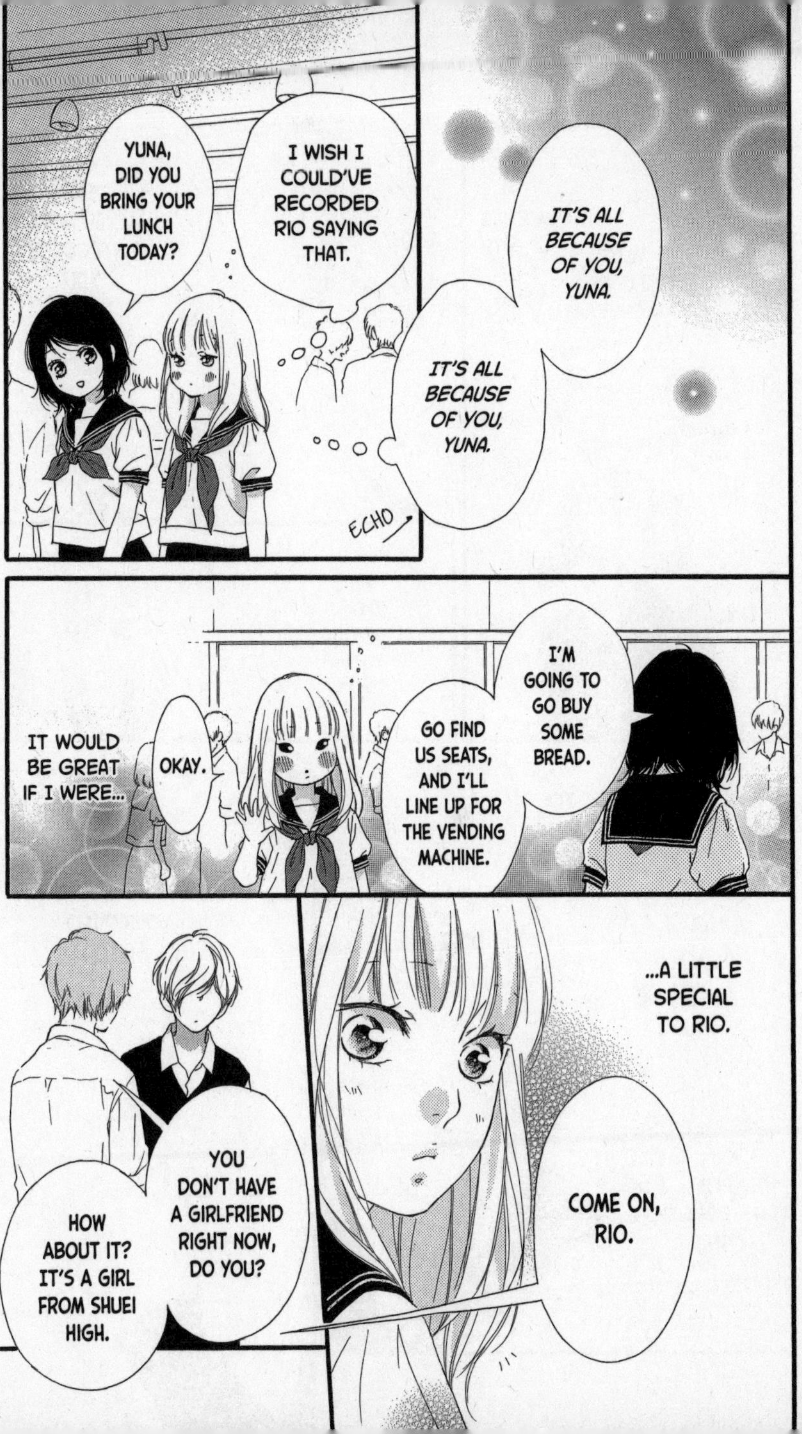
IT'S ALL BECAUSE OF YOU, YUNA.
IT'S ALL BECAUSE OF YOU, YUNA.
ECHO
I WISH I COULD'VE RECORDED RIO SAYING THAT.
YUNA, DID YOU BRING YOUR LUNCH TODAY?
I'M GOING TO GO BUY SOME BREAD.
GO FIND US SEATS, AND I'LL LINE UP FOR THE VENDING MACHINE.
OKAY.
IT WOULD BE GREAT IF I WERE...
...A LITTLE SPECIAL TO RIO.
COME ON, RIO.
YOU DON'T HAVE A GIRLFRIEND RIGHT NOW, DO YOU?
HOW ABOUT IT? IT'S A GIRL FROM SHUEI HIGH.

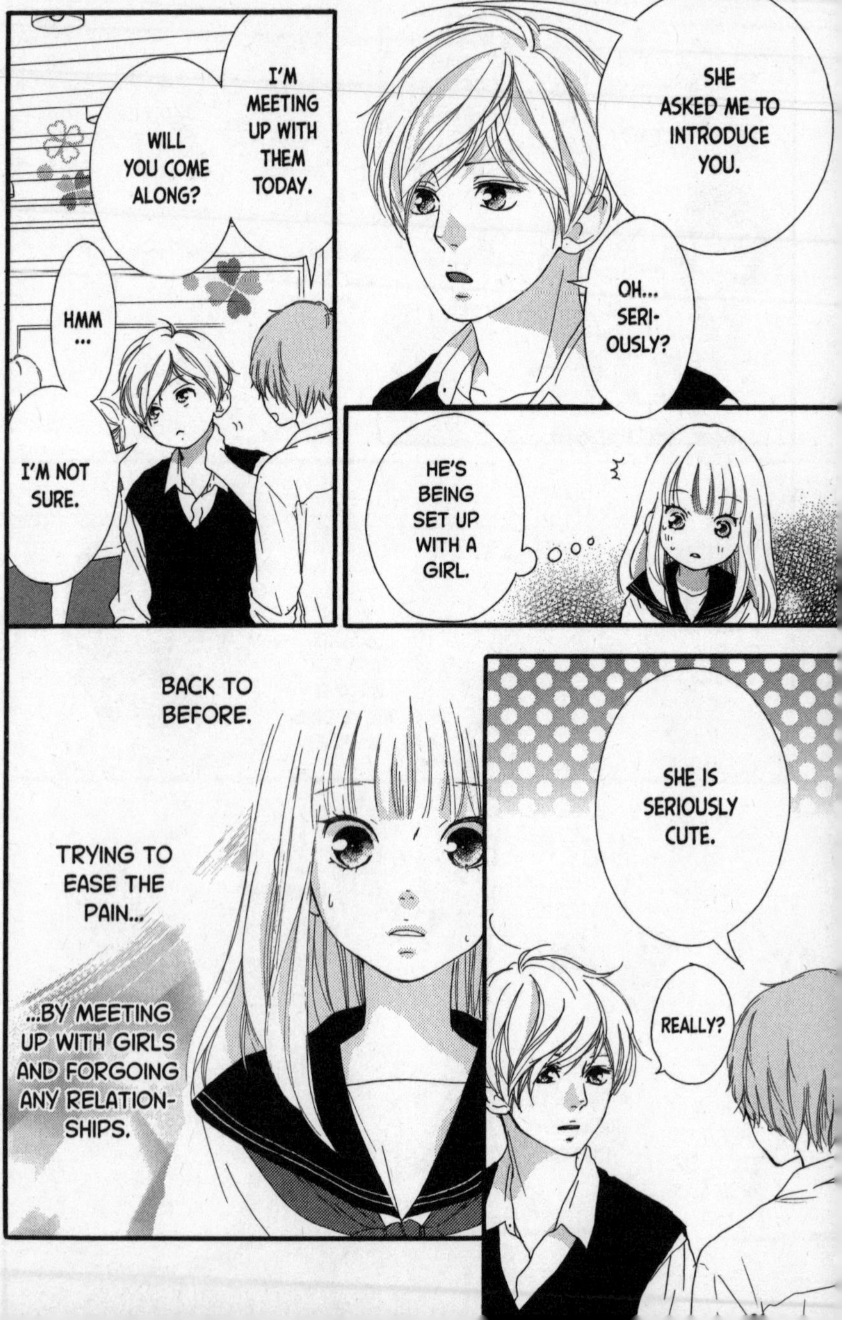
SHE ASKED ME TO INTRODUCE YOU.
OH... SERIOUSLY?
HE'S BEING SET UP WITH A GIRL.
I'M MEETING UP WITH THEM TODAY.
WILL YOU COME ALONG?
HMM...
I'M NOT SURE.
SHE IS SERIOUSLY CUTE.
REALLY?
BACK TO BEFORE.
TRYING TO EASE THE PAIN...
...BY MEETING UP WITH GIRLS AND FORGOING ANY RELATION-SHIPS.

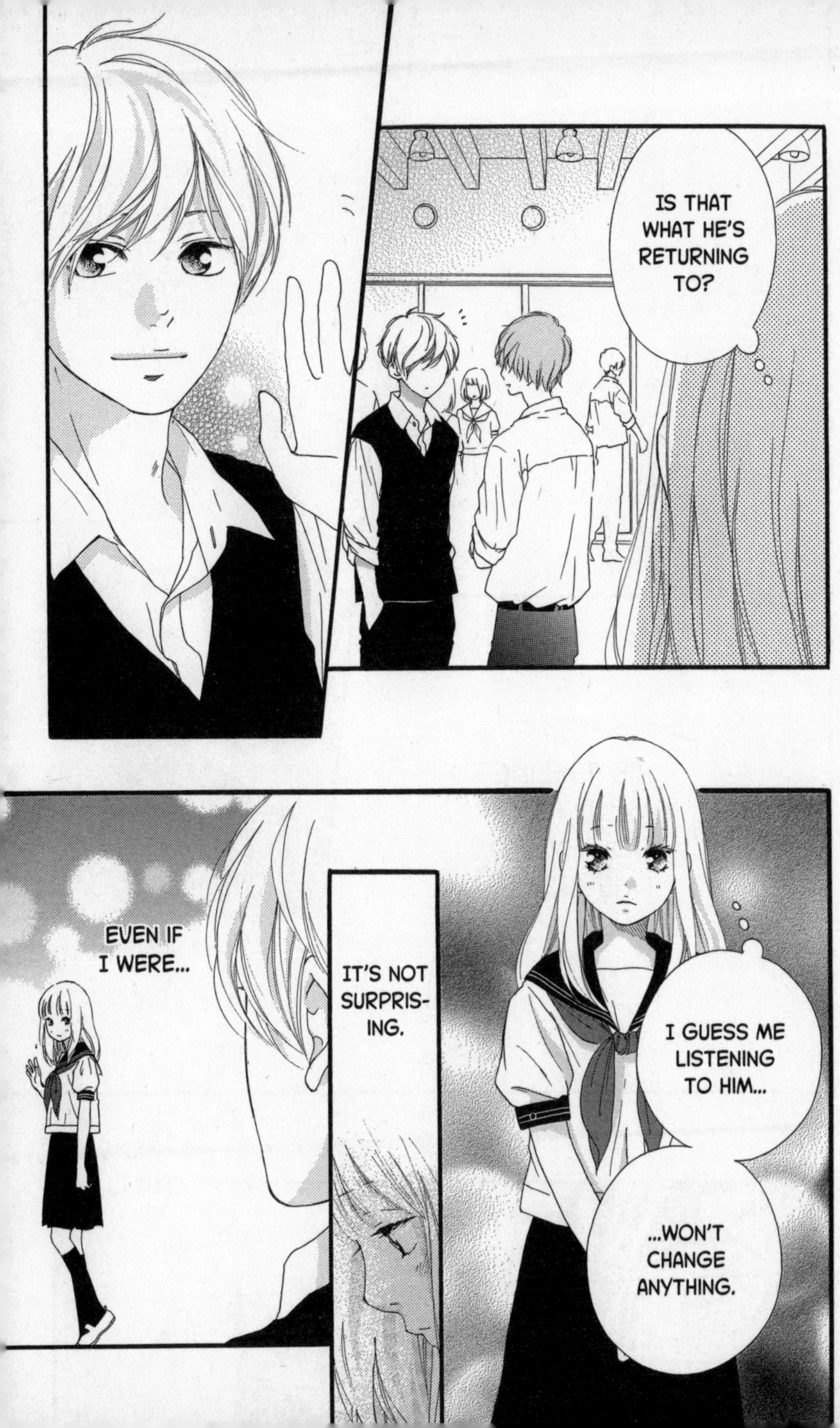
IS THAT WHAT HE'S RETURNING TO?
I GUESS ME LISTENING TO HIM...
...WON'T CHANGE ANYTHING.
IT'S NOT SURPRIS-ING.
EVEN IF I WERE...

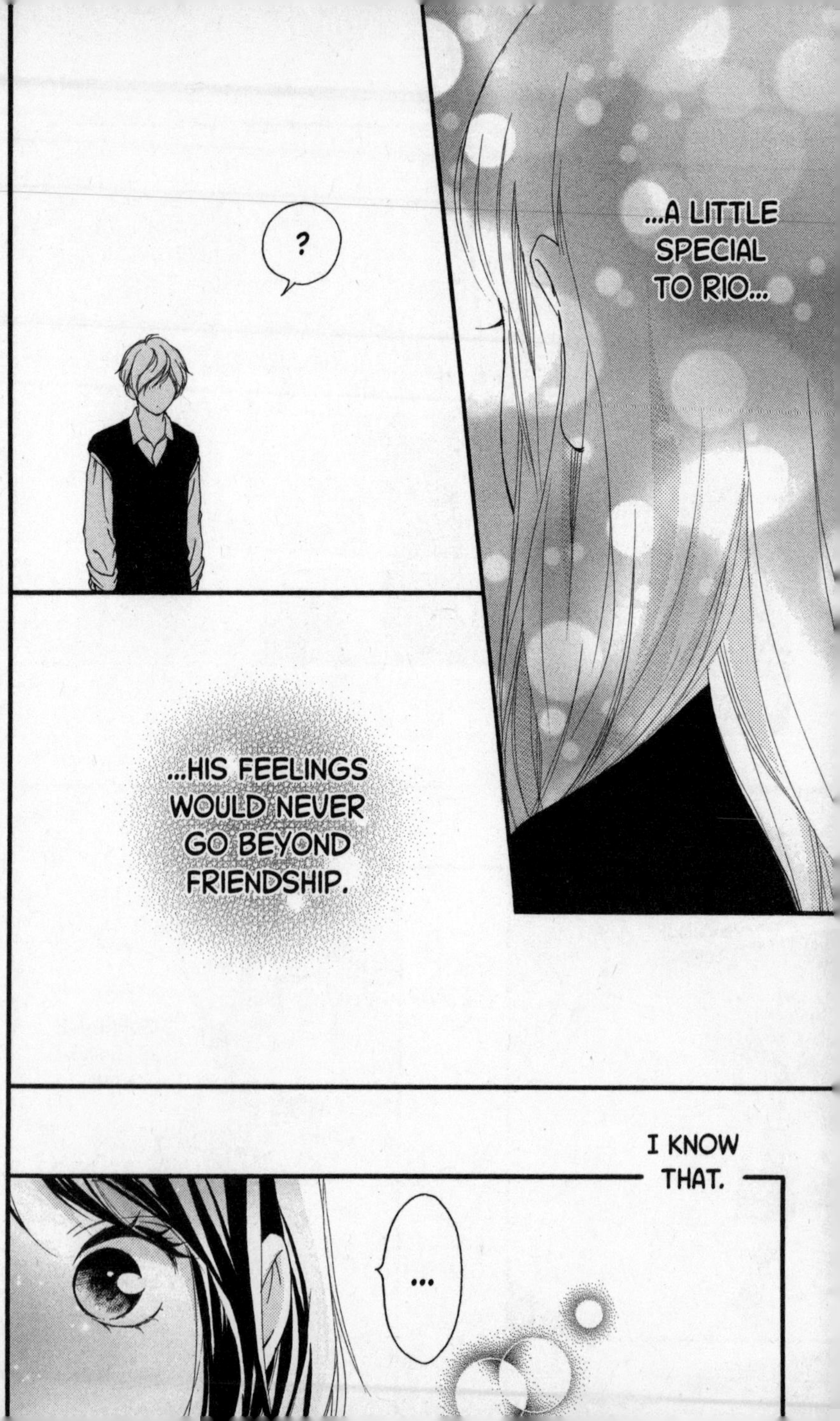
...A LITTLE SPECIAL TO RIO...
?
...HIS FEELINGS WOULD NEVER GO BEYOND FRIENDSHIP.
I KNOW THAT.
...

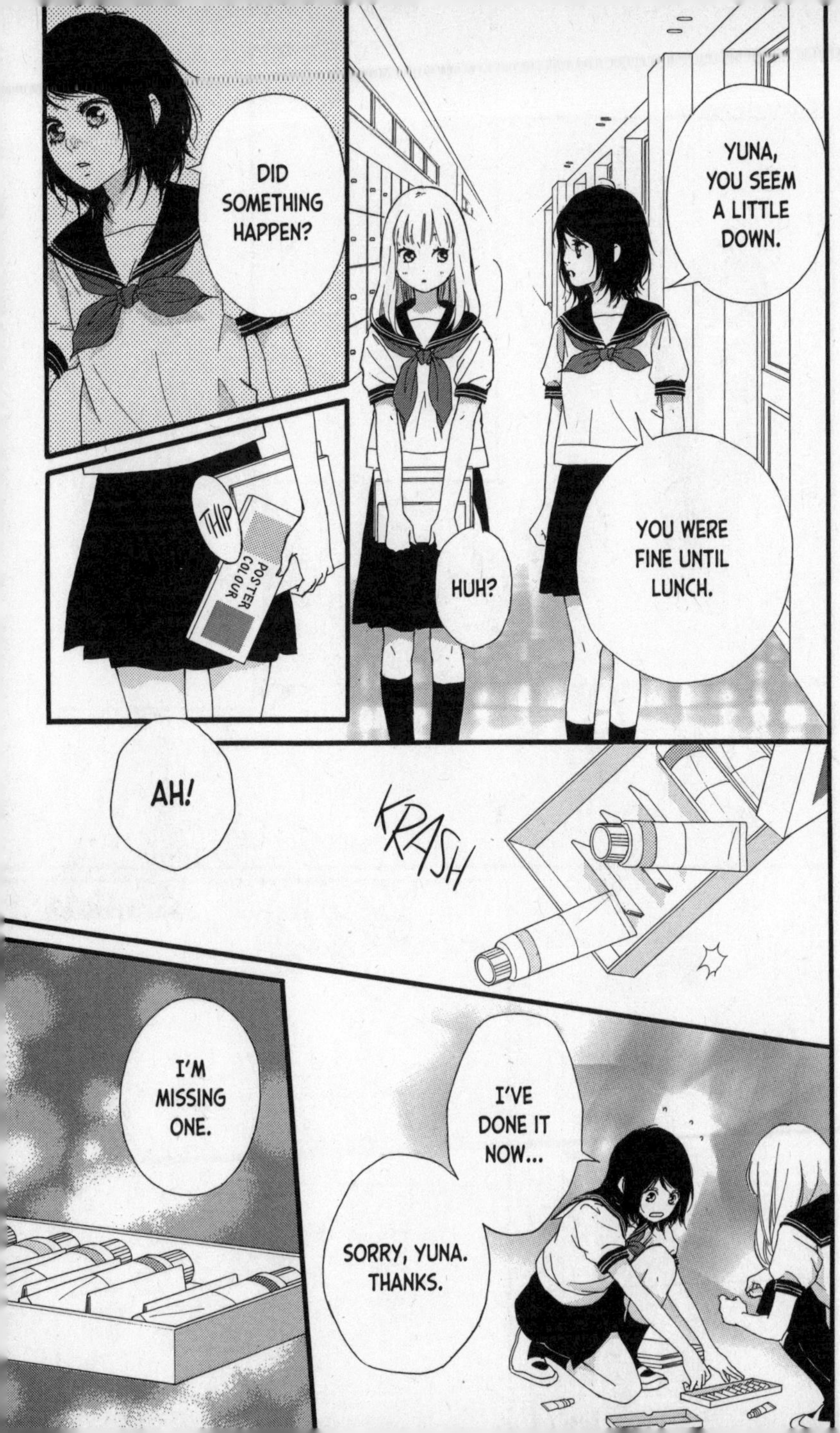
YUNA, YOU SEEM A LITTLE DOWN.
YOU WERE FINE UNTIL LUNCH.
HUH?
DID SOMETHING HAPPEN?
THIP
POSTER COLOUR
KRASH
AH!
I'VE DONE IT NOW...
SORRY, YUNA. THANKS.
I'M MISSING ONE.

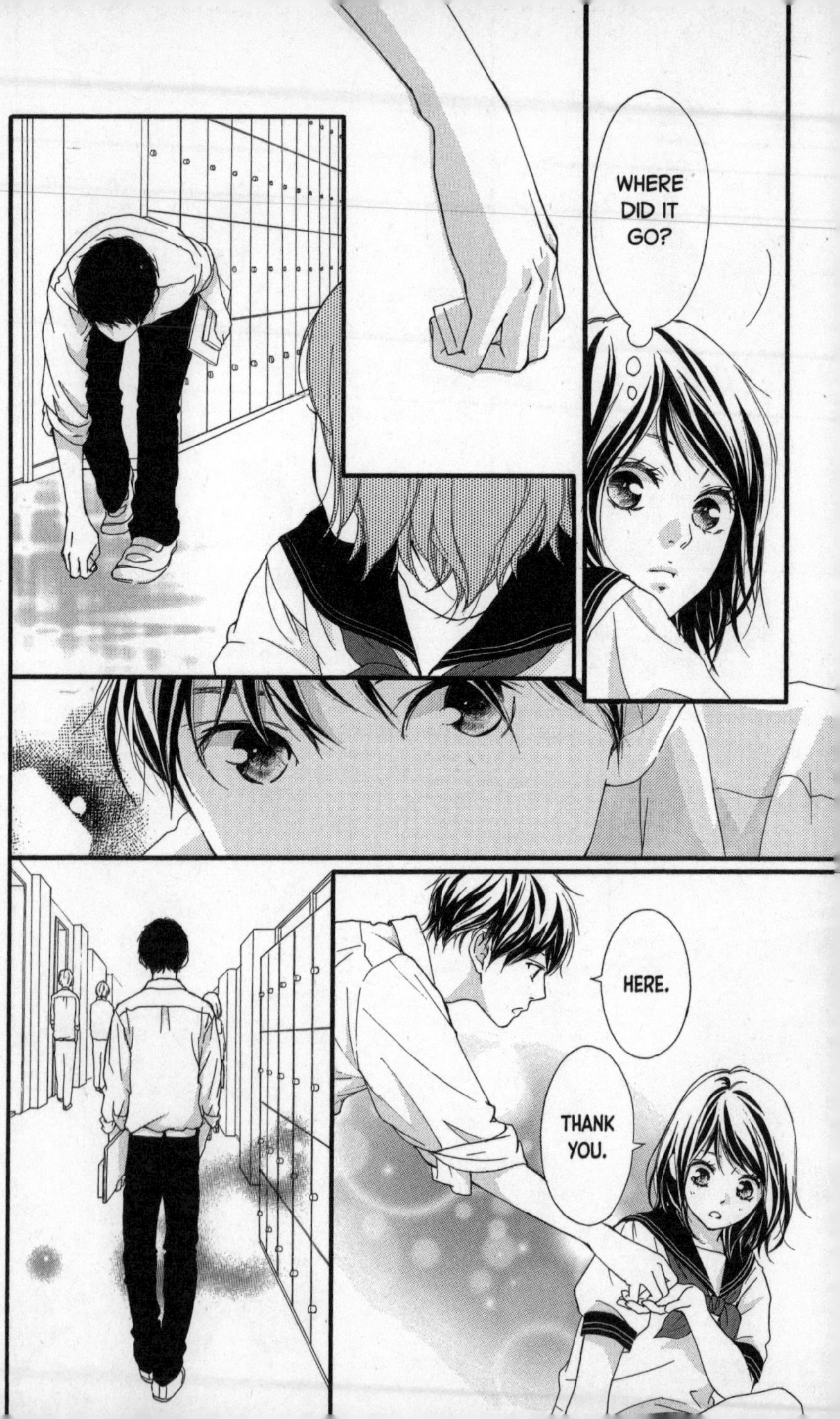
WHERE DID IT GO?
HERE.
THANK YOU.

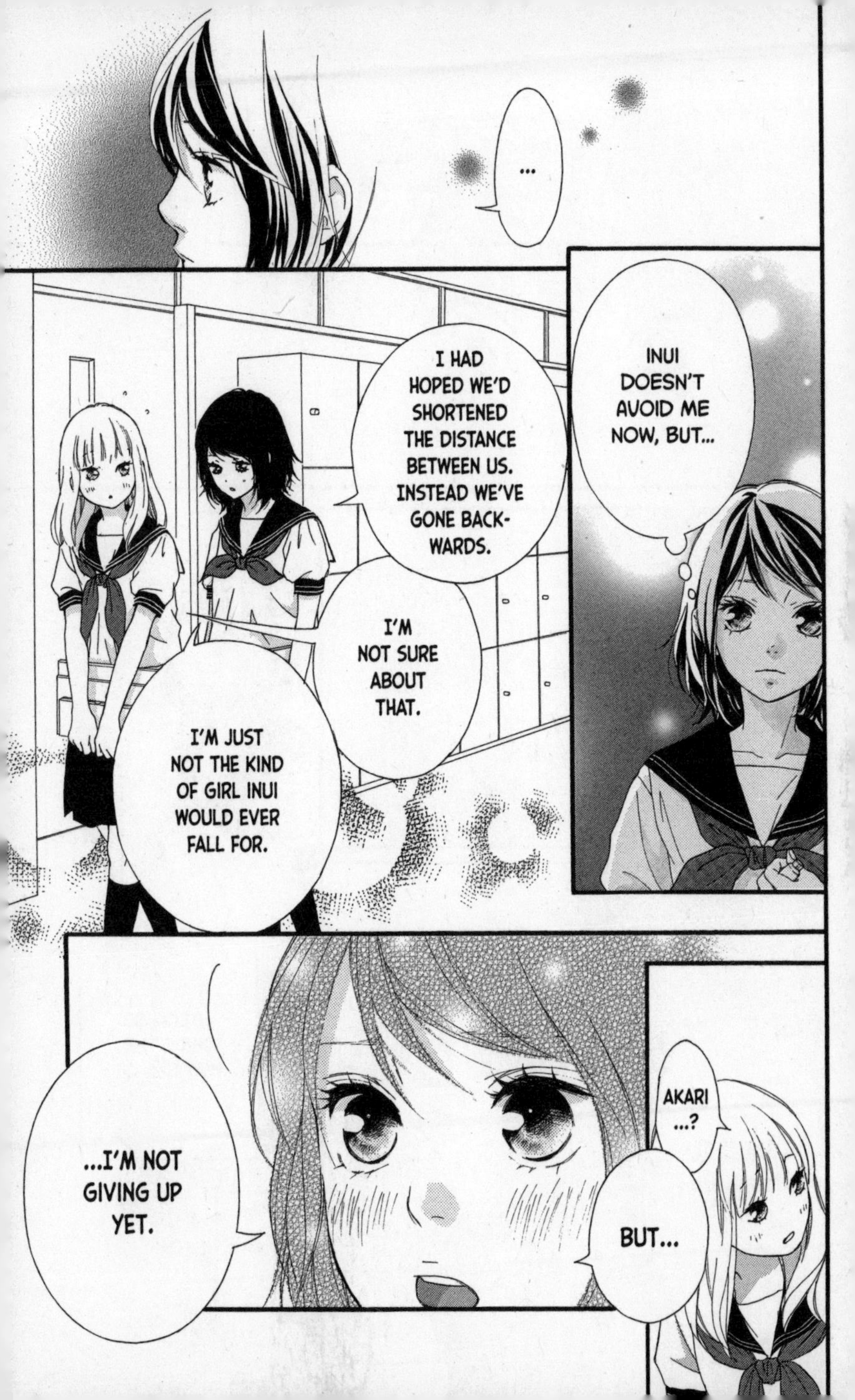
...
INUI DOESN'T AVOID ME NOW, BUT...
I HAD HOPED WE'D SHORTENED THE DISTANCE BETWEEN US. INSTEAD WE'VE GONE BACK-WARDS.
I'M NOT SURE ABOUT THAT.
I'M JUST NOT THE KIND OF GIRL INUI WOULD EVER FALL FOR.
AKARI ...?
BUT...
...I'M NOT GIVING UP YET.

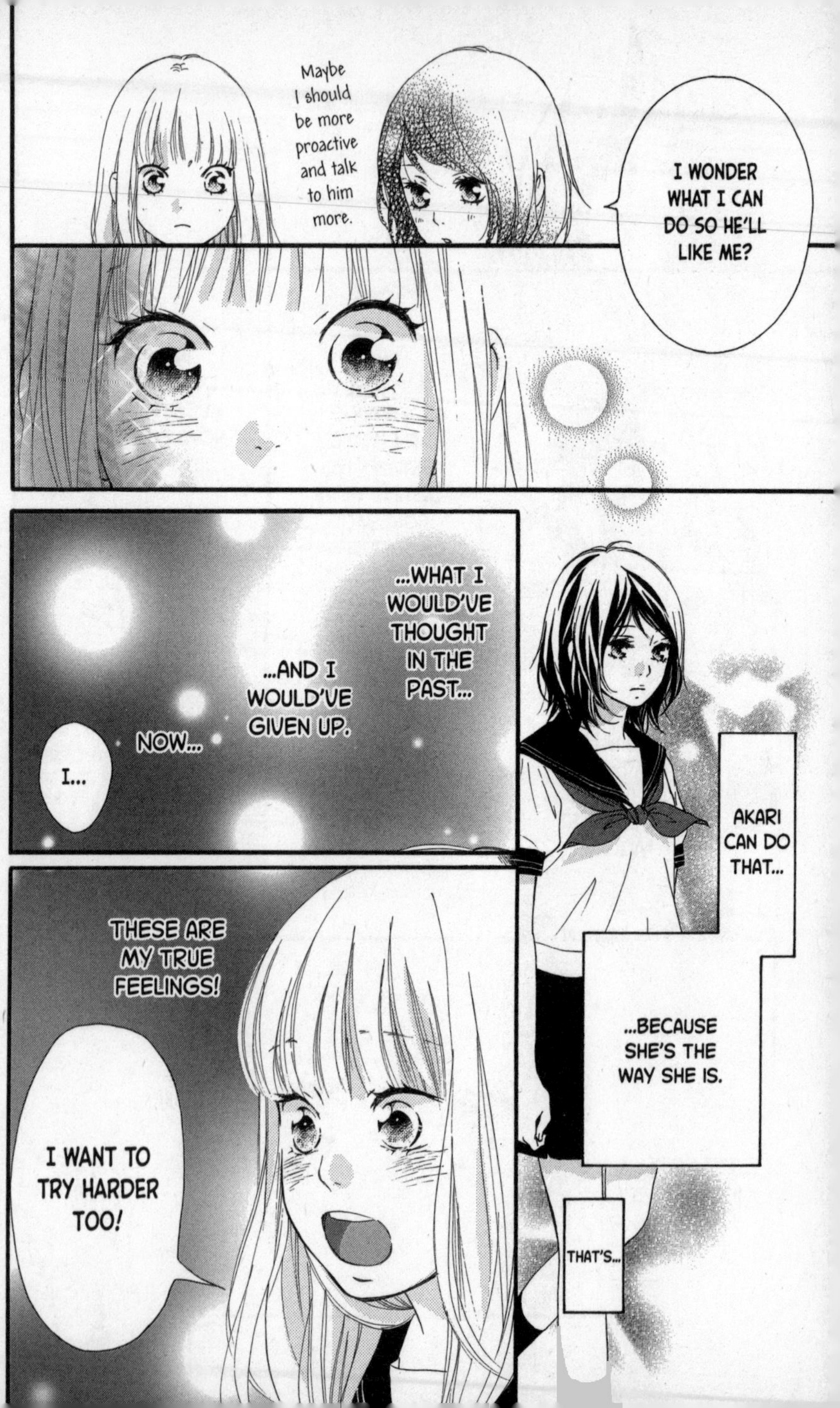
I WONDER WHAT I CAN DO SO HE'LL LIKE ME?
Maybe I should be more proactive and talk to him more.
AKARI CAN DO THAT...
...BECAUSE SHE'S THE WAY SHE IS.
THAT'S...
...WHAT I WOULD'VE THOUGHT IN THE PAST...
...AND I WOULD'VE GIVEN UP.
NOW...
I...
THESE ARE MY TRUE FEELINGS!
I WANT TO TRY HARDER TOO!

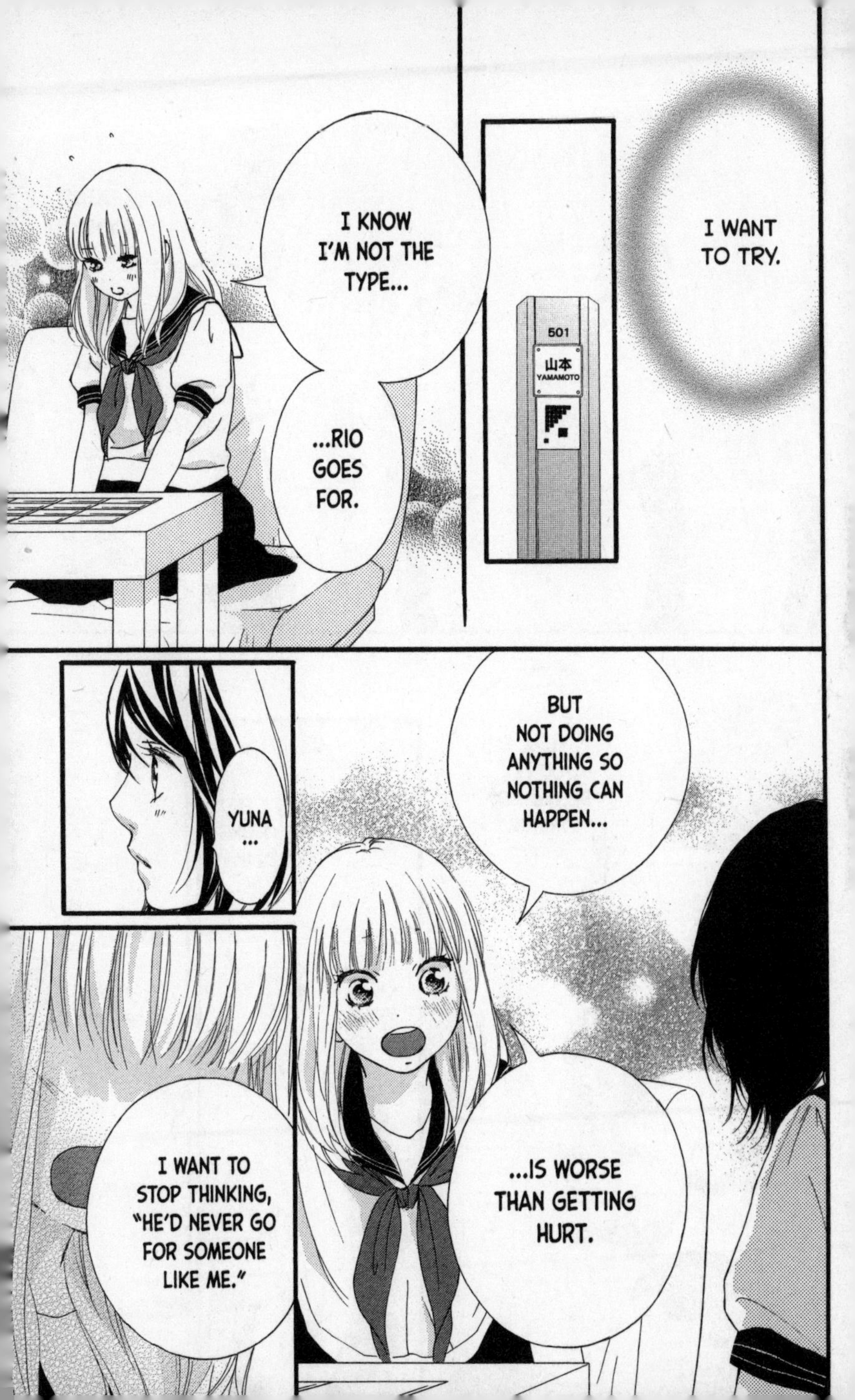
I WANT TO TRY.
501
山本
YAMAMOTO
I KNOW I'M NOT THE TYPE...
...RIO GOES FOR.
BUT NOT DOING ANYTHING SO NOTHING CAN HAPPEN...
...IS WORSE THAN GETTING HURT.
YUNA...
I WANT TO STOP THINKING, "HE'D NEVER GO FOR SOMEONE LIKE ME."

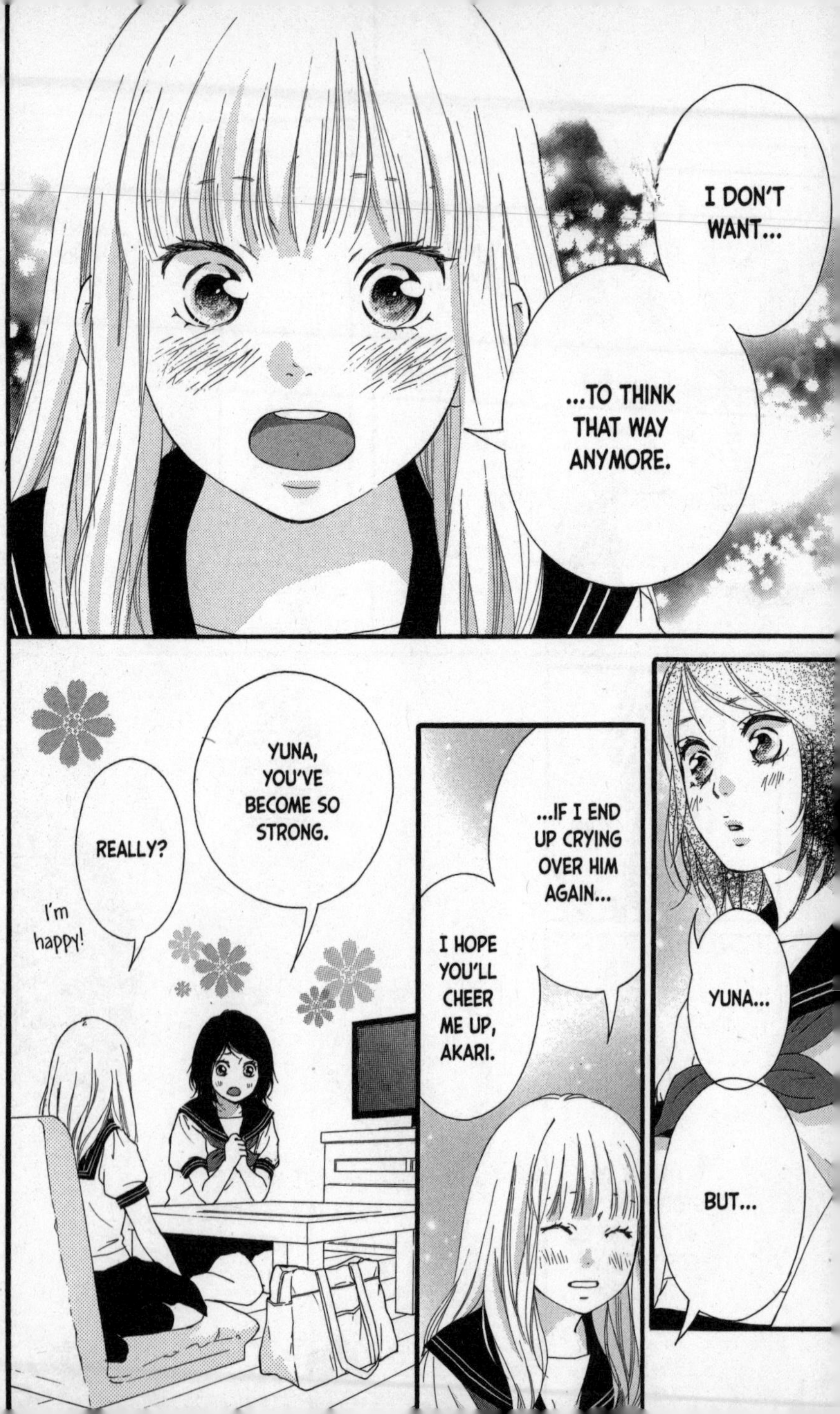
I DON'T WANT...
...TO THINK THAT WAY ANYMORE.
YUNA...
BUT...
...IF I END UP CRYING OVER HIM AGAIN...
I HOPE YOU'LL CHEER ME UP, AKARI.
YUNA, YOU'VE BECOME SO STRONG.
REALLY?
I'm happy!

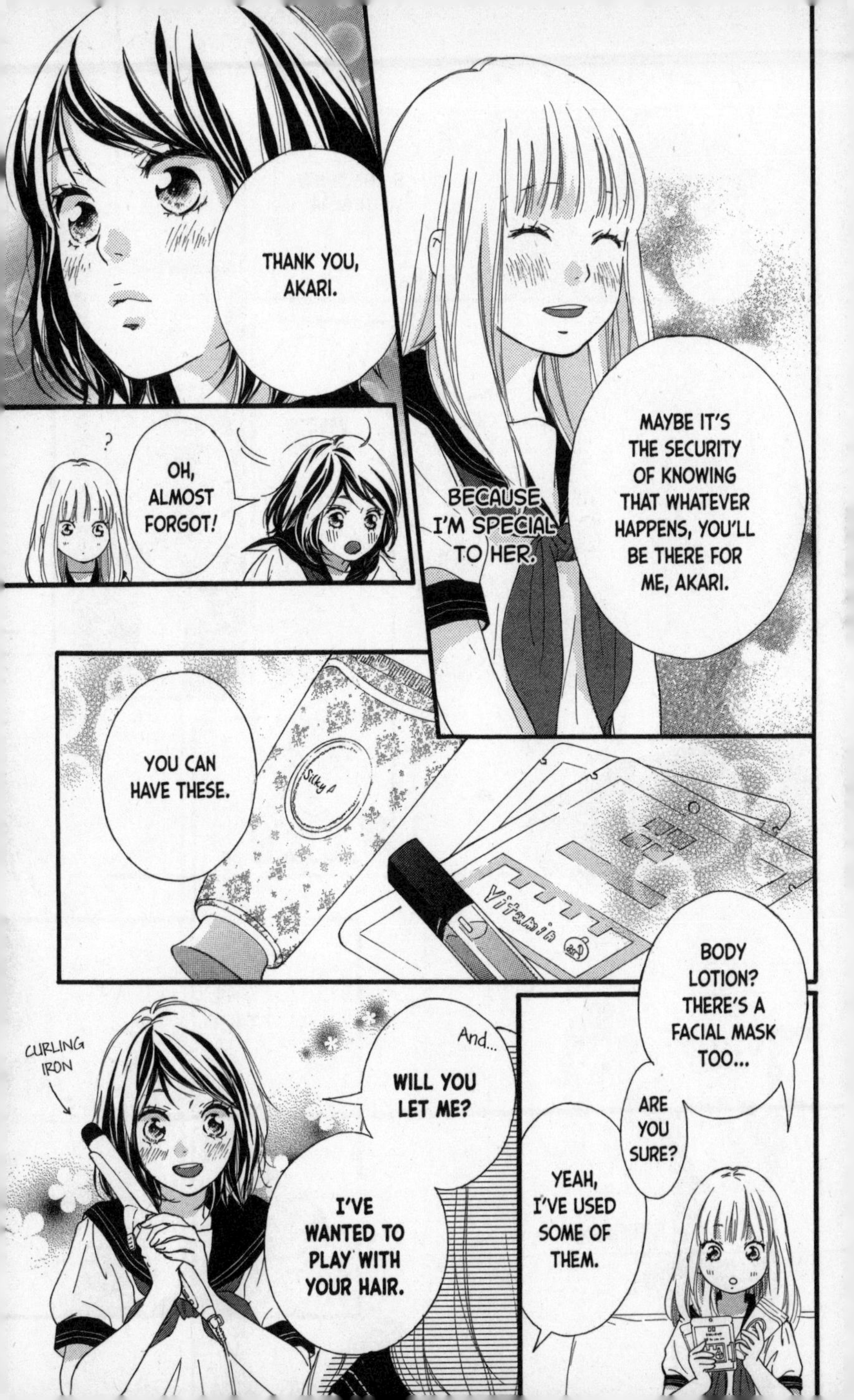
MAYBE IT'S THE SECURITY OF KNOWING THAT WHATEVER HAPPENS, YOU'LL BE THERE FOR ME, AKARI.
BECAUSE I'M SPECIAL TO HER.
THANK YOU, AKARI.
?
OH, ALMOST FORGOT!
YOU CAN HAVE THESE.
Silky A
Vitamin
BODY LOTION? THERE'S A FACIAL MASK TOO...
ARE YOU SURE?
YEAH, I'VE USED SOME OF THEM.
And...
WILL YOU LET ME?
I'VE WANTED TO PLAY WITH YOUR HAIR.
CURLING IRON

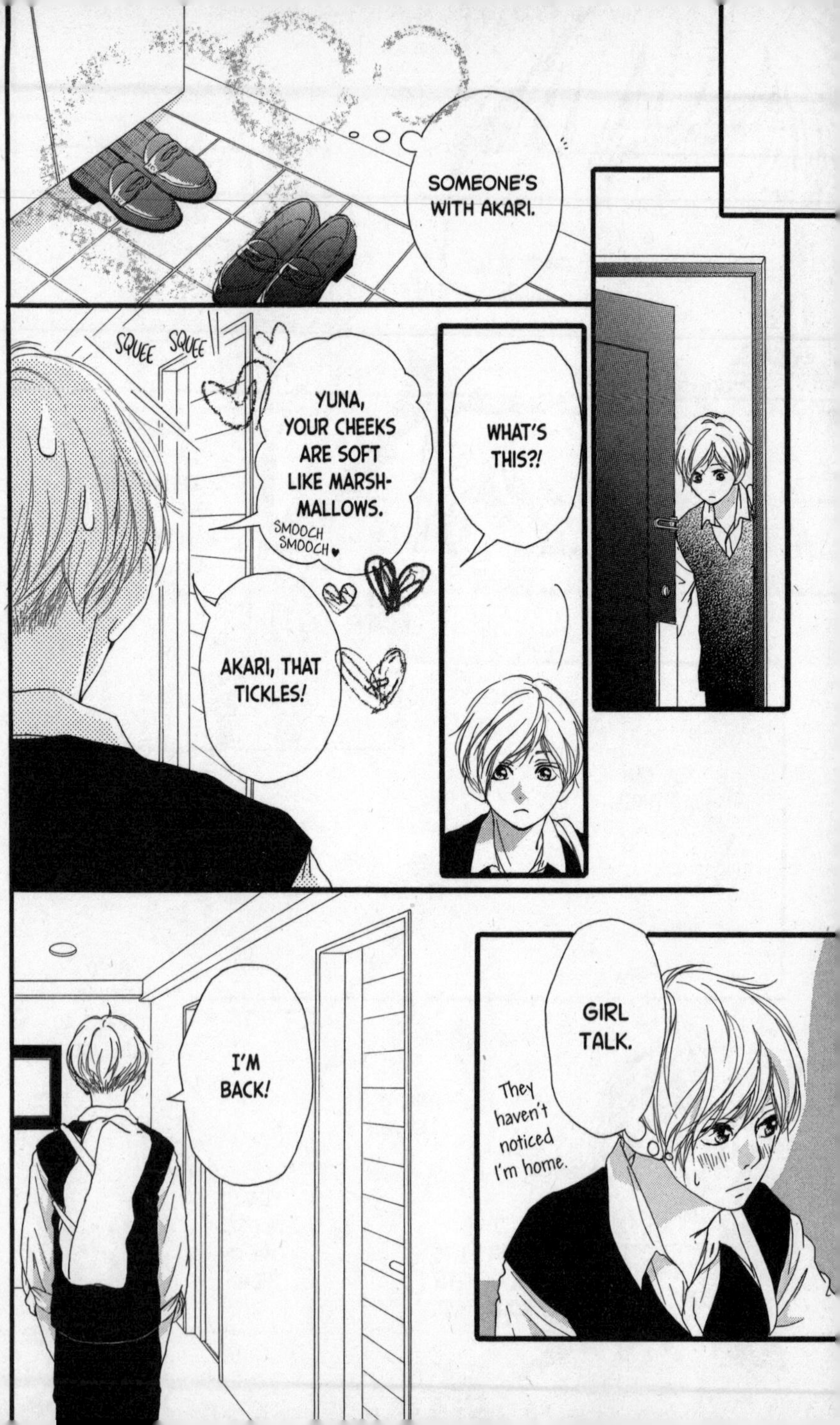
SOMEONE'S WITH AKARI.
WHAT'S THIS?!
SQUEE SQUEE
YUNA, YOUR CHEEKS ARE SOFT LIKE MARSH-MALLOWS.
SMOOCH SMOOCH ♥
AKARI, THAT TICKLES!
GIRL TALK.
They haven't noticed I'm home.
I'M BACK!

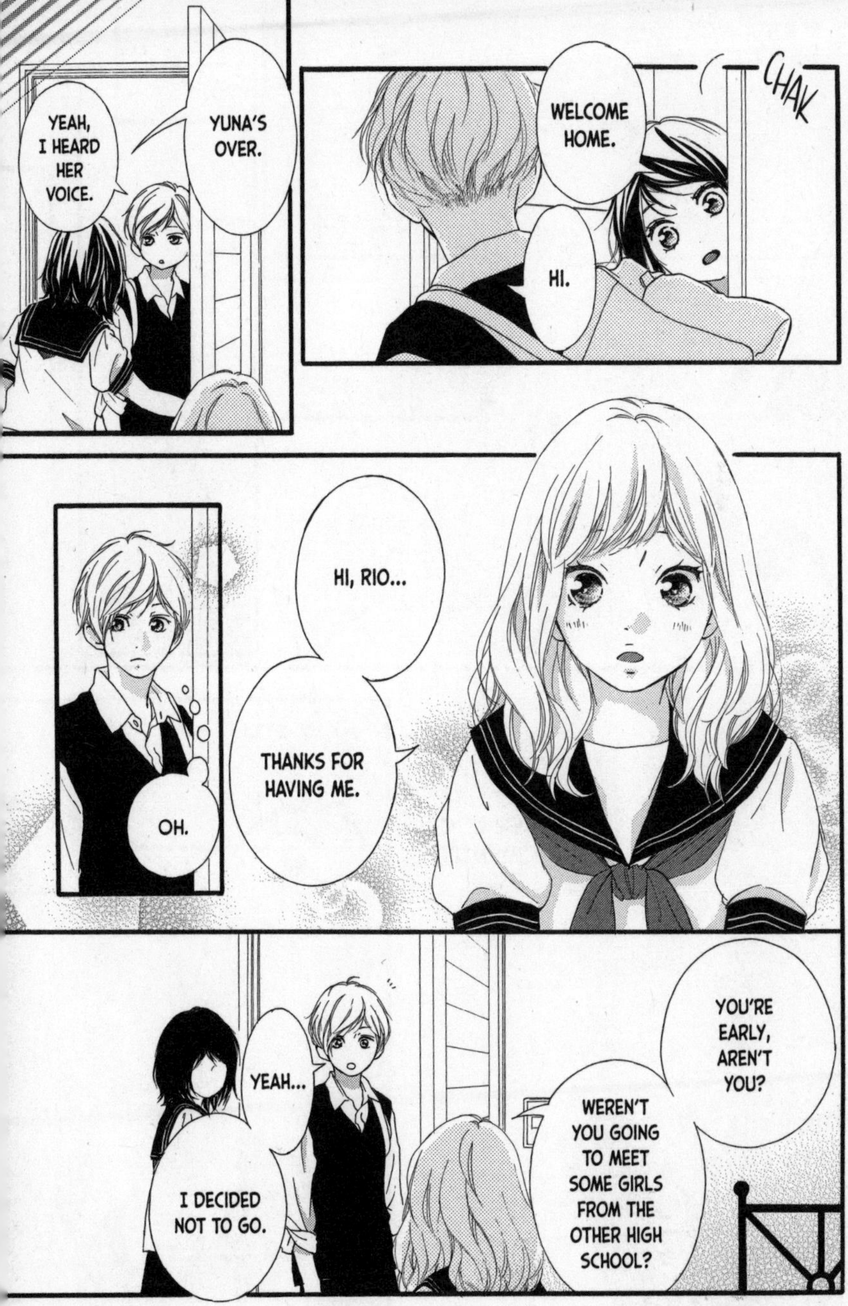
CHAK
WELCOME HOME.
HI.
YUNA'S OVER.
YEAH, I HEARD HER VOICE.
HI, RIO...
THANKS FOR HAVING ME.
OH.
YOU'RE EARLY, AREN'T YOU?
WEREN'T YOU GOING TO MEET SOME GIRLS FROM THE OTHER HIGH SCHOOL?
YEAH...
I DECIDED NOT TO GO.

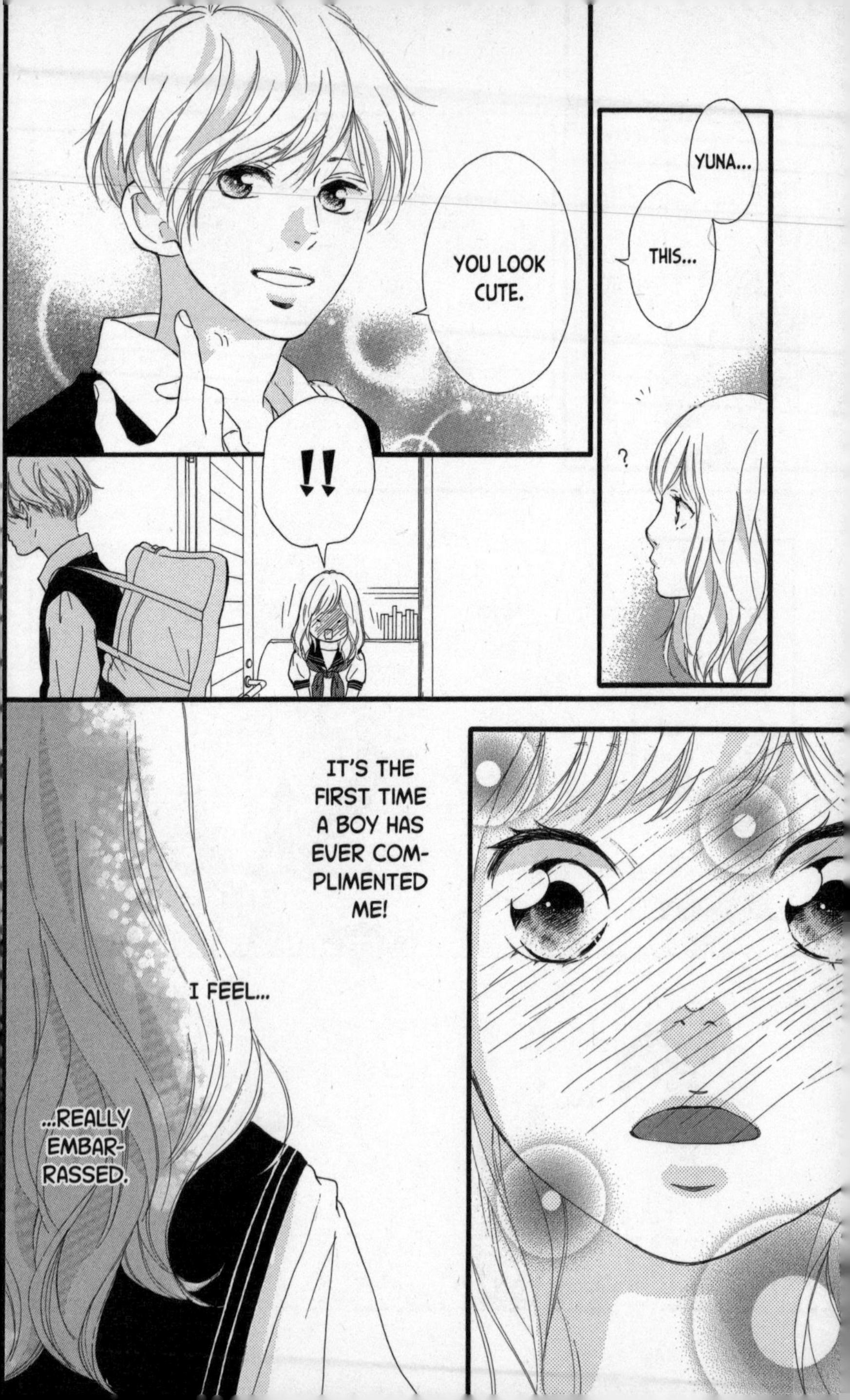

YUNA...
THIS...
?
YOU LOOK CUTE.
!!
IT'S THE FIRST TIME A BOY HAS EVER COM-PLIMENTED ME!
I FEEL...
...REALLY EMBAR-RASSED.

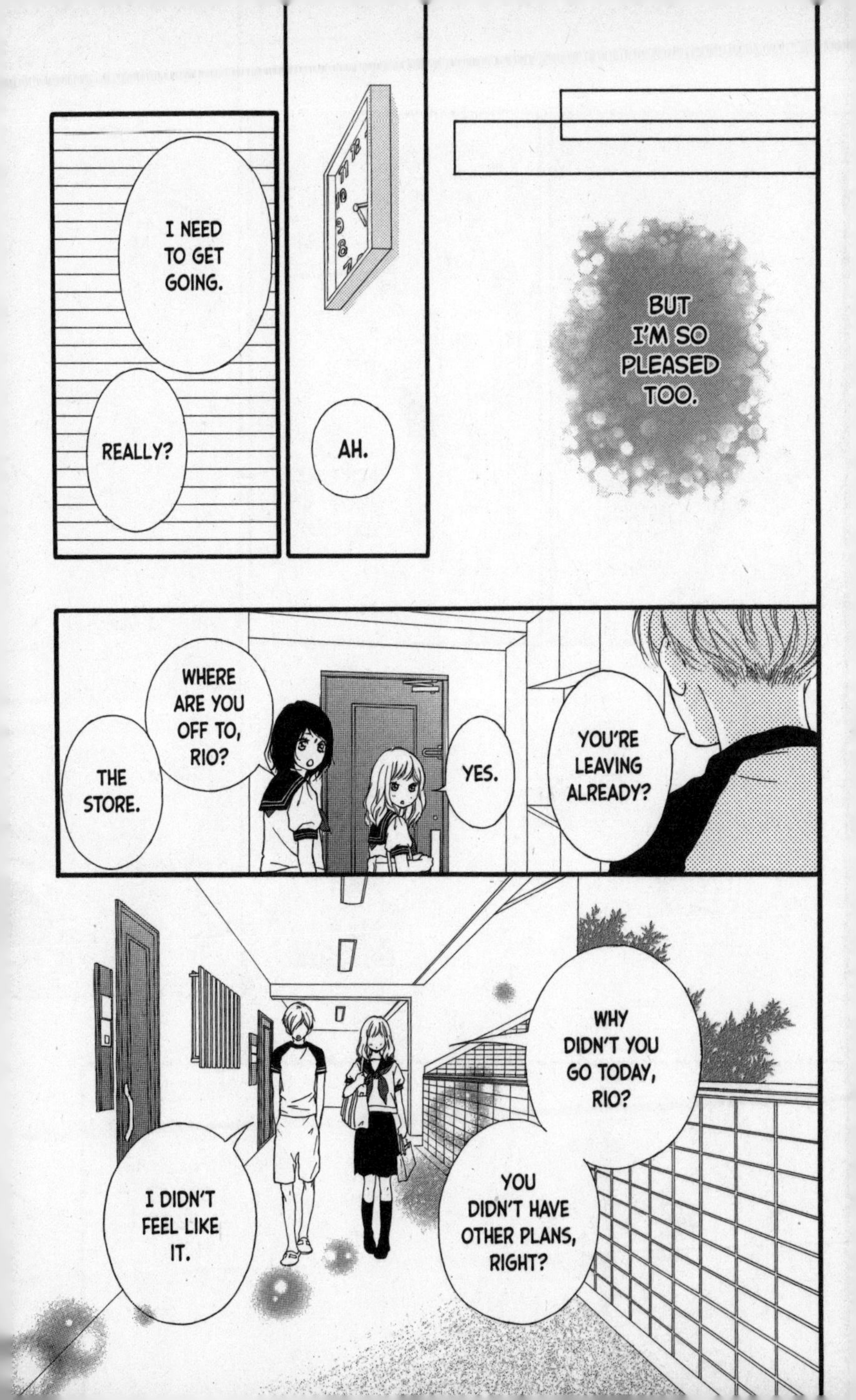
BUT I'M SO PLEASED TOO.
AH.
I NEED TO GET GOING.
REALLY?
YOU'RE LEAVING ALREADY?
YES.
WHERE ARE YOU OFF TO, RIO?
THE STORE.
WHY DIDN'T YOU GO TODAY, RIO?
YOU DIDN'T HAVE OTHER PLANS, RIGHT?
I DIDN'T FEEL LIKE IT.

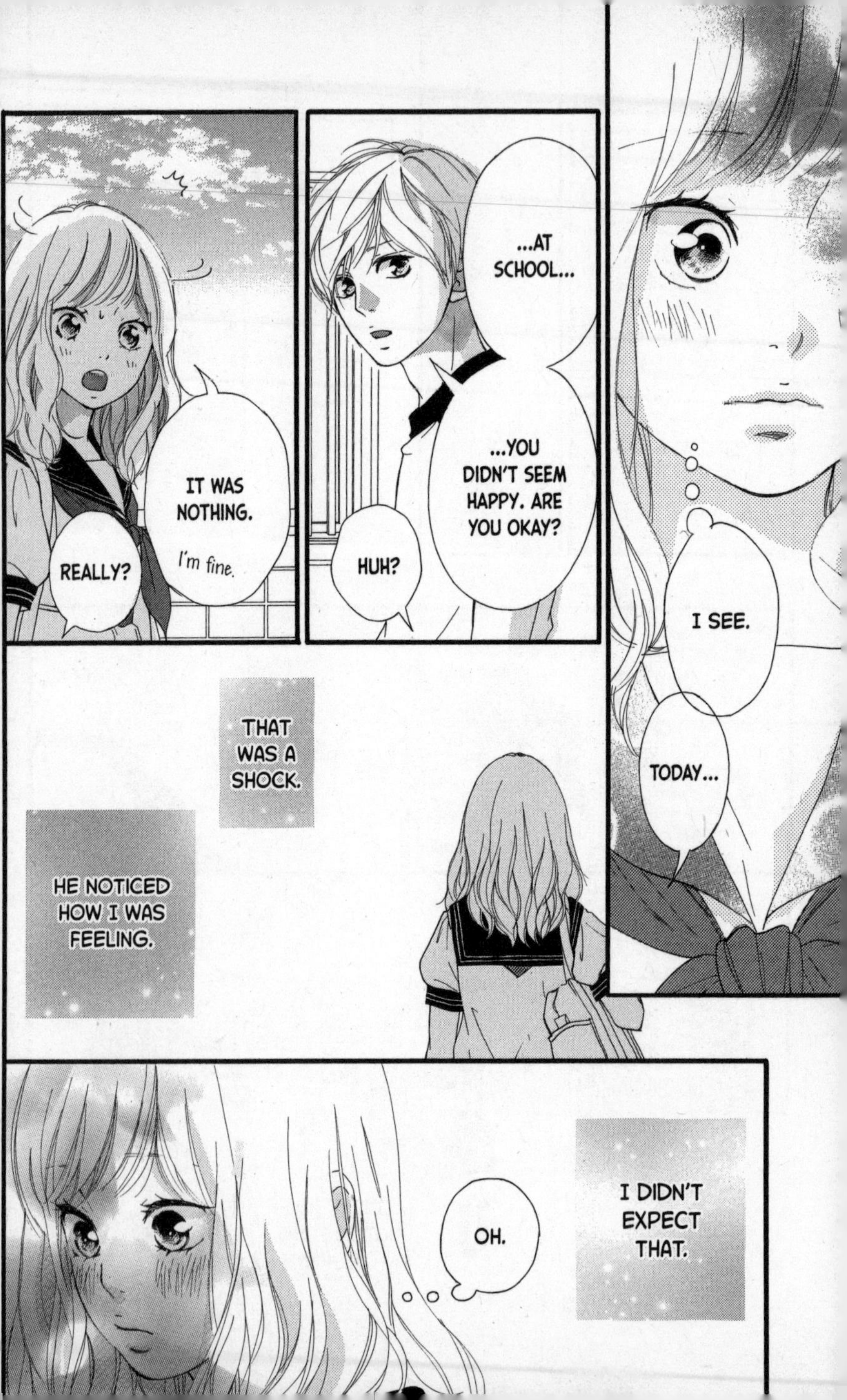
I SEE.
TODAY...
...AT SCHOOL...
...YOU DIDN'T SEEM HAPPY. ARE YOU OKAY?
HUH?
IT WAS NOTHING. I'm fine.
REALLY?
THAT WAS A SHOCK.
HE NOTICED HOW I WAS FEELING.
I DIDN'T EXPECT THAT.
OH.

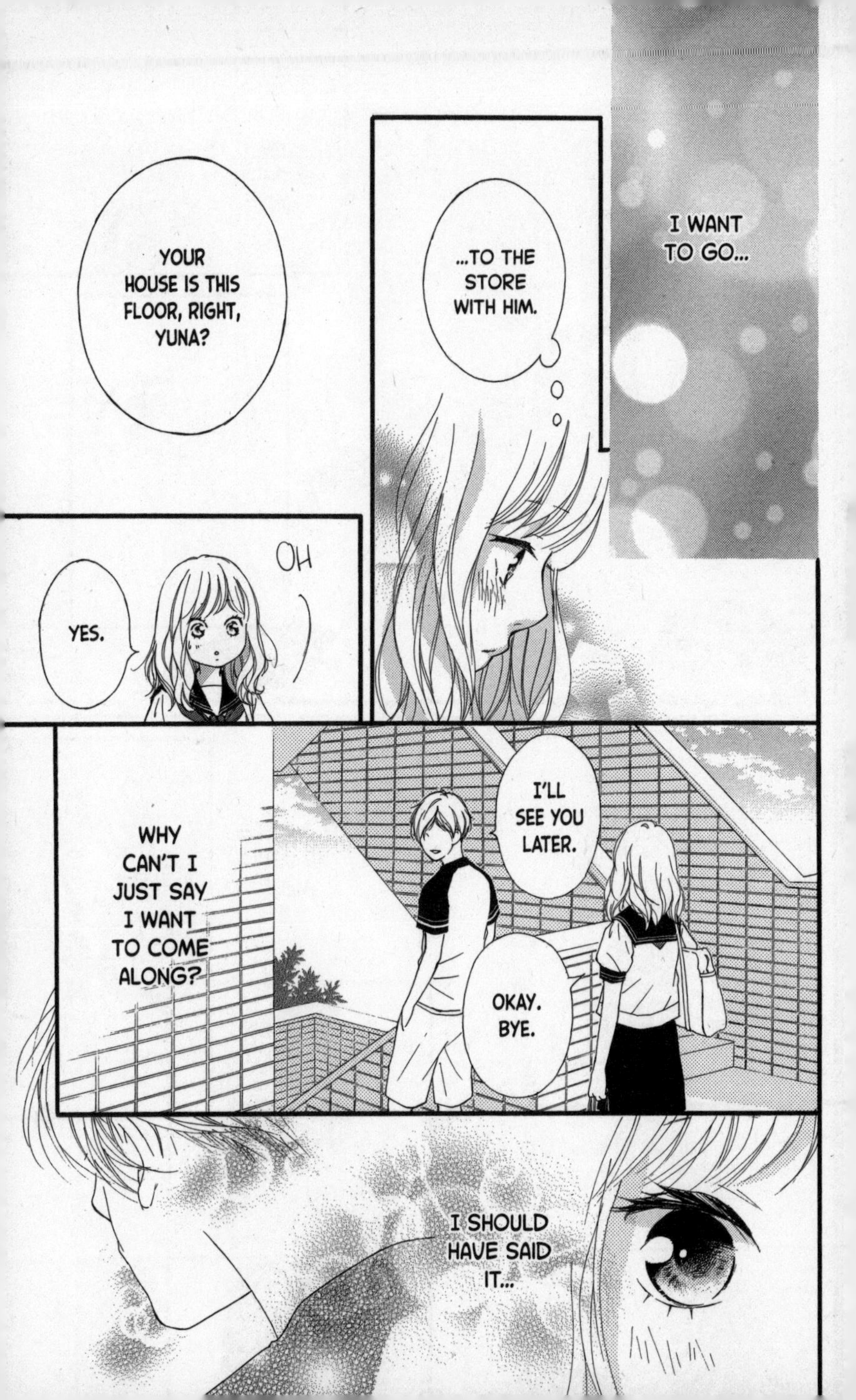
I WANT TO GO...
...TO THE STORE WITH HIM.
YOUR HOUSE IS THIS FLOOR, RIGHT, YUNA?
OH
YES.
I'LL SEE YOU LATER.
OKAY. BYE.
WHY CAN'T I JUST SAY I WANT TO COME ALONG?
I SHOULD HAVE SAID IT...

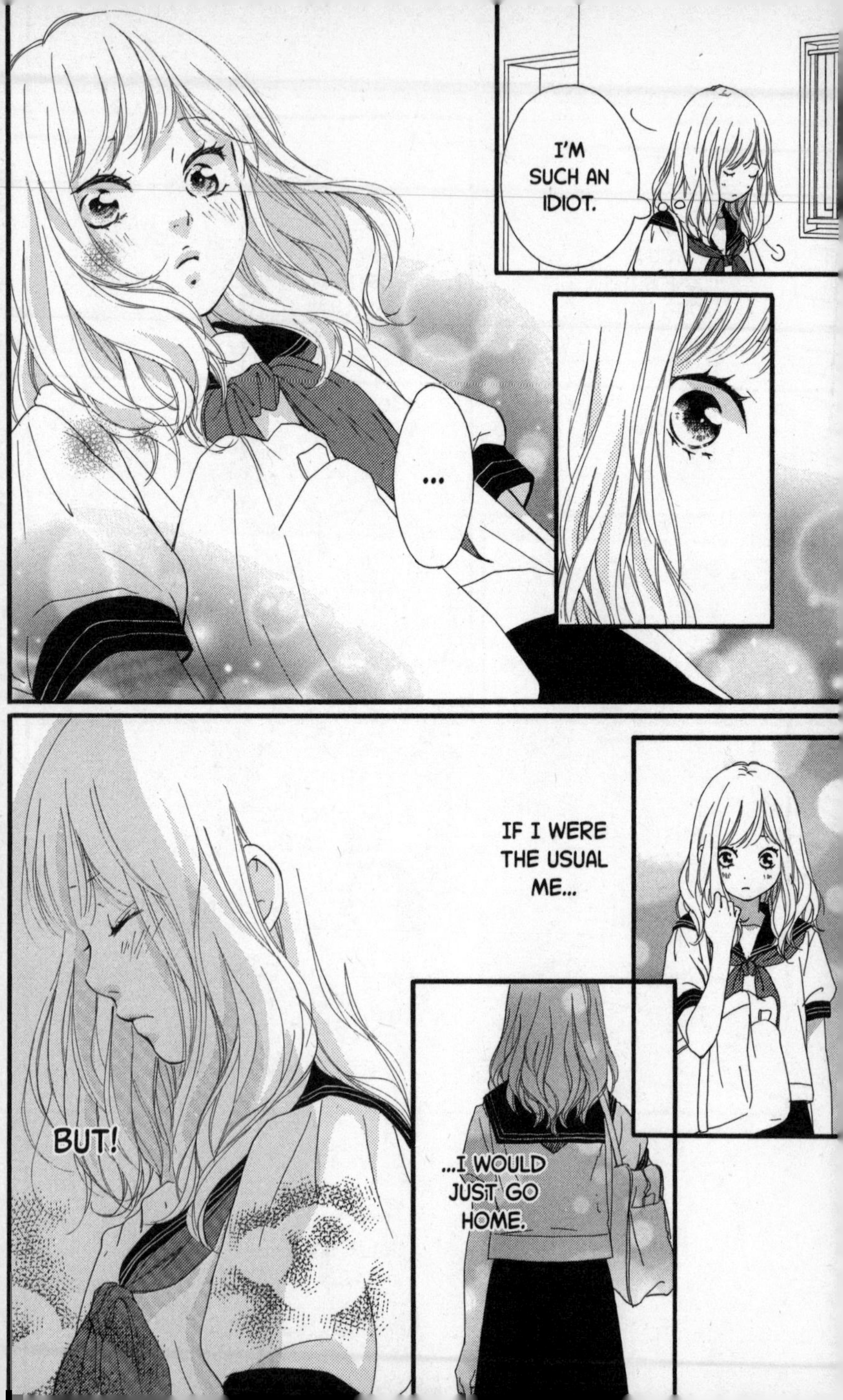
I'M SUCH AN IDIOT.
...
IF I WERE THE USUAL ME...
...I WOULD JUST GO HOME.
BUT!

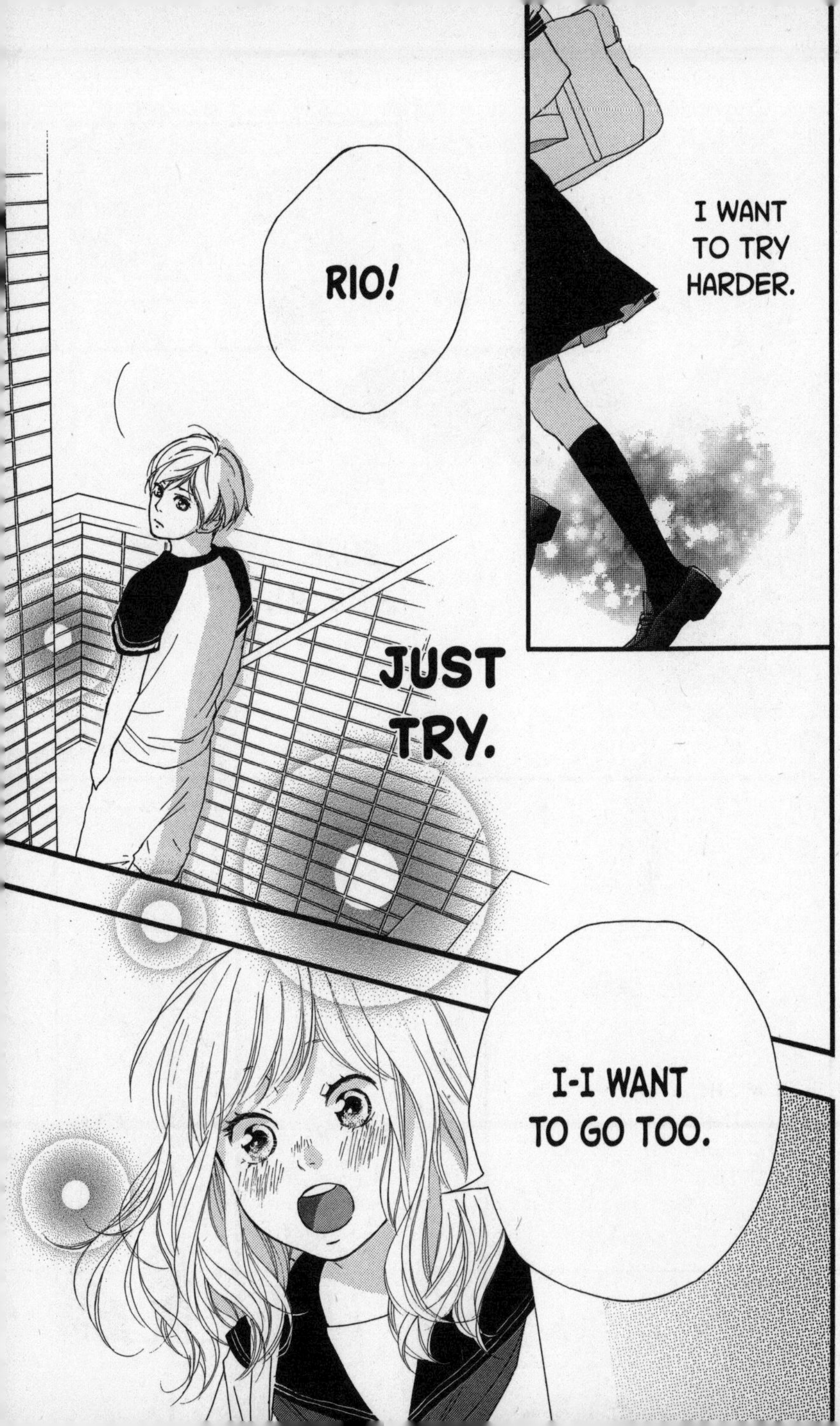
I WANT TO TRY HARDER.
RIO!
JUST TRY.
I-I WANT TO GO TOO.

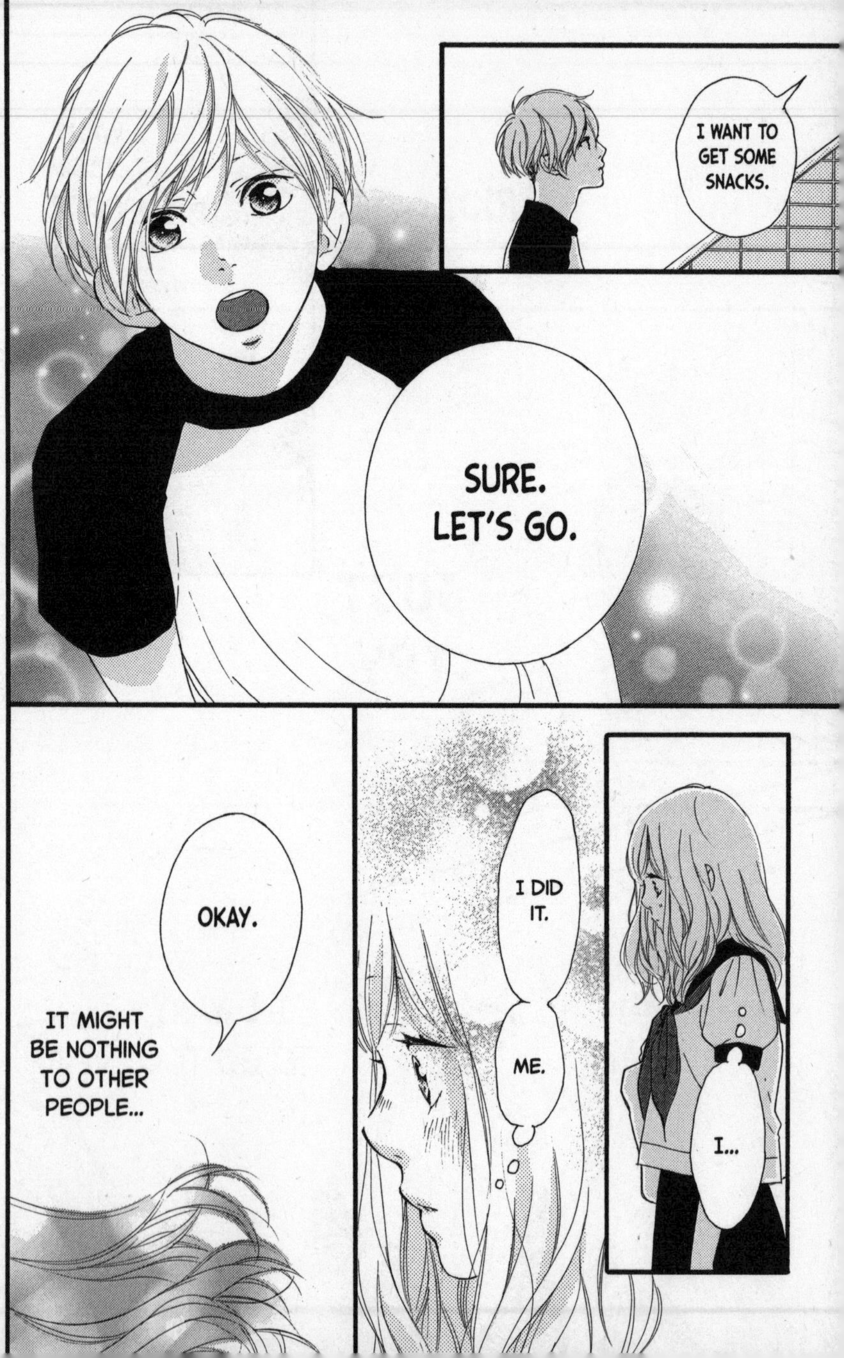
I WANT TO GET SOME SNACKS.
SURE. LET'S GO.
I...
I DID IT.
ME.
OKAY.
IT MIGHT BE NOTHING TO OTHER PEOPLE...

...BUT TO ME, IT FEELS LIKE I JUST TOOK...

...A BIG STEP FORWARD.

?

GRIN GRIN

I'M SO HAPPY.

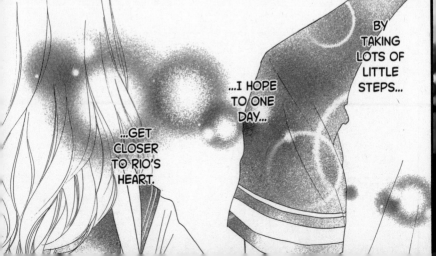

BY TAKING LOTS OF LITTLE STEPS...

...I HOPE TO ONE DAY...

...GET CLOSER TO RIO'S HEART.

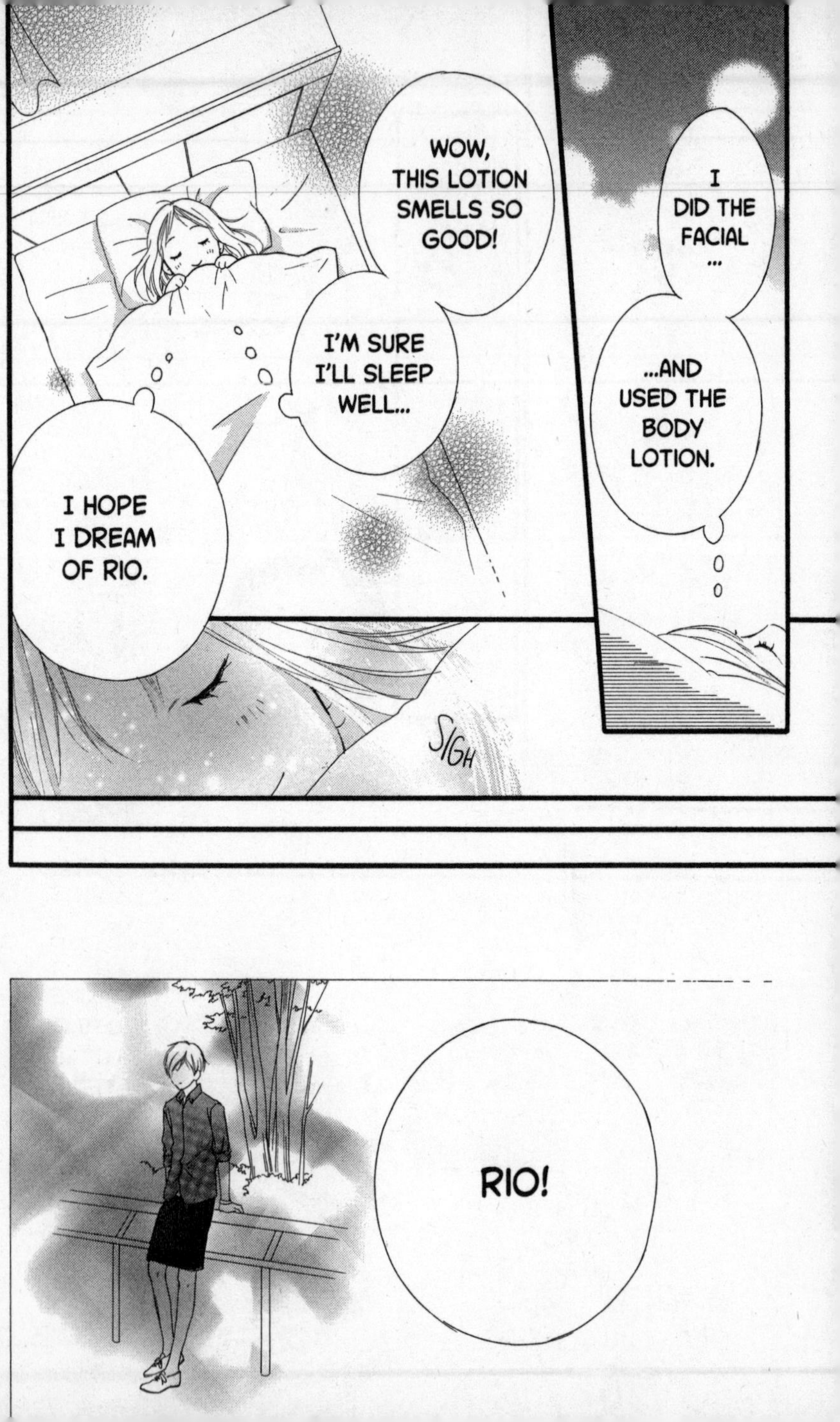
I DID THE FACIAL ...
...AND USED THE BODY LOTION.
WOW, THIS LOTION SMELLS SO GOOD!
I'M SURE I'LL SLEEP WELL...
I HOPE I DREAM OF RIO.
SIGH
RIO!

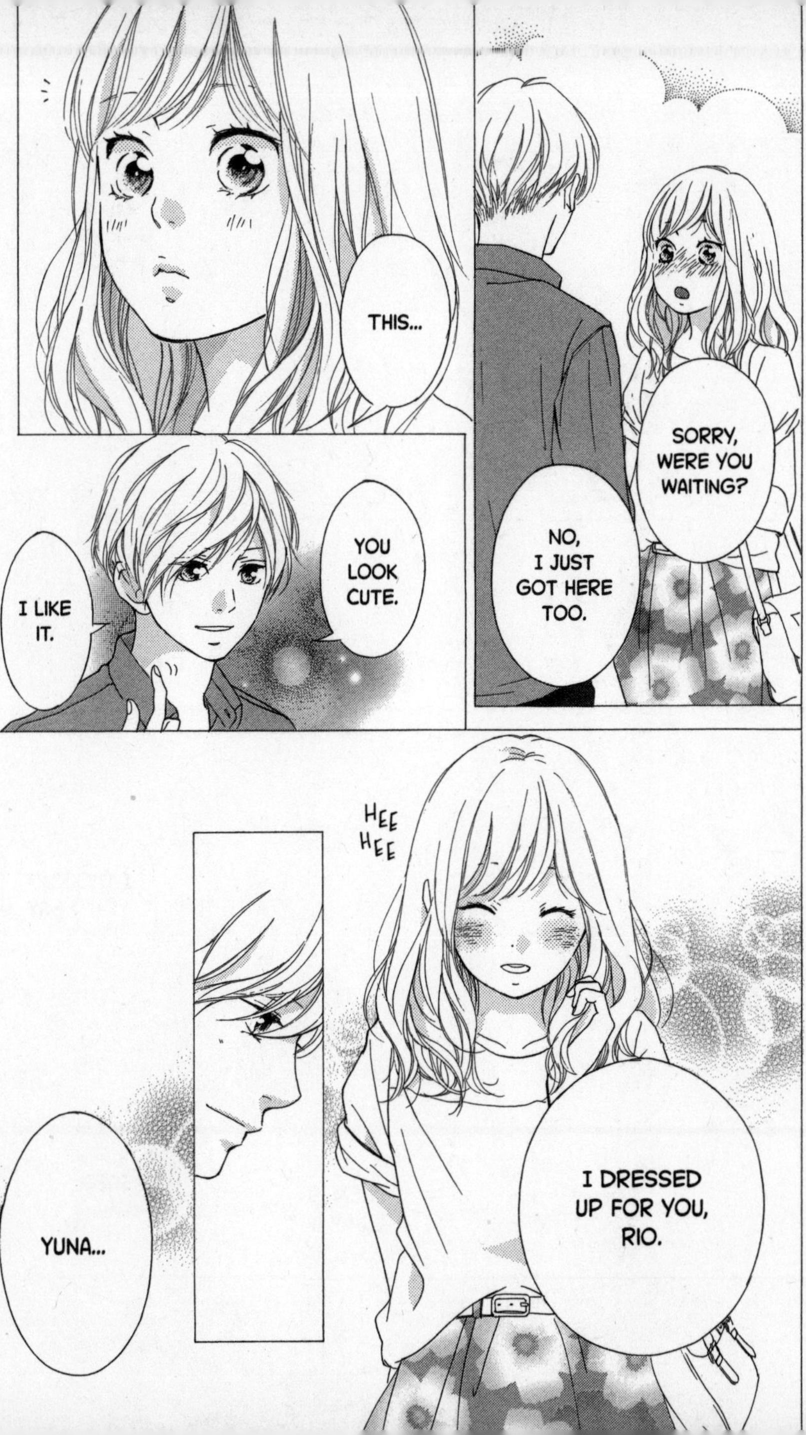
SORRY, WERE YOU WAITING?
NO, I JUST GOT HERE TOO.
THIS...
YOU LOOK CUTE.
I LIKE IT.
HEE HEE
I DRESSED UP FOR YOU, RIO.
YUNA...

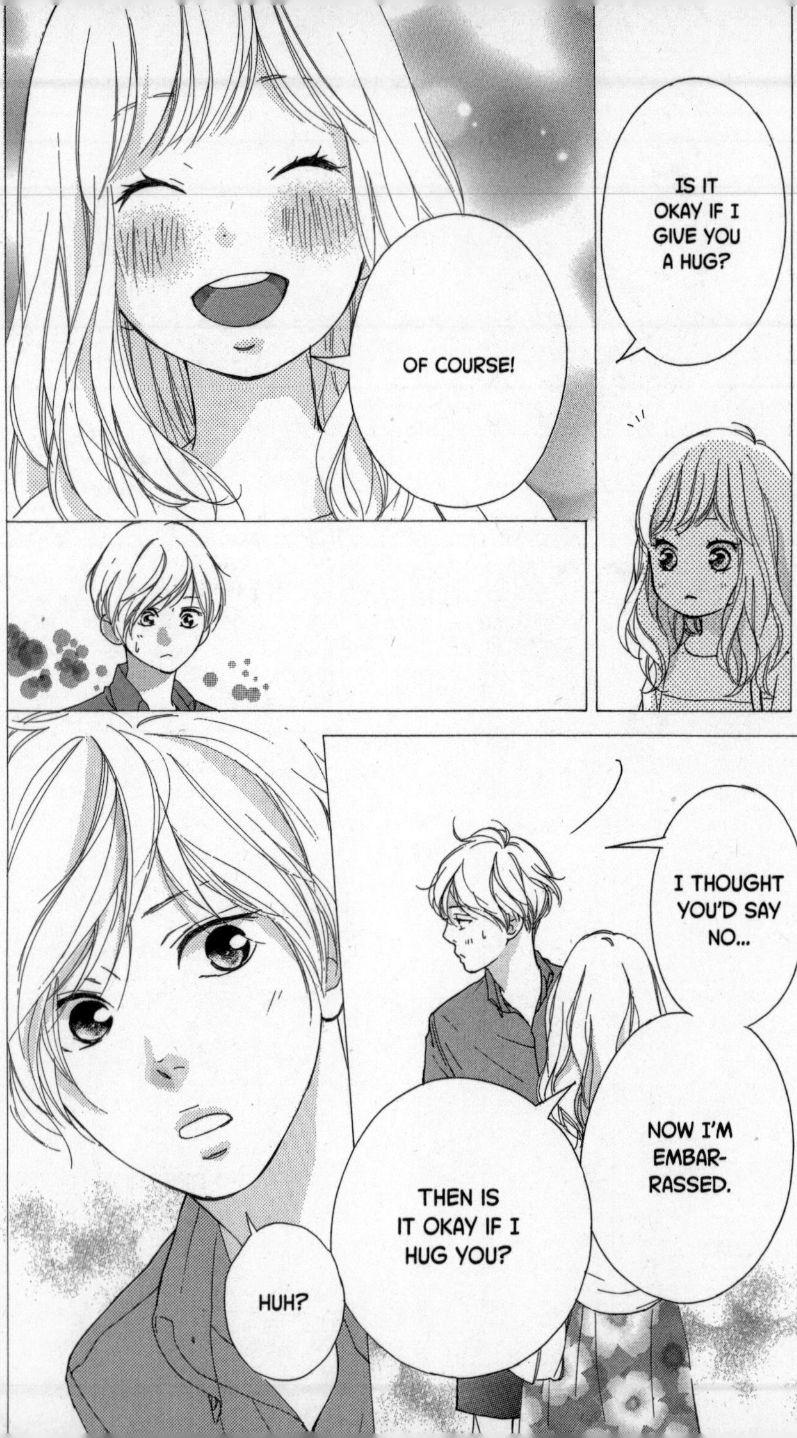
IS IT OKAY IF I GIVE YOU A HUG?
OF COURSE!
I THOUGHT YOU'D SAY NO...
NOW I'M EMBAR-RASSED.
THEN IS IT OKAY IF I HUG YOU?
HUH?

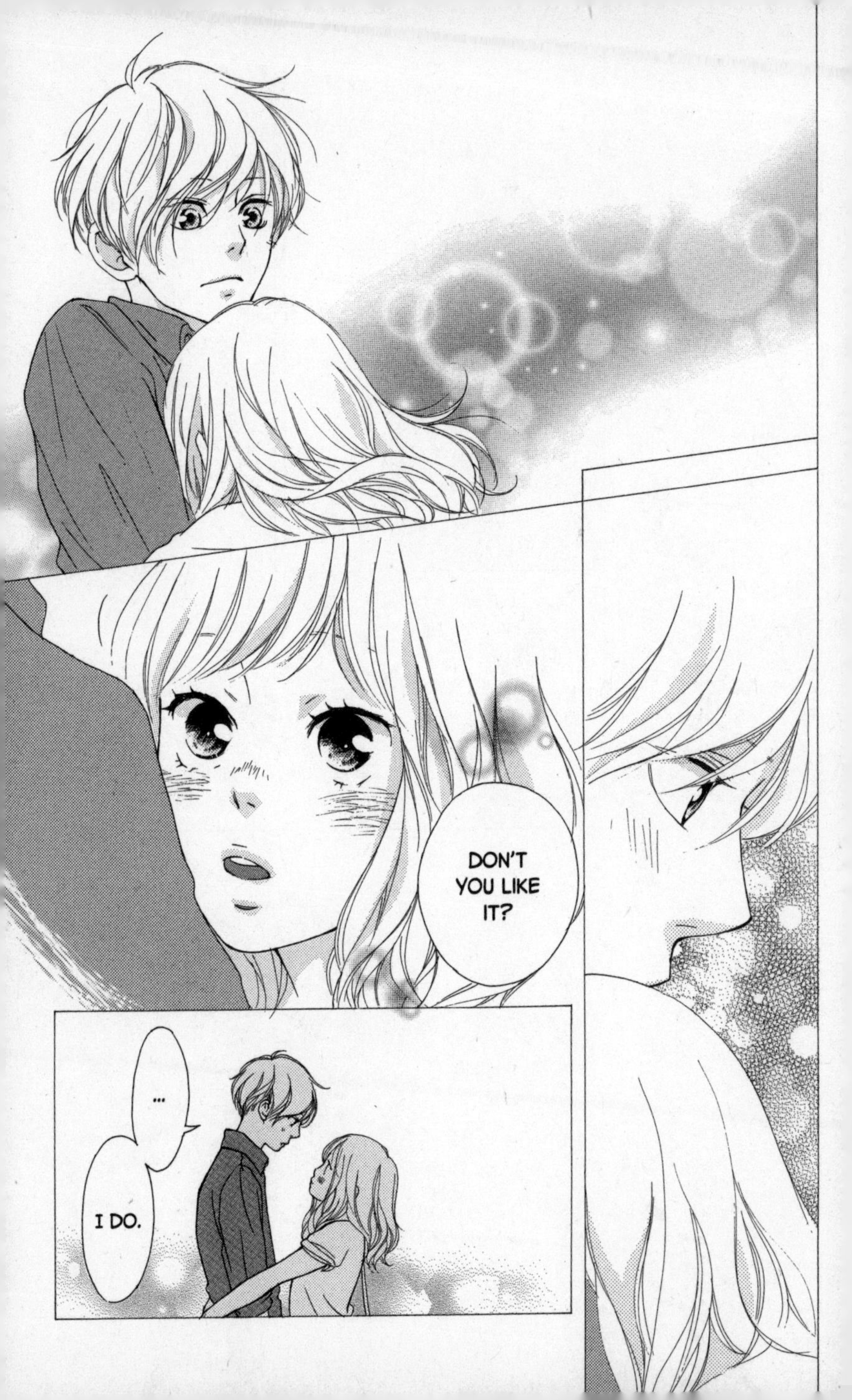
DON'T YOU LIKE IT?
...
I DO.

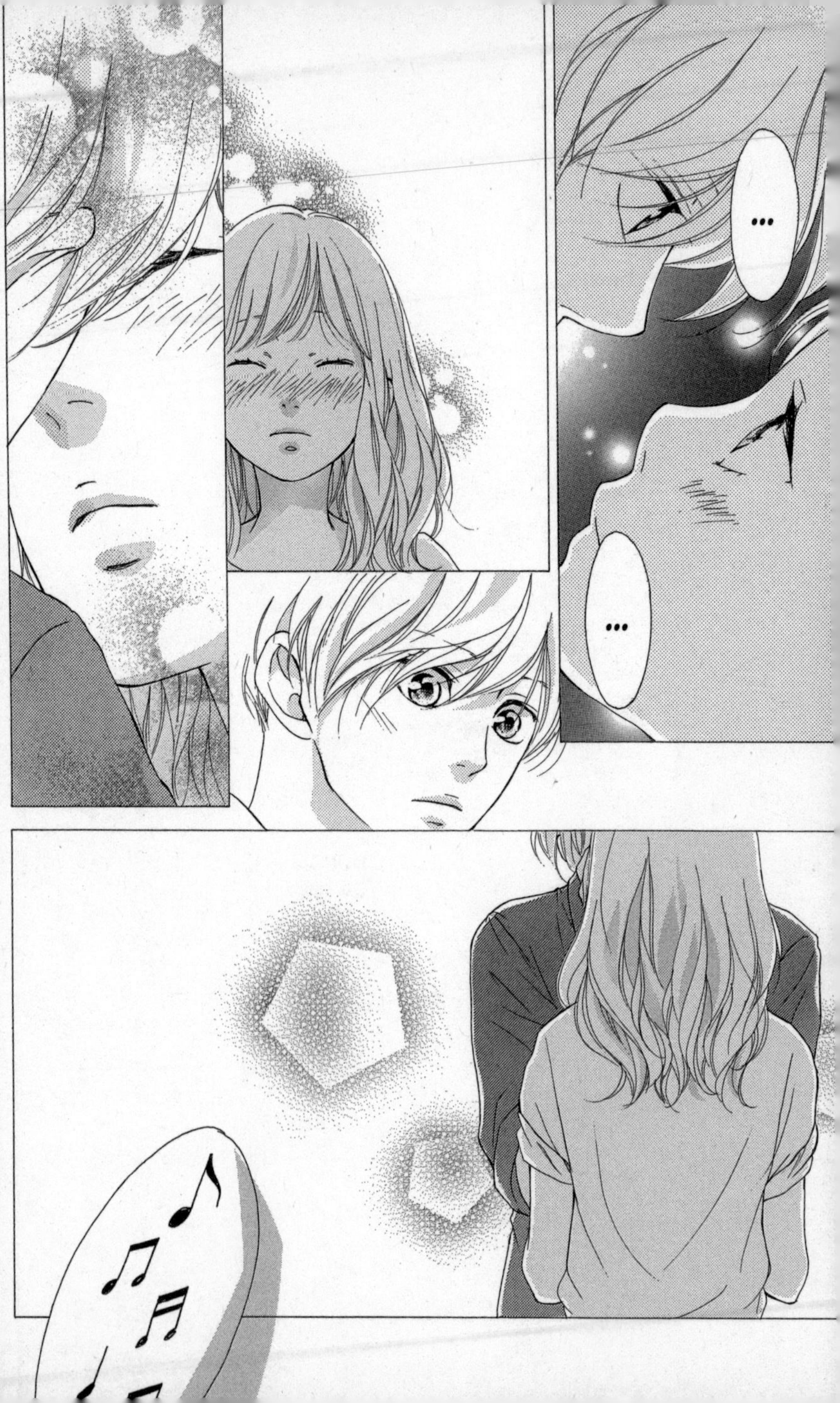
...
...

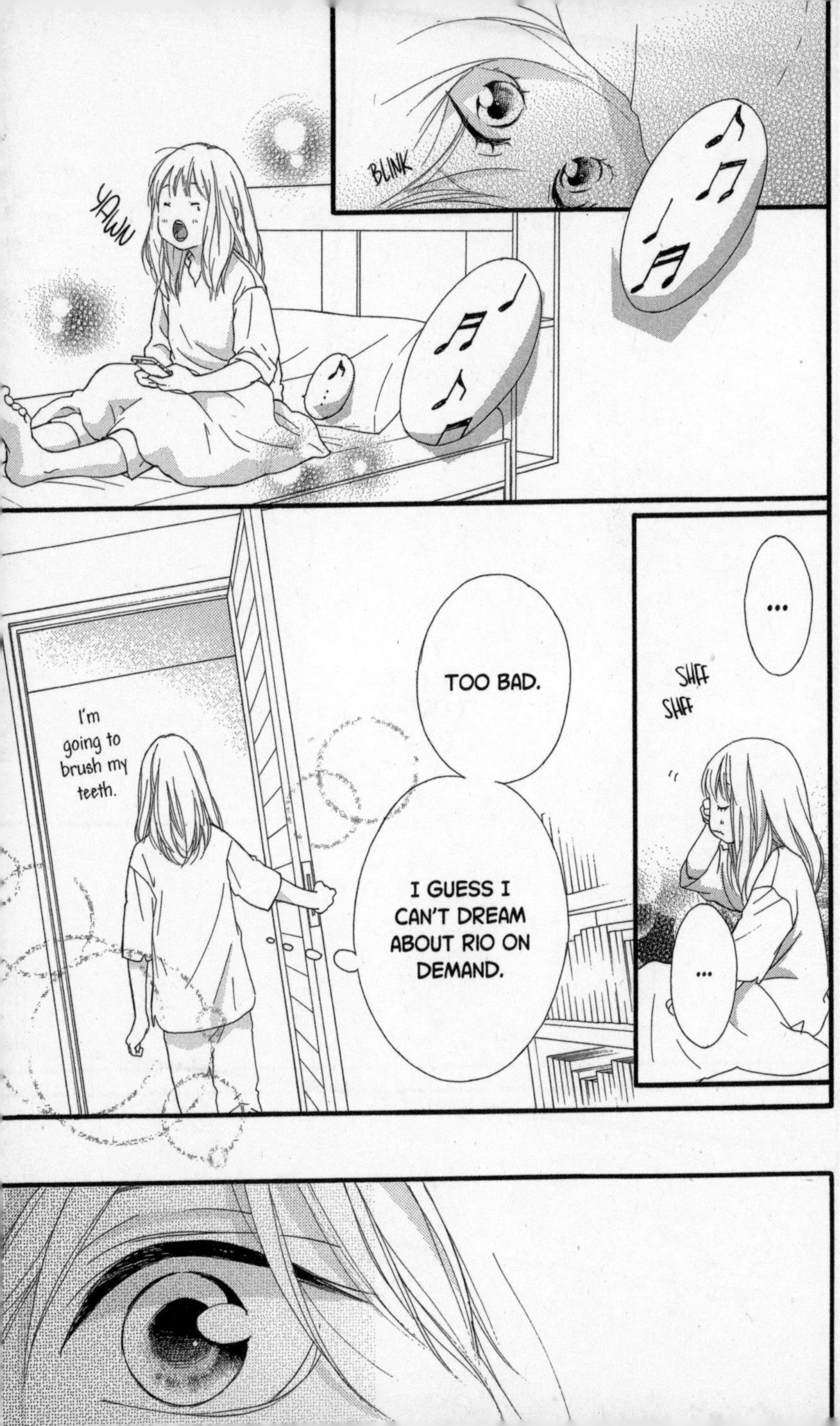
BLINK
YAWN
...
SHFF
SHFF
...
TOO BAD.
I GUESS I CAN'T DREAM ABOUT RIO ON DEMAND.
I'm going to brush my teeth.

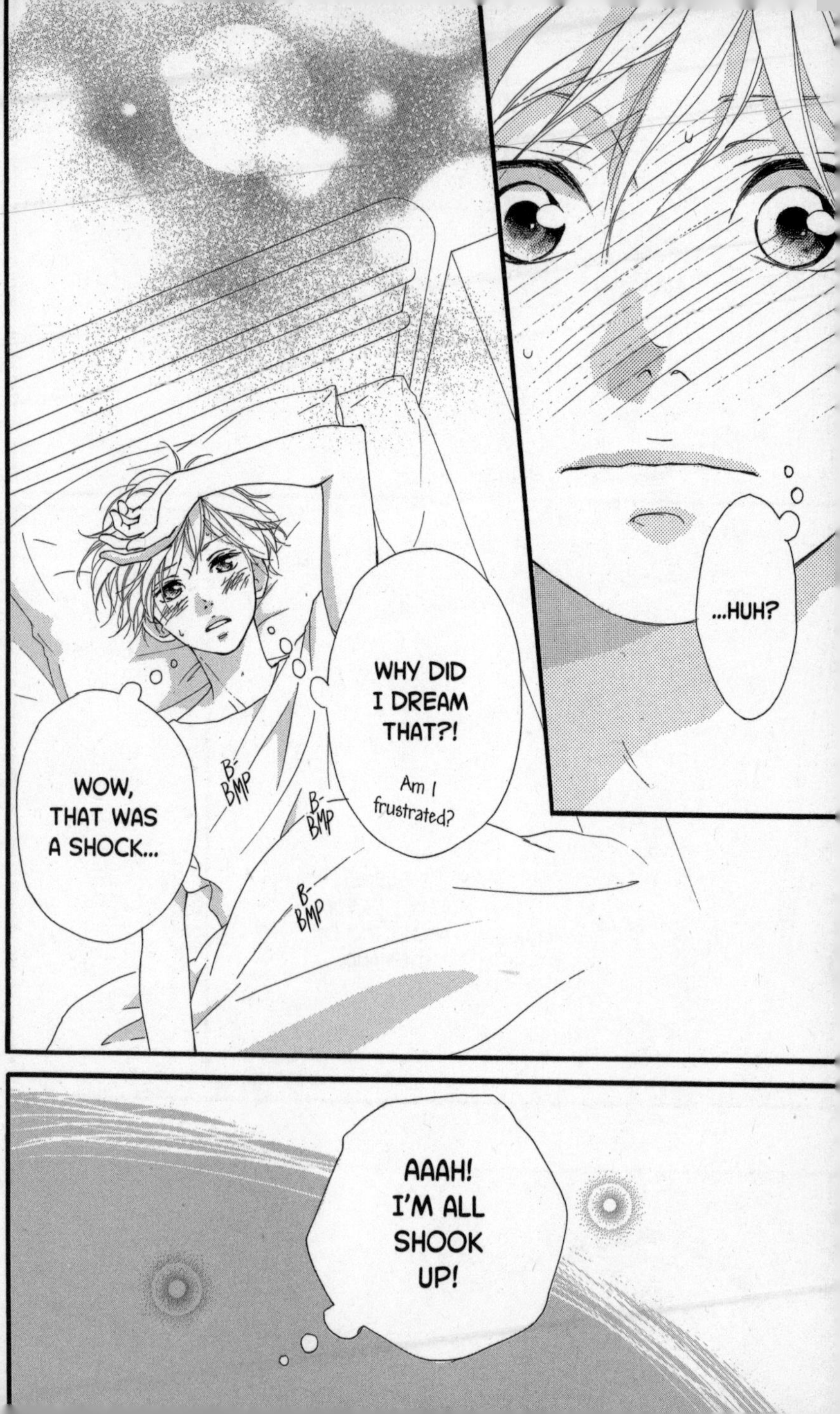
...HUH?
WHY DID I DREAM THAT?!
Am I frustrated?
B-BMP
B-BMP
WOW, THAT WAS A SHOCK...
B-BMP
AAAH! I'M ALL SHOOK UP!

AFTERWORD

Thank you very much for reading this to the end!

It was so much fun drawing Yuna and Rio's dream in Piece 16. It was so fun that I thought they should dream more—maybe for an entire chapter. When Yuna became more proactive in the dream than in real life, I was definitely more excited than Rio. I thought, "Rio, switch places with me." All the girls feeling shy who go for it are adorable. Boys feeling shy are cute too. It makes me feel warm and fuzzy. Therefore, shy girls + shy boys = ultimate cuteness! I want to write more about Yuna, Akari, Rio and Kazuomi as they become even cuter. With this in mind, I'm working hard on the next volume, so please stay with me. If I don't forget, I'm hoping to include everyone's profile in the next volume. (I'm sorry in advance if I forget. I will try hard not to forget.) I'll see you in the next volume!

 Io Sakisaka

I changed hair salons. The deciding factor was that the old salon took a long time to do hair treatments, but this new one can't do treatments and color on the same day. I haven't gone yet because it's hard for me to make time for separate appointments.

Io Sakisaka

Born on June 8, Io Sakisaka made her debut as a manga creator with *Sakura, Chiru*. Her series *Strobe Edge* and *Ao Haru Ride* are published by VIZ Media's Shojo Beat imprint. *Ao Haru Ride* was adapted into an anime series in 2014, and *Love Me, Love Me Not* will be an animated feature film. In her spare time, Sakisaka likes to paint things and sleep.

Love Me, Love Me Not

Vol. 4

Shojo Beat Edition

STORY AND ART BY

Io Sakisaka

Adaptation/Nancy Thistlethwaite
Translation/JN Productions
Touch-Up Art & Lettering/Sara Linsley
Design/Yukiko Whitley
Editor/Nancy Thistlethwaite

First published in Japan in 2015 by SHUEISHA Inc., Tokyo.
English translation rights arranged by SHUEISHA Inc.

Printed in the U.S.A.

Published by VIZ Media, LLC
P.O. Box 77010
San Francisco, CA 94107

10 9 8 7 6 5 4 3 2 1
First printing, September 2020

ratings.viz.com RATED T TEEN

PARENTAL ADVISORY
LOVE ME, LOVE ME NOT is rated T for Teen and is recommended for ages 13 and up. This story centers around teenage relationships.

VIZ MEDIA
viz.com

Shojo Beat
shojobeat.com

Shojo Beat Romances by **IO SAKISAKA**

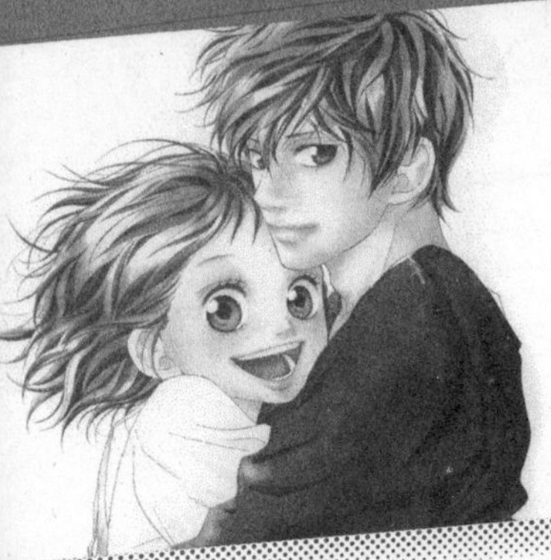

STROBE EDGE

When Ninako meets Ren, the handsome, enigmatic guy that all the girls worship, her life takes an unexpected turn. With just a few words and a smile, he changes her world...

Ao Haru Ride

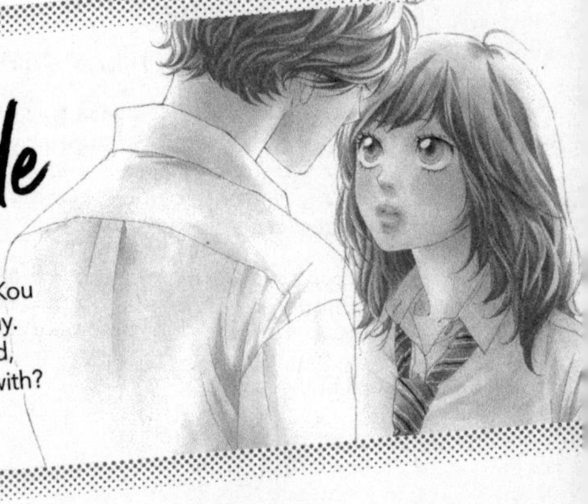

As soon as Futaba realized she really liked Kou in junior high, he had already moved away. Now, in high school, Kou has reappeared, but is he still the same boy she fell in love with?

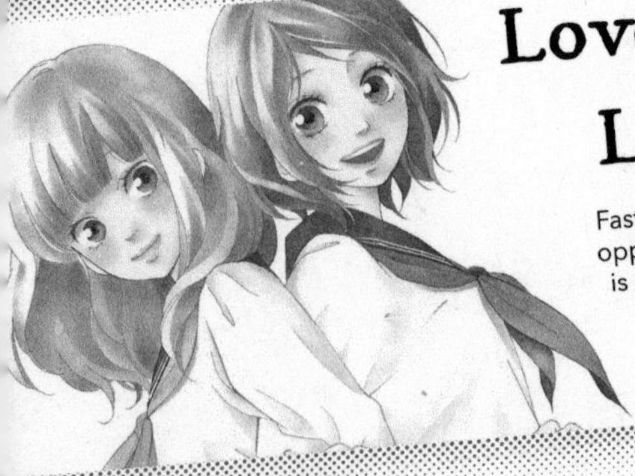

Love Me, Love Me Not

Fast friends Yuna and Akari are complete opposites—Yuna is an idealist, while Akari is a realist. When lady-killer Rio and the oblivious Kazuomi join their ranks, love and friendship become quite complicated!

RATED T TEEN

VIZ

Honey
So Sweet

Story and Art by *Amu Meguro*

Little did Nao Kogure realize back in middle school that when she left an umbrella and a box of bandages in the rain for injured delinquent Taiga Onise that she would meet him again in high school. Nao wants nothing to do with the gruff and frightening Taiga, but he suddenly presents her with a huge bouquet of flowers and asks her to date him—with marriage in mind! Is Taiga really so scary, or is he a sweetheart in disguise?

RATED **T** FOR TEEN
ratings.viz.com

viz MEDIA
viz.com

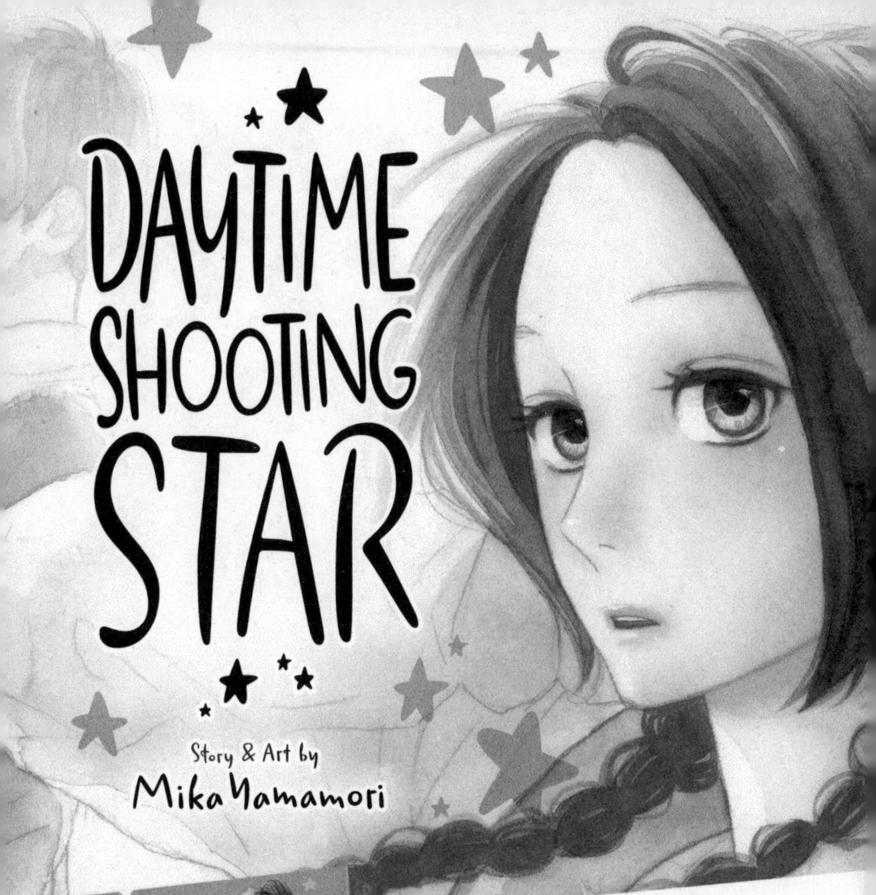

DAYTIME SHOOTING STAR

Story & Art by
Mika Yamamori

Small town girl Suzume moves to Tokyo and finds her heart caught between two men!

After arriving in Tokyo to live with her uncle, Suzume collapses in a nearby park when she remembers once seeing a shooting star during the day. A handsome stranger brings her to her new home and tells her they'll meet again. Suzume starts her first day at her new high school sitting next to a boy who blushes furiously at her touch. And her homeroom teacher is none other than the handsome stranger!

SHORTCAKE CAKE

STORY AND ART BY
suu Morishita

An unflappable girl and a cast of lovable roommates at a boardinghouse create bonds of friendship and romance!

When Ten moves out of her parents' home in the mountains to live in a boardinghouse, she finds herself becoming fast friends with her male roommates. But can love and romance be far behind?

VIZ

Stop!

You may be reading the wrong way.

In keeping with the original Japanese comic format, this book reads from right to left—so action, sound effects and word balloons are completely reversed to preserve the orientation of the original artwork. Check out the diagram shown here to get the hang of things, and then turn to the other side of the book to get started!

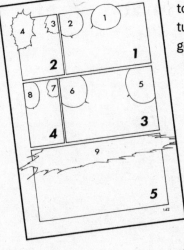